*invisible
men*

invisible men

Inside India's Transmasculine Networks

NANDINI KRISHNAN

FOREWORD BY MANU JOSEPH

PENGUIN

VIKING

An imprint of Penguin Random House

VIKING

USA | Canada | UK | Ireland | Australia
New Zealand | India | South Africa | China | Singapore

Viking is part of the Penguin Random House group of companies
whose addresses can be found at global.penguinrandomhouse.com

Published by Penguin Random House India Pvt. Ltd
4th Floor, Capital Tower 1, MG Road,
Gurugram 122 002, Haryana, India

First published in Viking by Penguin Random House India 2018

Text and illustrations copyright © Nandini Krishnan 2018

10 9 8 7 6 5 4 3 2

The views and opinions expressed in this book are the author's own and the
facts are as reported by her which have been verified to the extent possible,
and the publishers are not in any way liable for the same.

ISBN 9780670090143

Typeset in Dante MT Std by Manipal Digital Systems, Manipal
Printed at Replika Press Pvt. Ltd, India

www.penguin.co.in

This is a legitimate digitally printed version of the book and therefore might not
have certain extra finishing on the cover.

To Babu Mama, Maruthi, Ma, and my 'Dada', Dilip Mama

To Shwaanan Naïr, who changed my life with a single gesture of trust

To Simba, Pongo, Ouidah, Elvira, Ammukutty,
Kavery, Chaitanya, Mrityunjay, Meera, Karna, Dakshayani
and Ghatotkacha, who are my life

In memory of Sundari, Doofy, Snowy and Mona

For Piggy and Deepu, who keep me sane

Contents

Contents   ix

Foreword

Fluid Has Direction

This is the part of a book I usually skip. After the 'prologue', which is unnecessary, and the blurb, which is unnecessary and a lie, and the 'introduction', which is a ruse promoted by academics to appear in books that people actually read, the 'foreword' has to be the most spurious thing inside a book. But it has one respectable quality—the writer of the foreword usually is some kind of an expert, related in some form to the subject matter of the book, and he says scholarly things about his domain. But this foreword does not possess even that single redeeming quality. In fact it did not occur to me until I began to read Nandini Krishnan's manuscript that there can be genders within transgenders.

What did I think gender was? Male, female and a certain ambiguity? But then what exactly is the ambiguity? How many times have I met those amiable muscular Tamil 'eunuchs' in saris who have no ambiguity at all, who are rather very sure about who they are— women trapped in male bodies?

I first met them when I was twenty. *Savvy* magazine sent me to a small Tamil village called Koovagam to cover an extraordinary festival. Transwomen and transvestites from all around the nation arrived in spectacular bridal wear, and they stood in line to marry a minor god called Aravan. As the story goes, or at least as it was told to me then, during the Mahabharata's decisive Kurukshetra war, the good guys were losing and the sages said that for things to turn around, a 'perfect warrior' had to be sacrificed. There were only three men who qualified as perfect warriors—Krishna, who was a god and indispensable; Arjuna, who was the hero and indispensable; and Arjuna's son, Aravan, who was hence doomed. He was a virgin and he wished to enjoy sex before his death. So Krishna transformed into a beautiful young woman, Mohini. The transwomen of India worship Aravan because he married a woman knowing that she was once a man. And that is why they, too, marry him. On the wedding night, the brides offer free sex to the men and so the village swarmed with Tamil men in lungis, many of whom abused and molested the new brides of Aravan.

A quality of Tamil Nadu is that its transwomen are a part of mainstream life, yet they attract a dark and terrifying malice in Tamil men (once, in a train, a young and coy transwoman was seated beside me; a man came in with his bags and upon finding her, he kicked her on her chest, for no reason at all apart from that the fact that he could, culturally, kick her and get away with it). In Koovagam, after the raucous bridal night, the brides become widows to mark the death of Aravan. They wear white saris and they beat their chests and wail. As you keep staring at them, you slowly realize it is not for some mythical minor god that they mourn. They cry for their entrapment in male bodies. My time in Koovagam made me comfortable with them, and a few months later in Mumbai, at a traffic light, when a transwoman asked me for money and I didn't have change, I gave her twenty and asked her for ten back, which greatly baffled her.

The lives of transwomen are somewhat better now. Among transgenders, transwomen are the 'normal' people. The transgenders we think we know are in actuality transwomen; men who strive to become women. But there is the other kind, which is the subject of this book.

I have for long considered men and women who are 'normal', who are biologically, mentally, indisputably men and women, who claim that 'gender is a spectrum', as charlatans who want to state something esoteric even though they don't know what they are talking about. Gender is not a spectrum; gender is a definite state of being. The body is the spectrum. Some men and women are trapped in the wrong bodies, and they then proceed to transit. Transition is not a spectrum; transition is movement towards certainty. We imagine the people in transition as a single collective organism in weird clothes, whom we then place in our minds as the middle-people. What does not occur to us is that the transition is not only continuous, it also has a direction. To be precise, it has two directions.

It is not only men who strive to become women; there are millions of women who wish to become men. This exquisite book tells the stories of some of those women as they begin to transform—the hope and force of inevitability that subsume the torture of it all. You will read about women who use the latest medical advances to liberate themselves from their gorgeous female shape, who will cut away their breasts, destroy their long flowing hair, make stubbles spring on their faces, and fix agonizing penises.

Nandini uses a technique popularized by V.S. Naipaul and Svetlana Alexievich—of telling the stories of people through their own authentic voices. And she is such a trustworthy researcher that these stories she is about to tell also serve as an anthropological survey of Tamilians—how they deliver jokes, how they hurt and how they are fused with their grandparents, and in what ways they are subtle and what ways melodramatic. This book is, at times, the *Malgudi Days* of transmen.

There are, of course, large swathes of stories that she narrates herself, through her own voice. Her artistic talent alone would make the reading of this book an important joy, but there are two other qualities that I feel are more influential. She is a delinquent. No interesting aspect of life escapes the delinquent. Also, she does not need the farce of compassion to respect people. As a result, the book that you hold does not contain even a moment of the feudalism of the lucky masquerading as sympathy for the unlucky.

Above all, what the stories convey in every page is that our most corrupt and destructive idea is the notion of normality.

Manu Joseph

Preface

Every time I tell someone I'm working on a book about transmen, they assume I mean transwomen. So alien is the concept of transmen to the world that even when I explain they are female-to-male (FTM) and not male-to-female (MTF), the typical response is a puzzled, 'But then why do they wear saris?'

Finally, I resort to, 'Have you seen *Boys Don't Cry?*'

The film that won Hilary Swank an Academy Award was my first exposure to the idea of transmasculinity, and so it was for most people of my generation. I remember watching it in my teens and being stunned. Despite my familiarity with transwomen, it had never struck me that the converse could exist too.

Like most outdoorsy girls, I was considered a 'tomboy' as a child. Growing up with brothers and male cousins, I spent most of my childhood playing umpire or referee to their games. I had always loved watching and playing sports, but I had never nursed any desire to be male. Far from feeling any penis envy, I would shudder at the idea of an organ dangling between one's legs at all times. My G.I. Joes would have tea parties. My He-Man and the Masters of the Universe were constantly embroiled in family dramas. I was enrolled in Bharatanatyam classes as a five-year-old, and I loved its ultra-femininity. When I worked with transwomen much later, I found I could relate to them in many ways.

It was through my male friends in dance class that I first encountered alternate sexuality and gender identity. Some would tell me that they liked boys, and were as horrified by the idea as the rest of us were.

Some would tell me they wanted to be women, and were as confused as I was by the notion. All of us were terrified of the transwomen we encountered, at traffic signals and on beaches and on trains, clapping their hands boisterously, demanding money, and threatening to lift their skirts or feel up the boys unless they were paid. Indian cinema has used transwomen mainly in comedy tracks, and only reinforced our preconceived assessment of them as transgressive oddities, to be mocked and avoided.

In this context, *Boys Don't Cry* let me into a world I had never contemplated—the inner world of a transperson, a world where one's anatomy was at odds with one's idea of oneself and with society's perception of one.

A few years later, as a student of journalism in the United Kingdom, I chose to work on transgender rights for my final project, a video documentary. My documentary was a comparative study of trans rights in the UK and in India. It seems strange to think back to this now, but I—like most cispeople in India—had assumed transwomen were hermaphrodites or intersex people; I did not realize they had been 'fully functional' males until they chose to undergo '*nirvana*', the term transwomen use for castration and penectomy. In the UK, I met transwomen who had fathered biological children before transitioning. It took me a while to understand that Indian transwomen were not biologically of ambiguous gender. It took me longer to understand the *jama'at* system, under which transwomen formed quasi-families, a sisterhood to ensure their livelihoods and shield themselves against a cruel and prejudiced world. It was this system that gave Indian transwomen more protection than their counterparts in the West.

The narrative of transwomen dominated the discourse on trans rights. But I was keen to speak to transmen, and sought them out in both countries where my research was based. I met several transmen in the UK, all of whom had even more horrific tales to relate than transwomen I had interviewed anywhere in the world. If things were this bad for transmen in the UK, what was the situation like in India?

When I set out to make the documentary, in 2006, I travelled to various cities—Madras, Bangalore, Bombay—and several little villages of Tamil Nadu, to interview prominent transwomen and junior members of numerous jama'ats. I met only one transman in India. His name was Selvam, and I lost touch with him some months after we met. He did not have a phone at the time. The transwomen with whom he had lived told me he'd moved out of their community.

I'd always wanted to do a follow-up to the documentary after relocating to India. My search for Selvam and other transmen initially proved futile. I did hope to meet members of the transmasculine community when 'unnatural sex', under Section 377 of the Indian Penal Code, was decriminalized and then recriminalized, but all the non-cisgender spokespeople appeared to be transwomen.

Transmen were, and perhaps in the popular imagination still are, invisible.

It was entirely by coincidence that I was reunited with Selvam. I was interviewing Siva Kumar and Delfina of the non-governmental organization (NGO) Nirangal for another story, when they happened to mention Selvam. Could he be the same Selvam? He was. I met him in December 2016, and began to work on a long read on transmen for *Fountain Ink* magazine. It was an interesting time to do the story. The transmasculine community in India was beginning to form its networks, more people were coming out about their gender identities and sexual orientations after the Supreme Court's verdict in the *National Legal Services Authority vs Union of India* case on 15 April 2014, and the Transgender Persons (Protection of Rights) Bill, 2016 was due to be tabled in Parliament.

While working on my long read, I met and interviewed some of the people who would become close friends and subjects of this book—Selvam, Jovin, Satya Rai Nagpaul, Keerth, some who wished to stay anonymous—and heard about several others whose stories awed and often frightened me. They told me how much cruelty the world is willing to unleash, and how much endurance and resistance its victims find to counter it. I wanted to tell these stories.

The narrative of transmen has been typically restricted to before–after reports in the media, complete with pictures, and at best to discussion on transgender rights. In doing interviews and research,

I would come across various layers to their lives that are rarely understood. The stories I found most poignant were not those of the external, of how transpeople are perceived by the world, but the internal—their dilemmas and dysphoria, their struggles to explain their beings first to themselves and then to everyone else, and even inter-community and intra-community prejudice.

I would hear similar stories of growing up—of indulgence from parents, even pride at their 'daughter' scaling trees and playing cricket, which would suddenly transform into restrictions and sometimes rage once the child hit puberty. It was bad enough for a boy to grow breasts and deal with a monthly reminder that he was not biologically male; but even worse was being separated from his best friends because they were *boys* and *girls* should not interact with boys. It was traumatic not to be allowed to play cricket or cycle or wear shorts.

My interviewees are drawn from across various spectra—different ages, genders, regions, religions, convictions, socio-economic classes—and I would be struck by both the similarities and differences in their stories. The broad general issues I had planned to examine began to splinter into various other aspects of their lives that I had not even known existed.

At first, I was worried about how I would come across. Was I another journalist writing an intrusive story? I was particularly wary after I heard a talk by Gee Semmalar on trans healthcare, in which he expressed strong feelings about cis-curiosity with regard to trans surgeries: 'There's a kind of voyeurism that is involved in piecing together our lives. We're like lab rats. You place us on the table and you dissect us and you see what our bodies look like and how our bodies change and what surgeries are being done.'

I weighed my decision to speak to doctors in the context of Gee's talk. Would it be useful at all for transpeople? Would it violate their privacy in any way? Was I being voyeuristic? Gee says in several articles that it took him 'more than two decades of loneliness' to find other transmen, before the internet made social media support groups accessible. When he eventually found others, he realized most of them were clueless about surgery, hormones and healthcare.

During my own research, I met several young transmen who were not part of the network. I put some in touch with others, but the encounters told me there were people out there who had not come out, who were still confused.

As for cis allies like me, we rarely think about issues like trans healthcare—we tend to focus on rights. I finally decided that, under the circumstances, it was important to write about medical transition, healthcare, and trans experience that is not part of the mainstream narrative—because both cis- and transpeople could use the information Gee and other activists put out there.

As an ally, I've always felt like something of an impostor at LGBTQIA+[1] rallies and events. But I did think I knew enough through my friends from the community to not be offensive. Through the years I spent on this story, I would become aware of little subconscious gestures or comments or attitudes in myself that could indeed hurt my interlocutors. My lack of knowledge, my need to learn and unlearn, would be made apparent to me.

I would like to see a world where 'cis' and 'trans' are adjectives, but I have in the past casually used phrases like 'actual woman' and 'born woman' and 'natural woman' and even just 'woman' interchangeably with 'ciswoman', while talking to cispeople, without realizing that even allowing space in my head for this vocabulary was to negate the experiences of trans friends, who have been violated by their own families—forced into electroconvulsive therapy, cheated into taking the wrong hormones, and 'cured' by marital rape.

While researching the book and particularly while interviewing transmen, I found I had to be a lot more careful with my vocabulary than I had been while working on transwomen's issues. The term 'transgender' is largely acceptable as an umbrella term, but 'gender change' could be deeply offensive. I learnt, over time, that phrases like 'transsexual' and 'transvestite' did not necessarily denote physical states

---

[1] Lesbian Gay Bisexual Transgender Queer Intersex Asexual and others. While this is the politically correct term, LGBT, LGBTQ and LGBTQI are also often used to describe sexuality minorities.

of being. Someone who had not undergone surgery and identified as gender-fluid but preferred wearing clothes of a different gender could not be called 'transvestite'. Even a neutral pronoun like 'they' could be upsetting to some who identified within the binary. To say someone was 'trapped' or 'had the wrong body' could be offensive too. I met a transman who was deeply hurt because a psychiatrist had written that he 'suffered' from gender dysphoria. He did not like referring to his transition as 'treatment', because, he said, 'I'm not ill'. In interacting with someone who does not identify with the heteronormative binary, it is usually best to ask how that person would like to be addressed, in terms of noun, pronoun and adjective.

My friends and acquaintances from the trans community were patient. They did not tell me it was wrong to ask them for their 'preferred pronoun', because 'preferred' was moot. I learnt aspects of trans sensitivity in speech organically. I also became acquainted with intra-community issues, some of which I wondered whether I should reference in the book or not, because they could reflect rather poorly on the community.

For instance, patriarchal attitudes among transmen are rarely discussed, but toxic masculinity is something of an epidemic in parts of India, and transmen are perhaps even more susceptible to it than cismen. This is particularly relevant to their treatment of female partners, both cis and trans. But the context in which the patriarchal attitudes arise is also important—it has to do with the tremendous restrictions placed on a person who has been assigned female at birth, restrictions that could either convince one that a world which treats genders so unequally has to be changed, or convince one that this is the way in which women should be treated.

I also encountered prejudice within the community against relationships between people of certain genders or sexual orientations, against people who called themselves male without having surgery. Sometimes, surgery could be crucial—some transmen told me they were so traumatized just looking into the mirror that they simply had to alter their appearance. Others who want to have their surgeries are not able to because they cannot afford them. And there are still others who either don't want surgery or cannot have surgery because of other compulsions. None of them is any less or more of a man than anyone else, and doesn't deserve to be treated badly for the decision. I would call out such prejudices in the cis community, and so I should in the trans community too.

Do I have the right to such strong opinions? I did wonder at times. But the people I interviewed are no longer subjects. Many have become close friends. In some cases, I have been absorbed into the networks of quasi-families formed within the community. There are few people with whom I have only a formal relationship. These friendships have given me something of a right to ask questions, to search for answers, to debate issues. But they have also made me aware of other responsibilities.

I often caused my interviewees to revisit extremely traumatic incidents in their past. Many of them have been victims of forced marriage, even rape. Nearly all have been victims of some form of physical or emotional violence. Not one person told me he had never contemplated suicide. All of them had friends who committed suicide. I had to be careful while asking questions. How much pain was I unlocking? When my friends broke down, was it cathartic? Or was it indicative that I had triggered something I could no longer control?

And yet, how would I look at the layered aspects of being a transman without making them revisit these moments? Unless I could uncover those layers, how would the world know their lives, know about the support systems to which they turned, the legal roadblocks and the consequent red tape, their vulnerability to various kinds of exploitation in a system which did not recognize their existence, the difficulties of getting and keeping jobs, the loneliness, the love stories and the heartbreaks, the compromises in their relationships, the religious dilemmas that could lead to self-hate, the 'corrective' rapes? How would people know the stories of their partners, who often ached to have biological children with the men they loved? How would people know how the authorities, who were supposed to protect Indian citizens, subjected some of them to sexual harassment without even realizing it? How would I write about the other difficulties that could compound gender dysphoria, such as disability, caste, penury, geopolitical conflict?

Their lives were not all sad, not bereft of joy or even humour. Most of my interviewees had a keen sense of irony; they enjoyed political incorrectness within their little groups, and their wry observations could compete with the best stand-up acts. Once, as Selvam looked at his sideburns in some pictures I had taken of him as he worked on a terrace garden, he sighed. 'My *daadhi* looks nice in this. *Chedi valarkka vandhuttom. Seyrthu idhuvom valarppom* (I've got into the business of growing plants. Might as well grow this too).'

Another person I met, who had identified as lesbian for a couple of decades before identifying as a transman, told me about a visit to a gynaecologist over extremely painful period cramps and excessive bleeding. The doctor brought in a second consultant. 'They didn't ask, they assumed I'm married, they assumed I'm heterosexual and all that. So they checked me and then they were talking to each other. "Oh, but very sad, that this person cannot conceive . . . she has that PCOD (Poly Cystic Ovarian Disorder) and also hormonal problems, so it's very difficult to conceive. She has to take *lots* of medicines and all that." So I just intervened and said, "I'm very glad I cannot conceive; no need for the medicines. Can you just stop these periods for me? That's all I want." They were shell-shocked. Like, *what* are you saying? "I don't want children." Why? I said I *hate* children. They're like "What! How can you hate children? They're so important. But you *can* have children . . ." And I said I don't want (them), and I'm so glad that I can't have children. They just cannot take it when you say something like this. And finally, when I said that I'm a homosexual, they both drew back and stopped touching me. Two women gynaecologists. They gave me a painkiller and said please don't come back. Like I would go back to people who don't know how to treat you.' Things had changed of late, though. 'Now, when I went to a gynaec and told her I don't want insertive scanning, she was completely respectful. Like *complete* respect. Things have changed also, in the last twenty years. I was twenty-five when I went to those two. At that age, that day, when they told me I couldn't conceive, I was like yayyyyy, one more reason for not getting married. Officially.'

Between laughs and anecdotes, we would speak about deeper issues—about mental health problems, largely ignored even by people who suffered from them because the classification of gender dysphoria under psychiatric illnesses was so upsetting that they did not want to think about other psychiatric conditions such as depression; about phrases and assumptions that could be offensive; about NGO politics and hierarchies within the community; about the possibilities of a transperson's involvement in gendered fields like sports or the armed forces.

One of my primary preoccupations was the 'other'-ing that could so easily happen in such a context. My interviewees could not become specimens. I did not want to subject individuals and their lives to scrutiny. I wanted to subject the system which interfered with their lives to scrutiny. I did not want their stories to evoke pity. And yet, I would spend nights crying into my pillow, thinking of someone who had been forced into marriage with a man, or someone who had been disowned by his family, or someone who was having commercial sex with men in order to pay for his surgeries. Were they tears of pity? Were they tears of anger? Were they tears of empathy? Were they tears of helplessness? Were they tears of guilt?

At some point, I realized the lives of the people I was interviewing were tied into mine. The realization resolved one of my biggest problems—how would I deal with such a bulky narrative, how would I streamline it so that it made sense to the lay reader? Should I go in chronological order of my experience? Should I split the book by issue? Should I split it into chapters, each dealing with a personal story? I finally understood that I could not possibly streamline something that is so fragmentary. The only way to lead readers into the narrative was to leave the fragments and layers and contradictions as they were, to expose their nuances and fissures, to show them my own journey as distinctly or as vaguely as I remembered it. These lives had come to me in fragments. The stories were told in layers, often changing shape and form. Just as my interviewees went from strangers to acquaintances to friends, from people I approached for information to people about whose lives I cared, so I would like them to enter the consciousness of our readers.

When I hear the word 'transman', I think of the dimpled smile of a student who calls me 'Akka'; I think of a bodybuilder who spends four hours a day at the gym and has broader shoulders than any cisman I know; I think of a cinematographer and the heart emoticons with which he ends our WhatsApp chats; I think of the thoughtful eyes of an activist who does not subscribe to any pronoun, not even gender-neutral ones; I think of the brown curls and hazel eyes of a commercial sex worker cruising on Goan beaches; I think of the white teeth of a singer who jumped off a train; I think of the confident voices and happy laughs of their femme partners; I think of a person who twirled his moustache and flexed his biceps as he flirted with me from his hospital bed; I think of the intensity with which an interviewee asked me, 'Do you think my story is worthy of publication?' I think of a woman who sat next to her twelve-year-old child and testified in court that she wanted the child's Gender Identity Change certificate to state he was a boy. These are the images I hope will unfold in the next few hundred pages.

*invisible
men*

Blue Lotus

Long ago, in a time before time, when battles were fought by the book and won by sleight, a woman burned herself alive but retained her memory into her next birth, which she had determined would be dedicated to a single cause.

Amba is the archetype of the avenging goddess, a woman wronged and reborn for revenge. Her life had been wrecked on the rocks of male egos and so she turned to the manliest and most egoistic of the gods, the lord of destruction Shiva, and undertook a penance so severe it could only be followed by the violence of death by fire. Shiva had promised that Amba would inhabit a man's body and enter the battlefield to vanquish the warrior on whom she laid the blame for her fate, Bhishma: Bhishma, who had kidnapped her to wed his brother even as she was reaching out to garland her beloved, Salva; Bhishma, who had defeated Salva in his attempt to claim his princess before she entered the realm of another king; Bhishma, who had sent her too late to Salva, after finally giving ear to her story; Bhishma, who had refused to marry her when Salva, hurting in the shame of his defeat, turned her away.

Bhishma must die, she thought, and appealed to every king in the land, begging each to go to war, bearing a garland of blue lotuses that would serve as a badge of enmity against Bhishma. Every single one turned her away, and she flung the garland in disgust against the gates of the most powerful palace of them all, the kingdom of Panchala.

Bhishma must die, she thought, and immolated herself, over and over and over and over again, until the time was ripe for her heart's

3

desire—an act so visceral, born of hatred so unadulterated, its fury possesses everyone who hears the story of this woman scorned and soured through a series of lifetimes.

Spare a thought too for Shikhandi, the receptacle of her mind and memories, cursed with a body that would start a war so that it could end another. Shikhandi, who was born into the kingdom of Panchala, a man scorched by remembrances of ignominy and incineration, a prince who would grow the muscles of a warrior and the organs of a woman. Shikhandi, who, as a child, wore the garland of blue lotuses and marked himself as the destined slayer of Bhishma, he who could not die without desiring death. Shikhandi, who was banished from his home for fear of the prophecy marked by the blue lotuses. Shikhandi, who sought refuge in a forest to escape the delegation assigned to check his gender on his nuptial night. Shikhandi, who plunged towards another death as he wept for the humiliations of this life and those past, for the elusiveness of happiness and peace, for the dimming prospect of revenge. Shikhandi, who would have ended another lifetime of misery if not for the deus ex machina, the *yaksha* who emerged from the foliage and offered to swap genitalia with him, giving Shikhandi what is arguably the world's first undocumented sex change operation.

Millennia later, others traverse the same lands Amba and Shikhandi once crossed, with no garland of blue lotuses and no yaksha to work miracles, no lineage and no mythical precedent, born with the anatomy of womanhood and the conviction of manhood, desiring not to kill but only to live.

'I Will Erase Myself'

Unsettling Memories, Part 3

By A. Mangai

Performance in 2004

Selvam shows his photograph

The urumi *drum beats. Family gathers in front of the curtain and frame. Three actors face the audience. One has his back to the audience. Drumbeats slow down and trail off.*

PRIYA: Selvam, what is this? You've erased your face from your family's photo?

Selvam, the actor whose back is to the audience, swings around and walks out of the frame.

SELVAM: I will not stay with them. I have no place there. If I exist, they cannot. Appa, Amma, Thangachchi, they cannot exist. I have always been working. When I was nine years old, I used to go with Appa to break stones. We needed money, didn't we? If Appa was the only one who did hard labour, we would not have enough. Back then, no one noticed what I was at work. But once I came home, 'Wear a *paavaadai*, wear a blouse . . .'

Drumbeats resume. Selvam walks to a clothes line, pulls off a skirt hanging there, and ties it around his waist.

SELVAM: I used to wear a paavaadai. But I did not like wearing a blouse. I would wear a shirt. A collared one. I would roll the sleeves

6

up to my elbow. Like this *(demonstrates)*. As I walked, I would twist the paavaadai into a *veshti* and tie it up. Like this *(demonstrates)*. No one bothered me at work when I was a child. But then . . . later . . . would they let me be? They went on about this and that . . . I got so tired of it, I stopped working and stayed home. Then, there was a friend who accorded me the respect due to a fellow human being. After she came into my life, I cut my hair. If only I had stayed with her . . . if only I *could* have stayed with her . . . Let it be. I don't want to turn back the pages to chapters that have already been closed. Whatever I earn, however brave a face I wear, this body is at odds with my mind. I want a fierce moustache. I want a French beard. My chest must harden into stone. My hips must be ramrod-straight. This goddamned stomach ache, the blood that spills onto my thighs, must stop. My body must lose its wetness (its femininity and compassion); I must stand tall, erect, cold. Will I be able to? When? How? *(Laughs)* Don't know. I don't know.

Drum beats as he pulls off his skirt.

SELVAM: For now, I am alone. I hide my body and my face. And I am alone.

Beglaubigte Abschrift aus dem Geburtsregister

des Standesamts Arolsen -/-

Nr. 19

Arolsen , am 21. Mai 1885

Vor dem unterzeichneten Standesbeamten erschien heute, der Persönlichkeit nach

be kannt,

Kaufmann Bernhard Bär. -/-

wohnhaft zu Arolsen, ——————————————————————————————

——————————————————israelitischer Religion, und zeigte an, daß von der

Lina Bär geb. Löwenberg, seiner Ehefrau, ——————————————

——————————————————————israelitischer Religion,

wohnhaft bei ihm, -/-

zu Arolsen, -/-

am ——————————————zwanzigsten Mai -/-——————————— des Jahres

tausendachthundertachtzig und fünf, ————————————————vor mittags

um ——————————————————neun Uhr ein Kind ——————————weib lichen

Geschlechts geboren worden sei, welches den -/- ———————————— Vornamen

Martha -/-

erhalten habe. -/-

Vorgelesen, genehmigt und unterschrieben

Bernhard Baer

Der Standesbeamte

Waldeck

Die Übereinstimmung mit den Eintragungen im Geburtsregister wird hiermit beglaubigt.

Die Abschrift enthält einen Randvermerk.

Arolsen , den 31. August 19 93

Der Standesbeamte

——— Abschrift aus dem Geburtsregister vor 1900 (mit Religionsangabe)
Verlag für Standesamtswesen GmbH., Frankfurt a. M.-Hamburg-München H 105532-10

A 29

Das nebenbezeichnete Kind Baer ist männlichen Geschlechts und hat anstatt des Vornamens Martha den Vornamen Karl erhalten. Eingetragen auf Grund Anordnung fürstlichen Amtsgerichts Arolsen vom 08. Januar 1907. Arolsen, am 02. Februar 1907. Der Standesbeamte In Vertretung Müller

Missing Links

Transwomen have always had a place in history. They were called 'eunuchs' for a large part of it, but they held honoured positions as palace guards and literary characters, finding documentation in Persian poetry and Shakespearean drama. They were the confidantes of lovelorn heroines, teachers of princesses, protectors of harems.

There is no such lineage for transmen. Who were the first female-to-male transsexuals? There are few studies on the subject. I looked up online editions of journals, websites by transmen dedicated to tracing their heritage, and archives of newspapers to plot a sketchy history of transmen.

There are documented cases of non-operative transmen from as early as the 1820s.[1] But the first surgeries for female-to-male transition were only performed in the opening decade of the twentieth century, chiefly in Germany, on the patients of sexologist Magnus Hirschfeld. The details of these and of their successes are vague. It appears Dr Hirschfeld had been working by trial and error for some time earlier, but there is no related documentation.

---

[1] Some parts of this chapter were published in my long-form feature, 'To Be a Man', in *Fountain Ink* magazine, March 2017.

On 2 December 1829, Lucy Ann Lobdell was born in Albany County, New York. She was raised female, married George Washington Slater and had a daughter with him, but it was an unhappy, abusive marriage. In 1855, Lucy Ann swapped dresses for a man's clothes, lopped off her waist-length hair, and lived as a man called Joseph Lobdell for the rest of her life.

In 1855, Lobdell self-published a memoir titled *Narrative* and, perhaps as a consequence, was tried in Minnesota for 'falsely impersonating a man, against the peace and dignity of the state of Minnesota' in 1858. Lobdell would marry a woman called Marie Perry in 1861, a marriage recorded and reported routinely by the *NY Sun*, with no knowledge that this was, in fact, the first documented same-sex marriage in America. A *New York Times* article in 1879 hailed Lobdell in a headline that read: 'Death of a Modern Diana, Wearing Man's Clothing She Wins a Girl's Love.' But it is not clear whether Lobdell wanted to be a man or was a lesbian in disguise. Lobdell was incarcerated in a mental asylum in 1879, and died in one in 1912.

On 9 December 1869, journalist, adventurer and self-proclaimed soldier Jack Bee Garland was born in San Francisco. Under a series of assumed names, and often pretending to be mute so that his female voice would not give him away, he worked as a reporter, interpreter and cabin boy who accompanied the US Army to the Philippine War in 1899. Eventually, he became a nurse at military camps with the Sixteenth, Twenty-Ninth, Forty-Second, and Forty-Fifth United States Volunteer Infantry regiments. He does not appear to have had any

kind of surgery. When he died of natural causes in 1936, his family buried him in a white satin dress.

Martha Baer was born in Bad Arolsen, Germany, on 20 May 1885. As Karl M. Baer, he underwent one of the first sex-change surgeries, in December 1906, and was issued a new birth certificate reflecting his male gender in January 1907, thus becoming the first transman to be legally recognized. It was an eventful year for him: with Dr Hirschfeld, he authored a fictionalized autobiography called *Aus eines Mannes Mädchenjahren* (A Man's Years as a Young Girl), published under the pseudonym N.O. Body; he also won the legal right to marry a woman, and went on to remarry after his wife's death five years later. Hirschfeld wrote in a book that another of his patients had been granted the right to serve in the German military, and did so during the Second World War. Karl M. Baer died on 26 June 1956, at the age of 71, in Israel.

On 4 October 1890, Alberta Lucille Hart was born in Coffey County, Kansas. Alberta quickly changed her name to Alan, and always presented as a boy, except in school, where he was deeply unhappy at having to wear a girl's uniform. He would go on to become a radiologist and tuberculosis (TB) researcher who pioneered the use of X-ray photography to detect TB. In 1917, Hart approached Dr Joshua Gilbert at the University of Oregon, asking for a hysterectomy, identifying himself as a person with an 'abnormal inversion' who should be sterilized. Gilbert evaluated Hart as 'extremely intelligent and not mentally ill, but afflicted with a mysterious disorder for which I have no explanation'. The same year, the first recorded FTM transition surgery in America was performed

on him. In 1918, he married Inez Stark. They divorced five years later, and he married Edna Raddick in 1925, a companionship which lasted until his death on 1 July 1962, of heart failure.

Among the few transmen of international prominence today is Chaz Bono, perhaps more famous for his parentage—he was born to Cher and Sonny Bono—than in his own right. It was this inheritance that led a tabloid to photograph him with his girlfriend in 1995 and identify him as a lesbian. Chaz went on to self-identify as a transman, and in September 2011, competed as a man on *Dancing with the Stars*.

Thomas Beatie became famous as 'The Pregnant Man' in 2007, after undergoing transition in 2002. He bore three biological children after a mastectomy.

American swimmer Schuyler Bailar is the first transman to compete in the Division 1 category of the National Collegiate Athletic Association in any sport, a distinction he achieved in 2015.

Transman Laith Ashley became a hugely successful model within two years of going on testosterone, walking the ramp during New York Fashion Week 2016, and appearing on numerous magazine covers and ad campaigns.

In April 2016, German-born fitness instructor Benjamin Melzer became the first transmale model to make the cover of *Men's Health* magazine.

It has been largely impossible to find Indian transmen who are older than their fifties.

A work by Sunil Mohan and Sumathi Murthy (who now goes by Rumi Harish), *Towards Gender Inclusivity: A Study on Contemporary Concerns around Gender*, examines the absence of a lineage for transmen in India, citing several other scholarly works on the issue.

In William Penrose's publication 'Hidden in History: Female Homoeroticism and Women of a "Third Nature" in the South Asian Past' in the *Journal of the History of Sexuality*, he writes about how he learnt of the *sadhins*, women from the Gaddhi tribe in northwest India, along the Himalayan foothills. Penrose cites Peter Phillimore's 'Unmarried Women of the Dhaula Dhar: Celibacy and Social Control in Northwest India', published in the *Journal of Anthropological Research*, in speaking of the lifestyles of these women. Though the word 'sadhin' could be seen as the female derivative of 'sadhu', these women led a secular life. However, they were committed to celibacy and chastity for life. They did not take public vows, but it was a tacit understanding. In exchange for suppressing their sexuality, they lived with their families, but wore male clothes and did 'men's work'. They were often seen sitting with women, but they smoked with the men, which other women were not allowed to do. However, in addition to embracing celibacy, they must do so at puberty and no later, or they would be cast out of their villages.

The tradition of women becoming 'sworn virgins' and living as men seems to have been followed in various parts of the world, including Albania, Kosovo and Turkey. The last even has a similar word for them, 'sadik'. What female virginity has to do with the right to live as a man is not clear in any of these traditions; nor is it clear whether the people who became 'sworn virgins' did so because they did not want men entering them, since they felt their vaginas did not belong in their bodies, or whether they were driven by other motivations or compulsions.

It was the closest record history provided to transmen.

There is no clear enumeration of how many transmen—or even transpeople—there are in India. The 2011 census claimed the number of people who identified as third gender was 4.9 lakh, but there appears to be some confusion, since 55,000 of those were in the 0–6 years age category. Most transmen who live at home are not yet out, and it would be quite impossible to guess at the numbers.

Even mythology makes no place for transmen, Sunil told me. Transwomen had the story of Brihannala from the Mahabharata, which was the avatar Arjuna assumed following a curse; transwomen also follow the Koothandavar tradition of Aravan worship.

'But mythology has the Amba–Shikhandi story for transmen, right?' I said.

'Yes, but that story has been appropriated.' Sunil smiled. 'Ask anyone who Shikhandi is, and they will tell you he's a hijra, though he's not male-born. Because the concept of female sexuality does not exist. That too is an offshoot of the patriarchal system.'

I would come across instances of mythological transmen whose stories had been more or less usurped, perhaps inadvertently, by transwomen.

My own encounter with transmen in India came through the transwoman community. They found the young man I met quite bizarre—a woman who already had the body they so desired, and was desperate to change it for the bodies they had been so keen to discard.

Footboard Travel

If a film based on Selvam's life were to be made, he knew exactly how it would end—a smiling wife who would bring him coffee when he returned home after closing shop, a couple of children at whom he could snap for making a racket when their father had a headache, his parents at hand to coddle his offspring while he met his wife's eyes in silent spousal enquiry, and she giggled in shy acquiescence.

The narrative arc could be coaxed towards that end, but the beginnings of his story had rendered some parts not implausible, but impossible.

When I thought of Selvam, it was always at thresholds. I had first seen him in 2006, standing outside a tent and spitting into the ground before he strode towards me. I met him ten years later, standing outside the gate of a rented house in Madras, hands in pockets and a proud sprout of fuzz on his face. After another hiatus, I saw him at the door of the balcony of a newly acquired rental home, waving excitedly, reaching for a shirt to wear over his vest and *kaili*.

He was always on the verge—of a romantic commitment, of an entrepreneurial enterprise, of an operation that would take him closer to his ideal self, of collapse.

Once, as I was driving him to his parents' home about ninety kilometres from Madras, he said, 'It's a good thing you can drive. Otherwise we'd have had to go to Koyambedu because the buses are already full by the time they reach Ashok Nagar.'

'At nine in the morning?' I asked.

'What else? Everyone is going somewhere every day. There have been times when I've gone to Koyambedu and not got a seat, and not even standing room.' He stretched. 'Then it's footboard travel.'

'For a hundred kilometres?!'

'Hello. My entire life is footboard travel.' He grinned. 'How's my dialogue?'

'Makes me want to drive into the median.'

'Hello. I write super dialogues.'

'You could be the hero's friend.'

'Hero's friend?! Why not the hero?'

'I mean, like Vivek, Vadivelu, Santhanam. You've got great comic timing. You'd make a good comedian.'

'Do I look like a "comedy piece" to you? Everyone treats me as a "comedy piece".' He snorted. 'If you knew everything I've been through, everything I've got out of, you wouldn't say I should be the hero's friend.'

'Tell me your stories, then.'

'Did I tell you about the time I was surrounded by rowdies in a public toilet?'

15 December 2016

A strange house

'What they didn't see was what was so obvious to us—we belonged in the right gender, but had been given the wrong bodies. How could we tell them that what seemed odd to them was what came most naturally to us?'

—Selvam

The three rooms of the inconspicuous house were home to inhabitants who were the objects of the neighbours' curiosity: a bunch of boys with childlike faces, who smoked and drank like men with too much time on their hands; women with deep voices and tall statuesque figures, who wore beautiful clothes and expensive make-up before they went out to earn their livelihood; the women brought in the money, the men cooked and cleaned. What did outsiders think of this place, where gender norms were constantly subverted? What did its occupants feel about carrying out the very tasks they saw as markers of a gender to which they did not belong?

Selvam stood with his hands in his pockets, leg idling jauntily against a motorcycle which had been fortuitously parked by the gate.[1]

'Do you recognize me?' I asked him.

'Of course.' He grinned. 'Natarajapuram.'

11 May 2006

Bodyguard

I was setting up my tripod for a piece-to-camera. A group of transwomen had crowded around Priya Babu, who hushed their questions as I began to speak:

'I'm standing in the village of Natarajapuram, where the transgender community has been allocated housing space by the government, three kilometres away from the nearest town. It was transwoman Priya Babu who fought for this, on behalf of the community of *aravanis*, as they are called, after . . .'

'Hello! Foreign bitch! We're not aravanis or *kiruvanis*. We're *ladies*. A-haan!'

'Sssh,' Priya hissed, as I looked at the transwoman who was glaring from the frame of a house under construction.

'Don't "sssh" me. Ask that cunt to watch how she talks!'

I looked at Priya, who smiled encouragingly, and asked me to carry on.

'This community has not been able to find houses to rent. Priya has also successfully fought for voting rights and heads a drama troupe, made up of members of the aravani . . .'

'Son of a whore! You say that word one more time, I'll tear out your tongue and rub your pretty face with it'—she had a gift for graphic imagery—'You think sticking out your tits makes you special?'

---

[1] Some parts of my interviews with Selvam were published in my long-form feature, 'To Be a Man', in *Fountain Ink* magazine, March 2017.

'*Aiyo*, will you stop it?' Priya shouted. 'She is trying to help us. She's going to make a documentary that will be screened abroad, and we'll get money.'

'Ask her to give us the fucking money now!'

'Go inside, please,' Priya said firmly.

The transwoman spat on the floor. 'You've got her to do your *waqalat* (legal defence) for now. But you'll have to go alone to the bus stop, won't you? You won't see me coming. I'll kill you with my bare hands and leave your corpse to rot. By the time I'm done with you, people won't know whether you were a man or woman.' She snorted and disappeared into the house with no walls, and went to a windowframe from which she looked out at me.

My hands had begun to tremble.

'Don't worry,' Priya told me softly. 'Finish your speech. I'll send Selvam to escort you to the bus stop.'

I was relieved. Selvam, I assumed, was the *panthi*—cismale partner—of one of the women in the village. I hoped he would be formidably built, and I also hoped the woman who wanted to kill me with her bare hands and leave my corpse to rot would have a crush on him.

As it turned out, Selvam was six inches shorter than I, and his thighs were arguably slimmer than my arms. Wearing khaki shorts and a yellowed, once-white shirt, he looked like the student of a state corporation school. He was no panthi; he was, in fact, a pre-operative transman whose biological functions were identical to mine. I could not say what it was about this diminutive man, smaller and younger than I, that made me feel safe.

Documentary by Nandini Krishnan: M/F/?

Visuals:
Interview with Selvam
Commentary:
(interview in Tamil, with subtitles)
IN WORDS: 'I lived as a . . .'
OUT WORDS: '. . . people will find out.'
DUR: 00'36'

I lived as a woman until I was eighteen. Then they decided to get me married. I tried explaining, but it didn't work, so I ran away. I got my hair cut, wore boys' clothes and worked for a couple of years. Then people began to get suspicious, so I had to leave and come back home. Somehow, I managed to convince my family that I had actually become a man. They believed me, but we had problems in our village and we had to move here. So far, I haven't had any problems except low pay, because they think I'm a kid, but it's a constant fear—that people will find out.

The story was more complicated than a thirty-six-second sound bite, but Selvam did not trust people easily. All I knew then was that he had somehow found refuge with the transwoman community, and made a living doing odd jobs, disguised as a boy. In a village full of women who had been assigned male at birth, he was also the odd one out. 'I don't think there is anyone else like me in the world,' he said, firmly. When I told him about transmen I knew in the UK, he nodded nonchalantly and said, 'In India, anyway.'

He was stunned when I told him the transmen I knew in the UK had been operated upon and were undergoing hormone therapy. Then he frowned.

'Aravanis themselves cannot have their surgery legally here. They must go to quacks. How do you think (the law) will allow a freak like me to get operated upon? And what operation are you talking about? You can't *fix* a non-existent organ on me, right? Or can you make it grow?'

The world had changed for transwomen in the decade since I had last met Selvam. Sex reassignment surgery, or sex reaffirmation surgery as some prefer to call it, had been legalized. Transwomen did not have to put themselves at the mercy of quacks in seedy bylanes any longer. Selvam too was aware that the 'non-existent organ' could be created and fixed.

'If I hadn't met the transwomen, I would never have found out,' he told me, running a hand over his flat chest, 'I would not have even this body, though it's not really complete.'

It was at this time that he told me how he had first encountered the transwoman community into which he was adopted. His sister had happened to meet Priya Babu, who had come to an NGO near her workplace; she told Priya about the strange case in her family—a girl who had turned into a boy. Priya had not met a transman before, but knew of them through her networks. She decided to speak to Selvam. She was the first person, after his partner, with whom Selvam could be entirely honest. She told him about the settlement and suggested he move there with his family. The transwomen would help him out.

~

Documentary by Nandini Krishnan: M/F/?

Visuals:
Selvam walking down a road.
Commentary:
(interview in Tamil, with subtitles)
(Music fades in slowly)
IN WORDS: 'Even here . . .'
OUT WORDS: '. . . having children.'
DUR: 00'31'

Even here, people keep asking me why I haven't grown a moustache, though I'm twenty-two years old. My family wants me to marry a girl and prove I'm a man by having children.

~

A lot of transpeople have portrayed themselves as intersex in order to be more acceptable, and certainly the widespread notion that the hijra community is intersex, stands. Being intersex is seen as something people can't help and so, even though intersex children are subjected to horrible things and identifying as intersex doesn't make life easier, it's something that some transpeople have socially cultivated and that is socially understood of transpeople in India.

At a neural level, one can even argue that since behaviour emerges from the brain and we know of some neural correlates of trans identity, that trans identities emerge from intersex variations whose physical expression is in an organ largely hidden from public view, the brain. However, it is precisely the visibility of the external body to doctors and family that shapes the intersex social experience as very different from the non-intersex trans experience.

—Prof. Karthik Bittu Kondaiah

~

It was in the village that Selvam had met his 'sister' Aarthi. She was the 'daughter' of a transwoman who had adopted several youngsters. There was a system called *'reet'* among transwomen—the adoption and mentoring of young transwomen by their senior counterparts, who would become their 'mothers'. No one knew quite what to do with Selvam. It made sense for a 'mother' from the community to adopt him. But they would have to alter an age-old tradition to do so.

Unsettling Memories, Part 5

Directed by A. Mangai
Reet

Young kothi *comes into the jama'at. He touches the feet of the senior transwomen, saying, 'Paon padti.' They bless him with 'Jeete raho.'*
PRIYA: You've come here before, haven't you?

KOTHI: Yes, I have. Twice. You sent me away.

PRIYA: Then why have you come back?

KOTHI: I can no longer live at home. It's torture. They yell at me even if I wear kohl. I can no longer live at home. I've decided that if I am to live, I will live like you. Otherwise, I have no option but to kill myself.

PRIYA: Are you crazy? Do you think we're running a charity? We can't eat unless we go to the shops and beg. And then *bandhis* and *naaris* (men and women) call us 'ombodhu' and 'pottai',[2] this and that. And now you want to pile on? Go, go, go. Go home and be a good boy.

CHELA 1: Guru, don't say that. This kothi has told me everything. Its mind is made up. It can't go back home. And now, you're chasing it away. Don't do that. Let it stay on with us.[3]

CHELA 2: The pottai wants to stay on with us. Let's do a reet for it and make it a woman, why don't we?

PRIYA: Fine. Ramya, bring the *chattai*.

Drumbeats as Ramya brings the plate.

PRIYA: Take the blessings of the chattai.

Kothi touches the plate and says, 'Paon padti.'

PRIYA: Give me some change (Chela *passes her a five-rupee note*). And four annas (Chela *passes her a twenty-five paise coin*). Here, Gurubai, five rupees and four annas. Here, now, cover your head (*Kothi pulls a cloth over his head*). Put your hands on the plate (*Priya lifts the plate and Kothi bends to touch it*). Repeat after me. As the Aakaashvaani is my witness . . .

KOTHI: As the Aakaashvaani is my witness . . .

---

[2] Tamil pejorative words used to insult transwomen.

[3] Though 'she' would be the politically correct term, the Tamil word *'adhu'*, used to refer to very junior people, usually children, in affection or contempt or to assert seniority, was used in the play, which translates literally into 'it'. Since transwomen have told me several rituals must be undertaken for a kothi to become a *thirunangai* and earn the female pronoun, I have chosen to use the gender-neutral 'it' in translation for 'adhu' and 'he' while referring to the kothi before the reet ritual.

PRIYA: As Bhoomadevi is my witness . . .

KOTHI: As Bhoomadevi is my witness . . .

PRIYA: As the lamp of Kamakshi is my witness . . .

KOTHI: As the lamp of Kamakshi is my witness . . .

PRIYA: As the old and young present here are my witnesses . . .

KOTHI: As the old and young present here are my witnesses . . .

PRIYA: I . . .

KOTHI: I . . .

PRIYA: Consent to be the daughter of Priya.

KOTHI: Consent to be the daughter of Priya.

PRIYA: Through good times and bad . . .

KOTHI: Through good times and bad . . .

PRIYA: Through difficulties and sorrow . . .

KOTHI: Through difficulties and sorrow . . .

PRIYA: I will be by her side.

KOTHI: I will be by her side.

PRIYA: This . . .

KOTHI: This . . .

PRIYA: Is a promise.

KOTHI: Is a promise.

PRIYA: Is a promise.

KOTHI: Is a promise.

PRIYA: Is a promise.

KOTHI: Is a promise.

The transwomen do the 'thanaar thanaar' *clap, as the drum begins to beat.*

PRIYA: Take the blessings of all the elders, my child.

Her newly inducted chela *walks around, touching the feet of the older transwomen, saying* 'paon padti', *and they touch her head and say,* 'Jeete raho'.

GURUBAI: Henceforth, Priya is your mother. She will show you the ropes. Listen to her, follow her advice. Think of a name for yourself. Let's hope it's a lucky one.

～

The first time I heard the reet vows, it struck me as strange that the chelas promised to stick it out 'through good times and bad, difficulties and sorrow'. The phrase 'good times' was their only indulgence to optimism; why not 'joy and sorrow', why not 'difficulties and comfort'? So ruthless was the pragmatism of these transwomen that they would make no concession to euphony. And yet, they retained a sense of sharing misfortune and fortune, of creating a family. Would transmen be able to form a network of their own, families of brothers, of fathers and sons, of mates?

When Selvam first came to Natarajapuram, he thought he was an oddity, one of a kind. His only hope for community was to be absorbed into the family of transwomen, and he approached a senior member of the jama'at, asking if she would be his mother. His reet had to be carried out in secret, because he had moved to Natarajapuram with his parents and younger siblings—a brother and sister—who thought he had naturally transformed into a biological male. The 'mother' who adopted him was the 'sister' of the transwoman who had adopted Aarthi.

When Aarthi moved to Madras, Selvam asked to go along. They have now established a family with a complex network of relationships. Aarthi had several 'daughters' and many of Selvam's friends had become her 'sons'. The sons called him 'mama'—mother's brother—but the daughters called him *anna* (older brother), because 'mama' is also the word for a suitor or husband.

'Everyone in this area must be in *"semma* confusion",' Selvam declared, stepping over a mysterious figure in what seemed to be a human shape, prone on the floor, with the blankets drawn tight over it. 'But then, confusing people is an advantage when you have to constantly protect yourself.' He told me I had been the first to ever interview him, back in 2006. 'I must have prattled on and on,' he said.

'No, you were very brief.'

'Aanh, that's another problem. You would not have had enough material. Now, I've had practice. Everyone interviews me. See, I'll tell you so much you'll be able to write a book about me.'

Brothers in Arms

To most young transmen, Satya Rai Nagpaul is a vision of what they could become—broad-shouldered, with a thick beard, deep voice, and several awards for cinematography, he is a spokesperson for transgender rights. But his professional success has ensured that his gender is of no consequence except when he chooses to use particular labels.

'I can't wait to grow a beard like Satya's,' a transmale student told me wistfully. 'He came to my college for a lecture on film, and I just kept thinking, oh my god, how awesome it would be to look like him.'

Did Satya remember when he had first felt this moment of excitement in his own life, knowing that there was someone who had transitioned, and knowing that his physicality would one day match how he felt inside?

'There was no one,' Satya told me. 'At AIIMS (All India Institute of Medical Sciences), where I had started my hormone therapy in 1997, I had asked if there were others I could meet. My psychiatrist told me there were a couple of people he knew of, but they had asked not to be contacted, since they wanted to assimilate back into society and not be visible as transpeople.'

Satya knew he had to start a network. People who wanted to find others like themselves had to have a way to access each other. Soon after he began his transition, Satya reached out to lesbian and gay spaces in Delhi. He left his contact details with the gay collective Humrahi and lesbian group Sangini. Gradually, transpeople began to approach him. In the late 1990s, Sampoorna started with three transmen and one

25

transwoman as its first members. Today, the group, which calls itself 'a network by trans- and intersex Indians for trans- and intersex Indians across the globe', comprises more than two hundred members.

It has been nearly twenty years since the group began, but networks of transmasculine people are relatively nascent. Most transmen in India are on the Sampoorna Working Group mailing list. There are also various local and national social media networks, and private Facebook or WhatsApp groups, through which transmen have found each other in several cities across India. Satya told me these networks have been expanding, particularly over the last two years. Many are also connected to other networks across Asia. Because the numbers were still so few, they formed intimate connections over long distances. A transman in the United States could become close friends with a transman in New Zealand after meeting him at a conference in Sri Lanka or Thailand.

~

'Within this community, there's also a lot of humour. Among us. It's not just the sadness. It's not just losses that we have undergone. There's lots of humour. I mean, really shitloads of humour in terms of whether it's going to the hospital and experiencing something in hospitals, and you know, how the doctors call our names. There are lots of things which are very pleasure-oriented, plus-points which we really love. Well, you know, sometimes it is humour, sometimes it is trauma.'

—Rumi Harish

~

It wasn't all hunky-dory. As I met transmen and heard their stories, I would discover various aspects of these networks, some of which could be teething problems and others that indicated worrying trends. I would see the ways in which some of them tried to monetize their stories, and others rebelled against the concept of telling one's story, the politics within and between various organizations that represented or tried to represent transmen's interests, the chosen few who became spokespeople for trans activism, and the various ways in which other issues—caste, disability, language, class, education, family, religion— played into gender identity.

24 March 2018

Gee Semmalar added 2 photos

> Right (14 years old teenage), left currently.
> Whenever mainstream media wants to write about transpeople, they ask for before-after photos. They want to see our transition from point A to point B. They ask us, 'When did you know you are trans?' However, our lives are more complex than narratives set by them. Gender expressions and identities are not static or fixed, rather, they are a process. There is no particular moment we can pinpoint about our self-recognition. I was male identified without knowing the terms for it or the possibilities of transition at a young age. As young as 6 or 7 years old. So there is, in fact, no before and after. There is only the future, a future influenced by our past but not defined by it and our right to live a full life with happiness, love, and chosen families. In that future, I live with my brothers and sisters. For that future, I work for my people.
> #transjourneys #transmanindia #transmatter #transgender #transi sbeautiful#indiantransman #transmenindia #transmenofinstagram #transmenofcolor #lgbtpride#pride #testosterone #proud #asiantransman #transgender #ftm #ftmtransgender#ftmfitness #indian #femaletomale #equality #rainbowpride #rainbowflag
> —Facebook post by Gee Semmalar

On rare occasions, transmen do put up before and after pictures on their social media accounts, typically to indicate how far they have come, and to motivate others who are just beginning their transition. But many find it difficult to even look at their old photographs, particularly those who were compelled to wear their hair long or don female clothes.

Yet, most media reportage to do with transition is accompanied by before–after pictures, so that the focus is entirely on the body modification and not on the problems of being trans—a man with breasts and no facial hair, an unbroken voice, and a double life. Many reporters could also unintentionally spread misinformation and even myths about transitioning.

One of my interviewees sent me an article published on the website *Quint*, titled *Rajveer and Shivangi's Unique Love Story Will Make You Tear Up*.

The piece declared that Rajveer, whose assigned name was also mentioned, had decided to have his gender affirmation surgery in order to marry his ciswoman partner. A statement of this kind, that someone would go under the knife for love and not because of dysphoria, could give the impression it was entirely a choice, and that one could function perfectly well without the surgery.

The piece referred to them as a 'same-sex couple' whose relationship was not acceptable to their families, and that it was because of his partner's love and support that Rajveer had decided to 'change his gender'—careless phrases that make transpeople and allies cringe.

Could there be an argument in favour of media coverage? Did it only help create a voyeuristic narrative, or did it echo the stories of other transpeople, who might then reach out to each other? Did it bring invisible people into the public imagination? Was it important for the transmasculine community to have a place in the public imaginary?

Satya told me visibility in society, in law, and in life had somehow been replaced by visibility in media. In an age of 24-hour news channels, live website updates, hashtags, and the 'Insta' prefix, perhaps this was only to be expected. One could not quite dismiss these stories as fifteen-seconds-of-fame, though. The coverage had several insidious effects, and Satya would outline them to me.

'A certain bravado is attached to "coming-out" stories and a hierarchy of elites is created within the community, to whom the authority to speak and decide on behalf of the community is transferred overnight,' he said. 'All players get what they want—the media their stories, the funders their nods, the storytellers their "moment of glory and status", and the community remains where they are, where they always were. Outside of the career activists, it would be important to examine if the life of the common hijra person has really changed in so many years of hijra leaders coming to prominence of one kind or another. It's something for the emerging transmasculine and intersex communities to investigate as they devise their own strategies and positions.'

Who was getting the visibility? Whom did it serve? On whose terms and conditions? Was the visibility for the 'bourgeois press and audience'? And how did transpeople as a community benefit from such visibility? Did it help young transmen who were looking for role models? If so, what sort of role models were reaching them and how? Was the community interrogating these issues?

'The contemporary discourses being put forth by the current mainstream media are at their lowest,' Satya said. 'They seem unable to operate outside of the sensationalist mode and the engagement is at a very shallow level. For me, the idea that role models reach us in our actual lives is more powerful than reaching us through, say, television. If there is any bit of hope vis-à-vis the media, then I still have some from cinema and the newly emerging web media.'

'But can you actually think of examples of films that have struck you as positive?' I asked him. 'Like, in terms of representation of trans- and intersex people, what would you like to see in the fiction and non-fiction media?'

'None that match up to some of my favourites,' Satya said, and reeled off a list—'Hiroshi Teshigahara's *Woman in the Dunes,* Rolf de Heer's *Dance Me to My Song,* Wim Wenders' *Pina,* Humberto Solas's *Lucía,* Agnes Varda's *The Gleaners and I,* Helma Sanders-Brahms' *No Mercy, No Future,* Mani Kaul's *Before My Eyes,* Guru Dutt's *Sahib, Bibi Aur Gulam* and Roberto Minervini's *The Other Side.*'

Where were the real-life encounters, he asked. Transwomen were seen in life, not on television. Why, then, were transmen only really seen in the media?

'But then, most of our childhood memories of transwomen are restricted to seeing them begging on trains, at traffic signals, and shops, no?' I said.

True, Satya said. However, he felt the transman narrative in the media was even more problematic than our distorted understanding of transwomen from those childhood memories.

'"Coming-out stories" are a tiny, tiny part of the wider spectrum of the "trans discourse", which is the entire diversity of trans voices that exist and may or may not be available to us in a mediatized manner,' he said. 'The engagements go beyond "me and my struggle to become female or male".'

Trans discourse must raise questions about 'gender practice', he felt, and fired: 'Is the state creating the possibilities for self-determination of gender? Is it going beyond recognition in law and what institutional mechanisms are being established to ensure implementation? Has transmasculinity given patriarchy enough grounds for insecurity and self-reflection? Or has it only reinforced it? Does transmasculinity habitate misogyny at its core? What challenges has it brought to feminisms and feminist analysis? Has it transcended from the danger of *the* transmasculinity" to "transmasculinities"? Does it just feed off hegemonic masculinities or do its narratives destabilize them politically? What are its commitments to the larger intersectional space of caste–class–gender–ethnicity and other struggles? What kind of a "public sphere" does it imagine? And most importantly, what are the very constitutive values that transmasculinities are setting up for themselves?'

Those questions would encapsulate the various dilemmas I came across in transmen, the disturbing beliefs some of them seemed to nurse, and the susceptibility of the transmasculine movement—like all movements—to hijacking by vested interests.

Five-letter Word

If the invisibility of transmen from public life puts them at a disadvantage, their invisibility in law cripples them. In 2010, Sampoorna held their first legal rights awareness meeting for transpeople. The same year, Satya attended the very first international conference on Human Rights and Gender Identity, held in Barcelona.

Almost no conversation on transgender rights in India can be carried out without a reference to 'NALSA'. The acronym has become synecdoche for one of the most crucial court verdicts in the recent past.

The Supreme Court of India's judgment in the *National Legal Services Authority vs Union of India* case, delivered on 15 April 2014, is considered a landmark in recognizing the rights of transpeople. Essentially, the judgment allows one to self-identify with a particular gender, irrespective of what his or her birth certificate, hormones, or surgical history say. However, its implementation leaves a lot to be desired.

Dr L. Ramakrishnan, from the public health and human rights NGO SAATHII (Solidarity and Action against the HIV Infection in India), which works primarily with HIV/AIDS prevention and treatment, has been involved in the queer movement and is one of the administrators of the volunteer-run website Orinam. He has been advising several transmen on their health, and is among those fighting for transgender rights.[1]

---

[1] Some parts of my interview with Dr L. Ramakrishnan were published in my long-form feature, 'To Be a Man', in *Fountain Ink* magazine, March 2017.

He acknowledges that the NALSA judgment is crucial in 'making a clear distinction between a medicalized gender identity and a legal gender identity', but its interpretation in the popular imagination and non-implementation in government offices leave transmen at a particular disadvantage. Largely invisible in terms of national advocacy, they sometimes have trouble convincing officials they exist.

'They've been told, "You're just a modern woman who wears her hair short and dresses in boyish clothes,"' he said, and this refusal to accept their identity translates into the impossibility of getting their ID cards. When the cards are issued, the gender is often printed as 'T'—for transgender—irrespective of whether someone desires to be within the binary instead.

After NALSA, the Sampoorna Working Group had stepped up its interaction with the Ministry of Social Justice and Empowerment (MoSJE), and had been working with the Parliamentary Standing Committee on the Transgender Bill since 2016. The Bill should ideally have improved on the apex court's judgment, sealing with legislation what could be open to judicial interpretation. But it essentially ignores all the liberal aspects of that judgment, and till a recent amendment was added, made no reference at all to transmen, classifying all trans- and intersex people as 'eunuchs'.

'The implementation of the NALSA judgment has hardly gone under way, and the current version of the Transgender Rights Bill is badly diluted and distorted,' Satya had told me in February 2017. They were in the process of making depositions to the Parliamentary Standing Committee at the time, and were pushing for a clear and consistent inclusion of transmasculine and intersex people.

Several transmen told me that because the Transgender Boards even in the states that claim to be trans-friendly comprised mainly transwomen, there was some gatekeeping within the community. 'They fear losing what is perceived as a small slice of the pie,' an activist told me. 'They don't want it to be sliced up even further, so you have transwomen putting up all kinds of hierarchies of authenticity, saying transwomen who are post-operative are the most genuine, most authentic and most deserving transwomen and at the bottom of the totem pole are transmen, and somewhere in between are transwomen who are pre-operative or non-operative.' Changing one's gender identity on documents required proof of surgery before the NALSA judgment. Though the judgment upholds the right to self-identify without surgery, most government offices across the country are not aware of the case and will not accept requests from non-operative transpeople without explicit instructions from the 'concerned authorities'. I would learn from transmen I interviewed that no one, including the government offices that directed them to the 'concerned authorities', knew who these 'concerned authorities' were. Many have paid bribes they could barely afford to get their documents falsified. Others spent months, sometimes years, dedicating themselves to fighting various 'concerned authorities'.

Not only do many government offices insist on a sex reassignment surgery (SRS) certificate, they also deem whether or not someone has been surgically altered to a passable extent. Ramakrishnan told me about a transman who had applied to a regional passport office and submitted proof of having undergone a mastectomy, hysterectomy and oophorectomy.

'But the reply came, "You don't have a penis, you can't be a man", and his application (was) rejected—very, very cruel, and the fact *is* that the gender reassignment or sex reassignment surgeries that a lot of transmen opt for are limited to uterus and ovary removal and top surgery, because the phalloplasty or the metoidioplasty for construction of a penis is not a very well-developed surgery in India. There are very few surgeons with the skills to do that.'

The surgery is complicated, and prohibitively expensive. Worse, patriarchal notions of gender roles affect even medical professionals. Ramakrishnan told me about a surgeon who refused to remove 'the healthy uterus' of a transman, because she could not do so for a person 'who has not experienced the joys of motherhood'—joys to which no cisman is entitled.

When It Rains

18 December 2016

WhatsApp Voice Note 1:

'Hi, how are you? You asked me to tell you my story bit by bit.'

I was the third of a family that would expand to six children, and then reduce to five. My younger brother, born a year after I was, was my best friend. He loved dogs. He once brought a puppy home, and it was everything to him. He would spend the entire day with the puppy, feeding it and cleaning up after it. When he was six years old, the neighbours gave my brother poisoned milk. I think they were jealous that there were six of us—three boys, two girls, and me, the one on whom biology had played a trick—and they didn't have children. I still remember the way he died. His head literally burst. I remember the boils on his head, the way he would cry all day and all night. Since then, I can't bear to be around dogs, because they make me think of my brother and the way he would play with the puppy.

People ask me how I remember so much from events that occurred when I was not even seven. I remember everything. Sometimes, I wish my memory were less vivid. I wouldn't have had to start my story with such a sordid incident. But mine is a sordid story. Perhaps the episodes I treasure are sweeter for the bitter notes, like sugar after neem leaves.

20 December 2016

WhatsApp Voice Note 2:

'Hi! How are you? It's raining. Do you like the rain? I like the rain. It makes me think of love. I feel sad. But I feel happy too.'

I remember the first time I fell in love. I was four. She was four. She was my teacher's daughter, and I think I went to tuition only so that I could see her. I don't remember her name now, but I remember how pretty she was in her pink frocks and the red ribbons that always hung loose on her little plaits because she liked twirling them.

Real love happened much later, when I was fifteen. I'm still in love with her. Nothing mattered to her. As far as she was concerned, I had always been a man and would always be one. Every kiss from her was like a shot of Boost. I was a labourer, but if you saw me stride through the fields after meeting her, you would think I owned all the land you could see, and then some.

Perhaps that's how people remember me, as the guy who walked like Rajinikanth in Ejamaan through the fields.

I can't go back there any more. How can you go back to a village where a girl who loved you and whom you loved once was, and keep from killing yourself?

WhatsApp Voice Note 3:

'It's still raining. I'm still thinking about that girl. Do you know how much drama there is in my life? I became a man because of my girlfriend. I also nearly died because of her.'

I was always a man on the inside. But then I became one to the world the day we decided to run away. The plan was to change into a man's clothes, lop off my hair, and then become that most romantic of things—a couple on the run. It was the closest we had come to living the celluloid life we had so admired, but the guy who was to become its hero very nearly became a victim of the villains.

I went into the gents' bathroom near the bus stop, and changed into the clothes I had stolen from my brother earlier that day. I came out in men's clothes, and found myself surrounded by a group of rowdies.

'What's going on—you went in wearing a paavaadai, and you come out in pant-shirt?' one of them asked.

I knew I was fucked.

I could smell the sweat and alcohol on all of them, five, six, seven, I didn't know how many.

And here they were, towering over me.

'Oh, it's nothing, brother,' I said, calmly—I'm always calm when I know I'm fucked, because it's the only real option—and gathered some phlegm to make my high-pitched voice deeper. 'There's been some girl trouble. I've had to run away with her. So I wore women's clothes, and put on this wig. I'm going to remove it when we're far enough out to be safe from her family. They're following us with sickles.'

Now, their leers morphed into empathetic expressions.

The one thing you can trust our rowdies to understand is the unfairness of the world where love is concerned. 'Love' probably didn't have the same connotations to them as it did to me—with rowdies, love is usually one-sided; the girl's consent is of no consequence. What they do know is that outrunning an angry family armed with sickles requires ignominious improvisation, and passing off for a girl is as clever a disguise as any.

They told me where the first bus would come, and also suggested I wear my disguise a little longer, until we had switched buses at the next junction.

We shared a few beers, and then I went on my way. I'd had the foresight to stuff a sock into my trousers.

~

Selvam has a gift for narration. In person, he would tell me a linear story, leaving out the most dramatic elements. Then he would leave me voice notes and text messages with snippets. *'Appodhaan "effect" irukkum,'* he would say. His anecdotes were designed to have 'effect'. Usually, the most dramatic of these were relayed to me under the most casual circumstances, as he was adjusting the air conditioner from the passenger seat of my car or screaming into my helmet while riding pillion on my scooter.

He had 'nearly died' often, and he told me he liked the expressions of abject horror with which I greeted his accounts of narrow escapes. He would credit these escapes to his determination to live, and credit this determination to the love of his life. Without her, life was nothing, he said. 'I don't know why I'm alive now,' he would say with a sigh.

I marvelled at the importance of romance, its special place, in a community which was otherwise so cynical about the world. Most transpeople, men and women, expected nothing but cruelty and prejudice from the society at large. And yet, they would plunge into love, again and again, giving their all to a new relationship.

'There is a *lot* of love within the community,' the partner of another transman told me. 'Genuine love.'

There was love, there was heartbreak, and the drama around these relationships was invariably heightened. Possessiveness was proof of love. Forty-eight missed calls in a row were evidence of a significant other's concern. The slitting of wrists over an unreturned phone call, the carving of initials into one's skin to prove one's fidelity, were not uncommon.

I would see WhatsApp statuses that read, '*Sathyamaa en manasule vera yaarum illai* . . . I love you . . . please *ennoda pesu* (I swear there is no one else in my heart . . . I love you . . . please talk to me)' or 'My heart broken . . . she say don't call me' or even 'I miss you . . . you are my brother . . . I am sorry'. Friendships and fraternity merited public displays of remorse.

What prompted the histrionic, sometimes hysterical, declarations? Was it their absence from the public imagination that made them want to assert their emotions so emphatically? Or had this forced absence made transmen themselves feel their lives were illusory, like the films they watched, where all emotion and incident was transitory, and so could be indulged and experienced without lasting effect?

Of Love and War

Jovin[1] had offered me water twice, 'cool drinks' once, tea thrice, and *dosai* with sambar, which he said he had made specially for me, several times.

'Will you interview him also?' Selvam asked softly. 'He'll get upset if you interview only me.'

'Of course. I wasn't sure whether he'd be comfortable speaking to me right away.'

Selvam snorted. 'He's comfortable enough. *Dei!*'

'*Enna* (what), mama?' Jovin said, popping his head into the doorway on cue.

'She wants to interview you.'

'Me?! Whatever for? I don't have anything to say.' Jovin giggled and blushed.

'Thoo. Come and sit.' Selvam patted the bed authoritatively, and Jovin obeyed.

'Hello, ma'am,' he said, inclining his head.

'Please call me by name.'

'No, no, it's better to say "ma'am",' he said, and grinned at Selvam. 'At least in my case.'

'He doesn't know how to control himself around ladies,' Selvam affirmed. Jovin appeared to take it as a compliment. 'Tell her your story.'

---

[1] Some parts of my interviews with Jovin and Selvam were published in my long-form feature, 'To Be a Man', in *Fountain Ink* magazine, March 2017.

'What story?'

'Your "love-story-give-story", tell her everything.'

'Aiyo, mama, why, mama?' Jovin laughed, but didn't seem to need further encouragement. 'Do you want me to start at the beginning, ma'am?'

'You don't have to tell me your given name,' I said. 'Selvam hasn't. I haven't asked.'

'No, there's nothing to hide about my old name,' Jovin said. 'It's the name my parents gave me, so what's wrong with people knowing it? They called me Kalaivani. Now, Aarthi Amma has named me Jovin. When I was a child, I used to be like a boy. I would climb trees, run around . . . I didn't recognize this feeling within me. I never liked talking to "ladies". I always wanted to talk to "gents". "Ladies" used to ask me, Kalai, why are you like this, working all the time, not talking to us? And I would say, *"Thayavu senji enna thaniya vidunga. Pesa pidikkalaina yenna yen ippadi* "torture" *pannareenga* (For god's sake, leave me alone. If I don't want to talk to you, why are you torturing me)? Please, you can go."'

He passed Class 10, but it was hard to stay on in school. 'I'd find it very irritating to wear my school dress. Why did I feel like this, I used to wonder. While combing my hair, I'd think, why do I have such long hair, can't I cut it off? What would I look like wearing pant-shirt? These were desires within me. Was it a desire, or was this my life? I didn't know. I began to realize only after I came of age. I would feel a sense of *koocham*, shyness, when girls touched me. I felt nothing when guys touched me. I was a guy, and so were they. Then my cricket buddies asked me, "You hang out with us guys all the time. Won't they object at home?" At home, they said, "Our daughter is like a boy." But I didn't feel "like a boy". I felt I *am* a boy. And when my friends asked me this question, I got so angry I stopped talking to them. And I decided I would not go to college. I wasn't too interested in studying anyway.'

'Tension party,' Selvam declared.

'Yes, I get angry. Guys get angry, right?' Jovin looked at me for affirmation. 'My father had such a temper!'

His father also had a habit of getting drunk. He could not hold on to a job. Jovin had two sisters, and no brothers. 'If only there had been a boy at home, things would not have been so difficult,' he said. He made a decision. He would drop out of school and work in a biscuit factory. He was paid Rs 75 a day for a twelve-hour shift. In a good month, during which he had done double shifts, he could make up to Rs 3500, he said.

'We worked twelve hours a day, switching between day and night shifts,' Jovin said, 'Only Independence Day, Republic Day, Pongal, and Deepavali were factory holidays. When the machine doesn't get rest, how can the workers? It was delicate work. If the proportion of ingredients is wrong, the entire batch of biscuits is wasted. The married women worked eight-hour shifts. They were the only permanent staff. We were on contract, with no rights and no timings. We would have to wake up at 4 a.m., so we could bathe, eat, pack lunch, and be ready for the bus by 5.15 a.m. We would have to start work by 6 a.m., and it went on till 6 p.m. It would be 8 p.m. before we reached home. But those were good times. I made a lot of friends.'

To his excitement, the workers' union went on strike, demanding eight-hour shifts and increased wages, which were eventually granted. Payday was bliss. His friends and he would hang out at beaches and parks—'*sight-adikkaradhukku*'—to check people out. He would whistle at the pretty girls. His female co-workers found it odd. 'Why aren't you checking out guys, like we are?' they would ask. 'I swear, I only like girls, I don't like guys,' he would reply. 'You go your way, I'll go mine.'

They would spend a lot of their money, calculate how many days' worth of pay it was, and then lie at home that their wages had been cut. Selvam shook his head in disapproval as Jovin laughed.

'A girl there fell in love with me,' he said. 'When I was a "ladies". At the time, I found it funny. She asked me to make a decision. I said what decision, you're "ladies", I'm "ladies". How will we have a relationship? This is wrong. I should have okayed it. But then I hadn't done the operation. I didn't even know that there was such a thing as an operation. I still haven't done the operation, but I bind my breasts and I've cut my hair. So at least I *look* like a "gents".'

He began to avoid the girl. She was relentless in her pursuit.

'I got tired of it. I said, "Look, this is a workplace. We all have financial difficulties, that's why we're here. Let's do our work, get our money, and go home." And then I came to Madras to find a better job.'

In the three months he was away, the girl attempted suicide. When he heard about it, Jovin began to run a fever, he said. He couldn't get out of bed, but couldn't stop thinking about her either. He staggered back to his home town as soon as he could, and went straight to the biscuit factory. Her friends and younger sister, who worked there, surrounded him.

'Her sister caught me by the collar and said, "What did you tell my sister? She's fighting for her life because of you!" So I said, "I have to see her right away, where is she?"'

Selvam yawned, and snapped his fingers in front of his mouth. Then he looked indulgently at Jovin, who raised a hand to his forehead as if he were still running a temperature, 'I had a hundred and three degrees fever, ma'am. But I was determined to see her. It's the least you can do for a girl who attempts suicide for you.'

So a nearly delirious Jovin went to her home, where, in the presence of her bewildered parents, she ran out and embraced this colleague her parents saw as a girl. They both began to cry.

'She asked me, "Will you leave me?" I said, "I won't. I will never leave a girl who loves me so much. I will make money, build a house, see to my mother, my sisters, get my operation done, and come back for you. But all this will take time. If you can't wait, marry whomever they ask you to at home. I have all these commitments before I can come for you, but I will not marry anyone else."'

The girl clung to him and wept.

'She asked me, "How could you tell me to marry someone else?" This is how girls are, ma'am. Their lovers could praise them to the skies, but then they will only hear that one sentence which they don't like.' Selvam laughed in commiseration. Jovin turned to him. 'Right-aa, mama? Girls are like that.' Selvam nodded. Jovin continued, 'So then she said, "If you say such a thing again, you'll only see my corpse." I slapped her. I said, "*Thevaiyillaame loose-u maathiri pesathey* (Don't talk like an idiot with a loose screw). If not me, there'll be someone for you. If not you, there'll be someone else for me." She held on to my shirt and cried. "Why can't you say you'll live for me? Instead you ask me to die for you." So I hugged her and said, "Okay, I'll live for you."'

A fittingly dramatic beginning to a relationship that could have put Mexican soap operas to shame.

Jovin quit his job in Madras and rejoined the biscuit factory. His girlfriend was prone to public displays of affection, and she was offended when Jovin did not reciprocate. She had once pulled her slippers off her feet and beaten him with them, in the machine room.

'Don't worry, ma'am, I didn't take it lying down,' Jovin said. 'If a girl hits you, it's the ultimate humiliation. What I like about Selvam mama is, he won't hit any woman. If I get angry, I can't control my rage. I'll slap her and go right on. That girl's got a lot of slaps from me. All five of my fingers must be imprinted on her cheek.'

'I've never fought with my girlfriend,' Selvam said. 'If I checked out other girls, she would get angry with me. I would ask, "Don't you have any faith in me?" And she would cry and ask me to forgive her.'

'My girl was suspicious as hell,' Jovin said.

Selvam held out Jovin's arm. I saw an initial carved on it.

'I did that for her,' Jovin said.

'*Veera vilayattu*,' Selvam muttered. Dangerous games.

'She is a *sandhega praani* (suspicious animal),' Jovin said. 'She would not like my talking to any girl. Or to any guy, for that matter. She would want me to spend every moment with her. How can one be like that? Do you ignore people who ask you a question because you're in love with your girlfriend? It's like belittling them. Also, I'm a "social type". I can't change my character for you, I told her. I said, "If you like me, stay. If you don't, move on."'

'But why was she so suspicious?' I asked.

Jovin paused, blushed, and looked at Selvam, who began to laugh. '*Paarthiya, eppadi point-e piduchaanga* (Did you see how she hit the nail on the head)?'

'So . . .' Jovin began, 'There was this other girl who liked me. I liked her too.' Selvam mumbled something. 'No, mama, I didn't "correct"² both of them. This girl loved me, and I didn't know it. But my girlfriend realized. Actually, this girl was a lot prettier than my girlfriend. She was *semma* colour, as fair as you, ma'am. If you pinched her, the blood would rush to the spot.'

'You pinched her?'

Selvam laughed. 'Oh,' Jovin giggled, 'I like pinching the waists of women. I liked teasing her. She would call me "mama". She had no *thaimaaman* (maternal uncle). So I would play with her like a thaimaaman would have. I would call her *"chellam"* (darling) or *"kuttima"* (little girl). And I could never resist her waist. What a "figure". What a "structure". Not a chance. You'd see her walking, and you'd want to grab her. And her eyes . . . they were like our Silukku's (actress Silk Smitha's). A glance could have you bewitched. Everyone in the company tried to hit on her. She didn't fall for anyone. I don't know why she fell for me. I didn't even know then *that* she had fallen for me. But my girlfriend got wind of it. I guess someone told her. Or girls just know when someone else is gunning for their man.'

It all came to a head one day.

The girls had to wear the factory's uniform—a shirt—over their clothes. Usually, they would remove their dupatta scarves and wear the shirt. Typically, they would do this little swap in the storeroom. When the girl with Silk Smitha eyes was in the storeroom, Jovin happened to go in to pick up something.

'I averted my eyes immediately, and said, "Sorry, you were changing." And she said, "No, Kalai mama, it's fine. I only took the dupatta off. I had my kurta on." Some girl went and told my girlfriend that I had gone to the storeroom to spy on this woman changing her clothes. Man. I'm putting the seal on a packet when my girlfriend storms into the room and, in view of everyone, begins dragging me away by the shirt. Everyone's looking. I'm stunned. She drags me to the storeroom, starts removing her clothes and says, "If this is what you wanted to see, why didn't you ask me? I'd have shown you." And I'm going, "I swear, no, this is not what I wanted." And she says, "Why

---

² Tamil slang for 'seduce'.

did you peek when that bitch was changing? What has she got that I don't have?"

'And at this time, that poor girl, who had been running behind us, comes in and says, "Akka, Akka, Kalai mama didn't see anything. I had my top on." And my girlfriend says, "Who the fuck are you to call him mama?" And then they both began to fight. I tried to pacify them, and all their blows fell on me. So I finally slapped my girlfriend, twice on each cheek, and said, "You don't know what happened, and you talk such shit!" She had such bright marks on both cheeks that they must have turned purple by evening. Her mother even called me to ask what had happened that day. I said, *"Ponna valarkka thuppu ille, nee laan edhukku ammaava irukke, poyi sethudu engayaachi* (You don't know how to raise a girl to be a girl, what's the point of being a mother? Go die in some godforsaken place) . . ."'

In the days that followed, something had prompted a fight about whether Jovin was thinking of his girlfriend often enough. He heated a pair of scissors and branded her initials on his arm, saying he would no longer have a choice.

'And she was suspicious for no real reason. Once, when she got a pimple and was upset about it, I bought her two whole tubes of Vicco turmeric cream. And one day, she wanted a balloon. I bought two packets of balloons for her. I got anklets made for her. I bought a college bag for her sister. If she fell ill, I would rush to her with Horlicks and fruit. Her favourite colour was vermilion, and so I would wear only that colour, down to my vest and underpants.'

After one of his girlfriend's public displays of rage, involving slippers and slaps, the girl with Silk Smitha eyes had approached him in tears.

'She told me that she loved me, and that my girlfriend was angry because she knew it. I said, "What are you on about, I have no peace at home, and now because of the two of you, I have no peace at work." She said, "No one will love you like I do. And she treats you like a dog. I love you for how much you love her, and you deserve someone to treat you with respect. I don't like the way she behaves." And I said, *"Amma, enna thayavusenji Murugan-aa aakkidatheenga ma, thaikulame* (Oh, womankind, don't turn me into Lord Muruga, who had two wives)!" The thing was, she truly loved me. But I had made a commitment. I could not love her like she loved me, and I could not love her like I loved my girlfriend.'

When he and his girlfriend made their peace again, a new complication arose.

She wanted to sleep with him. He told her it was only right to wait until marriage.

'How could I sleep with her, ma'am? I haven't even got my top surgery done! And when I told her I could not, she got so angry she threw the remains of her half-eaten lunch on my face. Then she said, "You'll always be a girl!" And I said, "If I have to prove I'm a man by sleeping with you, I don't want that relationship."'

That was the end of that. Until the girl's family arranged a match for her, and she called him on the eve of her wedding.

'She said she had to see me. What kind of idiocy was this? She was to be married the next day, and she wanted to see me. I told her to stop calling me. She kept calling, and I kept cutting the call. Finally I got so angry I threw my phone against the wall and broke it. It cost me Rs 1500 to fix it. I went straight to Aarthi Amma and cried. She said leave it, let it go. I had beer so I could sleep. But I still lay awake the whole night.'

'Oh, this was just now?' I asked, surprised.

'Two weeks ago,' Selvam said. 'We had to knock sense into him. I told him, "You hang out with your friends, don't think about girls."'

'Yes. And I realized I was finally free.'

'And what about the girl who liked you so much? Silk Smitha?'

Jovin sighed. He looked at Selvam, who shook his head.

'Oh, that girl.' Jovin sighed again. 'She loved me so much. She cried when she learnt about what my girlfriend had said and done at the biscuit factory. She said she was willing to be celibate all her life, she just wanted me to love her like I had loved my girlfriend. I tried to make her see that I would only ruin her life. She kept rejecting suitors her family found. When they tried to force her into marriage, she attempted suicide. Her parents called me. I had short hair, but they thought I was a girl, that I was her best friend. So they called me to speak to her, not knowing I was the reason she had tried to kill herself.

'And when I went to see her, she took me to her room, leaned against me and cried on my shoulder, saying, "I need you, I want you, my life without you is pointless, no one will look after me like you do. My living and my dying are in your hands. I will wait for how many ever years it takes for you to do your operation. And I don't care if you never do it either." I said, "So many people in the company were in love with you, why did you fall for me, what do you like about me?" And you know what she said? "Everything." She said, "I like everything. All I want is for you to treat me like you treated *her*. I don't want money or wealth. I just want your love. I want to sleep on your lap and wake up to your face." I said I was still heartbroken over my girlfriend. I could not think constantly about one girl and marry another. I told her that if I'd known how she felt, I would have avoided her. "Forget me," I said. "Marry the man who is coming to see you today. I want to hear you say yes." She refused. I didn't know what to do. It was 2.30 p.m. The groom's party would arrive at 3 p.m. I had only half an hour. So I said the one thing I knew would work.

'I said, "Let me do one thing. I love my girlfriend. I know she and I will make up. So I'll marry her. But if you want, you can be my mistress." It was like she had been slapped. She looked up at me with these saucer eyes and said, "If you had hit me, if you had asked me to kill myself, I would have taken it. But that thing you said . . . okay, I'll marry this man, whoever he is, whatever he is. I'll live and die with him." And then she went, bathed, and changed. Her parents asked me what magic I had worked. And then, as the groom's party arrived, after all the horrible things I had said to her, she held my hand. And I felt like I was falling in love with her, but I couldn't let it on. Her parents saw me as their daughter too. What would they think of me if I said I would marry her?'

I turned to Selvam, who rolled his eyes.

'So, then,' Jovin continued, 'It was all fixed. She asked me to come in a week before her wedding. I went and stayed with her family. I was painting and cleaning, making idli for all the relatives who had come.

And as both of us were cooking one day, she said, "Mama, tell me even now to come away with you and I will." I told her I would throw the boiling oil on her face. I said I would leave right away if she spoke like this. She promised she wouldn't. She hadn't invited any friends for the wedding.'

'If you had told me, I would have come,' Selvam said.

Jovin laughed. 'Be serious, mama. It's a serious story. I put mehendi on her hands, squeezed lemon so it would darken, and then fed her in the flower garden at the back of her house. So there we were, surrounded by flowers, the sun above our heads, the breeze carrying the fragrance of these herbs. She said, "If only we were husband and wife . . ."'

'She sounds like a nice girl,' Selvam said. 'You could have given me her number.'

'That night, she leaned against me and slept. The next day was the day of her wedding. Both of us were in tears. She really loved me.'

'And you're the dimwit who rejected it,' Selvam interjected.

'There's a ritual where the thaimaaman has to garland the bride, and she will fall at his feet. Since there was no thaimaaman, her father asked me, as her best friend, to do it. And as I garland her, she says, in the presence of the photographer and her parents, "I couldn't get you to tie a *thaali* (nuptial chain) around my neck, but at least I've been garlanded by you." My hands were shaking. Her eyes spilled tears. I bit my lip so I wouldn't cry. She fell at my feet, and I picked her up.' Jovin sighed again. 'She has a daughter now. I bought clothes for the baby when she was pregnant, even though it's considered unlucky to do that. I said these clothes must be the first the baby wears. She told me, "I'll tell the baby this is what your *Appa* (father) bought for you." I said, "I'll kill you."'

'You should have introduced her to me,' Selvam said. 'I'd have given the baby my initial and your name.'

'Look at him, ma'am, look how he talks!' Jovin said.

'What, it's traditional to name your child after the person who got you together, right?'

As I was leaving, I noticed that the blanket-covered figure had not moved throughout my sojourn and remained still when I crossed it. I would never find out who it had been.

'Jovin has a tendency to exaggerate,' Selvam, who had walked me to my car, said softly, as Jovin waved to us from the door.

'You don't say.'

Jootha

Driving home from my first encounter with transmen in ten years, I wondered how I had seen them. Would I have laughed with them when they spoke of pinching the waists of women, when they spoke of slapping girlfriends, if they had been cismen? Did I feel sorry for them? Did I not see them as wholly male? Did I dismiss the possibilities of sexual violence from them because they lacked the organ most women have been taught to dread?

It was something that would constantly occur to me in the years I spent on the book. Why could I overlook such crude statements from transmen? I rather liked Jovin, for all his brashness, and I felt there were layers to him that were not easily discernible at first sight. But could that be an excuse?

Perhaps my interviewees' accounts of the violence they had faced made me sympathetic enough to forgive several transgressions, which I would not have in a cisman. Perhaps it also had something to do with the apparent youth of transmen, particularly pre-transition. The Peter Pan-like appearance could make Peter Pan-like behaviour acceptable.

Once, a transman told me he would only date a woman who had never dated before.

'Who wants *jootha*?' he said, using a word that is hard to translate. 'Jootha' is typically used to refer to leftover food or water that has been sipped. The implication is that by being tasted, the item in question has been soiled by saliva and spoiled for everyone else.

One of the issues that are being increasingly discussed in LGBTQIA circles is sexism among transmen.

Delfina, a volunteer with Nirangal, a non-profit for advancing the rights of individuals with alternate gender and sexual identities, told me, 'I am in no position to make generalized observations about all transmen, but based on my personal experience of limited interactions with a close-knit community of transmen who frequent activist and support spaces, I do have some things to say. I have worked with transmen who have quite some visibility and influence among the activist and support spaces for LGBT people in Madras, and I think most are inspired by toxic models of masculinity, which are very extreme, unrealistic, and harmful—the portrayal of men that we see in mainstream cinema. You typically have a man who can do anything and everything he wants to and women are supposed to implicitly obey him.'

They—Delfina identifies as non-binary and uses the pronoun 'they'—had once overheard a transman bragging to others about how several girls were in love with him, and he was leading all of them on. Delfina asked him whether he had a girlfriend, and it turned out he did. 'So I asked, "How many boys do you think your girlfriend should flirt with?" And he said, "She should not set her eyes on anyone other than me . . . *naan payyan dhaane, naan sight adippen . . . avo vera evanaiyaavadhu paarkkattum, naan adichipuduven* (I'm a guy, I have a right to check women out. Let her even look at some other guy, and I'll slap her)." That's the type of attitude they have.'

A ciswoman told me about an unpleasant experience she had had with a transman whom she had met at a queer community event. 'He added me on Facebook, which was fine, but then he started sending me these unsolicited romantic messages. I told him very clearly that I was not interested in him that way, though I was happy to be friends. But he kept ignoring it and kept hounding me on social media, to the extent that I finally had to block him. I feel very embarrassed about it, because that's not the kind of person I am.'

Delfina acknowledged that there were many transmen who did not subscribe to gender roles, and were very loving to their partners and were in committed and caring relationships, but the issues of aggression, domination, and wanting their way all the time did need to be addressed.

'Most of them have, from birth, viewed themselves as men. They've not felt they were women. But they've also experienced first-hand what it means to be seen as women in a patriarchal, heteronormative society. I initially thought that having gone through this experience, transmen would have some level of empathy with women, they would have seen how society treats women and they wouldn't want to treat women the same way. But unfortunately, I find that very few of them think so. There are many who think that okay, now that they have become men, they can do what other men in society do, and they don't care about the impact it has on women around them. Or that if they want to be men, they have to be like the men glorified in media and popular culture,' Delfina said. 'I see it as a broader problem and yes, there is a need to at least do a study on women partners of transmen, see what situation they're in, what help they need, and whether intervention is necessary.'

Cisfemale partners of transmen did not often find sympathy even when they tried speaking about violence in the relationship, Delfina said. The reaction of most people was either, 'But he has the body of a woman; why don't you hit him back?' or 'But he's gone through so much, obviously he will act out; the hormones do this.'

I was shocked when the interviewee in question essentially told me he could not date a woman who had been chewed and spat out by someone else. But I felt unable, at the time at least, to call out patriarchy from transmen the way Delfina could. I was somehow conscious of my cis privilege, as if I did not have a right to judge transpeople on account of being cis.

But it would often surprise me how oblivious some transmen were to their own prejudices, both in terms of gender roles and in terms of heteronormativity. Many of them believed it was wrong for a transman to be attracted to men. Several also found ciswomen and cismen who identified as gay unacceptable. Some went so far as to say gay men were closeted transwomen and lesbians were closeted transmen.

Non-gender-conforming or non-binary-identifying people use the terms Assigned Male at Birth (AMAB) or Assigned Female at Birth

(AFAB). The AMAB seem to outnumber the AFAB by some margin. I met only two people who did not call themselves 'transmen', and instead, spoke of being 'somewhere on the spectrum'. It seemed to me that there was something unacceptable about ambiguity within the community; that, having been on one end of the spectrum, perceived as ciswomen, many transmen gravitate to the opposite end, emphasizing their machismo.

~

I had first encountered Prof. Karthik Bittu Kondaiah through several pieces by them—Dr Bittu's pronoun is 'they'—following the suicide of Dalit student activist Rohith Vemula, whom they had known closely at the University of Hyderabad. Bittu had given speeches at several Ambedkarite forums, and was frequently interviewed on the YouTube channel Dalit Camera, though mainly on caste and not on trans issues. Bittu is perhaps the most highly educated person I know of any gender, with a PhD from Harvard University and having completed their postdoctoral research at the Centre for Ecological Sciences, IISc Bangalore. They are part of the Telangana Hijra Transgender Samiti as well as LesBiT.

Bittu is also among the very few transmasculine people who are open about their queer orientation. 'I am certainly attracted to men,' they said when I asked. 'And I've also spoken to people about labels.' In one case, a transman had had a quarrel with another over the latter's sexual orientation—he had said he liked having sex with men for fun— and wanted to remove him from a forum for transmen. 'So I said there's no reason someone should not do it for fun. Just because someone is interested in men doesn't mean he's a woman. I've been in relationships with cis- and transmen, and that obviously doesn't make me less trans.'

But alternate sexual orientation among transmen was not common. At a national meet for transmen a few years ago, there were only three–four people who identified as gay, Bittu said. There were two others who said they were bi-curious. 'There *are* other queer relationships in the community, but I don't know how many people are going to be willing to talk about it.'

In our first email exchange, Bittu had said, 'I should say I am not a transman. I am a genderqueer transboi . . . not quite the same and I wouldn't want to represent transmen since my dysphoria is not as strong as that of most transmen.'

Bittu's identification as male was strongest when they were around fourteen–fifteen years of age. 'One of the reasons why perhaps I'm different from some of the other people you've spoken to is that my dysphoria is something I deal with more and more as I grow older, but it's also not very strong compared to how strong it is for most transmen. And so I think that influences the fact that other people may be much more strongly male-identified . . . because the dysphoria that comes through not being identified as male is much stronger.

'You know, some people also assume that being genderqueer is about politics and if your politics is opposed to a sort of gender binary, that the enlightened thing to do is to identify as genderqueer. I disagree with that because I think it's really just a question of dysphoria, and I have very feminist transmen friends who do not want to identify as men, but that's how they identify—to the extent that the binary exists—and they're not personally genderqueer, even if they have radical critiques of the gender binary system.'

Unlike most of my interviewees, Bittu did not identify as male in childhood. Their dysphoria has only grown stronger with age, and now it has become 'a real thing that I battle'.

In school, their behaviour was seen as masculine, but they didn't find it unusual, and didn't think it reflected their gender. But, Bittu said, the fact that people kept remarking on it, saying, 'You behave like a boy, you behave like a boy', may have influenced the thought that perhaps they *were* a boy. It was not so much an internal identification at first, they said, but 'I found that when society slotted me this way, it was easier for me to just articulate what it was that I socially wanted'. They began to identify as male through school and college, but that changed when they met butch women. It struck them then that they did not have to identify as a boy in order to find people who were like them.

'I've always been also attracted to a somewhat butch aesthetic, and so in that sense, I am very gay, in that throughout my journey with gender, I've always been attracted to people who were, relatively speaking, kind of in the middle of the gender spectrum, rather than very much at either end,' they said.

Their identity varied at various points in time—as trans initially, as a boy later, then as a soft butch, and again as trans when they got involved in trans organizing in the US as a PhD student. The people Bittu met who identified in the same categories, but felt differently about their gender, would make Bittu rethink the labels.

'The transpeople I met in the US would be very, very strongly dysphoric and were very, very certain about wanting surgery and hormones. That was never the case for me,' Bittu said. 'So the fact that I was unsure of that made me think, okay, maybe I'm not trans in the way that these people are trans. My identifying as trans had been based on identifying with particular things up to that point. So, for example, I had identified with hijra women I had seen in India, and I used to think I'm something like them. When I watched *Boys Don't Cry*, for example, the fact that that was a trans narrative and I identified very, very strongly with it, that made me identify as trans.'

Perhaps the dysphoria of transpeople in the US was partially due to the transphobia they faced, which Bittu said was even stronger there than in India. 'Being trans is just seen as so unnatural and denied so strongly, at least (it was) when I was there,' they said.

But though Bittu began to question whether one could be trans if one was not as dysphoric, they were also interacting with groups of transpeople who seemed to recognize what Bittu calls 'my own trans-ness'.

'For many transmen, I think also some of their certainty (about surgery) comes from their heterosexuality. One aspect of their male identity is their interest in women. And for me, that aspect was never there, in that I was always very interested in women, but I was also always very interested in men. But I think that certainly had an effect on the urgency with which I thought of myself as trans, as being pegged as trans. So then when I came back to India, I met the trans community, I met a lot more people who were on the spectrum, and that once more made me comfortable with, in this context, identifying as trans. My identification has always been much more as trans and as opposed to gender than as male. And so I still use the word "transboi", because at the age at which I identified as male, I was a young boy. I was not a man and I never engaged or learnt or have strongly been influenced by adult masculinity.'

It was possible, they felt, that transpeople whose gender identity has been questioned might embrace it with a strength that comes from the denial of that identity. And while Bittu is 'deeply sympathetic' to binary transmen, having experienced some dysphoria, they are very clear that they are 'not empathetic to the point where I excuse or condone any form of toxic masculinity or misogyny'. But it is important to acknowledge an understanding of what masculinity means to transmen, or femininity to transwomen.

Some of this toxic masculinity, the imbibing of a culture that is seen as *male*, such as not doing chores or cooking for oneself, could be an effect of a collective perception. Several activist friends of mine have told me they tend to be wary of collectives of transmen, because certain notions about gender roles and a certain form of vocabulary which is derisive of women and womanliness do gain currency, and patriarchal attitudes are reinforced by the strength of numbers. Transmen who have negotiated the system by themselves and are not part of collectives, however, tend not to subscribe to this particular narrative of what it means to be a man.

Bittu had another interesting insight into the choice of some transmen not to socialize with others or be part of the community. In the case of transwomen, their femininity was noticeable, as something that should not be present in a male. Typically, they were outed without choice, and had nothing to lose and everything to gain by moving into the community. Transmen could lead a 'relatively non-stigmatized existence' because the phenomenon of transmasculinity is so little known and recognized that the stigma has not yet been socially constructed.

Was it this invisibility that inspired the particularly assertive brand of machismo that I had observed in many transmen?

People and Transpeople

Does a word exist when a MacArthur Genius and celebrated writer does not know it?

Chimamanda Ngozi Adichie—she who, in her viral TED talk 'The Danger of a Single Story', said, 'The single story creates stereotypes, and the problem with stereotypes is not that they are untrue, but that they are incomplete. They make one story become the only story'— was quite oblivious to the idea of stereotyping as she spouted a series of comments that felt like a violation of trans rights even to allies, let alone transpeople.

In an interview to Channel 4, Adichie, who claims to be an activist for LGBTQ rights, said, 'When people talk about "Are transwomen, women?", my feeling is transwomen are *transwomen*. I think if you've lived in the world as a man with the privileges that the world accords to men and then sort of change, switch gender, it's difficult for me to accept that then we can equate your experience with the experience of a woman who has lived from the beginning in the world as a woman and who has *not* been accorded those privileges that men are. I don't think it's a good thing to conflate everything into one. I don't think it's a good thing to talk about women's issues being exactly the same as the issues of transwomen. What I'm saying is that gender is not *biology*. Gender is *sociology*.'

Despite that last sentence, despite saying elsewhere in the interview that gender is about experiences and 'not about how we wear our hair or whether we have a vagina or a penis', she did make a distinction between 'transwomen' and '(real) women'. Ironically, she also said 'women can be many things' and that she believed we should get to a place where 'the world would be gender equal'.

The backlash was natural and swift, but more thoughtful than her remarks. On the same day the interview was aired—10 March 2017—trans activist Raquel Willis wrote a series of tweets about it. The thread has thousands of retweets and likes. In it, she compared Adichie being asked about transwomen to 'Lena Dunham being asked about black women'. Riffing on the danger of the single story that Adichie had spoken about, Willis said, 'She's just shown how dangerous cisgender hegemony is.'

Willis questioned the insecurity of ciswomen, which led to their feeling 'threatened by transwomanhood'. Were they not acting as 'a tool of the patriarchy' in 'ostraci(zing) and devalu(ing) transwomen', Willis asked, and went on to compare it to white women historically feeling threatened by 'black women claiming womanhood on their terms'.

The thread also dissected the notion of 'the validity' of various kinds of womanhood. A large majority of female-identifying people in the world are likely ciswomen. But does that make the experience of transwomen, albeit different from the experience of ciswomen, less *valid*? Adichie's comments hurt the transwoman community because they seemed to imply it was; Adichie even seemed to dismiss the womanhood of transwomen by suggesting they had grown up with 'male privilege'.

Willis pointed out that the experience of queer women was different from straight women, but their womanhood was not questioned in the manner of transwomen. Acknowledging that 'folks raised as girls are plagued with oppression in a different way than people not raised as girls', Willis then brought up the idea of cis privilege itself—was it not a privilege to be seen, accepted and respected in one's chosen gender from birth?

And in focusing on women while speaking about patriarchy, where did we leave transmen and non-gender-conforming young people, even children? How did we look at hate crime against transwomen by cismen? How would we examine the fetishization of transwomen in the media, or discrimination against transwomen in the workplace?

Nestled among the tweets was this mic drop moment: 'It's nonsensical and *privileged* to require transwomen to experience certain instances of oppression to prove their womanhood. If that were the case many of your rich, cis-het, white faves wouldn't be "real women" either.'

Willis finally concluded that transwomen should be allowed to speak for themselves, and that black women, both trans and cis, should begin dialogue with each other.

Over the next couple of weeks, Adichie consistently refused to apologize, and sought instead to 'explain' herself.

This privileged example of foot-in-mouth is somewhat similar to the Cambridge scholar Mary Beard's tweet on the Oxfam Haiti Scandal. Employees of the aid group Oxfam Great Britain allegedly sexually abused women and teenage girls in the aftermath of the 2010 earthquake, and Beard wrote a *Heart of Darkness*-ish 'I do wonder how hard it must be to sustain "civilized" values in a disaster zone.' Naturally, Twitter and columnists flung their wrath at her, and possibly having run out of defences, Beard tweeted a picture of herself in tears. Adichie remained defiant.

Speaking at the Women of the World festival, Adichie said she had been 'misunderstood' by people. She reiterated, 'I don't believe that we should insist on saying that the person who is born female and has experienced life as a woman has the same experiences of somebody who has transitioned as an adult', seemingly oblivious to the implication that 'biology is destiny', the phrase feminists have been taking on for more than a century. Naturally, that didn't win her too many points with the trans community and its allies.

On 13 March 2017, she posted a long note on Facebook, titled 'CLARIFYING'. It began with the loaded statement, 'Because I have been the subject of much hostility for standing up for LGBTQ rights in Nigeria, I found myself being very defensive at being labelled "transphobic." My first thought was—how could anyone think that?'

She said it was 'disingenuous' to say 'transwomen are women just like women born female are women', and that it stemmed from 'a need to make trans issues mainstream'. After discussing this 'strategy' and why it was wrong, she argued that it was important to acknowledge differences. She also wrote, 'Perhaps I should have said transwomen are transwomen and ciswomen are ciswomen and all are women. Except that "cis" is not an organic part of my vocabulary. And would probably not be understood by a majority of people.' After reiterating the 'male privilege' to which transwomen are, in her belief, entitled in their early years, she ended with a refusal to apologize for her statement.

'Nor do I think that we need to insist that both are the same,' she concluded.

The post drew more than 12,000 likes, nearly 4000 shares, and around 2000 comments.

The topmost comment, posted on 13 March at 9.46 a.m., was from Gee Imaan Semmalar:

Dear Chimamanda,
As a fan of your fiction writing, I was disappointed to see your initial statement on transwomen. But this clarification really takes the cake. You have used so many assumptions like your belief that people are 'born' into particular genders, that transwomen have 'male privilege' because they are assigned male gender by the rest of the world. As a transman with caste/class privilege living in India, I would like to say that transwomen, even as they are identified as men or boys mistakenly by the world, face misogyny. For being 'sissy', 'pansy', 'girly', etc. and after they transition (if they choose to or can afford to do so) then they face trans misogyny for not being 'woman enough'. Nobody is saying that cis and trans experiences are the same. But those differences should be articulated respectfully and in conversation with other transwomen. Transwomen, depending on their race/caste/class locations do not have access to health, social security, housing, employment, education and are at

increased risk of public and police atrocities. Very few laws
exist to protect transwomen whereas there are lots of laws to
criminalise them. Saying that cis is not part of your 'organic'
vocabulary is disingenuous. Because all social justice vocabulary
is learnt and constructed against the hegemonic and unmarked.
The biggest quality we look for in an ally is humility to learn,
unlearn and listen. I thank you for not talking about transmen.
Complete erasure is better than prejudiced statements followed
by worse clarifications. Hope you will have a conversation with
Laverne Cox or Janet Mock and show trans sisters that you are
serious about being an ally.

'You can't read,' replied Amy-Amanda Marr, clearly an Adichie-ite.

'Haha,' Gee replied. 'Thanks to British colonialism and my own
privileges, I have accessed English education. So no, Amy, you are
completely wrong about that. Lol.'

At 10.01 a.m., he added:

If an anti white supremacist writer like Chimamanda can think of
only Caitlyn Jenner and her experiences as representative of all
transwomen, it shows how powerful white supremacy is.

Adichie maintained that she had 'nothing to apologize for' and said, 'If
we can't have conversations, we can't have progress.' On 20 March, a
week after the post, speaking to a full house at Washington bookshop
Politics & Prose, she said, 'This is fundamentally about language
orthodoxy. There's a part of me that resists this sort of thing because
I don't think it's helpful to insist that unless you want to use the exact
language I want you to use, I will not listen to what you're saying.'
Referring to language orthodoxy as one of the 'less pleasant aspects
of the American left', she said the backlash had got 'very personal and
very hostile and very closed to debate'. She repeated that 'cis' was 'not
a part of (her) vocabulary—it just isn't', and that to 'deny difference'
was similar to 'colour-blindness'—to pretend that various races don't
exist is to deny racism.

Though she once said, 'I think white women need to wake up and say, "Not all women are white", three times in front of the mirror', she didn't appear to believe ciswomen could do with the same ritual.

What I find remarkable about the fallout of Adichie's statements is that there was no point at which the response prompted remorse in her—not for her words, not for the hurt they may have caused even inadvertently. She stuck to her guns, and refused to acknowledge that she had tied herself up in knots. Perhaps she did not even see it that way. I would revisit her statement with several of my interviewees, and encounter varied viewpoints.

Can we afford for 'cis' not to be an organic part of our vocabularies? If public intellectuals believe we can, what hope is there for the larger society, for families in villages who believe all transpeople are transwomen, and all transwomen are intersex? The families of most transmen believe the female-to-male trans child is an aberration, and a unique one—there is no child like him in any other family in the world.

Selvam once told me the only reason he had been able to weather various storms, even within the community, was the support of his family. 'But would they support me if they knew the truth about me?' he asked, rhetorically. 'They think my hormones changed naturally. If they knew the truth, they would think I brought this on myself; they wouldn't understand that destiny did this to me.'

I would find out, when I met his family, that that wasn't quite the case.

Boyhood

Sitting on his bed, Selvam sighed and began: 'My story starts when everyone thought I was a girl—everyone except me. Thankfully, though, I don't remember a time when I didn't wear pant-shirt. I should have worn my older sister's clothes, but I barely even looked at them. I used to wear my older brother's. And no one cared at home. My father is my entire life. I adore him, and he adores me. My mother loves me too. She knows I'm the most responsible of her children. I'm the one who stopped her from going to work. I was seven at the time.'

'If I'd gone to school,' he continued, 'I would have had to wear the uniform, a skirt-and-blouse, then *churidhar*, then *dhavani*. But thanks to my cousins, I didn't go to school after three days.'

The first day he went to school, he recalled having a bag, which must have held his slate, a piece of chalk, probably a book or two, and a few pencils and pens. His cousins were the same age as he, but each was twice his size, he said. Their chief source of entertainment during family gatherings was bullying him. Now they had him at their disposal for the whole day. He was prepared for their usual violations—pulling his hair, beating him, pinching him. But his first day at school was occasion for innovation in their tricks. When the students were called to collect their noon meal, Selvam stood in line. He returned with his food, to find his bag missing and his cousins grinning at him. He would never find out where they had hidden it.

His parents gave him another bag the next day, with new books and another slate. These met the same fate as their predecessors.

The events would be repeated yet again. When his parents asked him how he had lost his bag three days in a row, he said he did not know—'I couldn't tell on my cousins. I didn't want those *pehelwans* (wrestlers) ganging up on me.' So he told his parents he did not like school. They took him out, reluctantly. They did not care much for literacy, but the lunch was a free meal that they now had to source.

His father worked odd jobs, first in the fields, and when the government began to build highways that passed through the village, in construction. He left home before the children rose and rarely returned before they went to bed. Their mother would feed them and see them off to school before heading to the forest. In the little village where Selvam was raised, near Theni, his mother had to cross three, or four, or five hills to forest after forest, collecting firewood to sell. She would then go to the market in the evening, sell the wood, buy vegetables and come back home after dark. If she did not make enough money to buy vegetables, she had to wait until the stall closed and the seller could be persuaded to dispense with the unsold stock which would not last till the next day. By the time she had cut and cooked the vegetables, it was typically past midnight. With eight people in the family, there were rarely leftovers. But Selvam cannot remember ever going hungry or skipping breakfast.

When I met his mother for the first time, she was bent over a wood stove, heating a pan to make dosais for us. She kept up a steady chatter with me as she scooped generous ladles of dosai batter on to the pan, spread it into perfect circles, and flipped the dosai over until it was golden brown on both sides. In households where the shortage of food is not a looming threat, people strive to make thin white dosais. The half-inch-thick dosais his mother made told their own stories—she could not afford to waste oil on making three thin dosais per head, so it was better to make thick, solid pancakes; thin dosais would disappear in a trice, whereas one could chew her dosais, making a measly dinner last a little longer and sustaining the illusion of satiety.

'I did not like the fact that my mother had to work. The men of the house should provide for the house,' Selvam told me. 'So, as a child, I began to go with my father, looking for work. Back in the 1980s, the government was always building roads or digging tunnels all over the place. It was heavy lifting, but it earned me an honest meal at the end of the day. And it spared my mother the long walk through the hills and trees, picking wood all day so that her spine had begun to curve when she was not even thirty years old.'

Selvam was willing to put in the hard yards, but work did not come easily. At construction sites, men would figure out there was something strange about him, and find ways to brush against him to see if his anatomy was as it should be.

'The ideal job is a watchman's. Like a nightwatchman. No one else at work. But people look at me and they see a boy, and assume I won't be responsible. You must have a watchman in your apartment, right? Have you ever seen him awake on duty at night? The people who loaf around get good jobs. And then there's me. I worked at a morgue once. For a hundred rupees a day, I had to stand guard. No one was there at night. Just corpses. I spent most of the money on alcohol. You need to down a few to stay there through the night. But I couldn't drink too much, because I had to be up till 5 a.m., when the shift would change. They had all this expensive equipment. And for all the work I did, they would try to bargain with me, pay me less than I was owed.' He sighed. 'There's nothing you can do without an education. You can't win. I've done all right. If I were to look back at my life now, studies don't seem that important. It's all about effort. Effort will give you victory. But then the first thing people ask you is how much you've studied.'

His life had illustrated, if not shaped, his philosophy. He did not have an education, and so he worked hard and long.

'When you're poor,' he said, 'It's like you're on a treadmill. If you don't run, you'll fall. The treadmill keeps picking up speed. You have to run faster and faster. You can't ever get off. You can't ever move up. Not without intervention from the outside. When you're rich, you're on an escalator. If you run, you'll get there faster. Even if you don't make any effort, you climb up anyway.'

His sister and he had worked in a garment factory, saving up their wages from the sweatshop until they had enough money to get her married. He had decided to try his hand at tailoring, and apprenticed with several tailors, hoping to learn the trade.

'The master tailor will never let you see him cut cloth,' he said. 'Right when they are about to cut something, they will send you off on random errands—bring tea, bring biscuits, bring bun, bring idli. Or buy cloth. Without knowing the patterns, what can you possibly do?' He snorted. 'They're paranoid that you'll learn the craft and then leave, either go to someone else or start your own place.'

'Why don't you work in trans rights, though?' I asked him.

Selvam sighed. He volunteered with several non-governmental organizations, he said, and was keen on peer counselling, but he did not want a paid job. 'When you volunteer, no one can impose restrictions on you. I'm an outspoken guy. I can't be politically correct, and I can't be subservient. Set *aavaadhu*—it won't work.'

An NGO had given him a sewing machine. It was his pride and joy. I would meet it along with his family. His mother oiled it regularly. Selvam had registered for sewing classes in Madras, and would practise when he went home.

'How is this shirt?' he would ask me.

'Did you make it?'

'First, tell me how it is.'

'It looks nice. It fits well.'

'I bought it.' He would then grin and ask, 'Do you believe I bought it?'

'Yeah, why not?'

'I made it.' He then pointed to one of the shoulder seams. 'I prefer making my own clothes, because the boys' clothes have broader shoulders, and I look like a kid trying to fit into adult clothes. Sometimes, they ask me to go to the kids' section, and that's humiliating.'

'Have you begun to make clothes for other people yet?' I asked him.

'No. But soon, I'll make some churidhars for my sister,' he said. 'And once I'm confident about the cutting, I will start making clothes for other women. Tailors can make a lot of money.'

Money had always been important to him. A real man made money, he said. A real man built a home for his wife. A real man must inspire confidence in his in-laws.

'If only I had had that kind of money,' he sighed, 'I would have married her by now.'

~

19 January 2017

WhatsApp Voice Note:

'Hiiiiiii. How was your Pongal? I wanted to call you. But I went off to Bangalore. I had to meet my friends because I get depressed during Pongal. Call me when you have time. Let us meet.'

Selvam seemed to be in a good mood when I met him.

'Happy new year.' He beamed, holding out his hand.

He had just returned from his parents' home, a couple of hours outside the city. It was a rare family get-together—his sisters had arrived with their children, and his younger brother had made it too.

'How is this?' he asked me, showing me a gold-plated watch.

'It's new? I thought I'd seen it before on you.'

Selvam sighed. 'That's a *completely* different one. Only the colour is the same. My brother got me this. From money he saved.'

'Your brother? That kid I saw in Natarajapuram? He's working now?'

Selvam grinned. 'He graduated from music college. First rank there, as it was throughout school. Now he plays mridangam professionally, and also teaches.' He leaned back. 'I've done everything I set out to do. My sisters are married. My parents are settled in quarters in the same compound where my father works, in a cement factory. The owner has employed him as the security guard, in addition to his construction work. I built the house in Natarajapuram and it's on rent now. The loan is almost repaid. My plan is to get some land on lease in Theni, and settle them there.'

'You've done well.'

'Yes, I do feel a sense of pride when I think how far three days in school have got me. There are so many people who have a bunch of degrees and little to show for it. But then it will always be a regret—it will always trouble me, that I haven't studied. I could have done well. I loved my tuition class, and not just because of the teacher's daughter. I tried to teach myself things. My dad has passed the SSLC (Secondary School Leaving Certificate examination), so he taught me "A, B, C, D". I can manage to write a few sentences, talk a little bit in English, read a bit. But I'm not fluent. I don't know how to apply for grants, for funding, anything. Of all of us, only my younger brother has studied well. Serial first ranker. He would always be the first to get admission anywhere. But I wanted the best colleges for him, so I went and stood in every queue and got all the application forms. I stopped working to see to his college admissions. The next thing is to get him a stable job, and then get him married. Then I can see to my own life.'

'You told me you were depressed,' I said. 'You seem to have had a good time at home.'

'When everyone is celebrating Pongal, I miss the things we used to do back in the village. The girls would run away from us guys; they were terrified of me because I used to tease them so much. Those were the days.'

His family had never protested against his wearing male clothes. But, before he had run away from home, they would not let him cut his hair. It had been hip-length, and he had despised it.

'I even told them I'd get a tonsure at a temple, because I'd prayed for something. The people in my house went *"Aiyayo! How can a vayasu ponnu* (woman who has come of age) do this?"'—he imitated their horrified expressions, and then narrowed his eyes— '"*Vayasu ponnu" nu sollarappo evvalavu aathiram varum* (Imagine how infuriating it is to be called *"vayasu ponnu"*)! I decided I had to run away from home.'

But he was not single at the time, and the logistics of running away were complicated.

Girls had always seen him as male, he said. 'Since I was a kid, I've always liked pretty girls. And I knew how to "correct" them. I would make myself irresistible. And she came into my life when we were fifteen. We were together for three years,' he said. 'I can't think about her for long. I'll start crying.

'I've always had a loving relationship with my parents. But being in a body that is at odds with your mind is traumatic. So often, I'd pause and wonder what this life was for. I've attempted suicide lots of times. But I can't seem to die. After that girl came into my life, I felt it was worth living. But even then, Death seemed to obsess over me. A snake bit me when I was loading stones. I didn't realize it was a snake. I felt something sting me as I lifted a stone. I thought it was a thorn, and paused to check, and something struck me again. I could not find the thorn bush, and there didn't seem to be anything on the stone—the snake must have slipped away once it had emptied the poison—and I figured it was no big deal. I finished the loading work, and went home. My hand and then my arm began to feel heavy. I told my mother I had a strange pain in my arm. She took a look at my arm, and then gave me *pazhutha molagai* (ripe red chilli). It tasted bitter, not spicy. She told me a snake had bitten me, tied a rope around my arm, and rushed me to hospital. I don't normally faint—I'm sure I'd be able to walk even if someone physically drained all the blood from my body— but I must have fainted because I closed my eyes and I had no clue what was happening to me. Apparently, the poison had spread all over my body, got to my brain. They took me to a government hospital, and paid thousands of rupees in bribes so that they would tend to me immediately. My mother says they gave me four injections. I coughed up something and opened my eyes. Everyone around me was shocked—pleasantly, I should think. They told me I had died and been reborn. If I'd died and been reborn, I said, I wouldn't have chosen this fucked-up life again. What's the point of cheating Death and returning to a life worse than death?

'But I knew why I had come back. That girl was my reason to live. The reason I could not let the snake kill me was that she offered me more than any heaven could have. She gave me the confidence to be myself. She gave me courage. Women can do that. I've always wanted to settle down with a girl. I don't want a girlfriend; I want a wife. When you fall in love, it has to be forever.'

He was on contract for manual labour in her village. She would pass by the road he was laying, on her way to the fields.

They were in a relationship for three years, two long-haired people whom the village saw as best friends. Selvam would often stay at her home, sleeping in her room. Then, the girl's family began to search for a suitor.

'She had a plan. As we were lying side by side, she pressed herself against me, like I was a guy. She said if we were to unite—have sex—then no one could separate us. And that was when I told her about myself: that I feel like a guy, I *am* a guy, but I don't have the male organ. For hours, she stared at me in bewilderment, asking me to repeat myself, completely out of her depth. And then she began to cry. But even under those circumstances, she wasn't able to come to terms with the idea of separation.'

They decided to run away from home. He had grown up in Kerala, and had friends on whom he could rely. The first six months were blissful, he said. They lived as nomads, taking up work where it was available, making just enough money to live and eat.

'We moved in with friend after friend after friend,' he said. 'I was sure we were safe. But then my father borrowed Rs 2000 and traced me to Kerala. He would stop at telephone booths and call up friends of mine about whom he knew. I hadn't told my friends the entire truth about us running away, and I hadn't asked them to keep it quiet. So when he asked if I had come that way, one of my friends unintentionally gave me away, and my father was able to track us down. I didn't think my father was that resourceful. I don't even know how he got their numbers.'

His father knew he could not persuade them to return without deceit.

'He had a strategy,' Selvam said. 'The first time I'd run away from home, I had gone to stay at my partner's place. And he sent word that my mother was ill. So I rushed back, only to find it was a lie. He did a similar thing, but this time he said my partner's parents had died. You know what she said? She said, "They died when I left home. I don't have parents, I only have Selvam." Then my father said the police were looking for us. She got scared. I didn't want to go back. I knew my father was lying. But then she persuaded me. The moment we entered the village, it was all over.'

Her family was waiting for her. They dragged her away and beat her. Even as the blows rained down on her, she screamed, 'I don't care how much you hit me. I won't stay with you, I'll run away with him again. He's my husband.'

Selvam's father would not let him intervene in a 'family matter'.

'He said he would accept me as I am, but I had no right to run away with a girl,' Selvam said. 'My family is uneducated, right? So they bought my story, that something had changed in my body, and I had become a man. But the people in the village saw me as some sort of freak. Because the story is a strange one. Even here, people don't suspect anything when they see me. But then, once I tell them my story—which I have started doing these days, because attitudes must change—they seem to see me differently, as something strange, something new. I first began coming out ten years ago, giving interviews on television and print, thinking I could help change attitudes. But I haven't been able to.'

He paused and smiled. 'My father took me home, saying I should not take a girl away from her family. I replied, "You speak of moral right and wrong, but we can't live without each other." She heard me say that. That night, she managed to get out of her room and run away to my house. Her brother chased her down on a bike and dragged her home. They prised her mouth open with the wide ladle you use to stir vegetables, and then poured rat poison down her throat, and said she was better off dead. She said, "Why should I die? Let me live with him." She managed to throw up and survive. Then she went on a hunger strike, without drinking water, without bathing, without brushing her teeth. Finally, her mother phoned me. She said, "You have to save my daughter." When I went to see her, she immediately called off her strike.'

Her family began to consider marrying her off to him. Her brother, sister, sister-in-law, and mother were not opposed to it any longer. But her father had reservations.

'He knew I would work hard,' Selvam said. 'I'd bought her a gold chain with my own money during our six-month escapade. But he was afraid of what society would say. That is the problem with everyone in society. They're worried about what other people will say, without even realizing they're part of the machine.'

For a long time, he could not narrate the tale without breaking down, he said. 'But now I'm all right. Even now, when I think about this love that I had, so pure and so strong, I feel this odd sensation through my body, this ache in my heart.'

The story had not ended that night. He had promised he would work hard and buy a house.

'That makes you a man. No one can turn down a groom with a house, right?' he said. 'And she is so beautiful, the way she walks, her "style" . . . any man who sees her would want her. I needed to build a house to protect her.'

Soon after this, he met Priya Babu, moved to the Natarajapuram settlement, worked two jobs, and put down the initial payment for a house. When he went back to his village, having signed on the dotted line, he learnt that his girlfriend had just got married.

'The neighbours told me she had held out for a long time. Then her father put so much pressure on her that she finally gave in. This was 2004. We didn't have mobile phones or anything. We couldn't stay in touch, really. We only met when I would go back to the village. This time, I'd stayed away too long, because I wanted to save every last penny. And look how that worked out.'

Selvam told me he had been single for a long time. He couldn't bring himself to tell women the truth about himself, but he could not lie to them either.

'You know when I stopped liking Rajinikanth?' he said. 'After I watched *Arunachalam*. I saw it in Kerala, when we were on the run. I left the cinema disillusioned forever. "How could our Rajini do something like this?" I thought. I felt that his character had completely *played* the public—he joins a party and becomes big shit, and then he destroys it on purpose. But the people *trusted* Arunachalam, right? This is a world of cheats to begin with. When Rajini sanctions cheating, won't all of them think it's all right because Superstar has done it? I don't like the idea of cheating. So I cannot lie to these women.'

'But why must you lie?'

'Well, yes, there *are* women who don't care whether you're cis or trans. But then I feel this hesitation. Something has gone out of me. I've lost steam. I've lost courage. If only I'd been able to overcome it, I'd have got married and settled down by now.' Selvam shook his head. 'Now that I've made something of myself, everyone in the village has accepted me. I'd gone there for my cousin's wedding, and they told me, "Look, he's younger than you and he's married. Why don't you find a nice girl and get married? You should have had kids by now." You know my girlfriend has a child? But I know that if she sees me, if I talk to her, she will leave everything behind and come away with me. But it's wrong to break up a family. My father says it's wrong. And I've decided that, for once, I'll listen to my parents.'

He did not trust anyone to stay with him all his life. The first challenge was telling them about himself. What if they laughed in his face? What if they humiliated him by telling other people? And then, most of the girls called him 'anna', he claimed.

'The boys tell me the same girl who calls you "anna" must call you "mama". But once someone says "anna", I think of her as my sister. How do I ask her out? Other boys are not like me. They take it as a challenge. They go and fall in love with the girl who says "anna", just to make a point. I'm not that fickle. I want a partner for life. Most women are not ready to make that commitment. Particularly transwomen.'

He had a lover once, he said, who had transitioned from male to female. He had saved money for her surgery.

'I was her entire life. She could never be without me. If I'd gone to Bangalore or something, she'd call me and "torture" me. She would not let me attend a meeting in peace.' Selvam smiled, seeming to believe that her neediness was a crucial aspect of her love for him. 'How could I come back without attending the meeting? But she'd irritate the fuck out of me, saying, "I can't be without you, come, come, come." Someone who was that much in love with me, the people around her brainwashed her. They said, "Of all things, you're dating *this* creature." Among transwomen, there's this idea that they

can only be validated by being with a *real* man, someone who was
born a man. The same holds for transmen—most believe that they
can only be validated by being with someone who was born a woman.
She was so in love with me. She'd do anything for me. She was so
possessive of me, she would not let me even talk to other people. If
I were to sit with you and talk for five minutes, she'd start fighting
with me. "How dare you talk to another woman for that long?" If
someone came to interview me, I used to have to hide it from her.
She'd come and sit with me. She wouldn't let anyone photograph me
alone. She'd say, "I'm his wife" on video. She would tell reporters,
"You have to say husband and wife, otherwise I won't let you take
a picture." Her only flaw was that she could be influenced easily by
things people said. I wouldn't have thought it a terrible flaw if I'd been
one of her influences, but then she would believe their malicious lies
over my truths. I prioritized her operation over mine. And, after all
that, she dumped me.'

It had taken him years to move on. And now, he had other
reservations. The hardest thing, he said, was to pick the right moment
to tell someone the truth. If it were told too soon, you could overwhelm
her. If you waited too long, she would consider you a cheat. Most
transmen dated their friends. But Selvam believed in love at first sight.
'That's the only real kind of love. That's what I felt for my girlfriend.
During our time in Kerala, when she introduced me to people as her
husband . . . we never missed a single film. Whenever a Vijay film
released, I'd borrow a cycle, and ride with her for however long it took
to find a theatre screening Tamil movies. We *had* to catch the first day,
first show. Now, even if I see a poster for a Vijay film, I think of those
days and want to cry.

'I've shrunk into myself. First, there was the big heartbreak. And
then my transwoman partner's betrayal. It was too much to take.
There *are* women who like me. I've always had some quality that
draws women to me. But I don't want to make myself vulnerable
again. It's hard to curtail your desires, your anger, your emotions,
but I think I've managed to do that. It's too exhausting to put oneself
out there, to open oneself up to love and the heartbreak which

inevitably follows it. A strange lethargy has come over me now. My joie de vivre has gone. But then, I think, if I were to find a girl, the kind of girl with whom I can settle down, I think I'd find that "Boost Energy" again.

'I slid down because of a girl. I'll climb back up because of a girl.'

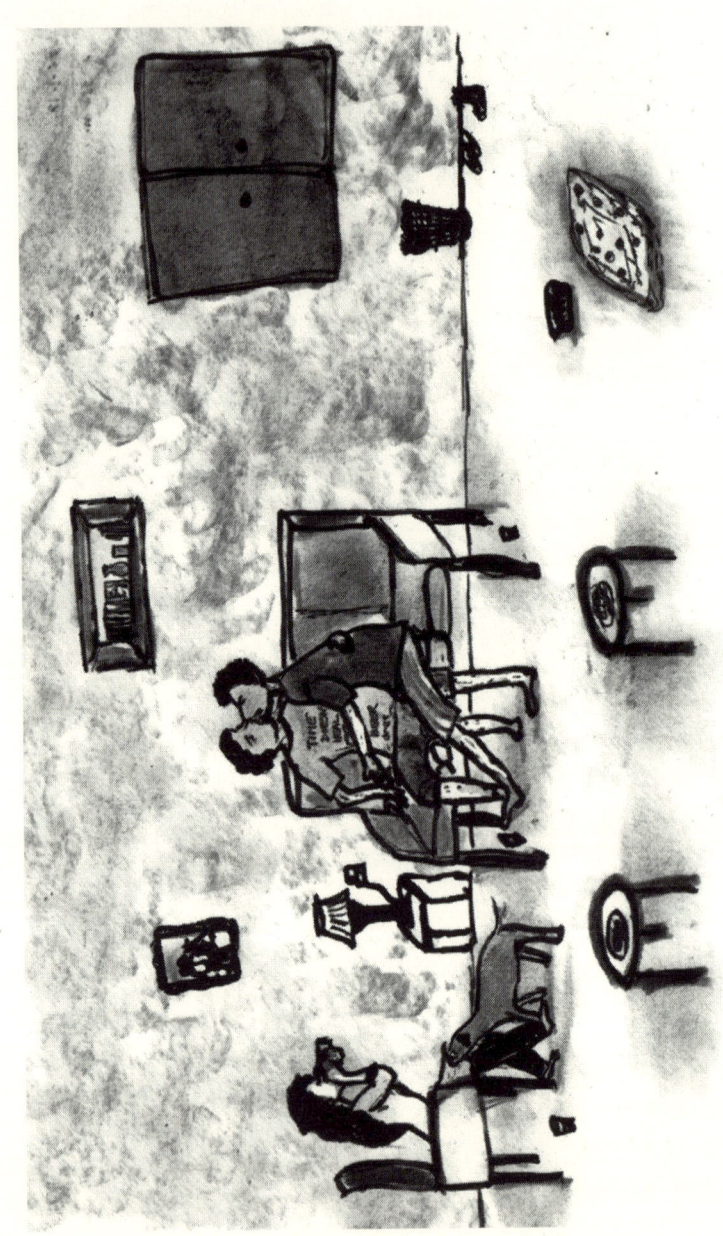

A Real Man

The transwoman was crying. Her panthi had slapped her, taken all her money, spent it on drink, and then gone home to his wife. He had not visited in a week. She lay against the shoulder of her trans brother, who sat fuming.

He had not wanted to be her brother. He had been in love with her. Once, she had asked him if he would marry her. It was the first time a woman had wanted him to marry her. He promised her he would. They would live in his village, he said. She had only one condition: that he should build her a house with a pucca toilet. She would not go in the fields. He was saving money, working three jobs in Madras.

And then her panthi had come into her life. He gave her nothing but dick. At first, the panthi was amused by the presence of the transman who wanted to marry her. 'She's our Draupadi, don't worry.' He would laugh. 'We'll share her like the Pandavas. I'll bring three more brothers too.'

He was married, but she didn't care. She loved him. He loved her. The boy who was saving money to build her a pucca toilet in his house in the village had become the Fool, maker of witty comments, foil to her King. She wasn't her panthi's only mistress. And he had not been joking about sharing her. Once, he had brought two others with him, and they had taken turns with her.

She told her transman friend all this as she lay against his shoulder, both of them trembling.

'I'll set this right,' he promised.

'I should have stayed with you.' She sighed. 'People said dirty things about us, because neither of us has had surgery. So what? You'd have kept me happy. The day the three of them went at me, I bled. And I wanted to commit

*suicide. He used to give me money, buy me things. Now he takes my money to
buy his wife things because he feels guilty about fucking me.'*

*When the panthi returned, the transman confronted him. 'You call
yourself a man, and you don't have the balls to earn money. You live off a
woman. A pimp is worse than a whore. You might as well sell your arse.
Listen, my girl, if you want a man, there's no point marrying this cunt. Marry
me. I became a man to marry a woman. You became a woman to marry a
man. This is no man.'*

The panthi left in silence. His mistress hugged her friend.

*The next day, the panthi returned with five people. They dragged both
of them out.*

*'You think you're a man?' the panthi said as he pulled off the transman's
trousers. 'We're going to rape you until we "load"[1] you. And then we'll see
how much of a man you are.'*

*The transwoman fell at their feet in turns, as the transman cried.
Everyone in the jama'at rushed out to beg them for clemency. They gave them
money and blowjobs. The transman pulled his trousers back on.*

~

'The thirunangais themselves ask how we will satisfy a woman
in bed, what the point of marriage is. When people who have
themselves faced so much hate, so much prejudice, say such
things about us, to whom can we go and cry?'

—Jovin

~

In Manipur, I would meet Santa Khurai, who headed the All Manipur
Nupi Maanbi Association (AMANA). Ramakrishnan had introduced
me to Randhoni Lairikyengbam, head of the SAATHII office in
Imphal, who facilitated several meetings with transmen for me in the

---

[1] Slang for impregnate.

state. I had wrapped up my interviews, and was lounging in the office, when Santa approached me.

'Hi,' she said. 'I wanted to ask you: did you happen to meet any transman with a transwoman partner?'

I had met several, across India.

'People should know about this, you know,' Santa said. 'Because one very sad thing happened here. Recently, a couple like that—a transman and a transwoman—eloped, and the entire community was very much against it, both the transman and transwoman community, and the two of them just disappeared.'

'It's sad when the community itself shows such prejudices,' Randhoni said.

'Yeah, exactly.' Santa shook her head. 'It was not society at large that was protesting, but the community. I was shocked. Because, even before I got involved in activism, I thought about this—a long time back. Because I identified as a female. So why should I not allow somebody who identifies as male to be a partner? What's the contradiction? I think it's important to speak about this. Because if someone wants to marry as per their wish, why should society, why should the community itself, compel them not to act on it? We *should* be there, to fight for them.'

The couple had met when the transman began to visit a hair salon where the transwoman was working. He would insist that she and no one else cut his hair, and soon the others began to tease them. They became very close friends, and one day, they announced that they wanted to get married.

'So then, someone called me up and asked me, "Is it correct for a transwoman and a transman to be together, in a relationship?" I said, "Why? Why not? It's very much okay." But then there was a lot of ugliness on Facebook and things. The girl spoke to me a couple of times, and I told her we were ready to help. I was even willing to go and meet them wherever (they were). But, suddenly, they deleted their Facebook accounts, switched off their phones and ran away. Now no one knows where they are. We discussed in office how we could help them, we were all prepared.' Santa turned to Randhoni, 'I feel *so* bad.'

'Yeah, if only we could meet them, we could see whether they need our help, whether they need certificates and all that,' Randhoni said.

'Because, as long as they're over eighteen, they can even get married, you know. They can register their marriage and it will be wonderful. All these gender constructs . . . they're so rooted in our thought. You know? As a transwoman, I cannot marry a woman. But then a transman is not a woman. He's my boy, and I'm his girl. That's how it works,' Santa said. 'We need to move together with this. We can't subscribe to such binary, heteronormative kinds of thinking; it's disgusting and ridiculous for the *community* to act this way. When a transman and his ciswoman partner are in a crisis, we all rush to support them. But when two trans partners are in a crisis, caused by the community, the (couple) are so scared they're afraid to even meet *me*. *Why?* We are actually . . . we are actually losing people, Nandini. We're talking about visibility, but *we*, the *community*, we have made them disappear.'

It wasn't the only case I'd come across. Among many transpeople, having a cis partner was considered validation of their own gender.

'The reality is that the community, instead of going deeply into their gender identity, just focuses on the genital part,' Santa said. 'Even the community sees pre-operative transwomen as girls with dicks. So to them, a transman is a boy with a vagina. Then where is the place for the emotion and bonding between two people? It's not all about sex. But even in the LGBTI community, they're always talking about sex. Sex, sex, sex, sexual orientation, sex, sex, sex . . . You know, like, even if you see a news report on gay rights or something, the first thing you'll notice is that the picture accompanying it is two nude or half-nude men hugging each other. Because then people will click on it. But they won't read the news. They only remember the picture, not the story, because they see it as abnormal. It's disappointing.'

She had known two transmen who had been in a relationship with each other for more than twenty years, she said. But they were constantly humiliated by the community. 'All the transmen resented them. They were like, "Oh, what are they doing, how can two transmen be in a relationship with each other? What is this?" And the pressure was so much that one of them broke it off and got married to a cisman. We have to stop thinking about sexuality and gender in such a rigid way. There are a lot of lesbian relationships among transwomen. What does it say about us if we cannot accept that?'

⁓

3 July 2017

Dear Nandini,
I heard about your book and read the note you put out on _____ forum.

My partner and I are really grateful that you thought about queer relationships in our community. There are very few people who are out.

We are not. If you're okay with not revealing our names or the city where we live, we would like to talk to you.

Both of us prefer face-to-face conversation. But if you want to chat before you decide whether we are worth visiting, my number is _____.

If it's any motivation, my partner makes the best brownies in the world, and I don't say this just because I love him. Our four-legged son Scooby also loves the brownies ;-)

Hope to see you in _____!

Warm regards,

_____

18 August 2017

They called each other Jaan and Tutu.

Tutu, who had written to me, opened the door and Scooby put his paws on my waist and began to sniff between my legs.

'So, there's one male in the house who likes women,' I observed.

Tutu laughed and pulled me into a hug. 'I like you already. Jaan!'
He led me into an immaculately clean apartment.

'Is it always like this, or did you guys clean up for me?' I asked.

'Oh, no, it's always like this. We tick every cliché in the box.
Except cats. Both of us are dog people.'

'Hi, Nandini!' Jaan called from the kitchen. 'I'll just be out. Sorry,
I'm baking.'

'So, well, I mean, every gay cliché, of course, not every transguy
cliché.' Tutu smiled. 'Jaan loves to cook. And I have right angle OCD.'
I eyed my slippers to make sure they were acceptably aligned. 'So, was
it the brownies that persuaded you?'

'The smileys, actually,' I said. Tutu and I had been in touch on
WhatsApp, and he had introduced me to an array of emojis of whose
existence I was unaware. 'I'm afraid I have to pass on the brownies.
I'm vegan.'

'Ah. Jaan and I have been thinking about turning vegan,' Tutu
said. 'I mean, on the one hand, it's like . . . vegetarianism is caste-
based, right, and all the Prides have been speaking out against this
government's cow agenda. You can't get into people's kitchens and
tell them what to eat, right? Like you can't get into people's bedrooms
and tell them whom to fuck?'

'Well . . . I just don't think animals should have to pay for the
government's idiocy. I won't win points with the *sanghis*[2] anyway. I'm
happy for them to drink all the urine they want, but the milk is for the
calf, not for them.'

Tutu let out a hoot of laughter. 'Dude, you totally talk like me,
man. I need to keep Jaan away from you. Or you could turn him
straight.'

---

[2] Hindu bigots. To be more specific, members, proponents, or fans of
the Sangh, as the Rashtriya Swayamsevak Sangh is often referred to—
they believe Hinduism is superior to all other religions, and to this end,
consider the cow a holy animal and believe India should be declared a
Hindu nation.

'I think Scooby has dibs on me,' I said, unsuccessfully trying to turn the still-sniffing Scooby's attention to my face, hands, feet—anything else.

Jaan insisted on making me vegan banana bread. Scooby's attention was successfully diverted to the brownies, and Tutu swore that cognac went with everything sweet.

'Also, Jaan only talks when he's drunk,' Tutu said, and Jaan smiled by way of acquiescence.

A quarter of an hour later, the bottle of cognac was half-empty, and my recorder had not yet been turned on. We had been speaking mainly about football, which Tutu followed, and cricket, which Jaan used to play.

They had been in the same school. Tutu was the star of all elocution contests, representing the school in debates, extempore, block-and-tackle, and Shipwreck. Jaan played cricket.

'I'm not good at talking,' he confessed shyly.

'You've been proving your point since she came, man,' Tutu said, and stroked his thigh and kissed him. He then turned to me. 'Obviously, we lost touch after school. I went to _____ to study mechanical engineering. And then I got interested in robotics, and went to _____ University. I moved back to India in 2012, so it had been . . . how many years, Jaan?'

'The 2014 Pride,' Jaan said, softly.

'Yeah, so we met at the 2014 Pride. And I'm like, what the fuck. You know? I always liked her—as in, I thought he was a she, in school, right—back then, but then I was . . . I don't know, we never spoke in school. Not a single word.'

'I thought he didn't know I existed,' Jaan said. 'Everyone in school knew _____ _____. Every time, it was _____ this, _____ that. _____ would be winning a prize every other day, and she'd go collect it at assembly.' He used Tutu's given name and assigned gender, and Tutu caught me glancing at him for his reaction.

'I don't mind. I mean, we kind of found it very hard to call each other by our chosen names. Even genders, sometimes. That's why we have nicknames, I think,' he said, reading my mind. 'You go to school with someone for fifteen years, and then you can't immediately switch to calling them something else, right?'

They had been in the same batch at school. When they met at the Pride parade in the city in which they both lived at the time—a different one from that of their childhood—they had exchanged numbers and decided to catch up. One thing led to another.

'At first, it seemed so wrong to me,' Jaan said. 'Because I was in touch with this NGO, and everyone was into girls-girls-girls. I was never into girls. And I thought, what is wrong with me, because I like boys, but I'm also a boy. But then I have this body.'

Tutu identifies as pansexual. 'You won't find a lot of transguys saying this, but I'm attracted to all genders,' Tutu said. 'I guess it's always been more about the person. But I've always liked the . . . well, I don't want to say "demure", but I guess the quiet kind?' Jaan pointed at himself, with an ironic smile. Scooby gave us the side-eye.

'Initially, we were open about it,' Tutu said. 'Like, we were part of these various transguy networks in _____, right? So we sort of were out. And we introduced each other to our circles. Then, I began sensing that this was causing some . . . shock, but also . . . something almost like offence, you know? As if we were mocking the cause, whatever the fuck it is.'

'Their point of view is not . . . it's not as if (they think) we don't have a right or anything,' Jaan cut in. 'I think they don't understand because they have all had to face struggles, like . . . all of us, right . . . we think we . . .'

'No, Jaan, I'm not invalidating the fact that they may have certain perspectives with which they've grown up, or that it's hard to understand. But this heteronormative bullshit is what all of us have been fighting against. And then suddenly they subscribe to it. It's fucked up.'

'But it's not exactly their fault. They just . . .'

'It is exactly their fault. How can you be fighting for rights on the one hand and calling people bigots, and then being bigots yourself?' Tutu slammed his hand on the table. 'I want to be able to tell people we're a couple. I want to be able to hold his hand and walk. I want to be able to put my arm around his shoulders and not be all "brother-dude-friend-man" about it. You know? I want to be able to do this'—and he spontaneously kissed Jaan on the lips—'and not be judged for it by my own fucking community.'

A Man's Job

At six in the morning, four of us were standing somewhere near the Red Hills reservoir in Madras.

'How long have you been driving, ma'am?' Surya[1] asked.

'Since I was seventeen,' I said.

'Without a licence?'

'With a learner's licence for six months, and then I got my licence when I was eighteen.'

'May I see it?' Kathir[2] stretched out his hand.

When I showed him my driving licence, he ran his hand lovingly over the plastic, and then passed it to Surya and Damu.[3] '*Gethaa irukku* (It looks powerful).'

'You're a real man only if you drive a car,' Kathir said. 'All these other jobs, they're all right. Being a mechanic is what comes closest. But the real thing, the *gethu* profession, is that of driver.'

A rattling noise made us look up. Damu's brother-in-law had arrived, in a car that had seen better days. He got out of the car, and looked at mine.

'Whose car is that?' he asked. 'Which one of you drove it here?'

'Madam,' Damu said. His brother-in-law noticed me for the first time, and stepped back as if startled.

---

[1] This person's name has been changed on request.

[2] This person's name has been changed on request.

[3] This person's name has been changed on request.

'Automatic-aa?' he asked, walking around my car. 'You know how to drive an automatic?' He whistled when I nodded, ran his hand over the mirrors and then gave the bumper an approving thump. 'We could have used your car if these useless fucks knew anything about driving. But even teaching them to drive a gear-shift car is "torture".'

We squeezed into his car, an Indica which he ran as a taxi.

He scolded the three transmen when they made mistakes. *'Makku payale!'* Dumb boy. *'Dei, loose-u!'* Loose screw. *'Maramandai naaiee!'* Wooden-headed dog. *'Enna da seyyare?!'* What the hell are you doing, da?

They looked admonished when he threw unisex abuse at them; they looked flattered when he suggested they were various genitalia that indulged in innovative forms of incest, epithets that were exclusive to male Tamilians.

'Have you met Charupriyan Anna, ma'am?' Surya asked me as we were driving back. 'He is my personal hero. He drives a cab. He's like us, but he's a real man because he is a professional driver.'

Livelihood

'I hate asking my parents for money, you know? I've always been a provider. But the last few years, I haven't been able to find a job.' Selvam was staring at the bed. 'My father doesn't make much money. I get some allowance when I travel on work, when I give interviews on television. I manage my expenses with that. In the months I make a little extra, I give it to my parents. When I have nothing, I have no choice but to turn to them. There is nothing worse than being poor. You don't want to look back, right . . . you want to look ahead. But when you're unemployed, you're stuck looking back, thinking about the problems you had at work . . . '

He was never paid at par with the other workers, irrespective of how much he did, because he looked too young. And once he got into trans activism, there were other challenges at work.

From M/F/?

Documentary by Nandini Krishnan

Priya Babu
(interview in Tamil, with subtitles)
IN WORDS: 'There isn't . . .'
OUT WORDS: '. . . in our plays.'
DUR: 00'31'

There isn't enough awareness amongst people about who we are. There's no point whining that people make fun of us, when the reason they do it is that there is no awareness. So we decided to start a drama troupe, because unlike television or cinema, drama happens right in front of you, and people will realize what the reality of our lives is. These were the origins of our group, Kannaadi Kalaikkuzhu. Kannaadi means mirror, and we mirror the way in which we are treated, in our plays. We do to each other what society has done to us, and show them how it affects us.

Selvam was the lone transman in the Sudar Foundation, of which Priya was secretary. He had always had a passion for acting.

'As soon as I came to Madras, I went and gave my photograph to studios in Vadapalani. I thought I could act as a boy in some movie,' he told me.

The movies did not work out, but he did become a member of Kannaadi Kalaikkuzhu, a group mentored by theatre-makers Mina Swaminathan and A. Mangai. A grant allowed them to pay the actors Rs 5000 a month. He loved the work.

During his time with the group, he met Siva Kumar of Nirangal. Siva asked him to come along to meetings where trans rights would be discussed. Many of these entailed travel. It was exciting for Selvam to go to cities of which he had only heard—Delhi, Bangalore, Bombay— and meet other transmen.

The travel meant he often had to ask for leave from work. Sometimes, he would simply stop showing up. He switched several jobs, either because he needed time off, or because his colleagues would look at him in a way that made him feel discomfited.

Had they seen an interview on television? Had a newspaper published his photograph along with an interview?

'The fear would show on my face, and as soon as someone spots that vulnerability, you're done for,' he said. 'You have to leave.'

But he didn't mind. This was a man's life, he told me. One had to face problems head-on. He had mixed feelings about the transwomen's jama'at system. Yes, there was a support system, but he did not think the interdependency was healthy. There were too many rules. It was all right for transwomen, because women could conform; but men should not be beholden to rules, he felt. An equivalent household of men would be strange. What work would they go out and do? They could not beg. They could not engage in commercial sex work. But he *was* envious of the emotional support, of the times transwomen would hold each other and cry, of the times they would tease each other, the relationships which were so defined, a quasi-family to replace the ones they had lost or left behind. Now, he was meeting other transmen. He was not alone. Soon, he had become a peer counsellor, whom others would put in touch with young transmen.

'I've always wanted to do social service. No one has come forward and said "I'm a transman", at least in Tamil Nadu. You know why. Because all of us think we're oddballs, we're one-offs, there is no one like us. If people knew that there were others like them, they would come forward. Just so that people will know, I've been open about this. I'm not afraid. I have no fear. Why should I be afraid, of whom should I be afraid? If they ask, I'll tell them. Yeah, what's the big deal? What will they do? People used to give my number to a lot of young guys like me. I spent most of the money I earned on the phone bill. They're young, right, they can't afford to make the calls. This is why I need a job. But then, jobs are a pain. Bosses are irritating. I want to be my own boss. I'll start something—maybe a tailoring unit, maybe a farm. But something that will allow me to stand on my own feet.'

It was hard to find jobs, and harder to keep them. The unskilled labour industry was exploitative by nature, and pre-hormone therapy, transmen even in their twenties could pass themselves off as teenage boys at best. They could make few demands.

~

18 January 2017

It was a hot day, and Selvam wanted to know if I minded his taking off his shirt.

As Selvam sat in his vest, Jovin sighed. 'I get so annoyed when I see him roaming around shirtless. I feel like saying dei, put your shirt back on.' He unbuttoned his own shirt to show me a crepe bandage. When I turned away, he said, 'No, no, it's fine. It's only after I get my operation down below that I shouldn't show you. If I were a guy, I'd be sitting without a shirt too, right? I don't mind if you see. What I mind is these.' He pointed at his chest.

'You're quite flat,' I said.

'Yeah, but not entirely. If I took this off, people could see. And then the other thing is that time, when you wash your hair?'—his euphemism for period—'I get irritated. I'm a guy. Do guys get this? They don't. Why do I get this? Why has god made us neither this nor that? Why does he make us suffer so much?'

Some months later, I would see a pack of sanitary napkins in a house where only men lived. It lay under a pile of freshly washed shirts, trousers, boxers, and briefs. I looked at them in surprise.

'I think someone's girlfriend left these behind,' I said.

'What?' one of them came over to look. 'Oh, these. They're his.' He waved in the direction of one of his housemates, and I realized I had forgotten the latter was not a cisman. For a moment, all of us looked at the sanitary pads.

'I'll go put them in the bedroom,' I said, finally.

When Jovin spoke about getting his period, it did not really strike me as bizarre—I had not met too many transmen then, and I was aware that his biological functions were identical to mine. Perhaps I had not begun to see transmen as male, at least not as *as* male as cismen. I did not realize, at the time, the deep humiliation a monthly period symbolized to transmen—a cruel reminder that they were not biologically male. I felt no embarrassment yet in associating the period with transmen.

'We say we're guys,' Jovin told me, 'But we're not able to walk as men on the road. Because we've cut our hair and worn pant-shirt, people can't tell that we're not boys. But then our voices give us away. I've done night duty. I've worked in petrol stations, I've been a watchman. At nights, I would find my colleagues looking at me. They would ask me about my voice. If they saw me smoking, they'd ask me what kind of age this was to start smoking, because they thought I was fourteen or fifteen.'

When he came to Madras, very few people could be trusted with the truth. One of them told a transwoman about him, and she put him in touch with Selvam.

'I feel like I've got my life back, just knowing there are others like me,' Jovin said.

He had been seen as a freak at home. The first time he cut his hair, his mother and two sisters stripped him down to vest and underpants, bound his legs, and hit and kicked him, as his father, uncle, grandfather and cousin watched. When they caught him taking his secretly purchased shirt and trousers in a bag, to change from his salwar-kameez at work, his father dragged him outside the house, stripped him naked and tied him to a pole.

'He spread me out like Jesus on the cross,' he recounted. 'My hands were bound to the grille of the windows on either side of me. My legs were tied together to the pole. I was standing there, not an inch of cloth on me. People were staring at the naked girl bound in rope outside her home. My mother came running out with a bedsheet. My father brought a sickle and said, "Look, you're a girl. Do you see? You're a girl, with a girl's body parts. You wear trousers again, and I'll cut you down with this." I said, "Fine, kill me. The entire village has seen me naked. There's no point my being a woman any longer. Either you let me be the man I am, or kill me."'

His father threw away the sickle in disgust. They burnt Jovin's trousers and shirts. That night, he drank kerosene. Nothing happened. The next day, he mixed rat poison into his food. His mother saw him clutching his stomach, made him throw up, and rushed him to hospital, where she bribed the doctors to hush it up. Jovin wasn't done. He mixed oleander seeds into milk and drank the concoction. This time, the hospital reported it to the police.

'Why did you do this? Was it "love failure"? Did some man cheat you?' a policeman asked the girl they saw on the bed.

'No, sir,' he replied. 'No one has ever fooled me. I am not in love with anyone. My father yelled at me for wearing clothes he didn't like, stripped me naked, and tried to kill me. Don't blame me for my father's sins. Ask my parents why they won't let me live the life I want. Tell me why death is not preferable to a despicable life.'

The police, he said, praised him for his bravery, wrote a case against his father, and warned his parents against yelling at him or beating him.

'I tried to run away so often,' he said, 'But my family found me each time. Once, I was working as a cleaner in a gym in Madras, for a woman who was very kind to me. They traced my employer to the market, where she was buying flowers, and asked her to make sure I was home between four and five that evening. They wanted to put me in a straitjacket and make me an inmate at a "mental hospital". Thankfully, my employer warned me, and sent me off to a friend's place. She told them I had run away.'

Through Selvam, Jovin got in touch with the organization Sahodaran, an NGO which works primarily for transwomen and gay men. They asked him if he was willing to be interviewed on television. Would there be problems at home? He wasn't sure, but he was tired of hiding.

'I don't have a life,' Jovin said on television. 'I'm not accepted at home. If we're not accepted at home and by the public, how do we live in society? We don't have a place there. Don't we have the right to live as we want? That's what we'd like, to be open about ourselves. Unless we have jobs, we can't live. And we don't get jobs if we're honest. How will we live if you push us aside at every point?'

Someone in his village saw the interview and told his family their youngest daughter was claiming on television that she was a man. Jovin's father was so humiliated he began to weep.

'He asked me, "Why do you take away our family's honour?" And I told him, "Your honour isn't putting food on your plate. I am. You choose between the money I bring home and the honour I take away."'

His father could never come to terms with Jovin's decision. But his addiction to alcohol killed him early.

'At the time, my sister, who was studying nursing, told my mother that Kalai is not a woman,' Jovin said. 'My sister told her that my

hormones have changed a hundred per cent. No amount of beating
and blackmail could reverse it. Whatever they said, I would not be
able to wear a churidhar or sari and be okay with it. Then, my uncle
told my mother to accept me—they had tried everything, and I hadn't
changed, so what could one possibly do? At least I looked after them
like a son. And so, I was allowed to light my father's pyre as the son of
the family.'

Jovin changed jobs frequently, and he knew several trades. He
could iron clothes, paint walls, string flowers together, do carpentry,
and make Rs 200 a day at a pinch with his skills.

'A carpenter employed me as a decorator, for a salary of Rs 15,000,'
he said proudly. 'I've got both my sisters married off. And one of my
brothers-in-law has a lot of connections—he's a driver. So he got me a
job at a petrol station. Then he got me a job as a watchman. That was
fun. I'd go to the site, sit around till everyone left, lock up and then
go home to sleep. If the owner was coming, my brother-in-law would
know because he was the driver, right? So he would call me and make
sure I was on site. I'd rush back and pretend I'd been there all along.
I'm clever like that. But I get tired of jobs where I don't have anything
to do. I prefer to work hard. It's because of the routine I got used to at
the biscuit factory.

'When I was at the gym, I would have to be up at 4 a.m., because
I would need to sweep and clean the gym, then make juice for the
instructors, then go and cook at my employer's house, feed the kids,
sweep and mop the floor, wash and hang out the clothes, and then
return to the gym. Lunch break was 2 p.m. to 5 p.m., and that's when
I slept. Then, I would return to the gym and make sure Housekeeping
was doing their job. I had to see what was in the fridge, maintain
accounts, count the cash, close at 9.30 p.m., and return home. I would
bring in the clothes, fold them, feed the kids, and then fill up hot water
for my morning bath. I would sleep maybe two hours at night. My
father was a good-for-nothing, right? So the other man in the house
had to work. The other man in the house had to look after the women.
Sometimes, protect them from him.'

Even as a teenager, he had defended his mother against his father's blows.

'He'd come back drunk and beat her. I would drag him off her. I used to wring my hands and plead with him. Then, once, he said something really ugly about me and my mother. That day, I lost it. I beat him almost senseless. I told him a real man fights men, not women. And then I hit him on the head with a fallen tree branch. He fainted right there, in the middle of the road. I dragged him to the side because my mother didn't want a bus to run him over.' Jovin studied his hands, and then said, 'Ma'am, that's not the kind of relationship I want. I will stop drinking once I marry. And I won't lie my way into marriage. Whomever I love, I must tell her the entire truth about myself. My aim is to build a house. If a girl puts her faith in me and marries me, I need to be able to protect her. I can't put her in a hut, where the rain will seep in. She needs a pucca house. She must be happier with me than she was in the house where she grew up. She must not have any trouble. I will do everything for her. I will cook for her. I will feed her with my hands. I will make coffee for her.'

'And what will *she* do?' I asked.

Selvam chimed in, '*Avunga* jolly-aa *kaalaattittu kudippaanga* (She'll swing her legs and drink it).'

'That's enough for me,' Jovin was indefatigable. 'She's leaving her family for me. You know, the only reason a woman leaves her own family and takes a man's hand is so that she will get a life and a child through him. I can't give her a child. What can I give her, what love, what wealth, what comfort, that could compensate for that failure? Won't she trade all of those for a child? So I must be her child, and she mine. I will not allow a single teardrop to spill from her eye. She must not work. I will work. We'll run the house on the money I bring in, even if we can only afford gruel. When I drink the gruel she pours out of her hands, I will be content. That is real love.'

'I thought *you* were going to cook?' Selvam asked.

'Yes, I'll cook, but she'll serve me the gruel.'

Selvam grunted. 'Cooking, cleaning, and washing is women's work. I'd like the women to do it.'

'But we do all of that here,' Jovin said, 'And the thirunangais go out and work. I don't like it when women go out and work. It's the man's responsibility to provide for the house.'

'I'm not as rich as he is,' Selvam said, sarcastically. 'Everyone must work. Unless you marry a rich girl. But I don't like rich girls. I like poor girls. Rich girls will expect us to be their slaves. Poor girls will be our slaves.'

'No one is a slave to anyone,' Jovin contended. 'A relationship is about "understanding". I must be able to tell her everything on my mind, everything I like, and she must be able to tell me everything too. That is compatibility. In such a scenario, sex doesn't matter. Sex is minor gratification, pleasure that lasts a second. You can go with a thousand people. If I wanted, I could sell my body for a hundred bucks. But I don't want that kind of sex.'

'Who said anything about sex now?' Selvam gave him a bewildered look.

'People will ask what marriage is without sex,' Jovin said. 'All I want is a woman who is true to me. Who puts her faith in me. Whether we have sex or not, whether she has desires or not, if we really want to be together, we'll find a way of making it work. We'll have our fights, of course. But there's a joy in fighting. For her to suspect me of being unfaithful, for me to scream at her and refuse to eat and storm out . . . and then to return home and comfort her, and beg her to forgive me, feed her dinner because she would have been too upset to eat, put her head on my lap, and lull her to sleep. Where will you find such pleasure?'

'So, basically, your idea of pleasure is a relationship based entirely on suspicion of infidelity.' Selvam smirked. 'I'm not like that. My girlfriend and I have never fought.' Ever pragmatic, he shook his head. 'Love will keep you happy, but it won't put food on your plate. Love won't last if you can't put food on your own plate. Before you think of love, you need a job.'

~

28 January 2017

WhatsApp Voice Note:

'Hiiii! How are you? I have some good news. I have got a job. It's in agriculture. They call it "terrace gardening". You grow your own vegetables. We help with that. I think it might be the "own business" I've always wanted to start. I'll go to work from February. If you want, drop in before that, and we can talk.'

Selvam would be on probation. His salary was Rs 3500, in addition to the bus fare, and lunch would be provided. Once he had become a permanent employee, his salary would be in the range of Rs 7000–8000.

31 January 2017

It was past seven in the evening. The house was livelier than I had ever seen it. Aarthi and her several daughters were getting ready to go out. They had to take turns with their showers. Jovin had gone to his village for a while, and another young transman, Vijay,[1] had joined the household.

Bathroom occupancy was subject to hierarchy, and so the daughters were awaiting their turn. Several of them were singing Bollywood songs and dancing with Vijay.

When I entered, they turned on the radio and asked me to join them. They assumed I was a Hindi speaker, and tried their broken Hindi on me. *'Kab aaya thha tu?' 'Betho*, sister. *Araam dedo.' 'Paani peeyega?'*

Their Pidgin Hindi, with its unintentional misgendering, suggested they had spent some time in jama'ats in west or north India, and had had to pick up the language to earn their living. What lives and what troubles, what happy memories and friendships, had they left behind?

They all crowded into the room where I was set to interview Selvam.

---

[1] This person's name has been changed on request.

'Why don't you interview me also, sister, I'm so much sexier than Selvam!' one said, and the others laughed.

A freshly bathed, stately transwoman wearing a sequined sari sashayed in.

'Take your seat, Ma,' said one of the younger ones, in English, making place on the bed by sweeping a pillow aside with a delicate gesture. The transwomen's movements often reminded me of dance mudras.

'Welcome,' the senior transwoman said, smiling at me.

'Are you Aarthi?'

'No, no, Ma is Mummy's sister,' the younger one said.

'Get ready, girls. Manju, go shower,' Ma said. 'I'm Sonia. See you after the interview.'

Sonia walked out with Manju. The others stayed behind.

'Don't you have any work to do?' Selvam snapped at them.

'Anna, have you told sister about Anni (sister-in-law)?' Monica asked. 'Sister, please help. He is in love, he isn't sleeping nights.'

Selvam half-blushed, slapped his palm to his forehead, and looked simultaneously annoyed and amused.

'Please help him,' Monica said.

'Ei, *ponne*, how will she help, make Anni fall in love with him?' another asked.

'Only we women can understand each other's hearts, no?' Monica contended. '*We're* his sisters, so we can't speak to her. We're family, right? She'll think we're prejudiced. But *you're* an outsider. Help him, please!'

Selvam physically pushed them out, and they left giggling. He closed the door. Monica opened it as we sat on the bed, and wagged a finger at him, 'Don't do anything with her. Anni will get jealous!'

'Listen, get out now, or I won't take responsibility for my actions,' Selvam snapped.

'Don't "mistake" us, sister,' Monica said to me. 'We're all crazy.' She disappeared, closed the door, and Selvam pulled the bolt across. 'Sorry,' he said. 'They're all crazy.'

'Who's Anni?' I grinned.

'She's a thirunangai.' Selvam smiled. 'It seems she's liked me for two years. She told me a couple of months ago. But we haven't got "close". Not like *that*, you know.'

'So you have a partner?'

'Well, sort of. I didn't lie to you. You know I don't like lying. But the thing is, she creates a lot of drama. She'll be all affectionate, and once I reciprocate, she'll disappear. I don't like these games. Actually, she's the reason I've decided to start working again. When you have a woman to support, you want to make money. If you give a woman that sort of comfort, she won't leave you. She's given me a certain confidence, but she won't commit to me. Sometimes, she says she's my wife. At other times, she asks me to forget her. That's why I haven't allowed any physical intimacy. When I get married, it will be forever. I'm capable of so much love. But the hurt you feel when a relationship ends is in direct proportion to the love you give when it lasts. So it should not end. I want a partner whom I can envelop in my love. But you know how it is. The guys who live an honest life don't get the girl. It's the bastards who will exploit them and ensure they're in tears for the rest of their lives that get them. And then ditch them.'

'Anna! Anna!' There was a series of knocks at the door. 'I have to change!'

Selvam undid the bolt. Monica was standing in a towel, her face made up and a folded sari hanging on her arm.

'Sister,' she said, 'Mummy will see you now.'

Aarthi and Sonia were in the master bedroom, surrounded by a flurry of 'daughters' putting the finishing touches on their make-up and hairdos.

'My mother's sister had adopted Selvam,' Aarthi said. 'So he's my brother, right? Now, I've begun to adopt his friends. Jovin, Vijay, Surya, a lot of them, some five or six. They are kids, they need someone to show them the ropes, to tell them what's good for them and what's not. So I have sons in addition to my daughters. Poor things, they have a lot of problems and can't come out to the public. We have problems too, but then everything becomes "normal". They can't go with women because they can't *do* anything, right? At least we have panthis because we can have sex.'

Sonia suddenly swept Selvam on to her lap and cuddled him close. I turned to them, the diminutive man in the arms of the large woman.

'Husband,' Sonia said, and winked.

'Really?'

'*Summa*,' Selvam said, shaking his head as he used the Tamil idiom for playacting. 'Sister.'

Sonia giggled and kissed his cheek. Watching him on her lap, smiling as he rested his cheek—just beginning to sprout fuzz—against hers, smoothened into hairlessness by laser removal, I had a sudden sense of the longing they had for lasting companionship. Of whom was each dreaming? And suddenly, the house, with its music and laughter and teasing, seemed incredibly sad.

The women left shortly after, the orange and black and pink and green and blue of their saris glittering in the street lights.

Selvam and Vijay stood at the doorway and saw them off.

'Poor things,' Vijay said. 'What fucked up lives they lead.'

'The bus stand where I first got down when we moved here,' Selvam said, 'that's where they work. Imagine. A bus stand.' He shook his head.

'Will the Government Allow My Wife to Live with Me?'

7 February 2017

I met Selvam at the office of the terrace gardening company. It was an old house, tucked into a street about a hundred yards from a highway. Potted plants and sacks of soil and seeds were everywhere. Flower beds had been cordoned off with empty liquor bottles, painted in different colours.

'We didn't drink all this.' Selvam grinned at me. 'You know Vijay, who was at the house that day? He works here too. He got married recently. You want to speak to him?'

Nineteen-year-old Vijay had not begun his medical transition, but he had very broad shoulders on an otherwise thin, even skinny, body. Only his voice betrayed his gender. He was the son of farm labourers from southern Tamil Nadu. His mother had asked him to leave home because his 'perverse' behaviour was ruining his older sister's prospects of marriage. His mother had tried everything—temples, astrologers, even doctors, he said. She had forced him to wear earrings and a nose ring, and beat him when he cut his hair. She had been terrified that his father, who worked in the unskilled sector abroad, would find out and blame her for not raising their daughter the right way. 'Get out of the house, get lost, I never want to see you again,' she had said. And so he had left for Madras.

His life changed because of a strange coincidence in 2014. He had passed his SSLC examination back home, and was studying hotel management in Madras. One day, he got a call from a stranger. 'The guy had dialled the wrong number,' said Vijay, with a grin. 'But he thought, "Ah, a girl has picked up. Let's talk for a while, let's flirt." I told him I'm not a girl. I told him how I felt. It turned out he was like me.'

The two of them met. Vijay heard the word '*thirunambi*' for the first time. His newfound friend took him to a meeting organized for transmen. 'I saw other people like me. I realized I wasn't alone. I wasn't a freak. I felt very happy. I thought, "*En life kadachiruchu* (I've found my life)." I suffered a lot back home. They used to call me "*ombodhu, ombodhu*" on my street because I liked wearing a kaili with a shirt at home. Only one person understood me.'

Vijay shyly held out his phone to me. It was a photograph of a girl in government school uniform, smiling coyly at the camera, a long plait over one shoulder.

'Your girlfriend?'

'My wife. I've tied a thaali. She was in my school. I fell in love with her when I was in the ninth standard, and she was in the seventh. I wrote a letter to her when she came to the eighth, saying, "I love you and want to marry you. I've always checked girls out, but you're the one with whom I'm in love." We've been together since. Then, when I found out about these other transguys and sent her photographs of all of us, she told me, "You've become a man now. Marry me."'

She wanted to run away with him to Madras. Her family found out, took away her phone, and locked her up in a room. She lied that she had stopped talking to him.

On her birthday, in November 2016, she asked him to tie a thaali around her neck. He fashioned one himself and tied it. He has the next few years of his life mapped out—'I want to get the hormone treatment, the surgeries, and then bring my wife here. I want to build a house for us. I need to get all this done before her older sister gets married, because her people will start looking for a groom for my wife once they've dispensed with her sister.'

She was the one happy memory he had of his native village, he said. His childhood had been all right, but when he got his first period, he was asked to sit in a secluded room. It made no sense to him. He went out and played cricket with his friends as usual, all boys, until one of them noticed he was bleeding and began to scream that Vijay was dying.

'Everyone in the neighbourhood came out into the street,' Vijay said. 'The beating I got from my father that day, I don't know how I survived it. My parents said I had ruined all the respect entire generations of my family had earned. That was the last time my friends spoke to me. Then, I became "ombodhu" to them. They would throw stones at me if I tried to play with them. After that, I had no friends in school till I met her. Everyone would tease me, but she would sit next to me at lunch. Naturally, I fell in love with her.'

Talking about her had made him want to speak to her. He dialled her number.

'Hello,' said a girl's voice.

'*Pillai, sollu di* (Babe, what's up?),' he said.

'Mmm, *iru di* (Wait, di),' the girl said, and we heard a rustling noise. Then she spoke again, softly. 'Sorry, mama, don't get angry because I said "di". I had to fool them at home. What are you up to?'

'I'm at work. A madam has come to interview me.'

'What work?'

I realized they hadn't spoken for more than a week.

When he was explaining what he did for a living, she interrupted with, '*Mama, kaduppa irukku mama* (I'm feeling irritated). I can't be without you. I keep thinking of how you tied the thaali around my neck.'

'What shall we do for Lovers' Day?' he asked. 'It's exactly a week from now.'

'I don't know,' she said.

'Shall I come?'

'And . . . ?'

'And see you, what else?'

'Okay,' she said, 'But . . .'

'I feel awful without seeing you, pillai,' he interrupted. 'Speak to the madam here.'

'I won't know what to say.'

'You're on speaker. Tell her what you like about me.'

She laughed. 'I like everything about mama.'

'Pillai, I had an accident.'

'What!'

'I was riding a bike, thinking of you. Someone rode across the road suddenly, and our bikes hit each other, and now my knee is hurt. It's all because you told me I must keep thinking of you.'

'Sorry, mama.'

'I can't live without you. If you were here, you could have taken care of me after the accident. I'm saving money for you. You can study nursing, and we'll be together always. Okay? I'm earning Rs 3500 a month now. I'll save enough, and I'll buy a house, and then we won't have anything to worry about.'

Suddenly, she said, 'Mama, I have to go. I'll call when I can. Look after yourself.'

They took a couple of minutes to hang up, though. She asked him to keep thinking about her, and not look at anyone else. Then she issued a series of instructions about his health.

'Kiss me, mama,' she said, and he made a series of kissing noises.

After he disconnected, Vijay paused. 'Madam, will the government allow me and my *thaalikattina pondaatti* to live together as man and wife?'

The Complete Man

11 May 2006

'*Saaptiya, da* (Have you eaten, da)?' Selvam's mother asked him.

Assuming I didn't speak Tamil, his father asked, '*Ivunga endha oorulerundhu vanthurkkaanga, da*? (From which place has she come, da?)'

The questions were unremarkable except for the use of 'da', an endearment reserved for men, the equivalent of 'di' for women.

The first time I met Selvam, he had told me gender was not necessarily of the body, but of the mind. He had told me a year after his mastectomy that it was the last surgery he would have. But it seemed increasingly that to him, life was about two things—surgery and a partner. Earning money was important, not just to live but to save for surgery.

He had his mastectomy, or 'top surgery', as it is colloquially known, in 2014. He had a benefactor, to whom he would only refer as 'Paatti'. She was willing to give him the money he needed for the operation. Back when he did it, very few surgeons performed the operation, and he had to travel to Gujarat, knowing no language except Tamil and Malayalam.

He has been on hormones since.

'I grew a super moustache,' he said. 'Someone told me it would grow faster if I kept shaving, but then it didn't grow back. The hormone replacement therapy is tricky. You can have all sorts of side effects if you don't take good care of your dietary habits and get your

105

supplements. My blood count sometimes goes down, and then I have to take a break between injections. It's upsetting because then my voice becomes less deep, the facial hair disappears . . . and I get very depressed. When you feel that low, it's even harder to regain your strength, and that sets off a vicious cycle.'

He intends to have a hysterectomy—'I only got my period when I was over sixteen, and I used to bleed so little I didn't need (sanitary) napkins. I used to have severe stomach cramps, and I didn't know why. I didn't know anything about periods. I'd never hung out with women, right, so I didn't know. Neither my mother nor my older sister had spoken to me about it. I'd always been with boys, and seeing this blood was humiliating. So I want to do away with the uterus'— and eventually a phalloplasty.

His sudden desire for a phalloplasty surprised me. 'I thought you wanted to stop with the mastectomy?'

'How will I tell a woman that I'm a man, but I don't have a penis?' he said, impatiently. 'I can't be a man unless I have the bottom surgery. Right?'

'I can't comment,' I said. 'It's not my place.'

'I can't think of myself as a man without it,' he said.

He had been among the first of his acquaintances, particularly from the working class, to take hormones. He was also among the keenest to have the top surgery, and would have done it a lot earlier if he'd had the money, he told me.

'The bottom surgery is dangerous, right?' I said.

'I would rather die on the table than live like this,' he replied.

I did not think of surgery as a Hobson's choice until I read a piece by Gee, in which he called it 'an integral part of the right to life of transpeople'.

The American Psychiatric Association's manual replaced the term 'gender identity disorder' with 'gender dysphoria' in 2017, after protests by the transgender community. Semantically, 'dysphoria' is the opposite of 'euphoria', and in context refers to a conflict between one's assigned gender and the gender with which one identifies. Dysphoria is often, but not necessarily, rooted in the physicality of the body. Most transmen experience dysphoria as hatred of the female sexual organs in their bodies and of other identifiers of femininity, such as long hair or womanly clothes.

Depending on the extent of one's gender dysphoria, simply looking down at one's body while showering can be traumatic—one of my interviewees told me he used to cry every time he bathed before he had his mastectomy.

It could also manifest as anger at misgendering through pronouns, at being asked whether one is male or female, at being touched in a certain way, or at being called by one's assigned name.

15 December 2016

Gee Imaan Semmalar was to deliver a talk on transgender healthcare at 'TransForm: Transgender Rights and Law', a conference organized by the Centre for Law and Policy Research (CLPR), held at the Indian Institute for Human Settlements, Bangalore.

I had encountered Gee several times without meeting him in person. When I emailed him asking to meet, he wrote that he would not want to be interviewed directly by me since he believes there is 'an epistemic violence inherent in knowledge production created on marginalized communities by outsiders', but for reasons of open sharing of knowledge, 'a core part of Ambedkarite politics', he would consent to the publishing of quotes from his Facebook page, articles, and speeches.

I was troubled by the notion that my writing this book could be seen as an act of violence. When I engaged in conversation about it with Gee, he explained that a cisperson playing the role of conduit for stories that were not her own, and being identified as the author of such stories, was in keeping with a history of knowledge production that has always been exclusionary.

How do we democratize from positions of privilege, he asked. Why could I not act as a facilitator rather than an author? The only right way to do this book, he felt, would be to collect stories as they are told by those who have lived the stories, translate them into English and then translate them back to the tellers, edit the book with them, and publish it as an anthology. This would be 'an act of democratizing knowledge production'.

There have often been times in writing this book when I have wondered about my own right to tell these stories. I have striven to keep the book from being voyeuristic and sensationalist, to prevent the 'othering' of the people I am interviewing. But when the stories do not belong to me, could my book help 'othering' those to whom the stories did belong? My interaction with Gee over his political stance— his reason for not consenting to be interviewed for the book—left me in a quandary at a very late stage in its preparation.

The book had led me to examine a lot of prejudices I myself had held, without even realizing they were prejudices, I told him. I did realize I was part of a system, a power structure; that, as a journalist and a previously published author, I had been entrusted with telling stories that were not mine. I had pitched the book as an anthology of individual narratives, but my discussions with my editor and publishers had changed the form the book was to assume. Perhaps there was something to be gained from the readers fumbling through the topic with me. Could a case be made for my being equipped to enable the readers to interrogate their own prejudices, as I did mine?

My mind was set partially at ease when Gee told me he would be interested in reading the book if it were about my journey—to write about how I 'fumbled through (my) prejudices' would make the book 'legitimately' mine. Was I willing to be vulnerable enough to insert myself into it? As a journalist, one has to constantly battle the propensity to appear omniscient about a subject, to relate more to one's interviewees than to the readers. In such a case, as an outsider, I had to be willing to tell my readers from outside the community that I knew about as little as they do when I started out writing the book; when they finish the book, they will know about as much as I do. How we chose to educate ourselves on the subject and engage with the community in future was up to us. But these were not our stories to tell. They were stories that we—they and I—were hearing, and which we were allowing to prompt us to examine our own understanding of a world to which we did not belong.

Gee is a film-maker, writer, activist, and stage actor who co-founded the theatre troupe Panmai with transwoman Living Smile Vidya. I had watched his film *Kalvettukal* (2012), which told the stories of three transmen from south India. I had read his chapter 'Emperor Penguins' in *A Life in Trans Activism* by A. Revathi (Zubaan Books, 2016).

Through an exchange of emails, and Facebook friendship, I would discover several aspects of Gee—his determination to leave the world a better place for young transmen, the no-nonsense beauty of his writing, his complete lack of reservation in taking on contentious issues, and how funny he is.

In 'Emperor Penguins', he describes his life in detail—his upbringing, relative privilege, how he went back and forth about his decision to medically transition until he realized the choice was 'one between life and death', and a horrific surgery he underwent in Bombay. In the talk, he would allude again to the surgery, mentioning the name of the doctor, and speak of the medical negligence and exploitation to which transmen are vulnerable.

'I have to say that there has been a lot of criticism about binarian trans identities, in the sense that we are willingly making ourselves legible to the state in terms of governmentality,' he begins. 'They say we have to make ourselves illegible because who is the Supreme Court to define gender, what is the definition of gender, etc. While at the discursive realm, all of this sounds fancy and radical, the ground reality is that for the majority of transpeople, we need to access benefits from the state. We are asking for legal gender recognition and state benefits, and for this we have to make ourselves legible to the state. And whether that is simplifying our identities or not, that is a different question. But politically, it is important for the trans community to make ourselves legible to the state in order to access benefits. The criticism comes from the position of privilege.'

Even with the privilege of caste and class, transpeople cannot easily access employment opportunities. Arguably the only community which benefited from the Indian government's obsession with collecting the biometric data of citizens, most transpeople got themselves Aadhaar cards with the names of their choice, and then began the tedious process of changing their education certificates, ration cards, and other legal identifiers to match that name and gender.

Gee pointed out that the binary was a 'place of safety'—those who were more gender non-conforming, which is increasingly promoted in progressive and academic discourse, tended to face public harassment on various accounts—but that neither being trans nor desiring to conform within the binary mandated surgery. While calling out the shaming of transpeople who identified within the binary by 'self-professed radical cis commentators', he also criticized the 'privileging of people who have had surgery as the authentic transpeople and other people as fake transpeople' and other such hierarchies within trans communities themselves. Gender is a spectrum, and there are multiple ways of being trans, he said.

But for those who do want to transition medically, the first challenge is finding a psychiatrist who does not 'advise cis-hetero patriarchy as a cure' for being trans. There have been psychiatrists, Gee said, who suggest that the best way to resolve the issue of bodily autonomy, ironically, is to get married—to a cisman.

In order to undergo surgery, or even start hormone therapy, a transperson will need at least one certificate from a psychiatrist. Some surgeons ask for two opinions. The process may be further complicated by the Transgender Rights Bill, 2016, the provisional version of which has sparked a series of protests across the country.

'In most counselling sessions, you're in fact educating them (doctors) on what it means to be trans,' Gee said. 'You're fighting with someone to convince them of who you are. And this is a truth that you've known throughout your life. To be who I am today, to have basic citizenship rights, I actually begged a psychiatrist to certify me as a mentally disordered person.'

Even with the certificate, transpeople often face so much prejudice in hospitals—Gee quoted an endocrinologist at Ramaiah Hospital in Bangalore saying, 'You know, after all, we are messing with god'—that many choose to self-medicate 'rather than go to ignorant doctors'.

Getting testosterone injections over the counter from pharmacies is not hard, since cismale bodybuilders often buy them. Gee did say in his talk that as long as one was fastidious about doing one's bloodwork, self-administration is 'completely safe'. But all the doctors whom I interviewed disagreed. There are too many ifs.

Online forums, chatrooms and seminars have made healthcare information accessible to transpeople. But medical expertise is usually irreplaceable.

The problem, Gee said, is that religion has destroyed the medical system. Nurses would refuse to give transmen the shots sometimes, because intramuscular injections can be extremely painful and they're worried the patients will curse them. Doctors have refused to perform hysterectomies on people they see as 'healthy women capable of producing children' because removing the uterus of a transman interferes with 'god's mandate'. To compound problems, parents of patients sometimes approach endocrinologists, asking them to 'brainwash' their children and tell them hormones are harmful.

There are those who prefer not to transition medically, but most transmen I met had opted for hormone replacement therapy as well as mastectomy and hysterectomy. Those who can afford it, and whose dysphoria is extreme enough to outweigh the medical risks associated with phalloplasty, opt for what is popularly called 'bottom surgery', or penile and uro-genital reconstruction.

'To transform into a *complete man*, like the Raymond's ad says,' Gee said, not without irony, 'you need at least five surgeries, if none of them is botched. If it's botched, of course, for the corrections that you do, you'll have to go through many other procedures.'

Doctors often give transpeople the impression that they are doing them a favour simply by consulting them. To provide healthcare, Gee pointed out, is a doctor's duty, not a favour. Transpeople who have saved money for years, even decades, for their surgeries end up spending exorbitant amounts on hack jobs that would trigger angry television debates and newspaper headlines if they were to happen to cisgender people.

It was not until 2009 that gender affirmation surgery was legalized in Tamil Nadu, a relatively progressive state as far as trans healthcare is concerned. Government hospitals were now teeming with doctors who had little experience in the surgery and were happy to experiment. Though the surgery is technically free, medicine costs, bed charges, and hospital fees do apply.

Because accessing subsidized healthcare is complicated and because of the track record of government hospitals in botching surgeries, transpeople spend several times as much money to go to private clinics. The doctors are usually more welcoming, but that is no guarantee that the surgery will not be botched.

At the talk, Gee showed a picture, saying, 'This is one of the better pictures, and I call it "reclaiming victimhood".' His mastectomy left him with craters on both sides of his chest as the nipple graft fell apart. He was bedridden for six months, and had three corrective surgeries.

'I in fact approached a lawyer to see whether a medical negligence case could be filed. He said, "In India, the loopholes are so big in medical negligence cases that you'll be wasting your time and money on the legal case." So I dropped it. So there's complete impunity in the medical system when it comes to transgender healthcare and these are the kind of surgeries that you have to live with for the rest of your life.'

There is no monitoring system for corrupt practices by doctors, Gee alleged. Trans healthcare is not in the syllabus in medical colleges. Transwomen face prejudice the world over—Gee quoted the instance of a transwoman who died of gunshot wounds in Pakistan because she was denied admission to both the male and the female wards—and hardly anyone knows about the existence of transmen.

Many transmen whom I interviewed would tell me how they were subjected to stares and questions when they visited gynaecologists, since cisfemale patients assumed from their appearance that they were cismen and could not figure out what they were doing at a clinic for women.

Despite the NALSA judgment, an SRS certificate is demanded at every government office to change one's gender markers. And even to fail the gender test, one must submit to a physical examination.

The latest version of the Transgender Rights Bill has removed the provisions for free SRS, and ignored the demand for separate wards for transpeople. There are no separate medical facilities for transwomen in prisons or shelter homes.

'The only transgender-specific surgery that is a little more accessible than the other surgeries is breast augmentation. Why? Because under cis-hetero patriarchy, under the cis pornographic imagery of the cismen, they want women to have bigger breasts. So transwomen somehow are able to access this surgery that is not designed for them,' Gee said, calling it a 'guerrilla tactic' to affirm one's gender identity.

What can cispeople do? 'Help hold workshops for medical professionals where we talk to them and we share our knowledge; let's educate them and sensitize them. Get doctors in your family to read (about) transgender healthcare and provide discrimination-free treatment. Help us make a database of trans-friendly doctors in every city.'

~

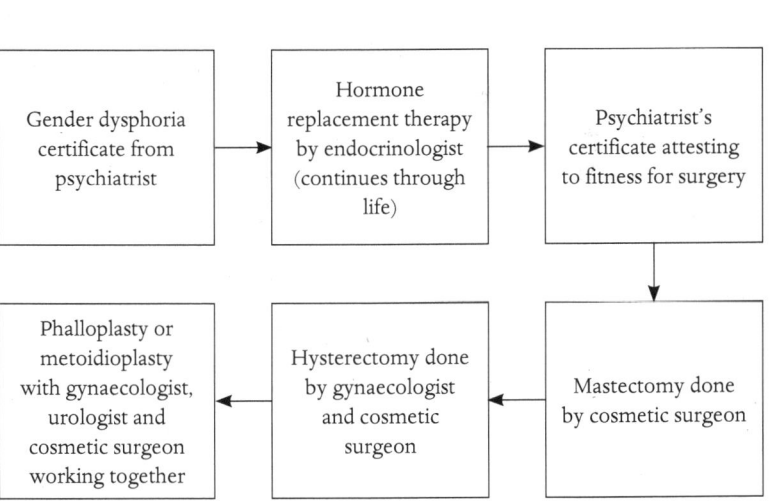

Transmen's groups on social media often recommend trans-friendly doctors to each other. There *are* psychiatrists who hand over the certificate in as little time as half an hour; there are those who ask the patient what he wants written, charge him for it, and sign it without an evaluation. Some run psychological tests on the patient, and others counsel patients for between six months and three years before giving them the certificate. Trans activists stress the importance of counselling, not just with the intention of getting a certificate but for continued support, since gender dysphoria does take a toll. Psychiatrists charge between Rs 500 and Rs 3000, sometimes higher, per session.

One can buy testosterone over the counter for as little as Rs 80–150, and have a nurse inject it for between Rs 50 and Rs 200. But this could lead to severe complications. It is important to have regular check-ups while undergoing hormone replacement therapy (HRT). The endocrinologist does have to run tests to check whether one's body is healthy enough to begin HRT. These tests could cost between Rs 1200 and Rs 5000. An endocrinologist will also determine the dosage of testosterone and the intervals in which it should be taken, as well as the method of administration. Testosterone is not necessarily administered only through injection. The endocrinologist will choose the route most suited to the patient—as an injection, as an oral tablet, or as a gel.

It is important to have tests done at least once in three months, because too high an intake of testosterone could affect the cholesterol, liver function, and blood count, and even trigger blood clots; it could cause an outbreak of acne, hairfall, hypermasculine appearance, and metabolic problems.

In some cases, the endocrinologist may recommend the GnRH injection (Gonadotropin-Releasing Hormone), which is far more expensive than testosterone shots, at Rs 11,500, but needs to be administered only once in three months. It removes the oestrogen entirely from the body, so that the effects of the testosterone are more pronounced and transition is quicker. It is not meant for long-term use, and is usually only administered as a stopgap before the hysterectomy.

Technically, minors can get their gender dysphoria certified by a doctor and begin transition, with the consent of their parents. But endocrinologists suggest waiting until one has crossed puberty, to ensure that it is not a phase.

Even for adult transmen, some endocrinologists insist on certificates from two psychiatrists to ensure that there is no underlying anxiety, psychosis, or depression, and that the patient is mentally equipped to handle the process of transition.

The endocrinologist also tells female-to-male transpeople that they can choose to freeze their eggs so that they may have biological children in future through a surrogate. Hormones could affect the quality of the eggs. Eggs can be stored for much longer than sperm, and so the issue of biological children is often specific to transmen rather than transwomen.

The guidelines recommend at least a year of counselling before HRT.

No endocrinologist whom I interviewed had ever had a patient change his mind about medical transition. But medical protocol in several countries mandates that a person undergo HRT for a year before opting for surgery. However, many transmen prefer to have surgeries before HRT, partly because the effect of hormones is more pronounced after the hysterectomy, and partly because it is impossible to remain inconspicuous when one has facial hair and breasts. HRT must be continued through life, or at least until one's fifties, when the natural testosterone production of the body in cismen dips.

~

So far, plastic surgeons willing to work with trans populations have been mostly in either corporate or private healthcare facilities and these, of course, already exist in a larger framework of 'exploitation'. The only way out is for state-of-the-art services with respect to trans healthcare to be made available through a public health system, but with the current government receding from its role in so many domains, it is not looking very hopeful.

—Satya Rai Nagpaul

~

With surgeries costing as much as they do, transmen often save money for years to go under the knife. Several states have instituted free sex reassignment surgery schemes, which are naturally tempting.

The problem is that these surgeries are not part of the regular medical syllabus. The expertise required is enormous, the complications that could arise are life threatening, and with transpeople often impatient to have their surgeries, there are quite horrific cases of surgeries gone wrong even in the private healthcare sector, let alone the public healthcare system.

Kerala-based Vihaan Peethambar told me, 'My mastectomy was not as horrible as the other cases I've seen. Just that it wasn't perfect, the way I wanted it.'

The liposuction hadn't been done thoroughly enough, he said, and he was left with hypertrophic scars—raised tissue formed because of collagen deposits. The doctor who performed his surgery had told him to continue to wear a binder and massage the area thoroughly.

He consulted another surgeon, who told him kenacort injections could suppress the keloid formation which was causing the scar. But since it was a steroid, he would not be able to administer enough to entirely remove all evidence of the scarring. Eventually, Vihaan had to get liposuction done again, make an incision and have radiation on the tissue to stop scarring.

'I initially just Googled and went to a surgeon, because I didn't have any contacts in the community,' he said. 'But this time, I'd asked a few transmen here. That's why the network is so important. Sometimes, even more than the success rate, you care about someone who is sensitive to transpeople, who knows how to talk. And most doctors don't even treat you properly. Like, they're just very rude.'

Each surgery must be tailored to the patient's needs. Not all doctors take the time or have the experience to consider every available option. For instance, depending on the amount of breast tissue that is to be removed, the mastectomy could be performed in several ways, of which the most popular seem to be keyhole surgery and double incision surgery. Depending on the hospital and the technique used, the mastectomy could cost between Rs 25,000 (under 'free' or subsidized schemes) and Rs 1,50,000.

The cost of a hysterectomy varies between Rs 12,000 and Rs 1,30,000. A hysterectomy requires a vaginal exam, and it is extremely important to choose a gynaecologist who is sensitive to transmen, because one could feel violated by a careless touch.

The final stage of surgical transition is the uro-genital surgery. Some transmen opt for metoidioplasty, which is essentially the enlargement of the clitoris to create a rudimentary penis. The biggest advantage of this surgery is that it allows for sexual gratification, though not through penetrative intercourse.

'But obviously, not a lot of transmen want that,' one of my interviewees said. 'The whole fixation is with a big penis, right, to go with your big male ego? I think the largest it can be stretched to with a metoidioplasty is about three inches.'

A phalloplasty is a far more complicated surgery, which involves connecting blood vessels and nerves. Though some doctors in Europe have claimed they have performed successful surgeries on patients, who are even able to experience orgasm, I did not come across any transman either in India or abroad who could attest to it.

There are several techniques that can be used in phalloplasty, which cost between Rs 4 and 6 lakh. But including medication, hospital stay and corrections, which are almost always required, the cost is usually in the range of Rs 9–16 lakh.

It is becoming increasingly popular in India.

The surgeons I interviewed told me there were three things all transmen wanted:

(a) Aesthetically, a penis should look convincing, with a shape that is pleasing to the patient, his partner, and to anyone else who may see it.

(b) It should function as a urinary channel, so that a transman can use a public restroom without any trouble.

(c) It should be capable of sexual function, including penetration during coitus.

The shape can be usually produced without much trouble, mostly in two surgeries.

The ability to pass urine through the constructed penis is delivered about ninety-five per cent of the time on average, one of the surgeons I interviewed told me. Since skin from elsewhere in the body is grafted to form the urethra, it may contain hair follicles which could cause blocks in the urethra. Corrective surgery is almost always required.

The demand for sexual function is more difficult to satisfy. Since the penis is made entirely of muscle and skin, it cannot become hard without stiffeners—implants, either manufactured or improvised using bone. Inflatable implants are also available, but they are much more expensive.

The surgery itself is not new, since phalloplasty has been performed on cismen for other reasons, such as following a surgery for removal of cancerous tumours.

During the phalloplasty for transmen, the vaginal passage is closed. The urinary passage is then connected to a manufactured urinary passage. The skin is folded using a 'Swiss roll technique', to form an inner and outer roll. The inner roll is the manufactured urethra, a passage for the urine. The outer roll is the penis.

This involves microvascular transfer, where a piece of tissue along with its blood supply is taken from one part of the body and connected to another part of the body. The blood supply must be established; if not, that bit of tissue is lost. In addition to the donor tissue having its blood vessels connected to those in the receiver site, the nerves must also be connected so that the patient can experience sensation.

By 'sensation', doctors usually mean sensory and not erotic sensation. It is unlikely that a transman will be able to experience erotic sensation after a phalloplasty, according to both plastic surgeons whom I interviewed.

The radial forearm flap—in which the skin to create the phallus was taken from the forearm—was the gold standard earlier, and is still considered a good option which yields consistently agreeable results. But since the scars on the arm would be visible, surgeons have begun to look for other sites for donor skin—the back, the thigh, even the foot.

The recovery period is at least eight months, and it is rare for a patient not to need corrections.

Surgeons recommend regular follow-up visits for at least five or six years after the surgery.

Most of my interviewees were hesitant to get their phalloplasties done, particularly in India. They hadn't met anyone who was entirely happy with the surgery, and the horror stories were frightening. Each of the three stages could be extremely painful.

'We're all waiting for a better technique to come in, for someone to say he is a hundred per cent satisfied,' an interviewee told me. 'We've heard of people who have had successful surgeries, without even requiring correction, in the US, Bangkok, Russia, Serbia, and a few other places, but not in India. Even those who say they're happy with it, they hesitate to share pictures, so we can't be sure. And since the healing period is so long, we can't be sure the surgery is really successful until that much time has passed.'

In several countries, the surgeons performing phalloplasty are highly specialized. In India, the surgeries were performed mostly by urologists or dermatologists who had learnt the techniques.

~

Among the most sought-after surgeons in India for phalloplasty is Dr Sanjay Pandey, currently with the Kokilaben Dhirubhai Ambani Hospital in Bombay.

When I met him at his office in Bombay, between a surgery and a flight to Calcutta, where he was to deliver an oration to the Bengal Association of Gynaecologists, I found him keen to talk about the various options surgeons had. He was relaxed, had several videos at hand to demonstrate what he meant when he went into the technical aspects of the surgery, and showed a fondness for metaphors.

He had patients from the deep south, from the northeast, and from as far off as Pakistan, he said.

'Frankly speaking, without boasting, we happen to be a destination for transgender individuals, both male-to-female and female-to-male, that is, transmen and transwomen,' he said. 'Even right now, I have three–four patients upstairs, all ready to go home. Some are doing very well, some not so well, some are taking time, and some come here after having major complications in other parts of the country.'

Several transmen whom I knew were his patients. They had told me he was particularly understanding and non-judgemental, and that was rare.

'First, we need to understand who transmen are,' Dr Pandey said. 'Transmen are those who are actually born phenotypically as females, that is, they have forty-four XY and two XX (chromosomes).' Flatteringly, he added, 'Like Aishwarya Rai and you. And they want to become Shah Rukh Khan. They dream of being men. And they've been trying to make that a reality for a decade, even two decades. They can't tell their parents. They can't tell their colleagues, they can't tell their peers, they can't tell their own brothers and sisters, and they live in that dream of coming out of entrapment. "Why am I entrapped? Why me?"'

Anything to do with gender and sexual orientation that did not fit the inclination of the majority was taboo, he said, and the umbrella term 'LGBT' had added to the confusion. 'They all have been grouped into one, whereas all are different identities. One is India, one is Pakistan, one is China, one is America, they're not all the same. But straight people like you and me regard everybody else as abnormal. And there's a chi-chi, thoo-thoo kind of attitude.'

He had been specializing in reconstructive urology for several years before he began to perform gender reassignment surgery. His patients were typically those who had been injured or had congenital malformations that required reconstruction of the genital region. But in the latter half of the 2000s, several transpeople began approaching him for surgery. In 2008, he trained specifically in gender reassignment surgery in Europe. During the first few years, he was rarely—perhaps never—approached by transmen. His patients were mainly male-to-female transpeople.

'Now, I think they are just forming their networks, and they have begun to look keenly for surgeons and so on,' he said. 'In the last couple of years, I would say I have had far more transmen patients than transwomen. And they are *so* focused. They know exactly what they want. They have read up on it, they have planned everything, they know what to expect. I counsel them, of course, but they are already well informed and very sure of what they want. What we as doctors have to understand is these organs don't belong to them—the uterus, the ovaries, the genitals don't belong to them. They're male. And we're here to provide them with male organs.'

They were investing their life savings, Dr Pandey said, and they were looking for various crucial results in terms of appearance and functionality.

He told me he did not usually give out his personal mobile number to patients, but made an exception for transpeople. 'I've even stored all their names, because what they need most of all is that 24/7 connection. They must feel wanted. Sometimes, they may feel awkward about coming in when there are other patients waiting, and they don't want to be stared at. I make certain special accommodations for them.'

Some of his patients could be in a hurry, and insist on surgery without a psychiatrist's certificate, and before hormones.

'I have to follow the WPATH rules,' he said, referring to the Standard of Care drafted by the World Professional Association for Transgender Health in 1979, and which had undergone seven revisions since, the latest in 2011. There is some criticism against the guidelines, particularly the Eligibility Criteria and the Readiness Criteria, because they assume that it is possible for a transperson to regret the surgery and want to reverse it.

'I have not come across such a case, but the rules are there for a reason,' Dr Pandey said. 'I'm a human being. I can have complications too. The surgery was, in the past, and still is, fraught with a lot of complications. And if something goes wrong, it will be a big article in all the newspapers and will be discussed in the Parliament and it might even be banned, which would affect a lot of transpeople. You have to be certain the patient is ready for surgery, and is fit for surgery.'

He no longer uses a radial forearm flap for surgery.

'You have the donor site, which you leave so dirty and scarred and sometimes functionally debilitated,' he said. 'A donor is doing a good service. Your first rule is you cannot harm the donor. So, the same way, you can't harm the donor site. I've been looking at ways to make this as scar-less as possible. What we do now is the skip flap. This cannot be done in a single stage. What we do is create the foundation for the organ in the first stage.'

Creating the penis, urethra, and urinary pipe in the same surgery involves very high risk—any complication could cause the skin that forms the organ to decay or become septic.

The first stage is the creation of the flap. The donor site is the hip joint, where a perforating vessel can be used to shape a penis. It would only leave a thin scar, on the pubic region. There is also a better chance of erotic sensation, since the donor site is among the body's most concentrated erogenous zones.

Dr Pandey showed me a video where the flap was cut out of the pubic region, between the stomach and legs. Since the surgery does not involve a microvascular transfer, but the use of a blood vessel as a perforator, anastomosis—the connection between two divergent structures, such as the joining of two blood vessels—is not necessary. 'The vessels are microvascular, and we're transferring them, but without anastomosis,' Dr Pandey explained. The flap is folded in on itself, and brought to the centre of the pubic region, with the perforator strategically fixed inside.

'The penis is taken *underneath the skin*,' he said, showing me a video of a surgery, 'And brought from the hip joint to the location of the clitoris, in the centre. It is buried through the skin.'

The clitoris was retained, though hidden behind the penis. This way, there was scope for transmen to feel sexual pleasure even after the surgery, he said.

'It is a complex surgery, but it works well. We've had some trouble too, since it is a new technique, but we've worked out the finer points now.'

The second stage is the creation of the urinary pipe, or the urethroplasty. In a video Dr Pandey showed me, after the completion of the first stage, I could hear him reassuring the patient that this would not be the final shape of his phallus.

The flap phallus is created from the superficial circumflex iliac artery, which serves as the perforator. The perforator-based flap is then rotated all the way up and brought to the midline. The phallus would take its final shape a few weeks after the surgery. There could be some torque or shrinkage, and it would have to stabilize before the creation of the urethra. The scarring would be hidden when the urethra was created and placed inside.

'We have to remember that the tube-in-tube is not a single structure,' Dr Pandey said. 'The organ is a shaft for sexual performance. The urethra is the urinary tube. They may have discrepancies because they are two different structures. Putting them in the same stage sometimes may not allow that kind of healing, or could cause disproportionate contraction.' This could cause a fistula, or even necrosis of the tubes.

'The urethra is made from the buccal mucosal graft,' he said. 'We lay the first-stage urethra as a buccal mucosa. We go ahead and tubularize it over 18 French catheter and make it as a complete urethra. It is being made from the native meatus all the way up to the level or tip of the shaft and has to be a staged surgery.'

In layman's terms, the mucosal graft from the inside of the cheek—preferred because of the absence of hair and the fact that it is already located in a wet place in the body—is used to create the urethra. The graft is slowly stretched from the point of origin to the end of the intended penile shaft using the 18 French catheter, so that it sets into a tube around it. The catheter is removed once the skin has taken on its shape. Since the shaping of the urethra will take time, the surgery has to be performed in stages.

The vagina is closed through a vaginectomy, to prevent urethral fistulas in the vagina.

Depending on the patient, the surgeon will decide whether to put the prosthetic penile rod before or after the creation of the urinary pipe, which is the final stage. The prosthesis, if a patient chooses to have it, is implanted from the opposite side to that from which the phallus was raised.

The gap between each stage could vary from six weeks to three months.

'The most important thing is to remember that this is not an emergency surgery,' Dr Pandey said. 'You cannot show bravado and agree to operate if there are big risks. The patient does not have a disease. He wants organs he feels he deserves, but does not have. So ethically, the first thing is 'do no harm'. Which is why we are very particular about staging the surgery, and not doing everything at one go, and being heroic about it. This is a new technique, a new world even to me, and we have only been doing it for four–five years. Each individual is different, and you cannot show me pictures of another transman and say, "You did this for him, do the same thing for me." It may not work. Your organs may not take the blood supply completely. Yes, I'm very proud of some of the surgeries. But let me confess that out of seventy-five, there are at least two patients whose perforator didn't take, and so we had to remove the first penis and create another one.'

Staging the surgery also allows the patient to get used to a new organ. In some cases, they found they were able to have intercourse without needing prosthetic implants.

'You look at a cisman,' Dr Pandey said. 'As a child, the boy only knows he has to pass urine through the penis. And in adolescence, he understands it's a sexual organ, capable of stimulation. So these are learned behaviours. It is possible that along with the touch stimulation on a reconstructed penis which we provide here, he may also begin to feel eroticism. Of course, most of them do not, and many of them also require the prosthesis to be able to perform sexually. And it's important to make the patient party to the understanding of his body.'

In some cases, it may not be possible to use a skip flap, and he had to use a back flap (where the donor site is the patient's back), Dr Pandey said.

'Just because you're capable of driving a Ferrari, you can't refuse to climb on a bicycle.' He leaned back in his chair. 'And I need to safeguard these techniques, popularize their use. So I do surgeries live for national medical conferences.'

He received several calls a day from transmen, he said.

'The thing is, it is hard for them to find jobs where their identity is accepted. And then, when they want to transition, no one is going to increase their leave quota. I have some patients who have had to shift jobs because they needed surgery and they had exhausted all their annual leaves. So they call me up to figure out the most suitable dates for them and we have to coordinate all of this. There are many roadblocks. For example, the penile prosthesis is not available in the country right now. The inflatable one is Rs 3.5–4 lakh, and it is imported. The cheaper, non-inflatable one is only Rs 25–30,000, but it is hard to get hold of.'

Dr Pandey has also been making videos on phalloplasty and the innovations in the field, which he puts up regularly on YouTube.

In one, which he played for me at his clinic, he says:

I think phalloplasty should always be staged, in my understanding, because we have seen the past gold standard, called radial forearm phalloplasty. A single stage phalloplasty of that kind, where from a donor site, we take tissue and create a phallus and create a urethra in a single stage and implant . . . it is probably history now. I've seen the complications of radial forearm phalloplasty both to the donor site and the recipient site. The donor site is such where the scar which happens around is almost non-recovering. The donor site is an exposed aspect of the body. And no one now is wearing a tie and coat. Men want to be in T-shirts, men want to dress well, men want—some of them—parts to be exposed, which are their forearms, their face and neck. And if a donor site on the non-dominant arm, which happens to be the forearms, is scarred to that extent which cannot be retrieved again, ever, either you have to cover it all the time in some elastobandages or wear coats like me. Possibly you never knew that radial forearm phalloplasty will give the donor that amount of scar.

With careful surgery, the possibility of urinary blockages could be completely averted. But not all surgeons are careful.

'I'm quite worried about some of the things we are dealing with,' he said. 'If I showed you some pictures, you would be very scared. A lot of people are just experimenting on patients. I've seen forearms which are practically all bone. Surgeries where the urine is constantly leaking out, and the patient is not able to pass urine properly. The kidney is ruined. Where there are so many blocks that even a catheter can't be inserted, and I have to create a new urethra. There are hundreds of botched surgeries. Six months after surgery, the organ hasn't healed. Grotesque scarring. They are spending more money on corrections than on the actual surgery. So I urge all of them to please do their research, and not go for something because it is free or inexpensive. Nothing is free.'

~

He was among the first to have his surgery done under his state's free SRS scheme. The surgery is usually done in three stages, over several months, with a year's recovery time. In his case, all three parts of the surgery were done together, with no time for the tissues to heal. The media reported that history had been made, and he was interviewed by various newspapers, television channels, and websites.

Within a month, he found that he could no longer urinate. There were blocks in his urethra. He went back to the government hospital, and they made 'corrections', which left him with a two-inch thick, thirteen-inch long penis attached to his right inner thigh; his back, thighs, and forearms were severely depleted of skin, which had been used for the graft.

He had spent Rs 3 lakh on a 'free surgery' which left him with such severe complications that he eventually went to a private hospital and spent a further Rs 12 lakh to get the phalloplasty corrected.

'They just experimented on me,' he told me when we met. 'I don't even remember what it felt like to be whole.'

~

'The biggest pressure is the social, since there is (as) yet no imagination of the possibilities of gender and sex being valuable and legitimate, beyond male and female.'

—Satya Rai Nagpaul

~

Selvam's surgery was performed by Dr P.K. Bilwani in the Maninagar area of Ahmedabad.

'Many media people to whom I speak ask me about the free SRS scheme that the Tamil Nadu government introduced for transpeople,' he said, and shook his head. 'It's impossible. The Aravani Welfare Board has to approve our applications. Technically, the surgery would also cover transmen, but they tend to prioritize transwomen. More importantly, the surgeons with the required expertise don't work in government hospitals. They have their own hospitals, where they make a lot more money. And this surgeon's hospital was all the way in Gujarat. I went to a place I did not know, to an unknown hospital whose staff could not speak any language I understood, because the idea of losing my breasts was thrilling. I didn't have much up here to begin with. People always assumed I was a boy. But I would hesitate to take off my shirt, because a part of me would worry that people would guess there was something fishy about this boy. They might see me differently.'

Selvam told me about his surgery in his improvised narrative technique—through voice messages:

When I got to the hospital, I was wearing these tight half-trousers, and a shirt over my vest. I went inside the room and took my vest off. It was a strange feeling, to stand like that. They asked me to lie down, and gave me an injection. I saw it all happening. But then I can't remember things after a point, so I must have fallen asleep. I think I dreamt of the surgery when I was asleep too.

Suddenly, someone was standing next to me, asking me questions that I didn't understand. They brought the flesh they had removed from my chest on a tray. It was the ugliest thing I'd ever seen. Having it out of my body gave me such a high—more than the best beer and the best cigarette could ever have.

On my chest was a bloodied bandage. I felt no pain, but the blood kept oozing. Each time I woke up, I would see various kinds of blood— the dried blood from the scabs I had scratched, and a viscous layer of blood underneath, and another shade of fresh blood that had seeped into my bandages.

For two weeks, I lay on the bed. The nurses would remove the bandage, spread some sort of medicine on my chest, and then tie fresh ones. I think they tied the bandages too tightly. The flesh on either side of my chest had hardened. I could not tell them this, because I did not know their language. I tried to make signs, but they only smiled encouragingly.

Yet, all the discomfort was as nothing compared to what I had experienced in childhood.

You can bear the pain of a physical wound; it will heal. But when someone hurts you with words, you can't ever forget it. Each time you remember the words, it is like the scabs peeling off to give way to fresh wounds, over and over again. People would ask why I thought I was a guy. People would tell me I was mad for wanting to become a guy. When they didn't pass judgement, they would ask questions.

Every sentence, every question, every look of bewilderment would make my heart splinter.

You're probably irritated because I'm spouting aphorisms when you want me to finish telling you about my surgery. I'm like that. I don't like straight paths. Every now and again, you should wander down tracks that crop up, and then, when you've seen all there is to see, you get back on to the main road and finish what you started. I've told you I like Tamil films. Think of all these asides as the comedy track. Even when I tell you sad stories, I'll make you laugh because of how I word them. Sometimes, I tell people about my most intense experiences and they laugh. I think, what the fuck is wrong with this person? I tell you about almost dying, and you laugh? *When I ask them, they tell me*, brother, don't take offence, it's the way you put things.

That's one talent, I suppose, to make people laugh. No one wants to hear someone whine all day. You look at films, and you think: if the shit that happens to the comedian happens to the hero, it would be depressing; but because it happens to the comedian, it's funny. The hero is the hero because of the heroine; the comedian is the comedian because he hasn't got his girl. I suppose I'm the comedian waiting to become the hero.

The surgery was the first step. It took me three or four months before I could feel any sensation on my chest. I would massage it every day, hoping I would one day feel my hand against the skin. I could not lift my arm—it would feel like my flesh was tearing. They did not teach me any exercises, so I made up my own. The doctor had asked me to go to the gym and lift weights. If I could speak his language, I'd have told him, 'Man, I don't have the money to go to the movies, and you want me to go to the gym.'

I knew that you needed to eat well to regain your strength. So I ate a lot, and then worked out.

Despite the discomfort that followed the operation, Selvam felt a sense of freedom he had never experienced. He could walk about with only a vest on over his trousers, and could remove that too if he was so inclined.

'For so long, I had wondered what this life and all its difficulties were for,' he said. 'And now, I finally had the answer. I've attempted suicide five–six times. I've died and been reborn. I've ground and eaten oleander seeds. But the moron that I was, I ate the paste on an empty stomach, and when my mother saw me vomiting though I hadn't had food, she knew something was wrong and rushed me to the hospital. If she had come that way a little later, it would have been "case closed". And then, of course, there was the snakebite. I've survived a lot of accidents. Sometimes, even now, I wonder why I'm alive.'

'You're an inspiration to a lot of people, you know.'

'Yeah, yeah, they tell me my story encourages them. But how long must I think of others? Sometimes, you want your life to move ahead. You want to *want* to wake up every morning.'

The Self-made Man

'Some men are born into their bodies. Others have to fight for it.'
—Vihaan Peethambar

~

My gender became my private affair
However my body became everyone's business
No I don't want to tell how my body looks like
Or how I do sex or my progress
I am not a lab rat
I am just another human
I am just tired of wandering from one government office to another
Just to get my documents updated and explaining everyone who I am:
a transgender
I feel vulnerable, I feel judged
First deal with the unknown, then search half a life for a name for it
as such
Oh gender dysphoria! Spend a fortune for surgeries and doctors fees
Then keep proving time to time I am a man, so no 'ma'am' please!
I want peace
I want an off button

—From 'I Am a Man Not a Girl!' by Jamal Siddiqui

'No one understands a transman except another transman.'

I would hear the sentence over and over again, so often that I wondered whether it was a WhatsApp group status message that all its members had adopted as a mantra.

No support system works quite like the transmasculine forums through which members can discuss common problems, medical professionals, and even mood swings while undergoing hormone therapy.

Jamal Siddiqui, a Delhi-based transman, has a YouTube channel and blog on which he documents his transition.

Jamal Siddiqui's YouTube Channel
Video 1
Posted on 15 March 2017
Transman India Introduction FTM

Hey. I am from India. This is my first video. And . . . I am (a) transgender man. Pre-operated. Been on hormone therapy. I've got two shots. I don't really see any change, much, right now. And let's see! This is my journey, this is my first video. Hope you like it. Bye!

On his blog, Jamal tracks his own transition in real time, reporting the changes in his body and behaviour, as well as his experience in society.

Muslim, Transman and a nerd. This blog is about my journey, my transition and my life. For me transition is not just about surgery which we go through; it is much more deeper than that. Changes, learning, fears, emotions, struggles and everything. From being daunted to being proud and accepting. This how I define my blog: it is all about the journey of my life and being me.

The blog has an entire section on how a pre-operative transman can pass for a cisman, which includes notes on how to figure out where one's dysphoria is most concentrated, coping with the barber's questions while getting a haircut, finding the right clothing, using a binder or improvising one safely—the wrong kind of binder could cause severe damage—and keeping it clean, how to 'pack' to give the impression of a bulge in one's trousers, where one can buy a stand-to-pee device, how to fake a five o'clock shadow, how to deepen one's voice, and how to 'learn masculine manners without being sexist'.

Jamal speaks candidly and in detail about each stage of his transition.

From his blog:

SEVEN MONTHS OF BEING A TRANSMAN
Physical changes: There have been many physical changes.

1. I didn't notice many changes after the first two shots; however, after two–three months, my voice started to crack, and it changed after six months. My voice is (a) work in progress.
2. I started noticing facial hair in four–five months, and before that, I used to shave so that I can have good facial hair. I have a light moustache and (a) French-cut beard that grows on my face. On my cheek and neck area, hair is still growing. I do not have a heavy facial hair.
3. My smell started to become strong at around four months. I sweat more than before, and my face has become more oily. I started getting pimples all over my body after six months, but still do not have a lot of pimples on my face.
4. I feel hungry all the time, energetic, and my libido has increased.
5. I still have a female body curve. I do not see any change there in seven months, and my body hair is still light. My skin is still not masculine, i.e., it is still soft.

Social changes: I bought a binder when I started my transition and got a haircut (buzz cut or military cut). Both of them help me a lot to pass as a cismale. Also, when my facial hair started coming, passing (for a cisman) became more easy. Nowadays, people treat me as a cisman. It has become quite easy for me to go through a male line in security checks and to use a male washroom, though I still do not have (a) stand-to-pee device; but people do not stare at me or pass any comments.

Psychological changes: After I have started transition, I feel my dysphoria is lowered to a certain level. Due to this, I feel more confident, calm, and not disturbed all the time. I have become (a) little impatient and aggressive. I am not sure (whether) it is because of testosterone or in general. I am getting more familiar with me as a person and understanding myself.

He usually adds a line or two of pep talk, asking transmen to hang in there—coming out to family is a process, physical changes do take a while to manifest, employers are becoming more accepting of transpeople.

Jamal Siddiqui's YouTube Channel
Video 5
Posted on 24 August 2017
Seven months on TFTM; Transman India coming out

So, it's been seven months on testosterone. And I have news. Recently I have changed my name and gender, legally—so through gazette notification. I'm one of the first transpeople who has done a gender change without surgery, on documents. I should also mention that in India, the procedure for name and gender change varies across states. I was able to do mine in Delhi. And on the basis of this, I have given my Aadhaar card for updation, on the third of August. There has been no update so far. I called the Aadhaar helpline, and they said it would take sixty–ninety days. So let's hope for the best. Fingers are crossed.

When I met Jamal, I would learn just how hard it had been for him to get his documents changed. It would not be the first account I heard from a transman of how miserably the NALSA judgment had failed to be implemented across states.

Red Tape

Vihaan Peethambar is feeling blessed.

11 November 2016

Hey guys, I have officially changed my name to Vihaan Peethambar. This is an exciting start to a new life and I feel so happy to share this with you. Cheers!

23 December 2016

Post by Vihaan Peethambar under his assigned name, deleted from: https://www.facebook.com/530171820/posts/10154071214906821/?hc_location=ufi

As many of you know, especially if you've seen me in the past few months—but just as many or more of you don't yet know, I began a huge new journey last year (July 2015). For me, this journey was a long time coming, with the seeds planted in early childhood and grown through my years in school and college. Though over the last five years I've found happiness and satisfaction without saying publicly what I'm about to say, something was always slightly off. I was never quite myself.

Finally, I found the courage to do what I had long been avoiding, thanks to my ever supporting mother, sisters, brothers-in-law and my best friend. (I thank God every day for them)

In short: I came out as transgender (Transman). This means that even though I was born biologically female, on the inside I feel like a male. I do not identify with my birth assigned sex/gender.

To that end, several months ago, I started the process of transitioning medically and legally to make my outside (body) match how I feel inside (mind & heart). This is not a decision that I'm making lightly. I've felt this way all my life but fought it to the extent that I tried my best to conform to society and live as a female (most of you know the phase of my life where I had long hair and wore female clothes) but I just could not do it any more.

And it's been a liberating experience that is already making me more genuinely myself and more happy than I have ever been in my life.

These past months, I have been living and presenting as male full-time. I have legally changed my name to Vihaan Peethambar and gender to male and use he/him pronouns. So to put it bluntly, if we talk (even if only from time to time), I ask that you abide by that change around the clock, whether I'm there to hear it or not. Change my name in your phone, your address book, and most importantly your mind.

I'm still the same person I was before I came out, though with the aid of modern medicine (Thank God!!), my physical appearance has changed to a great extent—but my old name and pronouns (she/her) are simply not mine any more. I don't identify with them, and I DO NOT respond to them. So even if it takes some extra effort, and it feels uncomfortable at first, and you slip up sometimes (in front of me or not), please put in the effort. It's important to me and it matters in ways both big and small. If you're stuck, I'm easy to reach and prepared to answer questions and field responses about any range of related topics, including my own evolving identity and trans issues more generally. Still like all those in my life (my awesome family and friends) who've already made the change, I think you'll find it's not as hard as you might at first imagine. It just takes a little practice and a bit of patience.

Like many transpeople, I've had to be patient with myself too. It's been a long road to feeling like I can share this part of myself with the world. Over the years, I've watched in horror as transpeople have been murdered for the apparent crime of trying to match their respective bodies with their minds. My heart has broken repeatedly as I've read and heard stories about transpeople pushed so far (beyond) their limits by their families, peers and society—so utterly broken by the process of coming out that they took their own lives (To be honest, I have felt that way several times). As most things with LGBT, things are slow but getting better, every day, month, and year at differing paces around the country and world. On that front, I will continue to be patient and I hope that in coming out, I can do my own small part in helping those who are trapped in their own battles in the ongoing struggle for trans-recognition and rights. I am now a member of Queerala—an LGBTIQ support group in Kerala and work for creating awareness for trans-rights in Kerala. Recently, I was a panel member (representing Kerala transmen) at Quest 2016—National Seminar on Queer Discourses and Social Dialogues at Trivandrum.

Big picture aside, these past few months have been the most liberating and alternatingly challenging/terrifying of my life. I am more myself than ever before. At last, I honestly say that this is who I am and I'm proud of it.

So hey everyone, I'm Vihaan. It's nice to meet you . . . again. I hope you'll stick around for the next chapter of my journey (and in turn, I'll stick around for yours).

I will be deleting this Facebook account (in a week's time so that enough people get the chance to read this post) as I move forward with my new life and would like for those who would like to stay in touch with me to add me on Vihaan Peethambar.

I apologize if anyone feels hurt that I did not share this with them earlier. The main reason I've waited so long to tell you all is that I just felt uncomfortable writing this post and that I really didn't know how it would (be) responded to if I told you this in person. Thank you for reading this. It's a grand step in my journey.

If you have any mature questions, feel free to talk to me or write me a message. I hope that I can count on you for your support.

28 May 2017

Vihaan is the kind of startlingly good-looking man most people would turn to look at again if they were to spot him peripherally—either to admire or to envy. He is tall and athletic, but there is a certain gentleness to his features that adds to his charisma. When we spoke on the phone, he laughed easily and often.

Unlike most transmen, Vihaan opted for a hysterectomy and mastectomy ahead of starting his hormone treatment. He was worried that growing a beard before removing his breasts may draw attention. He was able to convince his doctor that there was 'not an ounce of doubt' in his head—just as well, because within three months of starting his hormone therapy the next year, he began to sprout thick facial hair.

He had been working in Dubai for six years to save money for the procedures involved in transitioning. He underwent his first surgery in 2015, and returned to Dubai. But within a year, he saw that he had to leave. Gender transition, which is called 'cross-dressing' in the Middle East, is against the law in most countries in the region, including the United Arab Emirates. People would look at him oddly in public restrooms, and he had come across several stories of transwomen being found out and deported at best, jailed if they were not so lucky.

Even before Vihaan had transitioned, women would stare at the tall, broad person with short hair in public restrooms. Once he had his mastectomy, the suspicion increased. Some women would step back as if they were scared.

'I felt like it was just a time bomb waiting to go off,' he said.

The most sensible option was to move back to India. But it wasn't simple. His mother was living with him as a dependant. Both his sisters and their families were in Dubai. He spoke to his family, and said he wanted to legally change his name and gender. He wanted to complete his surgeries, and begin hormone replacement therapy. He also spoke to his psychiatrist, whom he had been seeing for six years. It was time to make the transition official. He quit his job, and moved back to India in June 2016.

He did not expect that getting his name and gender changed would be such a prolonged battle that it would be the only thing for which he had time in the next twelve months.

Despite the NALSA judgment having clarified that one does not need the SRS certificate in order to change one's name and gender, the gazette office, various press offices, and all government officials would study the printed copy of the judgment Vihaan carried with him, and shrug. 'No one is aware of it in Kerala. And even if people are made aware of it, they have a very callous response to it, saying the government didn't give us any order to follow it, so we won't follow it,' he told me.

He tried making his case. Did the Supreme Court's orders not carry any value? Well, sure, they did, but the government offices were helpless until the state government gave them particular orders to implement the court's judgment. But weren't they *government* offices? Yes, so they needed the Kerala government's orders.

'I would tell them okay fine, then tell me *who* is the Kerala government, you tell me where to go, whom to ask,' Vihaan said. 'But that, no one will tell. Ask this person, ask that person, no one knows anything. They don't actually tell you what to do or how to approach it. They say "ask the government". But I *am* at the government office. "No, no, ask some other government office."'

Laughing, he told me how he would meet ministers and officers of the Indian Administrative Service, carrying an increasingly tattered copy of the 2014 judgment. Sometimes, he would get calls from other transmen who had heard he was determined to get his paperwork done legally, without paying bribes. He would speak to them hoping for advice. They would instead tell him they had been trying to do this for the last couple of years, and could he please help them once he was done with his work?

'Afterwards, I came to know that there are at least ten–fifteen applications for every gazette that are stuck, *stuck*, that the gazette has put on hold because they have asked all these people to bring medical board certificates from a government hospital and none of them want to do it, because it is pure harassment.'

There was no information on any government website, and no document in any government office that outlined the process involved in changing one's name and gender. So the gazette and other offices followed their own bizarre, unofficial guidelines. 'I wanted to get down to the bottom of it. Like, who set this process?'

He submitted his application without the medical board's certification. Two months later, he was informed that the application had been rejected due to insufficient information.

'What certificate do I need?' he asked the officials, and was given a sample in response—a medical board certificate submitted by a transman in 2011, three years before the NALSA judgment made it moot. But the officials had 'not received any government order'.

He noted down the name on the certificate—Aashiq Koshy—and Googled him.

It turned out that the certificate had been the outcome of a case that went to the Kerala High Court in 2011. Koshy had had his surgeries in Bangkok and begun his HRT. When he was about to leave for the final stage of his surgeries, he was stopped at immigration. He looked very different from the photograph on his passport. His female name, 'Jaya Elizabeth Ninan', made no sense on the man with the beard who stood before the officials. When he tried explaining his situation to the staff, they insisted they could not let him leave without a change of gender and photograph in his passport. When he went to the gazette office to print the notification—which is necessary in order to get one's identification changed in India—he was told it was not legal to change his gender. So he filed a case in the high court, presenting his medical records. The court asked a medical board to examine him and file a 'gender status report'. The doctors who examined him wrote that he had become 'irreversibly male', and the judge ruled in his favour. The government had contended that there was no provision for formal notification of gender change in the gazette, to which Justice T.R. Ramachandran Nair said, 'That can be done within two months.'

Now the gazette office wanted Vihaan to get the same documents—a verdict and certificates.

He tried telling them this was a letter that the court had asked Koshy to produce. It was not needed for the gazette notification. He could not tell whether they were 'lazy, transphobic, pig-headed, nasty, or all of the above'. He considered taking the legal route, and a lawyer he consulted said there were already ten–twelve transmen with similar problems, and a Public Interest Litigation would almost certainly win a ruling in their favour. But it might take a while for the verdict to be delivered. Did he want to explore other options?

He went to the state's Social Justice Department, accompanied by several members of the LGBTQI support group Queerala, and submitted a petition, along with all the documents and medical reports he had. The staff at the department promised to send the petition to the minister for social justice. A week later, the Social Justice Department told him they could not do anything about it; the case would have to be handled by the state's Transgender Justice Board.

In 2015, the Kerala government had formulated a policy for transgender rights, which has been celebrated in both the media and political circles, usually with several complimentary adjectives —'progressive', 'path-breaking', 'radical', 'pioneering' . . . but they had left out 'unimplemented'.

The policy upheld the right of transpeople to 'self-identify'— identify themselves as trans without proof of surgery—a right already protected by the NALSA judgment. But all cases requesting name and gender change would be processed by a Transgender Justice Board in each district, which would comprise four representatives of the transgender community, a health officer, a law officer, and other government-appointed officials. They would interview the applicant and issue a gender certificate. This could be used to change all markers of identity, without the applicant having to line up at hospitals for physical examinations and medical certificates. No Transgender Justice Board had been set up in any district at the time Vihaan began the process of changing his identity.

'Now how do I approach a board that has not been formed?' He began to laugh.

Their answer was that he would have to wait for the non-existent board to be formed in order to change his gender legally.

So his only option was to get a certificate from the medical board.

'And how does the medical board meeting happen? They call all these people who have applied for various certificates to an auditorium in the government nursing school and there are ten doctors sitting at the front of the auditorium. As their names are called, the applicants go up to them, and explain their cases. What I heard is that at these meetings, they ask you to strip, basically.'

'In public?!' I asked.

'In public. In front of everyone. That's what I heard. But no one has gone for this because everyone is scared, you know. Obviously, they're basically violating every damn cell of dignity in your body. No one's going to go for such a meeting.'

He spoke to a friend who was with the Democratic Youth Federation of India, the youth wing of the ruling party in Kerala, Communist Party of India (M). The friend offered to accompany him, to ensure that he was not subjected to humiliation of any kind. Vihaan agreed. He wanted to find out what exactly happened at the medical board meeting.

It turned out that the meeting was actually for people who were physically challenged. Hundreds of people with various disabilities had turned up to get the certification, which one needs in order to apply for the state's pension scheme for differently abled people. The form Vihaan was given read 'Assessment form for the physically challenged'. He told the attendant who gave him the form that he was not physically challenged, and needed a gender change application form.

'He just gave me this puzzled look and said, "No, no, keep this", and went off,' Vihaan said. 'When my turn came, the surgeon seemed to know my friend who had accompanied me, so he just asked me a few questions like "Where did you do your surgery?" and he seemed a bit knowledgeable about SRS surgeries and all that, and he was telling another doctor what he knew—that it was expensive, and it was not just one surgery. And then, he tells me, "I want to see your chest", and he pulled at my T-shirt. I said, "Doctor, I can't open my T-shirt here and show it to you, so I'll show you a picture."'

Vihaan had shown him a picture on his phone. When he'd explained that he would need a certificate, the doctor had begun writing on the assessment form he had been given.

'So I said, "Sir, this is a form for the physically challenged, there is no use in writing on this,"' Vihaan told me. 'But he anyway wrote on that, and put his sign and seal there. So I went to the gazette with this, and at the gazette obviously they're just waiting for a reason to decline.'

He was told the letter had to be in the same format as the one Koshy had got. 'I said this is what they gave me at the medical board meeting. Then they said I need to go get a district medical officer's (DMO's) signature on this.'

The DMO had said the assessment form for the physically challenged was of little use, and he would give him a letter issued from his office. But first, they would need him to be examined by a gynaecologist and submit evidence that his surgeries had been completed, along with an ultrasound.

When Vihaan had shown him his medical reports from the other government hospitals to which he had already been, the DMO had seemed adamant about Vihaan consulting a particular Head of Gynaecology in the Women and Children's Government hospital. Perhaps that doctor was his friend, Vihaan told me, because the DMO quickly dismissed all the other reports and said Vihaan would need this specific government doctor's seal.

'The funny thing is, I've been to a gynaecologist's office three times. Every time I would go to a government hospital and tell them that I just need a certificate as a formality, they would say they cannot issue one without examining me, and put me through an ultrasound. So again, it's a form of harassment where a man has to walk through a gynaecologist's office where all these pregnant women are sitting and wondering what you're doing there.

'And when you're taken to an ultrasound room, all these women ask you questions. And I had to do that thrice, within a period of three months, because each government office I went to would ask me to go to *this* doctor from *this* government hospital. I had to do three different ultrasounds for the same fucking report—that I didn't have any female organs. So finally, this DMO again told me go to *this* doctor at *this* government hospital, and that he would issue me a letter.

'So I was like okay, chuck it, this is the last thing, he will give me that letter. So I went to that doctor, and that doctor was *hilarious*. He was *petrified* (upon) seeing me. And that's the thing—when you go to government hospitals, they have no idea. In Kerala, they really treat you like a terrorist when you go to government hospitals. It's like . . . I think their mindset is that you are changing your sex in order to do some criminal activity. And I have heard this thrice from three different doctors. They say, "You will ask for this letter and go. Later, if some problem comes up, it will fall on our heads." So I say, "What do you mean by problem?" And they say, "No, no, you don't know nowadays what all people do." So I'm like, "I haven't heard in the *history* of this world, someone has gone through five different surgeries and a lifelong hormone treatment in order to do some terrorist activity. I don't know of anyone who would go through so much shit and harassment just to commit a crime. If you know of someone like that, please enlighten me." At some point, they see I'm offended, so they say, "No, no, I'm not saying *you* will do it." And I'm like, "But you *are* saying *someone* will do it, and that's why they want to change their gender, right?"'

He began to laugh. 'You know, these are doctors, *doctors*, doctors whom the government officials send us to for certification, and they have no idea who transpeople are. Or what their journey is. Or what surgery is. These are the kind of gynaecologists sitting in government hospitals.'

The DMO had told the doctor he met about Vihaan.

'And this guy is standing there and trembling. He's like, "What do you want, *what* do you want?" I said, "See, chill, just calm down. I have done all these surgeries to transition, and I have *all* my doctors' reports, and you just need to assess them." He said he had to examine me. I was very clear that I won't let anyone touch me. I said, "I need a certificate from you saying I have done these surgeries so I can get the DMO's letter and produce it to the gazette. I'll leave. I'll get out of here, I won't trouble you." So he's like, "No, no, no, but the DMO said I have to examine you, I have to examine." I said, "Look at me, do I look like a female to you?" and he's like, "No, no, no, no, but DMO told me . . ." So I'm like, "Fine, what do you want to see, do you want to see my chest? I will pull up my T-shirt." And he's like, "No, no, no, no, wait, wait, wait . . ."

'And this is not in any private room, okay? We're standing in a ward next to an operation theatre with some ten–twenty beds. And he calls some two–three nurses, and then a sweeper lady also comes in, and all of them are staring at me like some show is about to start. And I'm just like so amused by what is happening, and there's no privacy, there's no privacy at all. Okay? So, I said, "What is this, I'm supposed to stand here and strip and entertain all these ladies?" So, then, he's like, "No, no, no, all of you go." And he's trembling. He just doesn't know what to do, he's petrified. And this is, like, the Head of Gynaecology at a government hospital. And then he went and brought one nurse and said she has to be there because tomorrow, I shouldn't complain that he sexually harassed me, which made me wonder whether there's a history of this happening.

'I was like, fuck it, I'll just get the fucking letter. Because this is the fifth time I'm going to a government hospital. So I explain to him that I need this letter so I can change my passport, and then go abroad where I used to live and work. And then he asks me, "What are the surgeries you've done?" So I explained all the surgeries with supporting medical reports from the hospitals where I did them. I told him all the stages, I explained everything to him. And then I pulled my T-shirt up and showed him my chest and all my other scars.'

Vihaan emphasized to me that what the doctor was making him do was against the law—a violation of privacy and dignity, going by the NALSA judgment of the Supreme Court. It did not end there.

'And then, after that, he's putting on his gloves, okay?

'And I'm like, "Why are you putting on your gloves?"

'"DMO told me to examine."

'I tell him, "What will you examine? I've just shown you everything."

'"But DMO told me to examine your genitals."

'So I say, "I have explained everything to you with medical records and also told you the legal implications of the process you are following here, and still you ask me such a thing?"

'And he's like, "Okay, okay, okay. But I will not write in your certificate that I have examined you." And I said, "I don't *care* what you write. Just say that you have assessed my report, and based on whatever surgery scars you've seen, this is what you've observed, and you write it."'

The doctor had said he would, and left. A few minutes later, he had returned to ask Vihaan if he had a template.

'So government officials send you to these hospitals where no one has a clue what to do. At three different hospitals, I myself went to the Personal Assistant's office, and I was sitting on the computer and typing out the letter. So all the letter templates that they have now are what I have set in their hospitals. So now, I gave him a letter I wrote for another government hospital.'

Half an hour later, the doctor had returned with a two-paragraph letter riddled with spelling and grammar errors. Vihaan had taken the letter to the DMO, who had barely read the letter, but noted that the doctor had signed off on it, and asked Vihaan for a template for the letter that he would need to sign for the gazette office.

'I obviously don't have a template. So he calls his PA, dictates what he feels like, this female writes it down and prints it out on blank paper. None of these government offices has a letterhead, okay? So he signs this and seals it and says this is the letter.'

The gazette office was reluctant to accept the letter because it was not the same as the medical board's 'gender status certificate' from 2011.

'Finally, they took it and that's how I got my gazette notification printed,' Vihaan said.

Vihaan's contribution to the gazette office was a newer template for the staff to wave at transmen who wanted their details changed. He told me he was hopeful those who had been in touch with him would have less trouble getting various medical officers to sign off on similar letters.

'This transguy I know, he got married to his partner two years ago, but the marriage couldn't be registered because none of his documents reflects his name or gender,' Vihaan said. 'Everyone was waiting in anticipation for me to get my gazette notification. I applied in December 2016, and I just got it, on 2 May 2017. So you can imagine what a torture it's been.'

How was it possible that the last letter the gazette office had had dated back to 2011? Had no one changed his gender to male in six years? Or was it being done under the table, with bribes? Vihaan is convinced they were hoping he would cough up some money to speed up the process.

His next fight is for unisex bathrooms in schools and colleges. He told me he was glad various NGOs working for trans rights were constantly raising awareness about the existence of transpeople as well as the fact that transpeople are not 'different'. In April 2017, a transgender sports meet had been held, and a beauty pageant for transpeople was scheduled for July.

With the government supporting transpeople, at least on paper, and opening up positions for them with the Kochi Metro, Vihaan was hopeful of more transpeople entering the mainstream. Soon after we had spoken, the media reported that all the transwomen employed by the Kochi Metro had quit their jobs because they could not find accommodation.

'The thing I find problematic here is that the basic grass-roots level awareness and the help that we need from medical people—in hospitals, in schools, especially in government offices—that is not there. Even if it's transwomen who got employed at the Metro, I bet most of them don't even have IDs. They have not legally changed their names, right? So these are the things that need to get addressed first, by the government.'

When I next spoke to Vihaan, he told me several transmen had got their names and genders changed without paying bribes.

'So when they tell me they've got it approved, I'm like thank god, some good came out of all the torture, right? I'm happy,' he said. 'I swear, when you go through this, you really wish no one else has to go through it, the kind of embarrassment and humiliation you're put through at government hospitals, with people who have no clue. Even if there was a proper process in place, however bad the process was, if you had a particular hospital which has been assigned the task of issuing these letters, with a doctor and team that is equipped to handle these cases, who are aware of transpeople, it would be all right. But they are not sensitized. They don't know how to talk to us, or what not to ask us.'

He told me about a gynaecologist he had once consulted, who had been teaching in the government hospital for more than two decades. Vihaan was the first transperson she had met, and she was bewildered that transmen existed. 'I explained everything like you (would) explain to a child, you know: I was female assigned at birth, but my mind and heart don't align with my body, and so on. And after all this, she looks at me and says, "So you were born female?" and I said, "Yes." She says: "You had all female organs?" So I said, "Yes, I did." And she said: "Then, what is the problem?"' He had to explain several times that he did not want to remove his organs because they were damaged, but because they did not belong in his body.

Another gynaecologist, after hearing him out, told a colleague who asked why a man had come to the clinic, 'Oh, he has come for the transgender process.' Vihaan began to laugh almost hysterically when he recounted the incident. 'I'm like, "Please tell me, what is this process?"' She believed he wanted to transition into a woman.

'No one is equipped to handle these cases of transpeople. You can understand (in the case of) the people in government offices, at least. You can't expect them to read and learn how our bodies work, or how our minds work, but doctors—you would expect them to, right, at least *doctors*? But every hospital I went to, I had to explain to them why this is like this, how many types of transpeople there are, it is not only transwomen. Because the media always emphasizes only transwomen, people don't even know transmen exist. Surely, if transwomen exist, the opposite must too, right?'

He is also aware of his own privilege—being fluent in English and articulate, he is able to get people to listen to him. Transmen from the working class are often treated poorly, sometimes even forcibly escorted out of government offices. Dalit transmen have it particularly hard.

Over the times we spoke, Vihaan began to tell me more about his past and his doubts about the future.

When he wanted to have his surgeries, he had no clue where to begin. He had no contact with the community in India—he didn't know any other transmen, and wasn't even sure there were support groups for them in India. So he Googled the contact details of a surgeon whose name he had come across.

'I chose the doctor because my mother had read some article in a Malayalam magazine a long time back, and she had cut it out and kept it for me, in case I wanted it.'

'Your *mother* did that?'

Vihaan laughed. His family had been far more supportive than he'd expected.

'I built it up in my head that it would be a problem, and I could not communicate to my family. But when I told them, they were completely fine. They all just wanted to help me, but they didn't know how. I was going through extreme depression and I was very suicidal. And some mistakes have happened from my mom's side just because she wasn't well informed.'

She took him to doctors, she took him to astrologers. And everyone left him feeling more humiliated. An astrologer even tried to sexually abuse him.

'So when we got into the car after that, I didn't tell her what exactly had happened, because I knew she would not have been able to take the guilt. But I felt extremely suicidal. So I went as if to ram the car into a wall, and I said, "If you want to kill me, let's just die now, don't take me to such people." And then she started crying, and she said, "No, no, I won't trouble you at all. I just want you to be happy. I won't try to help again. Whatever you want to do, I'll be with you." I realized she was trying to do me some good, but she didn't know how. Like any other distraught mom, she was just trying to help me in whatever way she knew. Right? So, after that, whatever I have wanted to do, she's been supportive. Then my sisters also helped. They kept telling her that this is completely normal, there are so many people like this in the world, just that we don't come across them. But she's very proud of me, like . . .'—he grinned at this point—'. . . now I'm completely involved with helping the LGBT community, I've become a board member of Queerala, so I'm giving talks and taking up projects, right? So she's extremely proud of me. I'm very fortunate.'

Not everyone is. Vihaan met a transman who had recently been forced to come out to his mother, because she saw him as a daughter and was keen to marry him off to a man. The transman's father had passed away some years ago, and his brothers were settled abroad. So it was just the two of them at home.

'Now, his mother is threatening to commit suicide unless he gets this "crazy idea" out of his head and marries a man. She's telling him he's bringing shame on the family. The thing is, this guy has just started his postgraduation. So I told him to buy time with his mother, tell her that he will get married as soon as he finishes. Don't start your transition in secret. Finish your studies, and then let's see what we can do—there's a whole community, a support group.'

The problem with most transmen, he said, is that they quit their studies halfway, partly because of depression and partly because they lose their families' support when they insist on transitioning immediately. However hard it is to live as a woman, one must finish one's studies and find a job before transitioning, he said. 'That way, you don't have to depend on anyone. If your family abandons you, you can stand on your own feet. So don't push it. The more he talks about transitioning, the more adamant his mother is. I've added him to a couple of WhatsApp groups, so he can interact with other transmen. We'll put him in touch with the doctors we know, who are sensitized to us.'

'You can't transition alone,' he added, shaking his head for emphasis. 'You need the support of your family, or a very close group of friends when you go through this, through surgery, or anything, for that matter. Because the fact is when you *are* going to surgery, when you're in the hospital, you can't do things by yourself. You need someone with you.'

The idea of transitioning, the realization that the source of one's unhappiness is the mismatch between mind and body, does not necessarily happen early. Vihaan was almost out of his teens when he began to accept that he could never fit into the gender he had been assigned.

Though he had dated women in his teens, and they were all women who identified as heterosexual, he did not think of himself as lesbian. And though he had never been attracted to men, he assumed there would be The One, one man who might make him fall in love. He was on the verge of being engaged to a man when it hit him that he did want to change his gender in every way, including his appearance.

'I was never someone who conformed to gender norms growing up. Like for me, up until puberty, I didn't have any problem with my body. I was flat-chested. And even pre-transition, I had a very well-built body, because of my involvement with sports, so I didn't have much of a bust. But whatever little I had used to irritate me, because I hated wearing a bra, even the sports bras, which would keep it very tight and kind of bind it. When I hit puberty, I found menstruation very humiliating. Every month, I would feel angry, I would feel suicidal. The hormonal changes really, really bothered me. As a child, I'd never bought into gender norms. I've always been someone who is kind of a feminist, not just for me, but for my sisters also. If someone said, "She can't do that, she's a girl", I would call it out.'

He thought of girls as 'them', not 'us', but he didn't quite realize he was a man. His girlfriends were confused about their attraction to him.

'But they used to tell me that I have a guy's vibe,' he said. 'So, in school, there would be rumours about me being a lesbian and I used to get very angry. But until I was twenty-two or twenty-three, I didn't really think about why I was angry. A lesbian is a woman who likes women. And I *do* like women. Why was I so angry? But only then, when I accepted that I'm a transman, I realized it was their calling me a woman that infuriated me. I'm not a woman.'

I held out my first poem to you,
It wept like a little child, from pangs
Of separation.

I searched out and held my child
Close to my heart.

As I raised him with love and chiding
In turns,
In the belief that even if he failed
To win the world; he would win
The one heart.

He won not one heart, but a hundred.
I am beholden to you, obliged
To thank you, for it was
Your heart that tattooed
The drumbeats of my awakening

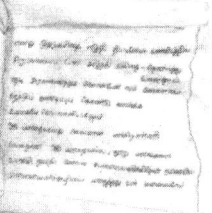

As the mornings nudge me awake,
And as the nights lull me to sleep,
It is you whose visions float into
A mind not quite aware,
Which yet dictates that for
Every hour, a memory of you
Must visit me as I lie.
And I send up a prayer,
Asking that, even on my deathbed,
You must be within reach,
My friend, you who are
Dearer than life, my love.

My eyes opened to the fluttering of my heart.
What is the time! My hands reached
For the mobile phone...

Within a quarter of an hour, in the exam hall,
My trembling hands received the paper.
And as I began to write, a surprise.
My pen woke up with a yawn and stretch.

Another surprise for my startled mind: my pen
Began to write the answers by itself
My dizzy head fell upon the table;
Or so I thought - till a far-off bell
Woke me up, with the
Disappointment that this was all a dream

WORDS WILL
SAVE ME
WHEN THE
WORLD SEEKS
TO FAIL ME

Loneliness

18 February 2017

The first time I met Keerththan Shiva,[1] an undergraduate engineering student at Indian Institute of Technology (IIT), Madras, he had the loping walk typical of teenaged college boys, enviably long eyelashes, large, expressive eyes, and a ready smile that woke up two light dimples in his as-yet-smooth cheeks. Curls straddled his ears, and he had cut off shoulder-length hair a couple of weeks earlier, he said.

'You can call me Keerth for short. Everyone does.'[2]

Keerth had the ideal start. From a middle-class family in southern Tamil Nadu, he was sent to an exclusive CBSE (Central Board of Secondary Education) school—his parents didn't mind taking loans to give their only child a good education. The school was a liberal one, and Keerth didn't notice that he had mostly male friends. His father was in the Tamil Nadu police, and they stayed in the government-provided quarters. Weekends were spent playing basketball and other sports at the facility provided in the police quarters. His father and he played cricket. When his grandfather visited, they would play 'terrace cricket' for at least an hour a day. He liked hitting the ball hard, and his grandfather would chide him for showing off when the

---

[1] Parts of my interview with Keerththan Shiva were used in my long-form piece, 'To Be a Man', for *Fountain Ink* magazine, published in March 2017.

[2] Keerththan was, for some time, 'Kirithick Rajkumar', and now goes by 'Kirithik Shiva'.

ball bounced over the parapet and into other houses. He didn't like part of his school uniform—the checked pinafore he had to wear— but loved the white shirt so much he would wear it when he went out to play with his friends, until his mother shouted at him for getting it dirty.

His mother would not let him keep his hair short. Until he was in Class 6, she used to comb it into two plaits. He refused to even touch his own hair. There came a time when he simply could not look at the mirror—the plaits were humiliating. 'So I did some *jugaad* (stopgap).' He grinned. 'I told her I had some *vendudhal* (vow) in Tirupati, and I'd promised to tonsure my hair. She's very religious, so she had to allow me.'

But one day would change his life forever.

'I was in (the) eighth standard when I attained puberty. I still remember, that's the last day I rode my cycle. The next day, they sold it off. I used to win cycle races and all. I used to go swimming, play with the boys. Suddenly, I could not go out at all, except to school. They didn't even like me going out with my girlfriends.'

He spent his time on video games instead. He and his father would fight over the computer—he had got his father addicted to *Project I.G.I.*, he said with a laugh. He has one happy memory of puberty: a grand function was held, and the trauma of being forced into a sari, and a half-sari a few days later, was offset by the number of people who turned up just for him.

He did not realize all this while that he was, in fact, a girl. Though there were signs throughout his childhood and teens that he was not 'like other girls', he did not feel 'different' because he was not different from other boys, he said. He had had crushes on three girls through school, as did other boys. Two of these girls became his 'best friends', and he was so close to each that people would tease them about being a 'couple'.

'How did that feel?' I asked him.

'Being teased?'

'Yes.'

He grinned, 'That was fun!'

When they were in Class 12, he asked his best friend, Nethra,[3] out. 'She didn't realize I had proposed. She thought it was a girly thing. You know how girls get emotional and say "dear" and "darling" and all that?' He thought she wasn't sure about her feelings, and so hadn't responded.

It did not occur to him that Nethra saw him as a girlfriend. 'I think subconsciously, I stopped looking at the mirror after puberty. Puberty was . . . I still hate the fact that it's there. Like a monthly reminder—"you're a girl, you're a girl, you're not a boy".' He would argue with his mother over the clothes he must wear, over the restrictions on talking to boys. 'And all this time, I did not know I was not a boy.' He laughed.

It was only when he got to the girls' hostel in IIT that he realized something was not quite right. 'I would feel very uncomfortable when they (would change) their clothes or when they'd come out in towels after a bath. I didn't know whether I should stay or go out of the room. And then all the girly chit-chat began.'

A group of freshers got together and began to ask each other about their crushes. When Keerth's turn came, he said, 'Nethra.' They impatiently told him Nethra was a friend; who was his *crush*?

'That's the first time I realized okay, they're telling this is a *friend*? Then I'm supposed to have a crush on a *boy*?' he said.

Soon, his hostelmates began to lose interest in him. He made no contributions to their discussions on clothes or make-up. They could not persuade him to go to the salon. Within eight months, he had no friends, though he shared a room with two girls. So complete was the isolation that when he was burning with fever for three days, neither his roommates nor their friends noticed he was shivering and crying on his bed. After three days, he called his parents and said he was too ill to move and needed help.

'Didn't your professors ask why you weren't in class for three days?' I asked.

He laughed. 'The professors here don't really care about you. They come, they teach the class, and they leave. We go to the website

---

[3] This person's name has been changed to protect privacy.

to check their names, because some of them don't even introduce themselves. If you have less than 85 per cent attendance, they fail you with a "W" grade, and then you have to repeat the course.'

His hostelmates didn't simply ignore him. They appeared to avoid him.

'I get the feeling that people here think I'll pounce on them or something, just because I like girls,' he said, wryly. 'So I mostly control my flirting with girls, but then it comes out, somehow. And when I say some things, they take it the wrong way. You know, guys make such sexist remarks all the time. I don't. But one incident happened, maybe some six months back. One of my roommates was telling me about a new friend she'd made, and I said, "Is she beautiful?" It was a spontaneous comment, and immediately this girl got very upset and she said I was objectifying women and all that. I wasn't. I mean, right *next* to us, there are other male students passing vulgar comments, based on the dressing sense of girls and whatever. I just asked if she was pretty. But after that, I've gone even more quiet. I mostly don't talk to these people.'

Even going to the hostel mess was traumatic. He seemed to have the Moses effect—everyone would bend away from him, leaving him to eat alone. It was only in the third year that one could apply to join the boys' mess, he said, and he felt a lot more comfortable after.

But along with the isolation of the first two years came time to browse the free internet the college provided. For the first time, he could look up things about which he was curious—his mother would sit beside him when he was browsing the net at home, so it had been out of the question.

Now he typed little phrases to see what Google turned up: 'I like girls.'

'Slowly, I got to know about lesbians. At first I found it very awkward, to tell the truth—girl and girl? How is that possible? Even *then* I didn't realize I'm a girl,' he said, with a sudden giggle at a younger, naïve self. 'I don't know how my mind was just fixed that I was a boy. I didn't identify myself as a girl at all.'

For the first time in years, he took a good look at himself in the mirror. 'I thought, "I look like a girl. Am I lesbian?"' But that didn't feel right either. One day, he stumbled upon an article about a transman. 'He describes how he hates his breasts, and he wears loose shirts to look like what he likes. That's when I realised oh-*kay*, this is what I have been doing for some time.' He began to search for stories of transmen. 'I realized many things after that. And I thought "Oh my god, I can possibly grow a beard" . . . and I felt very happy.' One of his favourite hobbies, growing up, was to shave with his father's kit in the bathroom, without his parents' knowledge.

What did he think of transwomen, growing up?

'I didn't know about any of it, LGBT. I mean, I've seen transwomen, but I thought that was just how they were born. Then once, I saw a show, *Neeya Naana* on Vijay TV, where they had invited some transwomen. That's when I first heard the word "thirunangai". And when they described growing up, I felt something—as if I could relate to it. Very different, but also very similar. I asked my mom why they were like this, and she said they're just that way, they're unable to control their femininity, it's a pathetic situation for them. Then I watched the whole episode again. I was fifteen at the time.'

Learning about transmen some years later was a revelation. He phoned Nethra—they spoke almost every day, for at least an hour—and told her what he had found; he also told her that she hadn't understood he was in love with her.

'She doesn't feel that way about me, at least not yet,' he said, a note of hope in his voice. 'But we still hang out as friends, and even now, we talk. Imagine, someone calls you up everyday and talks for hours. You won't want to pick up the phone if you don't like that person too, right?'

But when the excitement over the discovery waned, he sank into a terrible depression. He knew he was a transman now. But could he ever have the life the people in the videos from the US and Europe did?

This time, he missed classes for two weeks, and failed five of seven subjects. His parents were worried. They took him on vacation to try and cheer him up. He could not speak; he could not even smile. Finally, he came out to his parents. His mother's response was denial—'You're just imagining things,' she said. His father's reaction was to buy him several expensive 'girly' clothes.

For three months, Keerth tried being a girl—he wore the clothes, he tried to be affected by the compliments his hostelmates suddenly gave him, he tried looking at the mirror and feeling good about himself. But the person looking back at him was a girl who was miserable in these uncomfortable clothes and this uncomfortable body.

'I couldn't. I stopped trying. I said this is what I am, I have to accept myself.'

He put his efforts into something else—networking. He found the LGBTQI group on campus. He attended meetings, and then one of the members put him in touch with Orinam. Being part of the community cheered him up so much he felt his life had changed. He was able to focus on his studies. He managed to pass his exams without any problems.

'I have friends now.' He smiled, paused, and then said, 'I actually *just* turned twenty. On February 11. And for the first time, I celebrated my birthday here. My friends made a surprise visit. I used to get very jealous when (other hostel residents) would celebrate their birthdays. I'll be the photographer. This time, it was like . . . "My god, this is so nice!"'

~

22 April 2017

Keerth had been working hard. He had several papers to redo. The depression and breakdown from the previous year had made it near impossible for him to catch up. He could not attend the campus recruitment without having passed all his papers; his grade point average had dipped so low he would not qualify for most interviews.

'When you're used to being a topper, failing your exams is *very* hard to take,' he told me. 'And because of this eyesight issue, I have other problems too.'

Keerth had been diagnosed with retinitis pigmentosa (RP), a degenerative eye disease, as a child. Typically, RP is a genetic disorder that manifests slowly—its victims are born with normal eyesight, which deteriorates into total blindness. But his case was unique, he said. He had always had limited sight, with no peripheral vision, but he could read without difficulty; and it had not deteriorated either. It was difficult to see at night, but he could manage.

'I was bullied a lot in school because of this, on top of my other problems,' he said, smiling as if to make light of it. 'I couldn't catch balls when people threw to me. And I wasn't able to climb stairs. Day-to-day activities were hard. I wasn't allowed to go to the terrace after dark. So they used to play with my inability, bully me. They would stick their legs out and trip me up, and throw things at me, which I would see coming but couldn't duck or catch.'

He had taught himself to work around his vision. He used to practise catching a ball, first throwing it gently up into the air, then bouncing it against the wall at close quarters, and then aiming higher, and eventually asking his father to throw it to him.

'These are small, small things I achieved on my own. Even writing on an unruled sheet,' he said. 'And again, when I came to college, people didn't know about this problem, so I had to find my own way. In school, I had a few friends who would help me, particularly in the chemistry lab. Because if I accidentally spilled something, it would be a disaster. But here, suddenly, I was alone. And everyone has just come from boot camp, right, in preparing for JEE (Joint Entrance Examination)? So this whole competitive mentality is there. They tend to only think about themselves.'

In a strange way, though, his problems with his eyesight had given him certain liberties at home which his female cousins were not accorded. It had made his father particularly tender towards him, and indulgent of his insistence on wearing shorts and climbing lofts and playing with the boys—until puberty, of course.

'The other girls in my family, my cousins, they had *so* many restrictions, my god, you can't imagine,' he said. 'The boys can do anything. You come drunk in the middle of the night and vomit inside the house, it's fine. But then they would yell at the girls if they even stretch out when they sleep. This would happen after I hit puberty.

Suddenly, my mother would pinch me in the night, to wake me up and ask me, "Why is your hand on your stomach? Sleep properly." You wake people up to ask them to sleep "properly". It was total hell.'

The girls were expected to clean up after the boys, from taking their plates to the kitchen after they had eaten to washing their clothes.

'But I was something of a pet in the family, on both sides, because of the eye issue, I think,' he said. 'And maybe because I was born many years into the marriage. My mom had four miscarriages before me. So I was special.' He grinned.

A patriarchal set-up of this kind could influence transmen, he said. 'I won't deny it, I used to make vulgar, sexist remarks about girls until a year or two ago. That's what the men in the family do, and I'm a man, so it used to happen.' It would surprise and outrage him when his mother told him to behave like a girl, or set boundaries for him, or said he had to learn to behave so that he would be able to get along with a husband in the future.

Perhaps it was education that chipped away at the sexism that was ingrained into his thinking, he said, or perhaps it was the bullying, being made to feel like he was inferior. But he began to read about the feminist movement, about the male gaze, and that made him introspect.

'A lot of guys like me run away from home, right? I couldn't. Maybe if they had stayed on, if they had got an education, their minds would have been opened to things. It's happened very, very slowly for me.'

Keerth's stories of his upbringing would often confuse me. On the one hand, there were various rules he could not flout, particularly after he began to menstruate. 'They would not let me lie down on my father's lap, even,' he said. On the other, his father was so keen for him to be able to live independently that he pushed Keerth to make all his decisions for himself, down to whether he wanted to give the JEE a shot and which coaching centre he wanted to join. He was not allowed to browse the internet alone, but his parents were pleased when he looked up universities and figured out where he wanted to complete his graduation.

'My grandfather is also like that.' Keerth smiled. 'My father was into athletics, and he had also applied for the police recruitment trials. So he had to choose between a career in the police force and trying out for the nationals and going to the international level in athletics. My grandfather refused to make his decision for him. So maybe it's something to do with that.'

It was harder to convince his parents of his gender, though. 'My father is *trying* to understand. I think he'll come around sooner or later. But my mom . . . it's very difficult.'

It was not just 'society' she was worried about; she found it impossible to believe transmen could exist—she saw it as a figment of his imagination at best, and as betrayal at most times.

She had been speaking to him about marriage since he was twelve, he said.

'Everyone was always like, "You want to study in the US, right? Marry a guy who is settled in the US and you can study." And my mom would agree. And then she would say someone had to take care of me because of my eye problem, and my parents would not be around forever, blahblahblah. This marriage talk would freak me out. And I would shout back and say, "What is the guarantee that this person will take care of me? What if he marries me for the dowry and then abandons me?" This was the only argument I had, at fourteen.' He laughed.

~

Soon after, I would meet another transman with a disability, one far more evident than Keerth's. Usha Kiran Nayak was something of a role model in the trans community, having established various organizations that fought for the rights of several marginalized communities. He was also from the adivasi community.

'In what way am I marginalized? I don't know, actually.' He laughed. 'Am I marginalized because I'm adivasi, because I'm disabled, or because I'm a transman?'

To see them now, as part of a community, with a support system, gave me the luxury of visualizing a happy ending to their stories, neat little postscripts for chapters on them. But when they spoke of their childhoods, or when I met transmen who were just stepping out of adolescence, as Keerth was, the immense loneliness that ran through their early years would break my heart. The hairless faces and high-pitched voices of those who had not started their hormone therapy made it easier to picture them as little boys, confused that the world saw them as girls. I did not want to pity them. But how could one not feel protective of the children they had been?

Mohini's Men

She was a recurring character in Hindu mythology, her beauty ending battles and killing demons. Mohini's first appearance seems to have been during the Kurma Avatar of Lord Vishnu. A sage's curse had sent all the treasures of the earthly and heavenly worlds into the ocean, including the Nectar of Immortality. The only way to retrieve the nectar was to churn the ocean, and the mechanics of churning the ocean were complex. The only churn that was powerful enough to stir the ocean was Mount Mandara, and the only rope strong enough to turn Mount Mandara was Vasuki, the King of Serpents. The mountain had to be balanced on a pivot so it wouldn't sink into the ocean, and so Lord Vishnu took the form of a giant *kurma*, a tortoise. The churning of the ocean would require a coalition of armies, and so the devas and asuras, the gods and demons, made a pact—they would work together, and share the treasures equally. As is usually the case in Hindu mythology, the gods intended to play a dirty trick: they would ensure the nectar did not go to the asuras. And the orchestration of this fell to Mohini—Vishnu in the form of a woman, an enchantress so charming that the asuras agreed to let her distribute the nectar as she saw fit.

Mohini also appears in the story of Bhasmasura, a demon whose penance to Lord Shiva had granted him a bizarre power—he could turn anyone to ashes by placing his palm on their heads. Having had his fun with mortals and demigods, his cinder happiness found a target in Lord Shiva himself. Mohini came to the rescue. When Bhasmasura was chasing Lord Shiva through the cosmos, she sashayed across his path. Bhasmasura was so charmed, he paused his pursuit and asked Mohini to marry him. Mohini agreed on one condition—he must dance with her, matching her move for move. The duet went on for days and culminated in a gesture—Mohini placed her hand on her head. Bhasmasura, perhaps sleep-deprived and testosterone-fuelled, imitated her without thinking and reduced himself to ashes.

Mohini's love life saw highs and lows. She once took the fancy of Shiva, and reciprocated his interest. This rendezvous—between Vishnu and Shiva—produced a son, Iyyappa. Mohini was also called upon when Aravan needed a wife.

The Mahabharata legend of Aravan begins with the notion that a warrior's life had to be sacrificed to ensure the Pandavas' victory in the Battle of Kurukshetra. It was somehow determined that this warrior should be a prince called Aravan, one of Arjuna's many sons. He had been so busy attaining his warriorly perfection that he had not found the time to lose his virginity. His last wish was to know what it felt like to be with a woman. Since no one—not even prehistoric warriors—could justify marrying a woman off to a man whose life was to end the next day, Lord Krishna took on the female form of Mohini, married Aravan, and became his widow after the nuptial night, lamenting and cursing their fate. This episode is re-enacted at the Koovagam festival each year, with transwomen envisioning themselves as Mohini. The word 'aravani', which derives from the cult of Aravan, has now been replaced by 'thirunangai', which loosely translates from Tamil as 'divine woman'.

One wonders what the legend of Mohini says about Hinduism's take on homosexual relationships and gender transition. And why is mythological intercourse always procreative? Does any other religion believe gender transition is permissible?

There are disagreements among various Islamic scholars about whether the religion permits gender transition. One school of thought is that transition is allowed, but that post-transition intercourse must be procreative—ironically, the sort of mandate that would not be out of place in Hindu mythology.

If God Wills It

24 June 2017

It was Eid. I was to interview two Muslim transmen, and not by coincidence. They lived in Islamic countries where transition was illegal, but the pay was good enough to save for their surgeries. Bilal[1] is an Indian Shi'a Muslim based in another country, which he asked me not to name. Rommel Mohammad[2] is a Sunni Muslim from Bangladesh, who asked me not to reveal the country in which he was working, since he could be imprisoned. Both of them would have the time to talk at leisure that day since they had a long weekend for Eid.

My conversations that day left me feeling strangely drained. There was a sense of joy and warmth, but I also felt heartbroken. Both of them spoke about death, and they spoke about it in a manner that indicated they knew their lives would be short.

---

[1] This person's name has been changed on request.
[2] This person's name has been changed on request.

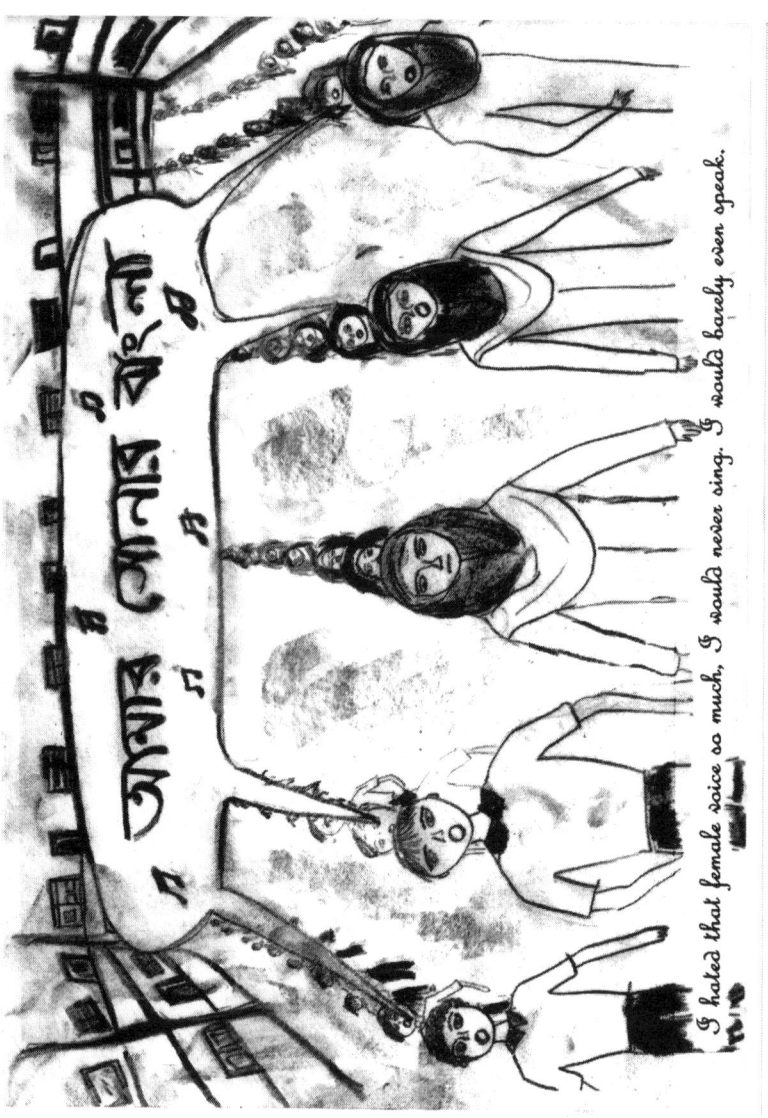

I hated that female voice so much, I would never sing. I would barely even speak.

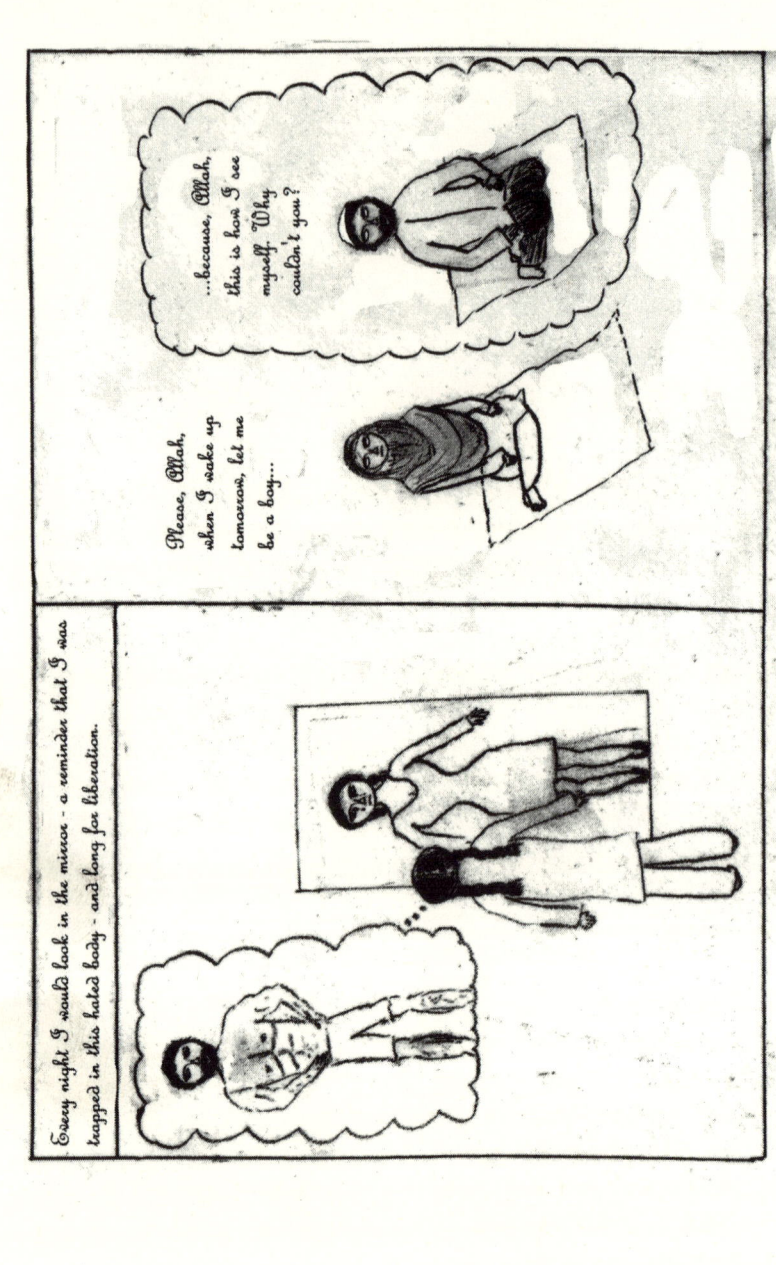

Tom and Jerry

On 18-06-2017, 11.53 a.m., Rommel Mohammad wrote:

Dear Nandini,
I was just going through your note that you are writing on Transman issues. I am really thankful to you for your creative work. Through Sampoorna, I came to know about you. I am a Transman. (from Bangladesh, now in _____) . I would love to talk with you, if u feel it will be worthfull. I am the first Transman from my country who started transition. And the journey was not at all smooth. Family, society and finally I was bound to leave the country.
Waiting for your valuable reply,
Dr Rommel.

On 18-06-2017, 9.54 p.m., Nandini Krishnan wrote:

Dear Rommel,
I'm so sorry you had to go through all this. It must have been traumatic.
And I imagine things are quite difficult in _____ also?
Yes, I'd love to talk to you.
How would you like to do this? Do you want to send me an email, or shall I give you a call, or a few Skype sessions?
Best, and looking forward,
Nandini

On 19-06-2017, 2.15 a.m., Rommel Mohammad wrote:

> Hey Nandini,
> I am glad with your warm reply,
> Its true things are worst in _____, But the thing is they still
> dont know that I am transitioning. Once they come to know
> they will terminate me. Anyways here I have contract upto
> December. I think skype conversation will be better. What about
> coming saturday?
> My skype ID is : _____
> Thankfully,
> Rommel

It took us a while to connect. Rommel had forgotten the password to
the ID he had given me, and after a frantic WhatsApp exchange, he
created a new ID and we finally managed to get online. The first thing
I noticed about him was his smile, which would lift his cheeks so that
his face looked almost cherubic.

Twenty-eight-year-old Rommel had completed his medical
training as a general physician a couple of years earlier. He planned to
specialize in surgery.

'I thought you were pre-HRT. But your voice seems to be
breaking?'

'Oh, it's been nine months,' he said. 'Today my voice is higher-
pitched because tomorrow is the day my shot is due. It will be deeper
tomorrow.' He winked and laughed.

Rommel was the fourth of five siblings. He remembers that his
father used to bring home toys for the children—lipstick and dolls for
the girls; cricket bats and cars for the boys.

'I would feel suffocated when I had to play with the girls,' he said.
'I used to play only with the boys before I went to school. But in school
there was no choice.'

He told me he had grown up in a family so conservative that I
could not possibly imagine it. Even now, he would not be allowed
into his home unless he changed into feminine clothing, complete

with the hijab, a garment he had always detested. For as long as he could remember, he was always looking to leave home. When he was as young as seven, he would escape to the houses of relatives for long stays during the school vacations.

'Right up (till) now, my family has been trying everything— mental, physical, financial—to stop me from transitioning,' he said, with a laugh.

'When did you know you wanted to transition?'

'I guess I always felt like a boy, right from childhood. But you know, when you hit puberty, the age when you can sense your feelings for someone? I realized that I liked one of my friends, a very beautiful girl. I liked looking at her. When she would come close, or hold my hand, or touch my shoulder, I would feel my heartbeat increase. At the same time, when this one boy liked me and proposed to me, I got so irritated I couldn't take it.'

He fell in love for the first time when he was in Class 12. A teacher noticed he and his female classmate were behaving like a couple, and told his family, who wanted to stop his education.

'I realized the only option I had was to pretend I was like other people,' he said. 'To study, to make a career for myself, to be independent. If I don't follow what they say now, they will stop me right here. So I behaved like I was "normal". I had to grow my hair long, and I hated it. I just wanted to get into medical college and go away to hostel, to be myself. I would feel depressed often, but I had to focus, I had to pass my exams, I could not allow myself to fail. Through my higher secondary and medical college, I made sure I only studied, every single minute, and I passed every exam.'

And even as he turned to logic to get him through the day, he turned to religion at night.

'Every night, I used to pray and cry that in the morning, I should wake up a boy. "In the morning, when I open my eyes, Allah, make me a boy, okay?" That's what I would say.'

And though it never happened, he didn't stop believing. 'I think it made me more strong. My religious view is that everyone's life has some problem or the other. My brothers and sisters may not have my problem, but they're not entirely happy either. I've been lucky to study this much, to focus on academics. My two sisters are married and have children. My older brother is a businessman, my younger brother is an engineer, and they're working. I want to study further, and I can.'

'Didn't they ever pressure you to get married?' I asked.

'Ah!' he said, with a laugh. 'Those days are finished. Some ten-twelve years ago, I stopped going to all family gatherings—weddings, functions, everything. And I broke off contact with most of my relatives because as soon as I talk to them, they will call up my parents with details of some boy they know who will be suitable for me. And then the pressure on my family also increases. They spoke to me about marriage a few times, and I said no, I can't do it, it's not possible.'

He made sure he only applied to medical colleges far from home, so that he would have to stay in hostel. His brother insisted that his going to medical college would be conditional on his living at home. Rommel pretended he hadn't got into any college that was a reasonable distance from home. Finally, he spoke to his father, who relented, leaving his brother no choice. Each time he came home, he would wear the hijab. Soon, he realized he could lop off his hair, and no one at home would be any the wiser as long as he wore a dupatta over it.

'The first time I cut it, I was afraid to go home because it was so short. What would they do? Then I decided I would just keep the dupatta on all the time. I think my brother was happy that I was being so feminine. But then once, I was reading and there was a mirror behind me. My dupatta had slipped a little, and my brother came in and realized what I had done. I was shivering. *Now* what he will do to me. Okay?' And he began to giggle. 'So he shouted. And shouted and shouted. A *lot*. And then the usual thing—"We will stop your studies. We will not pay your admission fees." And then they would get me married off to a man and throw me out of the house. So finally, I said, "Okay, if you want to get me married, get me married. Next morning, you won't find me. I don't know where I'll go, but I'll go somewhere."'

He began to laugh, almost hysterically, and I joined in, because I was too uncomfortable to do anything else. 'They stopped after that, because they realized that it would be far more shameful for them to face society if they had a runaway daughter than a daughter who behaved like a boy. So this is how it was. If they take one step, I'd take two steps. My whole life is like a *Tom and Jerry* cartoon.'

The first time he came across the concept of gender transition was in medical college. He had seen transwomen on the streets, but like most people, assumed they were intersex, born with ambiguous organs. He didn't realize they had had the same male bodies as any cisman.

In his third year, there was a list of psychiatric illnesses in his Forensic Medicine textbook. Being transgender, engaging in sodomy, sadomasochism, necrophilia, and necromania were listed one after the other on the same page.

He began to read up on the subject of gender transition, particularly about transmen, both in libraries and online. He learnt he could have surgery to change his body. And so he began to save money.

He began to offer tuition classes for junior students, and made about 2,000 taka a month. By the time he had finished his house surgeoncy, he had about 80,000 taka.

'I was planning to tell my father, because he and I were very close. I think he would have understood. He has always been supportive of me. But he was diagnosed with cancer suddenly, and he got very sick. For eight months, he was in such pain that I could not talk to him about this and give him more stress. Then, in 2013, one month before my final exam, he died.'

'How did you manage to write your exam?' I asked.

Rommel smiled. 'You're so sweet. You look so concerned. I think I studied very hard because I so badly wanted my father to see me become a doctor. He's the only one who wanted it. My mother and brother . . . their thinking is different. They don't see why I wanted to study so much, to be a doctor. My father was admitted in the same hospital where I was doing my residency, so I would sit with him, then go do my work, then sit in his room and study. Even my brother said, "Don't worry, he will not go before he sees you get your degree." But what to do, everything will not happen the way we want.'

After his father passed away, things became even more complicated. His brother was now the head of the family. He and their mother began to pressure Rommel to quit his internship, come home, and get married.

He decided to come out to his family.

'I had got a job, so now I would have some money. I told them I can't take it any more, and I am going to change myself. The first day, they were too confused to create problems. But from the second day it started. They said, "How will you get money for surgery? It's very expensive!" I said, "I won't take money from you. I'm working full-time in two hospitals, ninety-four hours a week. I'll save up and do the surgery. You don't have to help me. Just don't create problems, that's all the support I need."' He laughed again.

'You worked ninety-four hours a week? That's almost fourteen a day, with no leave.'

'Yeah, and I used to do duty also extra.' He laughed, 'So I can save money for transition. But then my brother said, "Okay, if you make *this* much money, why do you want to waste it on surgery? Give it to the family." They said they will stop asking me about marriage if I stay a girl. That was the condition.'

He told them he had no choice. It was biological. He was male. He would have to change his body. His family took him to a psychiatrist.

'I wanted to kick him. You can't imagine. He said I will become all right if I have sex with a boy. And later, he wrote in my prescription, under "Chief complaint", "Decreased sexual ability".'

'What the serious fuck? This is a doctor?'

'Oh, a famous one. He has two clinics in Dhaka.'

'How do these people qualify as specialists?'

'Oh, you know how amazing our medical books are. Being transgender is under the same category as necrophilia. So they read that in third year, and then there are two more years of study, and then internship and work, and then specialization, and the issue does not come up at all. So they don't know and they don't want to know. When I wanted to start my hormone therapy, I went to an endocrinologist here, who is a friend of my teacher's. That guy spoke to me, and counselled me, and then he said he will start the treatment if I come with my parents or guardian. I was twenty-five. I'm past the legal age for needing a guardian's or parent's permission. And I'm a qualified doctor.' He grinned. 'That is the state of affairs. Then I realized it is not possible to start here. It's not at all possible. So I decided to go to Bangkok for my hormone therapy and to ask about surgery.'

He made a last-ditch effort to convince his brother that transitioning gender was not against Islam.

He found a video where a scholar from Iran was explaining that men—cis or trans—could not wear a woman's clothes and vice versa. The scholar went on to explain that the government was obliged to subsidize the cost of surgery, because it was important for people to fit into the binary. It wasn't their fault—Allah had made them the way they were, and the only way to make honourable Muslims out of them would be to correct them surgically.

'I showed this to my brother, and my brother said, "They are Shi'a, we are Sunni, so I don't believe them."' Rommel began to giggle again. 'So then he took me to another scholar, who said no, no, being transgender is haram. Then I said let's go to a doctor and speak about it. So my brother said, "No, no, you're a doctor; so you'll take us to someone who will support you and lie for you." It's funny how many disadvantages there are to being a doctor.'

He made preparations to go to Bangkok in secret. His online research led him to the Transitions Hormone Clinic in Pattaya. He spoke to a doctor from the clinic, who seemed friendly and promised to help.

A Google review of the clinic reads:
I'd not recommend this clinic for transgendered men. Ran out of testosterone back in mid 2014, went to the clinic showing my bottle incl. prescription label as a proof that I really am from abroads. The staff didn't seem to care at all despite telling them that testosterone is important for my health.
They should have given me the advice to go to a real hospital.
Ended up visiting a real hospital (PIH) that took my problems seriously (sic).

'The thing was, this was the first time I was going abroad,' Rommel said. 'I didn't know anyone. And the money I had was what I have saved over four or five years. So I cannot afford to waste it. I have no backup. So I found out about an organization called Asia Pacific Transgender Network (APTN), and I noted down the address of the office and first went there. (At the time,) I didn't know who they are or what they do, even. So I just landed up, and one transwoman was there. She came out when she saw me at the door, and I told her my story. She suddenly took my hand and began to cry and said, "From so far you came, and you don't know anyone . . . what can we do to help you?" And I also started crying, and I said, "I don't know what you can do, but please do something."' He laughed.

Listening to him then, transcribing the interview later, and reliving it as I edited the manuscript, I would feel a lump in my throat. Rommel had a tendency to laugh when he was narrating the most painful episodes in his life, and over time, I would begin to well up each time he laughed.

He had to make the journey from Bangkok to Pattaya. He had no clue how to go, and most people he asked for directions could not speak much English. The transwoman had told him what she could, but she was not familiar with Pattaya, and once he got there it was a struggle to find the clinic. He was in Thailand for five days. The clinic ran blood tests on him, gave him hormone injections, checked his levels a few days later, and adjusted the dosage.

When he returned to Bangkok, the APTN had arranged for him to meet a transman member, Cianán Russell, whom he had encountered on YouTube.

'I felt like someone was coming alive from a dream, when I met him.' He laughed. 'That day was a memorable day. We became such good friends. Now we're always connected. They put me in touch with many communities of transmen in Asia. Like Satya from India. And in these nine months since I started my transition, I've come to know so many people, (so far) from literally knowing no one.'

He also got in touch with an organization for sexuality minorities in Bangladesh—Bondhu—and found other transmen through them. The hormone therapy had cost him nearly 90,000 taka, a sum few transmen from Bangladesh could afford. So he approached the Tangerine clinic in Bangkok, and asked if they could train him to administer hormone injections to other transmen. He is in touch with a doctor at the clinic, and sends across blood reports of the transmen regularly.

He was also selected to attend a two-week course on sexual identification and gender identity, conducted by the Sri Lankan Human Rights Commission. The workshop was to be held in Colombo, in December 2015. He had made his trip to Bangkok in secret, pretending he was travelling elsewhere within Bangladesh on work. But two weeks would be too long to explain away. His brother refused permission for him to leave. He said Islamic rules did not allow a woman to travel abroad alone. When Rommel began to argue, his brother delivered an ultimatum—if Rommel wanted to continue to live at home, he would have to stop his transition and all association with the community; otherwise, he would have to leave the family.

Rommel made his decision—he applied for the job vacancy in the country from which he was speaking to me. Transition was illegal in that country, but the pay was good. He was also desperate to leave Bangladesh—the hospital in which he was working was attached to the medical college where he had studied. His colleagues had known him for nearly a decade. They began to notice the changes in his voice, appearance, and demeanour once he started his hormone therapy. He was worried about the reactions he might receive.

He told me his future was uncertain. He was keen to have his surgeries, but there is no provision for changing one's gender in Bangladesh. His medical degree would be invalid if he were to change his name and gender. His identity card, which he needs to work and rent a house, might not be recognizable once his face changes.

'I can already see a lot of changes,' he said. 'My veins are becoming more prominent. My jaw is harder. My voice is different. I have to shave twice a day now. I had trouble getting through security the last time I went to Bangkok, because my face looked different in the passport. I don't know how I will manage everything. But the thing is, I can't wait any more, so I started.' He laughed.

Homosexuality is prohibited in Bangladesh, and since LGBTQI is seen as a single category, people assume transitioning is illegal.

'You heard about the murder of a gay activist there, Xulhaz Mannan?' he asked.

I had. In April 2016, Mannan and his friend Mahbub Rabbi Tonoy had been killed in the former's apartment by a gang carrying machetes. Mannan had been trying to organize a pride parade for the community. The day after his death, Bangladeshi Prime Minister Sheikh Hasina spoke of his writing as 'containing adult content'. He had come out as gay publicly a few weeks before his murder.

'Some days ago also, they attacked a group of gay men. And the police wrote a case against the men who were attacked. If I expose myself as trans, I will also have a case filed against me. I'm afraid, because I don't know what the public's emotions could be. If it's positive, Alhamdulillah. If it's negative, they could kill me. Maybe something will happen then.' He laughed. 'Maybe they will kill me. And then there will be some regulation. The law will change. But I will not be there. So I can't take that risk.' Another laugh.

Looking at him on the screen of my laptop, the grin on his face, the chunky ring on a finger, his dimples, the beauty of the adolescent face transmen in the early stages of their HRT had, I felt this image, this moment would always be frozen in time. I would remember his laugh, his expression, and they would haunt me forever.

I began to think of other books, set in the slums of Bombay or the alleys of Delhi or the ghettos of New York, in which characters we met when they were alive had died. I did not want that to happen, not while the book was being written, not after. The book was more than a book now. My subjects were friends, part of the fabric of my life. I wanted a happy ending for each of them. In context, a happy ending could even be escaping murder.

There is something about the face of the adolescent boy that inspires tenderness. It has an almost angelic quality—the last days of a hairless visage and delicate features imbue it with radiance, from which emanates a sense of excitement about the face and torso into which the boy is growing—the hardening of the jaw, the seven o'clock shadow, the cheekbones and shoulders, the angles that determine how they will look for the next decades. Something about them sings with the joy of no longer being their mothers' boys; they are their fathers' sons.

And in those faces I saw the vulnerability I had sensed in my own brothers as they morphed into men through teenage. I would drive myself crazy worrying about how I would protect them from this ugly world when they went out to meet it. How would I stop other kids from bullying them in school? What if they were ragged in college? How would I make sure no woman or man broke their hearts? What if one or both of them turned out to be gay? How would I protect them from the prejudice, the pain? In speaking to the boys I was now interviewing, I felt the same instincts and worries rise within me.

Rommel had moved on to other things. Even as I stared at him, barely listening to anything he said after he had spoken of the prospect of being killed, he was smiling and telling me about how he felt after hormone treatment. I had to rely on my recorder for his words. I have no memory of anything he said, and I felt disconnected from my own self as I responded to his revelations with questions.

'There's no point living as a girl. One day, my brother told me I would not be able to change my medical degree certificate, so what would I do as a man? I said I don't care, I would rather be a rickshaw puller, a daily wage worker, a jobless, homeless person than a lady doctor.

'Before HRT, I would never sing a song. Because the voice that came out, I couldn't tolerate. I just couldn't tolerate that voice. I would barely even speak. I laugh when I say this now, but then, every time I looked at the mirror, it would be so pathetic, you can't imagine—I would look at that face and think, "This is not me, this is not me." Whose voice was this, whose face was this? But now, every day, I notice some change. It's like, wow, this is changing, that is changing. My veins are more visible. I feel them throbbing sometimes. My spiritual belief, my confidence, all of that has gone up by 90 per cent since I started this transition. I know whatever comes my way, I will manage. It was not like that before. I'm finally going where I wanted to be. It's a very big relief.'

He had no family support. He rarely called home. They called up occasionally, and it was usually to ask his medical advice when someone in the family fell ill. He had stopped speaking about his transition to his mother. It upset her too much. One of his sisters was supportive, and she had told him not to bother trying to convince anyone else. It simply wouldn't work. His brother had only called him once, when his nephew was ill.

He didn't mind their not calling. But there were things his family said or did that hurt intensely.

'This Eid, I sent some money home for everyone. Not a big amount, but whatever it's possible for me to give. My brother refused to take it. He said my income is haram. The thing is, according to our belief, if one of your parents dies, there are a few things you can do for their soul. Like you can give money to poor people, or to the mosque. I asked my mother to give some on my behalf. My brother said if I give that money, it's wasted anyway, because my father will not be able to get any benefits of good deeds done using *my* money.' He began to laugh.

'It's hard to hear such things,' I said.

'Yeah, it is. I cried also. Nowadays, I don't feel like crying so much. Before I used to cry all the time. I think I feel more positive these days because I feel I know the solution to my problems, and I'm on my way.'

I wished *I* knew the solution. He was living in a country where it was illegal to be what he is.

It wasn't easy for doctors to practise in countries other than the one in which they had qualified as medical professionals. He had considered migrating to Europe or the UK, but the exams were intensely tough and the fees far higher than he could afford. The language requirements were more exacting for doctors than for other professionals.

'I don't know what I will do after six months,' he said. 'I can't go back home. And I don't have any other option also.'

'Are you safe where you are, for now?'

'For *now*, yes.' He laughed. 'People don't know about me here. I live in a remote place, very far from the capital and the big cities. I'm the only doctor here. The nurse and ward staff can't ask me personal questions. The only problem is, sometimes kids ask me, "Doctor, are you a boy or girl, are you a boy or girl?" I don't look like this when I go to hospital. I wear something across my chest, because I use a binder—I'm not able to stop wearing it. And I wear a dupatta around my face. Actually, when people from the community (came to know) I was going to come here, they said, "Go anywhere else in the world. But don't go there." They could even jail me if they knew. But, you know, I need the money and with my MBBS, I can't work everywhere. So I had to take this.'

He suddenly grinned at me, 'You know, I love talking to you. I feel I'm talking to a friend, not a journalist. Before this call, I was nervous, I was wondering how it would be to talk about this issue. But it was nice.'

I wanted to reach into the monitor and give him a hug.

That night, I cried into my pillow. How alone one must feel, I thought, how utterly alone to think of someone who does no more than listen with sympathy, without judging, as a friend after a single call on Skype.

I didn't know why Rommel had affected me so much. Perhaps it was the idea of someone doing everything alone, without the support of parents, enduring the nastiness of a self-righteous sibling. How desperate he must have been to access the hormone therapy, if he had decided to head to Thailand all by himself, armed only with addresses he had noted from the internet. How desperate he must be for surgery, if he had decided to move to a country that was even more hostile than home, hoping his disguise was good enough to live another day.

What must it be like to wake up every day in the 'wrong' body, to hate the sound of one's own voice? I loved the aesthetic of the male body. But could I have endured it on myself, the unwanted hair, the broad shoulders, the thick legs, the tapering hips, an ugly penis sprouting out of me? I had been considered a 'tomboy' as a child, as most girls with a love for the outdoors are. It didn't help that my mother would usually lop off my hair as soon as it grew below my ears, because it was just easier not to have to comb thick, curly hair.

I have never liked looking at my childhood photographs, because I have never liked the pixie haircut on me. For years after I had first been given a choice, I had refused to cut my hair.

When I was making my documentary on transwomen back in 2006, I had had a conversation with a young kothi, who had just been adopted by Priya and was yet to be allowed to grow his hair. I was asked to call him by his male name and use male pronouns. He carried the transwomen's luggage, and had tried to persuade me to let him carry mine. We sat outside the Koovagam temple, on mats. In the quiet hum of people settling down to sleep, of prospective clients negotiating with thirunangai sex workers, he asked me if he could touch my hair, which at the time reached my hips. I laughed, but refused.

'Is it because I'm not yet a "ladies"?' he asked. 'But think of me as "ladies".'

'No, I think I prefer men touching my hair to women touching my hair, that's why,' I said. He began to giggle. 'I'm averse to most physical contact,' I added.

'No, akka, it's just that your hair is so beautiful. How long did it take to grow this long?'

'I don't know. Some five–six years without haircuts?'

'You never cut it?'

'Not in that time. But I'm going to cut it now. It's getting hard to manage.'

He looked cheated. 'Don't cut it, akka. It's too beautiful. Or cut it and give it to me. I'll wear it as a wig.' A transwoman sashayed towards us and blew a kiss at a drunk man who was trying to decide whom to approach for sex. She winked at us and walked away with the man.

With an admiring glance at her, the kothi said, 'I want to look like that. When I was in school, I tried being a guy. I tried walking like one. It didn't work. I hate my body. I just hate it.'

I didn't know what had happened to him. How did he look now? And what would happen to Rommel in six months? I realized I was still in tears when one of my dogs decided he had had enough and licked my face till I began to laugh.

Of course I dream of having a son. Doesn't every mother want a boy? But what about THE CURSE?
Let this not be a boy, Allah. Who will look after my four if I were to die?
WHY ME? WHY ME? WHY MUST I CHOOSE BETWEEN MY HEART'S DESIRE, AND MY CHILDREN? ALLAH, A SON, NO!
Allah, let it not be a girl. I will never live down the ignominy of producing a FOURTH girl ...
A boy, a boy, a boy...a son to look after me in my old age. A son to keep our name alive. A son to...but what if I never get to see him?
NOT A BOY...I cannot fall victim to the curse...no, not a boy!
NOT A GIRL...not a fourth, no!

The Mercy of Allah

1975, Ahmedabad

Let it be a boy, please Allah, not a girl.
Let it be a girl, please Allah, not a boy.
If it's a boy, let me live.
If it's a girl, let me have a boy next.
Let it be a boy, please Allah, not a girl.
Let it be a girl, please Allah, not a boy.

Rehana[1] was pregnant for the fourth time. She had had three girls, each of which she had hoped was a son. Now, she dreaded a son. She also dreaded a daughter.

There was a jinx in her husband Mohammad Hussain's family, she had been told. If a woman had three daughters and then a son, she would die soon after the baby was born. It had happened to Hussain's mother, two of his aunts, and his sister. Hussain was a fourth child, and had lost his mother within a year of his birth.

A fourth daughter would be a further liability. But a son could kill her. What did she want? Hussain's family was conservative. And yet, the old women had told her to pray to Allah for a daughter. Seeing his wife so intensely troubled, Hussain sent her off to her mother's house in Ahmedabad, so that she could spend her pregnancy in peace. With his wife away, he prayed secretly, every namaz, for a son. Rehana

---

[1] All names in this chapter have been changed to protect privacy.

would sit for long hours outside the house, praying for a son, praying for a daughter, praying for neither.

~

Years later, she would tell her daughter Faiza about this dilemma. When Faiza became Bilal, he would tell me the story. 'My mother tries to deny it and say it was all rubbish. But when I was a child, the story was told to me multiple times. There's a theory, and it's scientifically proven too, that the state of the mother affects the baby when she's pregnant. What the mother thinks, eats, drinks, does, everything impacts the mindset of the child. I'm not saying why I am trans is because of this, but there are factors that influence (the baby) and this is one of the factors.'

~

Rehana gave birth to a daughter. But they so badly wanted a son that Faiza was raised as a boy for three years. Faiza liked short hair, and was never made to grow it. She could wear shorts and a shirt. She was not asked to wear a scarf like her sisters. She was allowed to play outdoors. Three years later, a son was born to Rehana and Hussain. They finally had the male heir for whom they had longed, a boy who wouldn't trigger a jinx.

Faiza was a 'tomboy'—she was an excellent sportsperson and topped her class in exams. They were proud of her. And they trusted her to protect her younger brother, the *heer*, the diamond, of the family.

'You are his guardian,' they told her.

Faiza took on the role. She taught her little brother to ride a cycle, to play cricket, to walk to school, to write—she was his assistant, tutor, babysitter and mentor, all rolled into one. The kinship between them was fraternal—he looked up to Faiza as a big brother, and she taught him what a boy would teach his little brother.

No one noticed that Faiza was running around in shorts and T-shirt and jeans until she hit puberty. Suddenly, her body became gendered. Her clothes were 'boys' clothes'. She had to wear 'girls' clothes'.

~

16 June 2017

Bilal had got in touch with me by email.

I am bilal from mumbai, presently in _____, i hv completed my transition and changed my documents. I am constantly on d search for more information with respect to islam's standpoint on trans and latest updates. I believe islam is a holistic religion and it is not possible that islam does not have a solution for trans. My goal is to first get valid information on islams standpoint and den support other muslim transpeople wid this information so that they are not viewed as evil and haraam by the family and the community

He was very particular about a few things—I would have to ensure confidentiality, and I would have to record our conversations because the words he used were 'very, very important', and everything he said was 'significant, very, very critical'. He wanted to know: How would I make sure his identity was kept secret? What if someone called and asked me whose story it was? Using a pseudonym was important to him for two reasons, he said—he was working in an Islamic country, under a completely new, male identity, and he could not afford for people to guess his past; and his parents were not comfortable with his speaking about his identity in public. He wanted to keep his name secret until the time was right.

'To be honest, I'm writing my own book, okay?' he said. 'The story of my life. And that's one of my goals, like before I die, I want to finish this book, and I want to get it published after my death—a posthumous publication. The purpose for me of writing this book is to leave a message for other Muslim transmen . . . for them to know what I'm going through. And the thing is, I can't write that book now, I can't publish it now because it will create problems for my family. So my reason for getting in touch with you is to anonymously represent myself. Because somewhere, the voice will spread, right, people will start talking about what is transsexualism, how do people struggle, do these kind of people really exist, does this happen in Islam as well, you know?'

Even on the phone, he exuded authority. When I told him he could choose to withdraw his story at any point if he felt uncomfortable, he said, 'Okay. But that won't happen, because I'm very sure about what I want to do. So that will not happen.' When I asked him about his reason for going to a country where the discovery of his identity could have dangerous ramifications, he said, impatiently, 'Okay. You're starting right at the end of my journey. I want to start at the beginning, because my objective in coming to you for representing myself in this book is not to talk about my challenges in this country. That's the least significant thing that I want to highlight. I will just make a mention of it. What I want to highlight is—there is such a thing as being trans Muslim. Like every trans goes through a journey of acceptance and coming out to the family and challenges. But as a trans Muslim, we go through a very, very big challenge, especially if you come from a family that is very religiously inclined. And that is the challenge of proving (that you are not) haram.'

He wanted to make sure my book was only about transmen, and not homosexuality. He was convinced homosexuality was haram.

'Because, in the Q'uran, it is clearly stated that homosexuality is haram. Before the Prophet Muhammad, there were 1,24,000 prophets, and every prophet came with a message from Allah. So somebody came with the message of honesty, somebody came with the message of being loyal and so on. Now, there was a prophet who came at a time when the community that he was addressing his message to turned out to be homosexuals, okay? So the men were with the men and the women were with the women, and at the time the prophet was to pass a judgment, Allah sent out his *azab*—his punishment—to the entire community. So it is very clearly stated in the Q'uran that homosexuality is haram. Now what the Islamic community has done is, they've just taken this one extract from the Q'uran, which says that this is haram, and they have broadly classified anything to do with gender as haram.

'So I want to represent two main things—one is what the religion says about transsexualism; and the other thing is about social fear.'

It was 'blinkered', it was 'like being blindfolded', he said, to call anything that was stated as haram in the Q'uran 'haram', without interpretation. People tended not to distinguish between transsexualism, homosexuality and gender identity. That particular statement would niggle at me through several of our conversations—if he believed 'haram' was open to interpretation, why did he subscribe to the notion that homosexuality was forbidden? But I would not confront him about it until several months later.

The first time we spoke, Bilal told me the other issue trans Muslims faced was 'a big, big social fear', higher than that of any other community. Muslims in India were community-bound, community-conscious, he felt. Anything someone did would affect everyone in his or her family.

'Suppose I come out in the public as something which is not acceptable in society, then nobody will marry my siblings, we will be outcast, and this will impact the future generations in my family. So it's as if everybody's destiny is dependent upon my actions, which is completely unfair. So at one point, they say that they believe in Allah and Allah is taking care of them and Allah is their provider and Allah is blah blah blah. But at the other end, more than Allah, they have a fear of society. So this is the debate that I always have with my parents: I tell them, "You're so religious and you have so much faith in Allah, but then you tell me if I go public with this, what would be the future of my brother's children and my sisters' children. If Allah is their protector, are you not contradicting yourself? And then you say that because of my actions, that kid won't be able to get married. If somebody has to marry your kid, Allah will create that for you, in spite of everything, that person who will marry your kid." You know? This kind of hypocrite mentality that people are carrying today, in my family and other families . . .'

He trailed off. Transition could not be stopped, he said. Not living one's identity was like not living. If he were to lose his eyesight, he could learn Braille and live. He could take up a job that allowed visually impaired people to work. If he lost a limb, he could wear a prosthetic. But if his entire body did not belong to him, how could he compensate?

'People like me have to find alternate ways of living our identity,' he said. 'Because we cannot even represent ourselves, leave alone find acceptance. The moment you sit across the table with your family and open such a dialogue, they will say it's haram and they will start crying and there's a whole emotional drama around it and they will force you to stop. When you don't get support from your family, you try to hide it from them. We seek support from other people. Because the identity needs to come out, right? You can't live it behind closed doors. Identity is the representation of how people perceive you and how you perceive yourself, both ways, right? So as long as you perceive yourself as somebody like this and you don't have other people who perceive you like this, it doesn't serve the purpose. So this is what I'm going to talk about. I'm going to tell you my story: about how it's moved from feeling that guilt to accepting my own self. Before other people accepting me, I have to accept myself.'

~

Even as a child, Faiza hated wearing her convent school uniform. When she was nine years old, she began to carry a shirt and trousers to school. When the children played sports after school, she would change out of her uniform in the toilet, play for an hour, change back into the despised uniform and then go home. Many of her friends pitied her. They thought her only problem was that her parents expected her to play in a skirt. They did not realize wearing the skirt was a problem. They did not know Faiza was Bilal.

When Bilal was in Class 7, he had a crush on a girl from school.

'It was like I'm Shah Rukh Khan and she's Madhuri Dixit, you know, at that time,' he told me. 'She was an extremely good dancer. So every cultural programme in school, she used to dance. And everybody used to tell me to come in at the end, like the hero. So the final hugging scene used to happen between me and her, and I used to think that I'm her boyfriend.' He laughed.

In Class 10, they began to pass around 'autograph books', in which one had to write one's favourite memory, one's best friend, one's crush, and so on. She wrote 'F_ _ _ A'. Bilal was thrilled, until he realized there was a boy in her building whose nickname fit. She liked him, not Faiza. It was the first heartbreak of Bilal's life. He began to cry, in class. Several girls in his class had a crush on him, and they surrounded him to console him and try their luck.

Bilal eventually applied for a degree in medicine. He lived close to a large park, and would tip the watchman five rupees to allow him to use the restroom on the way to and from college. He would change from the salwar-kameez he had to wear while leaving home, into jeans and a T-shirt. In college, he was part of a gang of boys who would have fights with other gangs from other colleges, complete with sticks and threats. He had already begun to live two lives, even before he had learnt about gender identity.

And then he fell in love again.

'It was always love at first sight for me, I don't know why,' he said. 'We were done with some two–three weeks of orientation, and then this extremely beautiful girl enters class—a late admission. And I just look at her and I'm like oh my god, she's so beautiful, this is the girl I want to be with and, you know, I make a decision right then and there that I want to marry her.'

He began to include her in group discussions. She was painfully shy, and could not understand why a female cohort was so keen, almost determined, to be friends.

'I started doing that college *pataoing* thing with her, and finally I managed to *patao* her (win her over). Because one day we were playing a truth-or-dare kind of game in college, and someone said "go kiss a girl" and I went and kissed her. She also developed feelings for me, and we started talking to each other. I used to have a two-wheeler back then. Now, I lived five–six kilometres away from college. And she lived ten–eleven kilometres away from college, in a different direction. And still, I used to go every day to pick her up and drop her back and every day I would buy her roses. My life revolved around her.'

She began to visit his home, as a friend, and Bilal would hang out at hers. When they were in their third year of college, her parents decided to get her married.

'Even at that stage, we were so innocent that we didn't understand what will happen after she gets married,' he said. 'So I asked her what she wanted to do.'

She had a younger sister who could not be married off until she was. Her parents would not be able to understand that she was in a relationship with Bilal—Faiza to them.

'She said, "I have to do what my father says," and I said, "Okay, do what your father says." So, yeah, I'm at her wedding and standing there as if I'm her best friend and trying to help and in my heart I'm crying, crying, crying, crying . . . and everyone can see me going to the back of the stage and crying, and then her *bidaai* is happening, and everyone is crying. I couldn't go home that night. I went to another friend's place and I cried, cried, cried the whole night.'

They were in touch for some time after the wedding, but they could no longer be in a relationship. She was another man's wife. They had never been friends. So they could not have a platonic relationship, and drifted apart.

'Now, all this time, no one in my family knew I used to dress like a guy when I went to college. I come back home, and I am what they want me to be. Why? Because I did not have the balls to come and tell my parents that this is what has happened to me,' he said. 'Even I wasn't sure of what was happening to me. I just know, like, I like women, I'm a boy, and I'm supposed to be a woman.'

He did not know one could transition medically. He had seen hijras, but assumed they were hermaphrodites. All the time he was with his girlfriend, he was tormented by the idea that this was haram.

'All the time, in my mind, the only thought that struck me was this is haram, I will go to hell, this is haram, I will go to hell; and I can't be going to hell, I can't be going to hell, I can't be going to hell. So every day, I would pray to Allah, every namaz, that "Oh my god, Allah, please don't put me in hell because I don't know why this has happened to me, I know this is haram, you've said in the Q'uran that this is haram, so I'm going to go to hell."'

This was the main reason he couldn't confess to his family, he said: because he was ashamed of the feelings he could not curtail. He used to pray for a miracle. He would read books in which the miracles Allah had worked through his prophets were recounted.

'I would read about people with diseases and blindness and disorders who were cured, and I would think, why can't I have a penis and (a) flat chest when I wake up? I would ask, "Allah, why can't you perform this miracle for me, why can't you transform me into a complete man when I wake up?" Because I didn't know about surgeries and all at that point.'

He learnt about transsexualism for the first time in medical college. There was a chapter on gender identity disorder, and he began to read about it in more detail. Biology had seemed to suggest he was a woman who liked women, and so he was a lesbian. But lesbians did not hate their bodies and want to change them for male ones.

'Also, at no point in my sexual life, even till date, have I ever got gratified by any woman in terms of she pleasing me as a woman. Okay? So this thing was very clear in my mind, that I don't want to be pleased as a woman, because I'm not a woman.'

Nothing he read at the time spoke about gender transition. Even in his textbooks, transpeople were conflated with intersex people and hermaphrodites. He was living with the guilt of being inclined to sin, when his parents began to speak of marriage. He had finished his degree, he was a doctor. It was time to find a groom, preferably abroad. His older sisters were all married and had children; his brother would have to be married off too. He was already in his mid-twenties and could no longer put it off.

'And why did I get married? That was also foolish of me, because I didn't have the guts to face my family at that point, and I had not found out about transsexualism and what the Q'uran had to say about it,' he said.

They settled on a groom who was planning to migrate to Canada. He would not be able to take his bride with him; he would come back in a year or eighteen months, once his work permit and her visa were sorted. Bilal's parents were hesitant, but he thought this was a great opportunity. His brother would be married off by the time the husband returned, and he could find a way out of his marriage to a man without ever having cohabited with him.

'So I said okay, I'll get married to him on the condition that the marriage will not be consummated until he has taken me to Canada,' he said.

He would get married for the paperwork, and they would live together as man and wife once the visas came through. In the meanwhile, Bilal would not have to meet or speak to his husband. The husband left for Canada within two days of the wedding.

As it happened, there was a 'glitch' in the husband's paperwork, and his work permit didn't come through. He had to return to India within two months of marriage, and wanted his wife to live with him. Bilal finally relented.

'I stayed with him for five and a half months. That was the most traumatic time of my life. When I went, my weight was seventy-two kilos. When I came back to my parents' house, I weighed fifty-nine kilos. I was in trauma because I didn't know what was happening. But I was not able to have one episode of intercourse with him. Whenever the intercourse was attempted, it would not happen. Because I used to get into a spasm. As a woman, you probably understand it?'

Bilal's husband took him to a doctor, who could not diagnose the vaginismus—the clamming up of the vaginal muscles during attempted penetration—and told them they would be able to have normal sex over time.

I found myself thinking about the humiliation of it all—for a man to go to a gynaecologist and have a part of his body that he did not want in the first place examined for shortcomings; for a man to lie naked below a 'husband' who wanted to penetrate an organ that did not belong in his body.

It turned out to be fortunate for Bilal that the husband was a cheat. He had lied about his education. He did not have a job, and was trying to swindle money from Bilal. He had said he would apply for a visa and work permit again, but there was no sign of his making the attempt. Finally, Bilal's parents decided they and their daughter had endured enough.

'Seeing their child go through so much shit, you know—I'd lost (a) significant (amount of) weight, I developed autoimmune thyroiditis, and I was under severe stress—my parents had a soft corner for me.'

Once he moved back in with his parents and now-married brother, the restrictions they had once imposed on Faiza were loosened for Bilal. He could wear what he wanted. He could go out and work, he could stay out late. Now that their son was married, they did not have to worry about society. Hussain had recently undergone a bypass surgery after a cardiac arrest, and had become calmer and more reasonable than he used to be. He did not object to Bilal wearing trousers in his presence. That was the last time Bilal wore women's clothes, he told me.

His parents were so focused on his brother and their only daughter-in-law that it was six months before his mother asked where all his clothes were. Why was Faiza dressed in trousers all the time? What had happened to her trousseau?

'I said, "No, I just don't like wearing those." I never told her the real reason. I just kept avoiding that conversation. But I started living my life—I started enjoying my life and the identity that I wanted.'

He had realized quite early, even before he learnt of gender dysphoria, that his sexual orientation would eventually cause a rift with his family. He knew he could not make enough money to sustain himself independently as a doctor. And so he switched careers and got into management. He was earning well, making friends, dating women. He was not financially dependent on his parents.

One of his friends, who had moved to the UK after marriage, told him she had seen people like him in London—he should move under the Highly Skilled Migrants Programme, and try to find a job. He would find acceptance in that society. It was in London, at the age of thirty, that he met other transpeople for the first time.

'Realizing that, "Oh my god, I'm not the only one on earth who's like this, there are so many people who are just like me, going through the same shit" was the most delightful moment in my life.' He laughed.

People from the community gave him literature on the subject, and he realized surgery could give him the body he had always desired. But would religion allow it? He had always felt Islam was the most practical religion in the world, and that the Q'uran provided a solution to everything. He began reading religious opinions on gender transition. Sunni clerics felt there was no scope for transition—it was haram, as was homosexuality. But he came across an article that said members of the Shi'a community—to which he belonged—were permitted to undergo gender transition surgery, according to Q'uranic research by a group of clerics from Iran.

'It was the moment of greatest relief in my life. The guilt of doing haram ended. I could accept myself now. I could live my identity without guilt.'

That was the starting point of Bilal's own research. He began to write to Shi'a scholars of Islam, inquiring in detail into the difference between homosexuality and transsexualism.

'I'm a very god-fearing and religious person. So had I not known about this aspect of my religion, probably I would have just lived my life as what I was. But if my religion accepts me, then there is nothing on this earth that should stop me. So I made a decision for myself at that stage that now, I'm going to start my journey. I'm going to transition myself to my identity and I'm going to start living my real life.'

He began to dream of growing a beard, of having a man's body, of marrying a woman—'building castles in the air', he said—and he had only one goal now: to make enough money.

He reconciled himself to inhabiting the woman's body for a while longer, until he had the means to support himself once his parents disowned him, as they were bound to do. He had made the decision to transition later than most others he met—some were as young as seventeen—and he did not mind waiting a little longer.

'The majority of transmen make that mistake, I would say. And then they end up in a situation where they have no money for their own surgeries and their families are not supportive and so on. I'm a god-gifted planner, and I always plan things strategically in my life. Once I make a decision, I won't go back.'

He could not find a job that paid well enough in the UK, and returned to India. He worked at a media conglomerate as part of the human resources team. Some of his colleagues were aware of his identity, and kept it confidential. They would often 'protect him', he said, from gender stereotyping. During 'Sari Day' in office, they would publicly urge him to dress up as a man for laughs. He worked in an all-male team, so everyone in the office would assume he was being ironic when he showed up in male ethnic wear.

When he was in his early thirties, he tried having a conversation about his gender with his mother and sister. They dismissed him, saying someone must have put bizarre ideas in his head, that he should stop thinking perversely, and that he should not even talk about such nonsense.

He was doing well at work, but realized he needed another qualification to make his next jump. He joined a part-time MBA programme.

'I met this girl, a psychologist who was also in the programme,' he said. 'We first became very good friends. I told her my story. She's the one who really helped me in life, who gave me strength, and told me I had to shape my life in a particular direction. That I needed to stand up for myself and make those hard decisions. I had to confront my parents; but every time I tried, the answer would be, "No, no, don't say that, haram, no, haram, no, haram."'

He wrote a letter to a cleric in Iran, asking for a fatwa permitting gender reconstruction surgery.

From: <withheld>@hotmail.com
To: fatwa@<withheld>.ir
Sent: Sunday, 1 June 2008 3.35 p.m.
Subject: Istifta

Salaams

I am a shia muslim suffering from sexual identity disorder, being a female i have always felt and lived and wanted to be like male since childhood, i am just not comfortable with my female body and do not get attracted to men at all, Pls let me knw that SRS surgery is one solution to this prob but is it permissible in Shia faith, your answer will clear my confusion and wil be great help for me. Thank you. May Allah bless you.

From: fatwa@<withheld>.ir
To: <withheld>@hotmail.com
Subject: Re: Istifta
Date: Mon, 9 Jun 2008 18:18:22 +0430

Salamun 'alaykum wa Rahmatullahi wa Barakatuhu.
The answer is as follows:
Bismihi Ta'ala
There is no harm in undergoing the said operation if the end result would be determining of the true sex of the person provided that it does not lead to the commission of any ḥarām act or a vile consequence.

With prayers for your success,
wassalam.

He also found a blog in which an Iranian transman was documenting the process of counselling and applying for a permit to undergo sex change. In June 2011, the licence was granted.

He learnt that a Maulana from Iran, who was of Indian origin, would be in the country to conduct Amaal (prayers) on Shab-e-Qadr (The Night of the Decree), which is observed in the last week of Ramzan. It was believed to be the night on which the Q'uran was revealed to Prophet Muhammad. It could fall on the nineteenth, twenty-first, or twenty-third night of Ramzan. In 2011, it was on the nineteenth night. It is believed that prayers offered on Shab-e-Qadr are more powerful than the accumulated prayers of a thousand nights.

So it was for Bilal. On 22 August 2011, he wrote to the Maulana. He had come across a fatwa issued by Ayatollah Khomeini in 1975, which seemed to sanction sex reassignment surgery. He had also come across the research of a cleric from Qom, Hojatoleslam Kariminia, who had written a book about transsexual rights to surgery in Islamic law.

The Maulana replied within a day.

Dear Faiza

Alaykum as salam

Thanks for your e mail. I appreciate your love towards religion and the sharia of Ahlebait (as). Mashallah.

I would love to help you in this problem of yours, if I could. Inshallah.

You know the case is sensitive and should be handled with extra care. Dr Kariminiya and few others in Iran are approachable and I know him and we can consult to them if needed. Basically he is known as a hard worker for such kind of people.

I hope you will not mind if I ask you few questions for studying the case thoroughly and possibly find a solution for it. Inshallah

Find my queries in red.

Fi amanillah

The Maulana followed this up with two more emails.

Suggestions:

Plz send a question to Ayatullah Sistani also, so it can be useful to show the other people in the society who will then cause any type of problem for you.

In Iran, there are (a) few tests which proves that a person is trans sexual. I know the best judge could be yourself in the matter but for society where u would like to live and work for it, should also get convinced that you r really suffering from this and is all proved by neutral medical tests.

Once I m back to Iran, will try to link u with other fellow friends suffering from the same nature.

Most important suggestion: Plz be calm and patient until the things happens as u wish. After all u r part of the society and we need all of u to b an active member of the society. Until that time changing the name and not wearing Hijab and.....will not move the things forward in a rational way.

Fi amanillah

23/08/2011

Alaykum as salam

I would like to suggest you to send two questions to the office of Ayatullah Sistani:

1. *What is the ruling regarding sex changing without any reason and undergoing sex reassignment surgery?*
2. *I am a Shia Muslim female suffering from sexual identity disorder. Is it permissible for me to undergo through sex reassignment surgery?*

By the way, if I m taking any interest in your case is due to the impression which I have that no one would b helping you in the matter bcoz of being a unique and a typical case. So I thought I should help you. May Allah swt help us to get a solution which He likes.

Fi amanillah

Bilal then wrote to the office of Ayatollah Sistani and received this reply:

The purpose of gender reassignment is a form of resurrection, in which the genitalia are surgically removed from the transsexual, and replaced by artificial uro-genital systems. It is injection of hormone to give the impression of a woman, such as shedding facial hair and appearance of breasts, or in the case of a woman who is transitioning gender to male, to give the impression of a man such as the flattening of the chest and appearance of facial hair. This does not affect one's true gender, and so the religious law governing gender cannot be modified. It is not permitted to touch or explore such a body for purposes of pleasure.

However, if the purpose of the surgery is not simply to change the external genitalia, but only align them with the internal mechanisms, then it is permitted. But this has not been achieved so far. Only the outer appearance has been changed, which is forbidden by Islam. Of course, people who have abnormalities in the reproductive system, such as a man who has a concealed penis in a body with a feminine appearance but no female reproductive system, or a woman who has a masculine appearance but internal female organs, are allowed to undergo surgery as it does not carry the mala fide intention of changing the true gender as accorded by God.

In such a case, the surgery is deemed necessary as living with this anomaly is a departure from the decreed gender, and intercourse is also permissible. Good luck.

بسمه تعالی‌اگر مقصود از تغییر جنسیت این باشد که با عمل
جراحی آلات تناسلی مرد را قطع کنند و به جای آن برای او
مجرای بول و آلت تناسلی مصنوعی بسازند و با تزریق
هورمون علامات زنانگی از قبیل ریختن موهای صورت و
برآمدگی سینه در او ایجاد کنند یا در مورد زنی که تغییر
جنسیت می دهد مقصود این باشد که برای او آلت تناسلی مردانه
مصنوعی قرار دهند و با تزریق هورمون علامات مردی از
قبیل کوچک شدن سینه و روییدن موی صورت ایجاد کنند این
امر موجب تغییر واقعی جنسیت نیست و احکام شرعی او تغییر
نمی کند و از جهتی چون مستلزم کشف عورت و لمس آن است
جایز نیست.واما اگر مقصود تغییر دستگاه تناسلی داخلی
وخارجی باشد که معیار اختلاف زن ومرد است پس این امر فی
حد ذاته با قطع نظر از لوازمی که ممکن است حرام باشد اشکال
ندارد ولی تا به حال این امر محقق نشده است و آن چه تا به حال
صورت پذیرفته همان تغییر ظاهری است که تاثیری در تغییر
احکام ندارد.البته ممکن است در مورد کسانی که دچار ناهنجاری
در دستگاه تناسلی شده اند با عمل جراحی آلت تناسلی مردانه را
که مخفی شده است در مردی که ظاهری زنانه دارد ولی دستگاه
تناسلی داخلی را ندارد نمایان سازند یا به عکس آلت تناسلی
ظاهری مردانه را از زنی که دستگاه تناسلی زنانه داخلی دارد
قطع کنند. واین کار فی حد ذاته اشکالی ندارد و ارتباطی با تغییر
جنسیت ندارد و البته اگر مستلزم نگاه یا لمس حرام باشد در
صورتی جایز است که ضرورت داشته باشد یا ترک آن مستلزم
حرج ومشقت شدید باشد. موفق باشید

For years, he would continue to search for answers from both religion
and science. Not much research had been done on female-to-male
transpeople, but Bilal found various studies online that suggested that
the brain function and responses of transwomen were closer to those
of ciswomen and unlike those of cismen.

He came across a paper called 'A Sex Difference in the Human Brain and Its Relation to Transsexuality', published in the journal *Nature* on 2 November 1995, which posited that 'in a region of the brain called the bed nucleus of the stria terminalis (BSTc), a region known for sex and anxiety responses, MTF transsexuals have a female-normal size while FTM transsexuals have a male-normal size.'

Another study, led by Dr Hare, found transwomen had longer androgen receptor gene sequences than cismen, which made it harder to bind testosterone and prevented 'complete masculinization of the brain'.

A study titled 'A Polymorphism of the CYP17 Gene Related to Sex Steroid Metabolism is Associated with Female-to-male but Not Male-to-female Transsexualism' by Bentz et al. was the only one he read that focused exclusively on transmen. The study had found a variant genotype for a gene that acts on sex hormones, as well as an allele distribution—the fraction of chromosomes containing the variant—equivalent to the male control subjects and unlike the female control subjects of the study.

Religion too seemed to be on his side. He looked up various religious forums in which questions about gender transition were posted.

But there *were* ambiguities. Everyone seemed to agree that in the case of people with anomalous genitalia, or those who qualified as 'hermaphrodites', surgery was not just permissible, but mandatory. In the case of gender transition for those with 'functional' female or male internal and external sexual organs, things were less clear.

From 22 April 2010

Religious authority: Makarem Shirazi

A fatwa permitting sex change surgery from Ayatollah Shirazi:

Sex change is not inherently against Islamic law and it is allowed. However, it should be done according to Islamic rules. For example, the forbidden parts should not be seen and touched unless and to the extent necessary.

Question: Some homosexuals have a completely feminine or masculine body, but they are emotionally inclined to the same sex. Many of them wish to make an ostensible sex change that is not real, and they threaten suicide otherwise. May a doctor conduct the surgery in order to prevent his or her suicide?

Answer: Sex change has two forms: it may be a mere formality that although makes the opposite sexual organ appear, the organ does not really work. This is not allowed. But if the sex change is real and the real sex organ appears, this is allowed by Islamic law.

In response to another question about changing gender and gender identity, Grand Ayatollah Yusuf Saanei had said it was not permissible for 'legal and Foreign Affairs-related reasons'—I was reminded of Vihaan's account of doctors theorizing that transition was a way of escaping imprisonment—and it could not be allowed in the case of someone with perfectly normal biological functions that were in accordance with one's assigned gender; it was only allowed in a person whose internal organs were also in sync with appearance.

Some clerics said the change could be cosmetic, but then the person would remain a man or woman internally and so was not permitted to have sex with a person who was of the same gender as the transsexual had been assigned at birth—this would qualify as homosexuality, which was haram.

After a series of exchanges with the cleric who was receptive to him, and discussions with his partner, Bilal decided to come out to his family. He had it all planned.

His entire family—three sisters and brother, along with their spouses and children—would be in Bombay for a family wedding. It would be the perfect time to speak to them. He prepared a PowerPoint presentation, with thirty-three slides.

He spoke about the dilemma his mother had undergone in pregnancy, and the fact that both his parents had turned to Allah and begged Him to do what was best; he wrote about how he had always liked to dress like a boy, wear his hair short, and play outdoor games with boys while the girls played indoor games; he wrote about the confusion and depression puberty and periods brought—how he could never reconcile himself to his body bleeding like a woman's. He said he had given in to the family's pressure to change the way he dressed, 'but did not compromise on my hair—my hair was my asset, my sign of manhood'. He wrote about how he focused on his studies and postponed marriage until he had to obey his parents, but could not consummate a physical relationship with a man.

He detailed the guilt and confusion in his mind—'My body is female but why do I think and feel like a male?', 'If this is how Allah has created me, then why has He not created a solution for me?'—and how he had visited two psychiatrists who diagnosed him with transsexualism. 'The guilt began,' he wrote, 'I am abnormal, I am cursed, will go to hell, lived with the burden of this guilt.'

His 'ray of hope' came from research. He read about transsexualism, and was particularly struck by an article he found online, which said 'a person experiences impaired functioning or distress as a result of that gender identification'.

Most importantly, he discovered that gender dysphoria was different from homosexuality. A cisgender homosexual did not despise his or her body; s/he was attracted to people of the same gender, but did not want to transition into the opposite gender.

He wrote about how gender dysphoria was characterized by depression and suicidal thoughts; how his fear of social acceptance had stopped him from coming out; how he persistently desired hormone therapy and surgery. He wrote an outline of what hormone therapy and surgery would involve, complete with before–after pictures. He made it clear that while surgery and hormones could realign the body to suit one's own sense of gender, and remove the distress of being misgendered, it could not make a transwoman produce eggs or a transman produce sperm.

He included the emails he had exchanged with the cleric, copies of the gender change permit issued in Iran and the fatwa he himself had received, questions and answers from the religious discussion forums, and the scientific research papers he had found.

He was hopeful that his family would be receptive. He sent the presentation to his brother-in-law and asked him to make sure everyone in the family went through it, so that they would be prepared for the meeting. He knew they would shut him down before he began to speak if he tried to explain in person everything he had put down in the slides. He was hoping their curiosity would keep them reading, and allow education by osmosis.

'But right after he read the presentation, he calls me and says, "We don't want to meet you, this is all rubbish. What you're doing is haram, we're never going to accept you as a guy; you're a girl and you'll always remain a girl. You're Faiza and you'll always remain Faiza. Just forget about all this shit."'

Bilal convinced him to allow him to speak to the family, just once. After a long conversation, his brother-in-law agreed to invite everyone to his sister's home. Bilal could make his case.

Or so he thought.

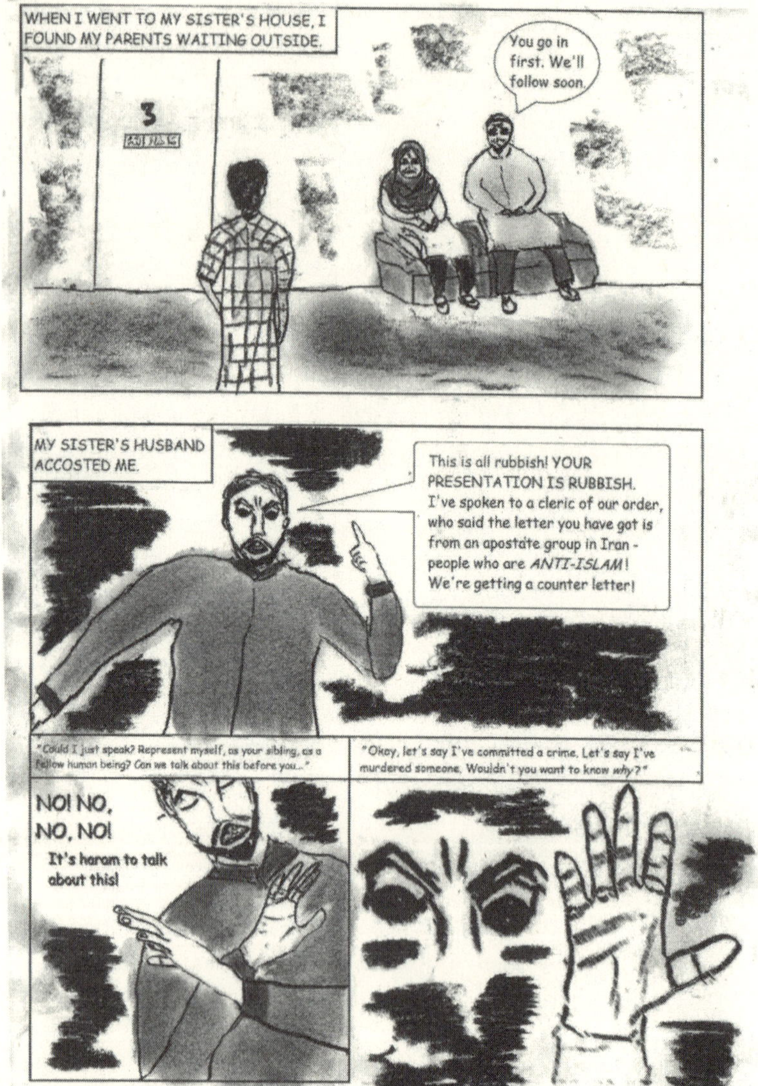

8 September 2011

Full name: <withheld>
Country: India—Mumbai
Gender: Male
Age: 33
Email: <withheld>@hotmail.com
To: <withheld>@alsistani.org
Subject: sex change

─────────────────

Question text:
PLEASE REPLY TO MY QUESTION IN PERSIAN
RESPECTED AUTHORITY SALAMUN ALAIKUM,

I WANT TO KNOW WHETHER SEX CHANGE
OPERATION IS ALLOWED IN ISLAM, (BY SEX CHANGE I
MEAN TO BECOME A MAN FROM A WOMEN BY DOING
SOME OPERATION) , ACTUALLY THERE IS A GIRL AGED
35YEARS IN OUR FAMILY WHO WANTS TO DO IT, SHE
SAYS THAT SHE FEELS LIKE A BOY SINCE CHILDHOOD
AND SHE CANNOT LIVE LIKE A WOMEN ANYMORE.

OUR WHOLE FAMILY IS AGAINST IT BUT SHE IS NOT
READY TO LISTEN TO US, SHE SAYS THAT IT IS ALLOWED
IN ISLAM AS IRAN ALLOWS THE SAME AND THAT IT IS
VERY COMMON IN IRAN.

PLEASE ADVICE AS TO WHETHER THIS SEX CHANGE
OPERATION THAT IS CONVERTING FROM WOMEN TO
MAN THRU SOME MEDICAL PROCEDURE IS ALLOWED
IN ISLAM OR NO.

THANKS IN ADVANCE, REGARDS

From: <withheld>@alsistani.org
To: <withheld>
Subject: RE: sex change
Date: Sun, 18 Sep 2011 12:52:32 +0430

بسمه تعالی
فی نفسه اشکال ندارد

There is no problem in it by itself.

May Allah grant you success.

http://alsistani.org/e/
Board of Istifta
Office of Grand Ayatollah Sistani

His family found an influential cleric from the same region as the cleric who was helping Bilal. His brother sent a series of questions to the board of Ayatollah Sistani in Najaf.

Subject: Maulana sahab
From: <withheld>
Date: Thu, 19 Jul 2012 19:11:03 +0530
To: <withheld>

Maulana sahab
Respected Ayatullah Uzma haaj Sayyed Ali Al Husaini As-Sestaani
Salaam Alaikum wa rahmatullah
I present congratulation to you on the occasion of the wiladat (birth anniversary) of Imam Husain (a.s.), his brother Hazrat Abbas (a.s.) and Imam Mahdi (a.s.) in the holy month of Shabaan and pray to Allah to Hasten the reappearance of Imam (a.s.).

Nowadays, a lot of discussion is being done about changing the sex of a person, these are some of the question pertaining to it
1. *What is the order of changing the sex of boy to girl or vice versa*
2. *What is the order for encouraging some one to undergo sex change?*
3. *If some one has changed his sex, then what is the order about namaaz, hijab, inheritance etc?*
4. *After changing sex, what is the order about marrying?*

5. *What is the responsibility of the parents and the society in this regard?*

In view of the above, you are requested to give a reply which becomes the cause of satisfaction for the followers of Ahle Bait (a.s.).

May Allah hasten the reappearance of Imam (a.s.) and include us among his servants.

Wa salaam Alaikum was rahmatullah was barakato

Yours sincerely
<Withheld>

They received a handwritten reply, or so they claimed, producing one with a seal and stamp for Bilal:

Rajab 30, 1433 ah
Reply

In His Name, the High

1. *A girl cannot become boy by operation or taking hormonal injections and vice versa. This act is HARAAM.*
2. *It is not allowed (not jaaez) to encourage someone to undergo sex change*
3. *There is no change in Fiqhi masael*
4. *Not allowed*
5. *Responsibility of Nahi anil Munkar (Discouraging from evil). And Allah knows the best.*

Seal
Office of Ayatullah Sestaani
Najaf

Shabaan 11, 1433 ah

On 4 July 2012, Bilal wrote to the cleric he knew, asking for advice. He received a reply within two days:

Salams
I had a good talk with the advisory board of the Ayatullah Sistani's Office and asked for the clarification of the fatwa of Najaf and they came up with this points:

The question asked in that letter is incomplete. It is regarding a person who just want to entertain him or her by changing the sex which is not permissible to some extent.

They were not sure about the nature of this process. They believe that change of sex is impossible. No one can change the sex in such a way that internal and external private part of the body could get the harmony. Apparently its just a change of the outer part of the body and the inner sex of the person would be the same as previous even after the surgery.

When I discussed that according to the new research it might be possible. They said: If such is the case, then there wouldn't be any problem unless of Mahram Na mahram issue of the surgery and etc which could be bypassed if the person proves that he/she is in real need of the surgery.

Their answer was this:

واما اگر مقصود تغییر دستگاه تناسلی داخلی وخارجی باشد که معیار اختلاف زن ومرد است پس این امر فی حد ذاته با قطع نظر از لوازمی که ممکن است حرام باشد اشکال ندارد ولی تا به حال این امر محقق نشده است و آن چه تا به حال صورت پذیرفته همان تغییر ظاهری است که تاثیری در تغییر احکام ندارد.

Now plz clarify your status that what actually this surgery would be? Will it make a real change in your inner sex apart from the change in the outer part? They fail to understand this but they say if its possible, they do not have any objection.

Fi amanillah

<withheld>

The question of 'mahram na mahram', Bilal would explain to me later, had to do with the gender of the doctor who would perform the surgery. Islam mandates that any medical procedure that requires a woman to expose her private parts must only be carried out by a woman, unless it could be proven that no female doctor had the expertise to perform the procedure, or that the condition was life-threatening and had to be sorted out under any circumstances.

The fact that there was a provision for this requirement to be 'bypassed' gave him hope.

Bilal replied to them:

Modern medicine does not understand sex as only inner or outer but as a combination of genital, secondary sexual characteristics, genetic, hormonal, as well as brain sex (identity of gender that the person has of himself or herself).

Advanced medical technology can help a transsexual person to harmonize his body (genitals, hormones, secondary sexual characteristics) to his brain sex.

If required by the board, I am willing to submit a certificate from a registered medical professional that the above information is true.

The various replies I have received have left me with a confusion towards the ruling of Shariah for case of transsexualism.

I therefore request you to approach these questions keeping in mind that the rulings are for a female to male transsexual person and not just for someone who would like to change the gender for no reason.

Your guidance will go a long way in not only resolving my situation but also helping my family understand it and accepting me. Lastly, it would also continue to offer guidance to any other Shia transsexuals who would like approach this question anytime in the future.

The cleric he knew even visited his parents and brother when he was in India next.

'They started influencing him against me. They said I don't do namaz, I'm not religious, I don't wear hijab, how can he help someone who is not religious, and so on,' Bilal told me. 'They thought portraying me as anti-religious would help their cause. But he was very sensitive. He tried to reason with them.'

And so his family turned again to the other cleric who was from his home town, in order to influence his opinion. 'They started giving *dhamki* (threats) to him, pressuring him,' Bilal said. 'They wrote a letter in Gujarati and asked him to translate it into English and send it to me as if he was writing it. It said something like he was taking back all his words and I must listen to my parents, and if I don't, I will go to hell.'

From: <withheld>
Date: Sunday, 2 September 2012 8.42 a.m.
Subject: Your Gujarati letter is translated
To: <withheld>
Cc: <withheld>

Bismillah hirrahma nirrahim

Dear _____

Salamun alaykum

Trust this email finds you in the best of your health.
I have translated the letter in to English. Plz verify it.
I strongly suggest to think and rethink on this letter. Plz consult Brother _____ before it. Sis Faiza will clearly understand that this letter is written by you and not me and that will create hatredness of you, her brother and the whole family in her heart.

I have nothing to do with Sis Faiza. She doesn't know me and neither me knows her. I just have sympathy (The genuineness of the case has to decided by the doctors and not me) for such victims and I understand that it is my religious and humanitarian duty to help such persons.

The way the family is dealing with the issue is not appropriate. (By the way, I do understand the feelings of a father and a brother on such cases but the matter is not to solve it with emotions rather to solve it with sharia rulings and intellectual basis).

I would also like to emphasize that we should not misinterpret sharia rulings for the cause of our social and family issues. I am ready to talk to respected Maulana _____ too on the issue. If Ayatullah Sistani (May Allah swt give him a long life) doesn't have a clear stance, then we have many other Mujtahids who permits it as well as we have others who deny it. So this is not as haram as adultery or backbiting where all of them say that it is haram.

Anyways, I would send this letter just for the sake of her parents and NO one else. I understand that they are aged and if they take some steps which are not appropriate after the surgery, I will feel guilty about that. In the same way, if Sis Faiza takes inappropriate steps after the settlement you all will have to be guilty for that.

My best regards to all and best wishes and duas to all for solving the problem which pleases Allah swt.

NOTE: IF you feel appropriate, plz forward this email to Br _____

Fi amanillah

_____

They asked him to make some changes to the letter, which they felt had not been worded strongly enough in translation.

From: <withheld>
Date: 6 Sep 2012 9.30 p.m.
Subject: Re: Your Gujarati letter is translated
To: <withheld>
Cc: <withheld>

Dear _____

Salamun alaykum

This is an edited version. Plz check and let me know how should we go forward to end up the discussion. Your efforts to end up is really appreciated.

Thanks
Fi amanillah

_____

Bilal was upset when he received the letter, but decided to follow up by writing to yet another scholar of Islam.

From: Bilal
> *To: <withheld>@almahdi.edu*

Dear Sir:
As salaam Alaikum. I have been following your lecture series on you tube and I am very much fascinated by your approach to the concept of humanity the way it should be understood. I have found answers to many questions through your lectures and I believe the whole Muslim community should be open enough to respect collaborations and thus expand Islam in a righteous ways.

I am from Mumbai, India. The reason I am writing to you is there is a question on my mind for which I am looking for the right answer/ perspective since very long and there is immense confusion when you look for reference to the Ulema, maybe since you are approaching issues differently you could have a perspective on this.

The question is as follows:
It's about a condition called 'Transsexuality' which means a person has a gender identity disorder, wherein he belongs biologically to a particular gender, but his mental gender is not same as his biological gender and hence he cannot conform to the gender he is born with and always strives to be in the opposite gender role. The way to deal with this medically is a procedure called Gender Reassignment Surgery where the body gets aligned to the mind.

Now, there is a fatwa of Ayatollah Khomeini in 1975 which allows for sex change surgery for such people since it is not against the religion to disallow it. The man, Hojatuleslam Kariminia in Qom, Mashhad is doing research on the rights of transsexual in Islam and has also written a book on this.

The current government of Iran is supporting this and allowing for sex change surgery.

However, if you write to the Iraqi Marjas, like Ayatollah Sistani and others, they are not approving of such a surgery and call it against Islam, in which case if a person suffers for gender identity disorder he is supposed to suffer till he dies and live with the guilt of not conforming to the rules which he has to follow due to the gender he is born with.

Sir, you as a research scholar with a different perspective, could throw some light on to this subject. I am aware that you may not be able to write which Marjah is right and which is wrong, because that's not going to be politically correct for you, however, you could probably look at the right perspective and throw some light on this subject.

You may not be aware but this could help me a great deal and Allah SWT will grant you immense sawaab for this act.

Sorry to bother you without permission.

Fi Amanillah
Regards,

Bilal.

From: <withheld>almahdi.edu
23 December 2013 at 5 p.m.
To: Bilal

Salam
My apology for a very brief response.

Ayatullah Khomaini's view appears most accurate in terms of the traditional norms. He has probably resorted to the judicial precept of 'Humans have full rights upon their wealth and selves' whilst the Iraqi scholars probably see this principle conflicting with another principle where gender is seen as the right of God.

In my own system of thought and my understanding of the tradition there would be no problem at all for people to opt for such surgeries.

He then forwarded the reply to the cleric he knew, asking what he was to do. Bilal wrote that he had received the cleric's own letter, but here was a contradiction. Could he help him out?

The cleric was troubled enough to tell him about his family's deception. He apologized and said he could no longer help Bilal; there was too much pressure. He could reassure Bilal that religion was on his side, but he could not interfere in what was 'a family affair'. Bilal thanked him for the help and advice he had given, and for connecting him with clerics in Iran. There was little he could do about the embarrassment on both sides—the fact that his family had forced the cleric to write a letter which was essentially a lie left Bilal shamefaced; the cleric himself felt guilty about succumbing to such pressure.

'On that day, I made this decision that I will not go back to my family and try to reason with them. I will start my journey and I will live with whatever limitations. I was financially independent.'

He moved out of his parents' home. It broke his heart to leave the house in which he had grown up, which was now also home to a niece he loved as his own daughter.

'First, my parents refused to let me go. My mom cried and said, "Forgive us, from now on we will not say anything". But I was firm. My brother said he was sorry, but I'd decided to leave. This was the only way we could still be family.'

He began to save money to buy a house, and rented a flat in the meanwhile. He would visit his family on weekends.

He scheduled his first surgeries—the hysterectomy and oophorectomy. He made the journey to and back from the hospital in Ahmedabad by himself. His family did not know he had gone. Neither did his colleagues. He had taken a week's leave from his office, and was back at work on the sixth day.

'Isn't it a two-week healing process? Two weeks to a month?' I asked.

'Yeah, but I had no choice. I had twenty-eight stitches on my abdomen, but I had to summon all my mental strength and force myself to work.'

He would come back home and collapse. His partner and his friends helped as much as they could. Following the surgery, Bilal began to take hormones, but shaved twice a day, so that no one would know he had begun to sprout hair on his face. He was also wearing a chest binder. People at work had begun to notice. Finally, he came out to his boss and some of his colleagues.

'They accepted it very gracefully,' Bilal said. 'They started calling me by my male name and gender. I really started enjoying that validation of my identity.'

He reduced the shaving to once a week. He would allow his stubble to grow, socialize as a man on Saturdays, and shave before his weekly visit to his parents.

The transition was taking a toll on his relationship. He now wanted to go out in public with his partner, but she had reservations. They both worked in human resources, and she was worried that their network would find out.

'And I said, "What if they get to know?" She definitely loved me a lot. I don't think there's any girl in my life who loved me the way she loved me. But she was not ready to come out with me in public and that's the (point) where we started developing conflict, like I would tell her, "Look, I want to live my identity, why don't you come out with me, why are you ashamed?" Like if we're going to a shopping mall, she will not walk beside me. She will walk either ten steps ahead of me or ten steps behind me, because she doesn't want anybody to notice that she's with me. And that kind of made me paranoid. As I started developing confidence in myself, I became more and more demanding with her. I wanted her to come out with me. I wanted us to meet each other's parents.'

They decided to take a vacation to sort things out. He happened to leave his laptop open, on a weekend when he was visiting his parents. His brother snooped into his emails, and found a series of chats with his partner. He saw that she would often make plans to come over to his place—Bilal had now bought a flat in Andheri—and that they were planning a holiday together. He noted down her email address, and spoke to his sister.

'So, my sister sent her an email,' Bilal said. 'She told her not to tell me, but said since she's a friend, the family wanted to speak to her about me. They invited her to dinner. Obviously, she told me, and I said okay, they've called you, go and explain to them. So she thought this was going to be a friendly dinner, where she will explain what's happening with me, and she was very confident.'

She was also under the impression only his sister and parents would be at dinner. She entered his parents' home to find something of a courtroom assembled.

'So my sister, brother-in-law, brother, sister-in-law, and parents start bombarding her. "Look, *this* is the email we found"; "*You* are the girl behind our daughter's problems"; "You're *influencing* our girl"— they just start blaming her for everything I am, because they didn't want to accept that their child is actually like this. And it became a typical drama like they show in the movies. On the one hand, my brother threatens her, saying if she doesn't leave me now, they will tell her parents about us tomorrow. On the other, my mom falls at her feet and says, *"Please mere bachche ko chhod de* (Leave my child alone)."'

She held her own. She told them their threats would not stop Bilal from transitioning. It was best for them that they had an open conversation with him. They began to curse and swear at her, upset that she was referring to their daughter as a man.

'She told me what happened in the evening. She was very upset, obviously; they'd thrown insult after insult at her. She was also upset with me, though she loved me. She said my family was like this junglee family, and she couldn't deal with their threats and insults.'

His partner began to drift away from him when he was most in need of support.

'There *was* love. There is love even today. Even now, we could probably work (things) out. We kept in touch, of course. We kept fighting, kept coming together, kept fighting, and this continued.'

He was temporarily single when he had his mastectomy. He began to change all his documents—his Aadhaar card, his driving licence, and eventually his passport. He had started his transition later than most people; his life insurance and medical insurance policies, his property, were all in his given name, and he had to have each changed individually.

His parents noticed that his chest was flat, even without a binder. His facial hair was noticeable even after he shaved. His voice was changing.

'But they didn't ask me, and every time I tried to bring up the conversation, they would bring out the Q'uran. They would ask who would marry my nieces and nephews. I saw there was no point. I was feeling suffocated. I just couldn't live that dual life any more, and I was looking for a way out.'

He stuck it out for a year. He spoke to his girlfriend about migrating. They could leave India, and perhaps get married. But she could not make the commitment. Eventually, he made the decision alone. He sold his property. He began to apply for jobs abroad. The best offer came from the Islamic country in which he now lives.

'I took the risk, though I would have to live in this constant fear,' Bilal said. 'Like what if I meet with an accident, or I have a medical condition, which requires physical examination? I haven't had my bottom surgery done yet, so I will be exposed. Should I go, should I not?'

Eventually, he did. He could no longer endure the double life. He was looking forward to being a man, without prefixes. He wanted to pray at the mosque.

He doesn't regret it. 'But I'm always living in this fear. And at this point, I'm stuck because I cannot quit my job and suddenly come to India. If I come back, I'll have to live the same life that my parents wanted me to, or I have to move to a different place and live another life. If I keep staying here, I will always live with this severe, severe insecurity, feeling unsafe all the time, not knowing what could happen to me. As of now, I've not made a decision. I'm still struggling with what to do next in my life.'

He does visit India, but isn't able to see his family. It upsets him to be called by his old name and gender. His parents visited him once, and he was traumatized.

'I mean, they're seeing me, that I'm living like a male and have a beard and a moustache and my passport says "male" and everything is male. But still they call me by my old name, and they call me by my old gender. I have a driver here, and they were using the female gender on me in front of him. When we went out, to shopping malls, everywhere, they address(ed) me in the female gender.'

His extended family doesn't know about his transition, and visiting his parents could make things awkward.

'At one point, I told my parents, "At least accept me behind closed doors. I'm not asking you to accept me to the extended family; I get it. For them, I will be what you want me to be. But at least tell me that yes, we accept you. I've been fighting this, I've been on this journey for twelve years." But they say, "Whatever you call yourself, you'll always be Faiza to us." Sometimes, my mother comes to me and cries and says, "Please forgive me, but I can't sacrifice my other four children for you." And I'm like okay, you're asking me to forgive you, but at least accept me in secret. Call me by my new name. Use my new identity, use my gender correctly. No, that's not possible.'

He once passed his street, and saw the home where his parents lived. He could not bring himself to climb the stairs. He would not be allowed in wearing the trousers and shirt he was in. He could not shave and wear a salwar-kameez.

'It hurts me. It pains me. I had tears in my eyes. They just have to understand that I'm a human being with a problem. I'm not mad. I've not gone and done surgeries one after the other without any support for no reason at all. Tell me, do you cut your body for no reason? I love my parents. I really love my family. And that child who was brought up like my own child, I cannot stay away from her. I mean, my heart *cries* when I go to Bombay and I cannot see that child. I just love her so much.'

He said, without resentment, that his parents and siblings contact him when they need money. 'But when I want them to support me or understand, the doors are closed. So I've accepted the fact that the doors will always remain closed. I have only one main aim in my life now. That I want to become so famous, I want to do something that makes me world famous, tomorrow, world famous and respectable, so much so that my parents have no choice but for them to come in front of the world and accept that yes, this is our child.'

'But you shouldn't have to do anything,' I said.

'I don't know. That's the only way I can get an acceptance from them. I'm hoping one day my father comes and refers to me as his son. Some day. I don't know whether that will happen.'

~

I met Bilal after a long day in Bombay. He had been attending a conference, and had had a twelve-hour day himself. I wasn't sure how he looked, and everyone in the lobby of the hotel where we were meeting had the confused, enquiring expression of strangers trying to find each other.

Eventually, I saw him, wearing a backpack and bearing a samosa.

'It's for you,' he said. 'I figured you'd be hungry.'

I was touched. In many of the transmen I had met, I had observed a certain ease in taking charge, in making decisions, in looking out for other people. A little plate of food could say so much about someone.

After we had spoken for a while, about his work, about his family, I finally brought up my old quibble. Bilal had spoken to me on the condition that my book was about transpeople and not homosexuals. I found it odd that someone who faced a certain kind of oppression because of a certain inclination should not fight oppression because of another inclination. Why did he find homosexuality wrong?

'Because the Q'uran says so,' he said simply. 'It says explicitly in the Q'uran that people of the same gender should not be together.'

'But surely that's not something which one chooses?' I said. 'Surely that's how Allah made them too?'

'If someone can prove that to me, I'm ready to accept it,' Bilal replied. 'If it can be scientifically proven.'

'Even if the Q'uran says it's wrong?'

'The Q'uran is not against science. If it is natural, I'm sure there is some provision for it,' he said.

Suddenly, he leaned back in his seat, as if the exhaustions of the day, of his life, had caught up with him at that moment.

'You haven't met your family here?'

He shook his head.

'They don't know you've come?'

He shook his head again.

'But . . . they will come around, right? I'm sure they do love you.'

'Of course they love me. I'm their child. My parents love me. But the question is, do they love me more than they fear society?'

His transition was complete, and his voice was so deep I could not imagine it had ever sounded female.

Leaning back in the armchair, his arms and legs spread out in a way that was effortlessly masculine, the lounge lights marking out the stubble on his face, his rolled-up sleeves exposing the thickness of his forearms, the only feminine features on Bilal were his large eyes and soft mouth. I wondered how he could possibly be taken for a woman. How could his family even see a daughter or sister or aunt in him?

I was reminded of another friend, from Pakistan. She was a transwoman, and had moved to a different country pre-transition. It would be her home for decades. Her father lived in Lahore, and when she had come to terms with her gender, her siblings discouraged her from telling their father the truth about herself. For a long time, she would write letters to him under her old name. At one point, her dysphoria became so extreme she could no longer sign her given, masculine name. She wanted to speak to him on the phone, and her brother discouraged her. She had not been in touch with her father for six years, but one day, felt an impulse to write. She wrote him a seven-page letter, ending with her phone number and saying she would understand if he chose never to accept her. She signed it with her chosen name.

Ten days after she had posted the letter, she received a call from Pakistan, asking for her by her feminine name. She did not recognize her father's voice at first, and he did not know her voice had changed. When they realized they were talking to each other, they cried for several minutes.

'How?' Her father sobbed. 'How could you make the decision that I would prefer a son who did not care about me enough to write, to a daughter who loved me so much she did not want to hurt me? Who gave any of you the right to make my decisions for me?'

When I told Bilal, he smiled. 'If that happens to me, that will be all I want. My life will be complete.'

'Maybe they will miss you enough to reach out.'

'Yeah, I think cutting off is very important.' He sighed. 'Right now, I feel I'm in the worst stage of my life. It's been one setback after the other, one setback after the other, and I've been feeling betrayed, and I feel very lost in life, very broken, at this stage.'

'Is there anything I can do?'

'Write the book. Please write the book. And please show people that this is what we go through. I want this book to reach my parents or my family in some way. I want them to read it. I want *my* community to read it and understand.'

Boys Do Cry

'A woman shall not wear a man's garment, nor shall a man put on a woman's cloak, for whoever does these things is an abomination to the Lord your God.'

—Deuteronomy 22:5

'Does not nature itself teach you that if a man wears long hair it is a disgrace for him, but if a woman has long hair, it is her glory? For her hair is given to her for a covering.'

—Corinthians 11:14–15

'I have huge problems with the Church,' a friend who was raised Catholic had once told me as we sat on a veranda in Goa, drinking cheap alcohol. 'The guilt. The constant fucking guilt. You can't take it.'

'What guilt?'

'Starts with Original Sin. Goes up to the Crucifixion. You're made to feel guilty about everything—living, breathing, eating.'

Five years after that conversation, almost to the day, I was at the same hotel where I had stayed at the time. The rooms were nice, the weather was lovely, Goa was pleasantly crowded, and I was waiting to meet another 'lapsed Catholic', as Cass had described himself.

The name was a derivative of the middle name he had been given at birth, 'Cassandra'—the name of his grandmother, he had said on the phone. She was the most non-judgemental person he knew. He wished she had lived long enough to counsel his parents, because she would have.

Cass drove up in an old red scooter that belched smoke. His hair was curly, relatively long for a transman. His hazel eyes and delicate bone structure gave him a femininity he didn't try to disguise.

It helped in his present line of work, he said. The men who paid for sex liked his smooth face and flat chest.

~

'The worst thing that can happen to a transguy is sex with a man,' Cass told me. 'It's what we want to escape from, right? So I tell them they can't treat me like a woman. I'm okay with Greek.' By 'Greek', he meant anal sex.

He was raised in a posh neighbourhood in Bombay. But his parents are 'strict Catholics', who 'believe the devil has possessed their daughter'. Like most others, it was easy enough in childhood. Who doesn't love a tomboy? But when the tomboy never becomes a lady, the narrative is skewed.

'They want to be able to show your childhood pictures and say, look, how cute, look at her wearing her brother's clothes! Look at her with the painted moustache! Look at her with the short hair! It doesn't occur to them that maybe children think about gender differently. That we don't know we don't have options.'

He was given an ultimatum when he was twenty-two. He had to accept that he was a girl, or he had to leave home.

'You can't accept something that is not true,' he said, earnestly.

He moved in with friends for a while.

'But, you know, everyone is cramped in Bombay. Everyone is struggling to make rent. You have to work. And work was pretty damn hard to find. I was in an ad agency for a while. Then I worked with a production company. Everywhere, there was harassment. And if a guy made a move on me, I would fucking break his bones. Like smash his face. You're my boss, you're the watchman, you're the managing fucking director, I don't care, man.'

He tried to freelance, but things didn't work out. His résumé signalled troublemaker. He had not worked in a single company for longer than five months. He had held seven jobs in four years. Everyone who hired him wanted him to take a pay cut.

'And then I found sex,' he snorted. One of his friends, a cisman, had been moonlighting as a sex worker. His clients were mainly older women. But 'that didn't work out' for Cass. They were horrified at the idea of 'sex with a female'.

'Not like I wanted to eat old pussy either. But it's a lot better than having a dick up your ass,' he said. And then a transwoman whom he had met while cruising had a suggestion—with his delicate features, he looked like an adolescent boy. If he got his top surgery done, he might find a steady clientele among men. It worked.

'It actually worked too well for my safety,' he said. 'I had to relocate. You know how it is in Bombay, right? You have to pay people off. And I'm trying to save up for my phalloplasty. So I can't afford to pay people off. I can barely afford to live.' He was threatened with rape. He was beaten up a few times. And then there was an assault so bad, he said, that he knew he would not live to tell the tale next time.

'I can't go back,' he said. 'And this is going to last for as long as I need to collect the money for my phalloplasty. Then, I'll do something. Anything. I can't wait to leave this behind.'

And how far along was he? He shook his head.

The money came easier in Goa, with the foreigners. The best days were when he was hired by women, he said. It had only happened twice. There were some terrible days with men.

'You know what people tell you, all those stories about how you think you're going with one guy, but then there are four of them? All of them are true. I carry a knife with me. I'll cut their balls off. I'm not afraid. *I'm* not the transphobe, right? I'll turn them into trannies if they try shit with me.'

He missed home. There was no significant other in his life. He had had partners through school and college, but he didn't want to be with anyone until he could leave 'this life' behind, he said. He spoke to his mother, occasionally, always from a different number, so that his father wouldn't know. She called him when she could. And every conversation ended with a fight. The same fight. On the nights he spoke to his mother, he could not bring himself to go out and work, he said.

'Friends?' I asked.

Cass smiled ironically.

'Within the community? Do you have support?'

'I don't want support,' Cass said. 'I just don't want to be judged. I know what they say about me. I know they say I'm not really a man, I'm a girl selling myself for sex to men. Tell me, you're a girl. Would you save money up to throw away your boobs? Would you be doing anything, *any fucking thing* someone asked, one guy up your ass, another guy down your mouth, just so you could get a fake fucking dick? I'm "not a man" until I get my surgery. And I'm "not a man" if I try to make quick money to get the surgery. *That* is the community. If I wanted support from them, I'd kill myself. Then they'd hold my posters and candles and sit together. That's *support* from the community for you.'

～

I was often surprised by how many transmen subscribed to heteronormativity, both in terms of sexual orientation and physical appearance. A transman was often considered less masculine if he was in a relationship with another transman or a cisman, instead of with a woman.

I also noticed, particularly among the younger transmen, a keenness to get their surgeries done, to put their lives on hold basically until they felt they were 'complete men'. The notion of 'completing transition' struck me as problematic, because it was suggestive of reaching for a particular body rather than acceptance of self. But most troubling was a certain kind of triumph over—and at times even contempt for—people who choose not to have surgery, and pity for those who cannot afford to have surgery.

'Do you think this a trend, where surgery is prioritized unreasonably, over almost anything else?' I asked Satya.

'This is indeed a very, very worrying trend,' he told me, and then recounted a recent incident on a transmasculine WhatsApp group. A member of the group had kept up the pretence of having gone through phalloplasty, describing in detail the size and functions of his organ. He was eventually found out by other transmen to have been lying about the phalloplasty—no such surgery had ever been undertaken by him. Because transmen relied on each other so much for medical information, what seemed like white lies could be dangerous.

'Having followed his advice, these transmen had already been damaged for life,' Satya told me. 'It's clear what could have led to this. Having "come out" in the media, there was no other way he could keep up the idea of "masculinity"—neither to his own self, nor to others in the community—without having to put out and sustain such a lie.

'In many ways this trend reaffirms to me that the "coming out" format not only encourages an unhealthy, counterproductive and competitive identity politics amongst transmasculine persons, but that in the final analysis, it is an apolitical format. Coming to terms with oneself as trans is not necessarily a moment of politicization. And this can only be attributed to the largely apolitical environment that we all live in, as well as the political histories we have inherited. The glaring questions that face our transmasculine communities (are) about the sheer poverty of affirmative masculinity models culturally available to us. What models have hegemonic masculinities given us? Did feminisms do anything productive with the masculinities they criticized, other than largely demonizing them? What did the lesbian–bisexual–queer women spaces do? Only extended the already internalized hatred towards cismen? The transmasculine communities are at the receiving end of the absolutely unenviable position of "no positive cultural models of masculinity".'

Satya himself had not been without what he called 'the after-effects of such an all-pervasive "lack".'

'But I have also been very lucky to find, within my profession, feminist ciswomen, some of whom were queer, (and) that allowed me entry into a rich resource of questionings and possibilities,' Satya said. 'I count myself as having been partially saved by these encounters from the very spectre that all hegemonic masculinities are bound to doom one to; the rest, I continue to struggle with. There is no way out other than the hard route of continuous politicization and consciousness-raising.'

~

Deathbed

He was twenty-two. He was happy with his mastectomy. His parents were supportive. He decided to have his hysterectomy done at a private hospital in Delhi. When he was being anaesthetized for surgery, something went wrong, and his corpse was rolled out to the waiting room where his parents sat holding hands. They could not read. They did not make much money. Their savings had been spent getting their son the body he desired. They were asked to sign blank papers in order to take custody of their son's body, the torso hiding a vestigial uterus. No death summary was given. The hospital has no record of a person being admitted for a hysterectomy that day. There was no scope to pursue it legally.

'Why Didn't the Indian Army Want to Search Me?'

'That profile picture on WhatsApp . . . it was taken at Coffea Arabica, right?' I asked.

Zubair's[1] eyes widened. 'You know Coffea Arabica? You've been to Srinagar?'

My friends and I would hang out there nearly every day of my visit to Srinagar. When I told him, Zubair grinned. 'So you know what used to happen there.' He winked. 'I think after the floods, everyone in Srinagar was single.'

Coffea Arabica had been something of a live Tinder before Tinder was Tinder. I found myself in a group of boys, comparing notes on all the women at the tables there. My verdict usually was that all of the boys at my table could do better. One of them believes I was jealous. He was probably right. They were very good-looking boys.

I had rarely encountered women on Srinagar's streets whose heads were uncovered. 'It's the culture,' one of my friends had explained to me. I found it rather strange, since most Kashmiri women I had known in Delhi were uncovered.

'My family used to insist on the hijab. It was bad enough when it was part of the school uniform,' Zubair said. 'It's humiliating. Who asks a son to dress up as a daughter? I kept telling them I'm their son. My father slapped me. They took me to a dargah to see what spirit had

---

[1] This person's name has been changed on request.

got into me.' He laughed. 'It's funny. Religious people can believe the devil has possessed their child; but they cannot believe that god made their child a certain way.'

Zubair had learnt to work around his problems early. He knew he could not discard the hijab, or the long brown hair that mushroomed under it. And so he decided to kill two birds with one stone.

'Every day in school, I would cut off a few handfuls of hair in the toilet, and throw it in the dustbin on my way home,' he said. He told his mother that his hijab was making his hair fall out. Her response was to oil Zubair's hair, make him soak it in for an hour, and then wash it off herself. But clumps of hair continued to fall. She took him to a doctor.

'I think the doctor was not very good.' He laughed. 'She just recommended some vitamins. I thought maybe they will make more hair grow elsewhere, but that didn't happen. I even broke the capsules open and tried rubbing (the powder) on my arms and legs.'

The clothing gave Zubair one refuge—the freedom to grow hair on his arms and legs. He would shave ferociously, hoping to roughen the skin, get the hair to grow in thicker, masculine clumps as they did on the limbs of his brothers. His sister tried to talk him into waxing. So did his friends.

'So I escaped to hostel as soon as I could.' Against the wishes of his parents, he insisted on studying engineering. He went to a college in south India, 'as far away from Kashmir as I could go.' Yet, his family managed to find friends who would keep an eye on him.

'You have to take three flights from there to reach Srinagar. And still, there was someone whose house I had to go to for lunch once a month.'

Zubair had dreamt of a college where he could switch the salwar-kameez for T-shirt and jeans, the hijab for a crew cut. But the engineering college had a dress code, not very different from the one back home. 'Salwar-kameez with dupatta,' he said, grimacing as he made air quotes. He had also dreamt that he would be part of the sports teams.

'Not a single women's team,' he said. 'And, of course, they would not take me in the men's team.'

He got into a couple of fist fights in college—one because he supported Pakistan against India in the latter's last tour there.

'You know it's tradition, right? Of course we support Pakistan in Kashmir,' Zubair told me. 'And most of my classmates were these north Indians who had come down. The south Indians don't give a fuck, honestly. They're not going to beat you up over whom you support. But these Delhi-type fucks, too little grey matter and too much dick-show. Sorry, I should not use these words in front of a lady, but that's how it was.'

The second fist fight was over a girl.

'I liked her. I knew it could not go anywhere'—because she was not Kashmiri or Muslim—'but then this arsehole was hitting on her, and I couldn't take it. So I told him to stay away. Of course, they branded me a lesbo after that. I'm not a fucking lesbo, man.'

Zubair worked in Bangalore and Delhi after he graduated.

But he never reached out to the community in Bangalore, he said.

'I didn't want to be involved with any organization. I had some relationships in Bangalore. One girl had dated a transman before, and she offered to put me in touch with him. I said it's too weird. And it took me a long time to actually come out even to the community. The thing is, especially in Bangalore, they have this thing about female-born being together. Like lesbos and us. And some of the lesbos even hit on you. That is really humiliating. And it's haram. I'm still a Muslim. I still pray. And some things are not okay.'

But he missed home. He missed his family, he missed the Dal Lake, he missed his friends—a group of boys from his 'first neighbourhood', where they would play games of cricket. He returned for a year. Home did not feel like home.

'You know that song, *Summer of '69*?'

'Who doesn't? If you were born in the '80s or '90s.'

Zubair laughed. 'Exactly. So that's what happened, actually. Two guys had got married, one had moved to the US; one guy was in Delhi. We didn't really meet any more. And the girls in school and college were reaching out. They all wanted us to start meeting. Us, our husbands, our children.'

What was it like growing up in Kashmir in the '90s, I asked. After the Indian government set up its army camps.

'We were kids, right? I mean, now I understand how horrible everything was, how people used to disappear,' he said. 'But back then, I didn't know much. My family didn't suffer too much, but then yeah, searches used to happen.' He laughed suddenly. 'It used to bewilder me when they would ask all the boys to line up and take them to the fields, and I was not asked to come with them. My father would look mournful, and my brothers would look important when these ID searches happened. I was too young to know why they were going. I was too young to know what happened. And when people spoke about their *susu* (penis) being electrocuted, all I could think was, I don't have a susu. I remember my younger brother's circumcision. I asked my mother when I would have it done, and she laughed so hard and told everyone, who laughed. They told me girls can't have it done, and I cried all day and all night.'

As he grew older, his manliness was less amusing. He was not against the hijab—he believed it was quite right and proper for women to dress 'modestly'—and his only quarrel with it was that men were not required to wear it. His family did not understand why he was perfectly happy for his mother and sister to wear the hijab, but refused to himself.

He could live away from home after college, but he could not avoid marriage forever.

At twenty-six, Zubair had caused his parents some despair. Did he have a boyfriend, they asked. Why had he rejected everyone they had found for him? What did he want? One of them was a doctor, another was in the IAS—'It's like the cardinal sin for Kashmiris, right? Either you become a doctor or join the IAS, or you marry someone who has, preferably all of the above. And I had done engineering in the other corner of the country, and come back with short hair, and now I was not even getting married to IAS people and doctors.'

And so he moved back to Delhi. 'I fucking hate Delhi. It's shit. It really is. How can you like it? You can't stay on, right? After a few years, you have to leave.'

He did fall in love—Delhi gave him the partner his parents could not find for him: a Kashmiri Muslim doctor. Except, she was not husband material. She was definitely wife material, Zubair said with a smile. 'But we don't know what's going to happen. Because she and I both have sisters and brothers who have to get married. We can't tell our parents until it happens. I really don't know what will happen. I go home for two days, fight with my parents, and come back. I'm thirty now. She's twenty-four. They will start pressuring her also soon, na? Her sister knows about us. But nobody in my family knows.'

His plans for the future? 'I'm looking at migrating to Canada,' he said. 'Then we can be free. I've just got all the information on it.'

The Land of Jewels

The warrior princess lived in this land, the only heir to the king and so raised more as a warrior than a princess. She fell in love with Arjuna, the Pandava prince, when she saw him, but wept in despair. How would this fantastic specimen of masculine beauty, he who could have any woman he wanted, he who had won a wife through a feat of archery, he who rarely left a land without marrying its princess and breaking hundreds of hearts, he who loved the curves of bows and women, desire her? Her body was bare of voluptuousness. Her arms and back and thighs and chest were rippling with muscles, her face had hardened from long hours on the training grounds and battlefields. What claim did she have to Arjuna's love?

As is to be expected in the Mahabharata, Chitrangada found the gods pliable to her pleas. And so, Kamadeva, the god of love, granted her the power to transform at night, her tough arms turning into delicate white limbs, her chest ballooning into breasts, the hair that had been thinned by a protective helmet shooting out into luxurious locks, so that she could seduce the archer for whom she lusted.

Her disguise had to be abandoned when her land was invaded. She discarded the feminine form for the warrior's body, and led her army against the invader. Arjuna had never been more in love, he declared, and would have always chosen the warrior over the damsel. He fought by her side, gave her children, and left the land. She ruled her country after her father, and trained her children to protect it after her.

In Manipur, the legend of Chitrangada could be appropriated by anyone. Did she belong any more to transmen than she did to transwomen? Did she belong any more to anyone than she did to the militants fighting for secession from India?

~

11 August 2017

The first thing I saw as we drove out of the Bir Tikendrajit International Airport at Imphal was the curved barbed wire fence that marked a Central Reserve Police Force (CRPF) camp. The signboards across town alternated between the Bengali and Meitei scripts. Old manuscripts in Meitei had been destroyed in a fire at the library, and several of the tribes wrote their languages in the English or Bengali scripts. A few years ago, the state government had decided to piece together the Meitei script and make it the official one. Randhoni had told me that she was learning it by teaching her son. The prime minister's larger-than-life face grinned out of posters everywhere, promising free housing, governance over government, safety for women, development, and pipe dreams as we rattled over roads ruined afresh that year by the monsoon.

Close to my hotel was Kangla Fort, the site of the Ima Protest— the Mothers' Protest. On 16 July 2004, a group of twelve middle-aged women had arrived at the Fort, then a camp of the Assam Rifles paramilitary unit. Five days earlier, the bullet-riddled and mutilated body of thirty-four-year-old Thangjam Manorama was found between her home, from which she had been arrested earlier that night, and a police station. The twelve women were soon joined by eighteen others. They had planned a protest against the Armed Forces Special Powers Act (AFSPA), which gave the forces sweeping powers with impunity. Manorama, the paramilitary had claimed, was a dangerous operative of the separatist group People's Liberation Army. Her family maintained that she was an activist, who had never indulged in criminal activity. Years before investigations revealed that Manorama had been tortured and raped before being shot at close range, the thirty Manipuri mothers silently walked to the gates of the Kangla Fort, once the residence of the King of Manipur and now the headquarters of the Assam Rifles. Holding up a placard that read 'INDIAN ARMY RAPE US', they began to strip until they were naked, shouting, 'Indian Army, come rape us too', 'We are all Manorama's mothers'.

It is one of two enduring images most Indians from the 'mainland'—as the people of the seven states that comprise northeast India refer to the rest of the country—have of Manipur. The other is of a frail woman with a large face, curly hair, and feeding tube up her nose—Irom Sharmila Chanu—who had recently called off a sixteen-year-long fast in protest against the AFSPA. The Act was not repealed. She had been bestowed with the epithet 'Iron Lady of Manipur' by the rest of India and 'Mengoubi' by Manipuris. Having called off the fast and announced she would marry her long-time partner, she was now the subject of contempt, resentment and trolling in her home state.

There is another image, which often slips the mind of mainland Indians: the boxer Mary Kom, standing at the podium with her 2012 Olympic bronze. The only female boxer to have won a medal in each of the six world championships, she is famous enough for her face to be recognized. But most Indians, including actor Amitabh Bachchan, who had carried the Olympic torch ahead of the opening ceremony the same year as reward for being famous and popular and not connected in any way with sports, cannot remember which of the seven states she is from. Bachchan tweeted: 'Mary Kom!! wins boxing bout, insured a Bronze! What a story! A Mother of two from Assam, creates moment of pride for India!!' (sic)

I had not imagined I would be in Manipur to cover anything other than the insurgency and the AFSPA. And yet I found myself in the lobby of my hotel, chatting with Randhoni and Hemabati from the Imphal SAATHII office, planning meetings with the transmen of Manipur over the next week.

No Man's Land

Manipur's transman collective ETA (Empowering Trans Ability), headed by Hemabati Oinam, had started its work fairly recently, and owed its origins to SAATHII.

Since its inception in 2000, SAATHII in Manipur had focused mainly on the care, support and treatment of HIV/AIDS patients. From 2008 onwards, they had been involved in a UNAIDS programme, Decentralization of HIV/AIDS. They worked in close collaboration with the Manipur State AIDS Control Society (MSACS) and the National Rural Health Mission (NRHM). Their targeted interventions (TIs) focused first on Men who have Sex with Men (MSM), and then transwomen.

In 2008, several community-based organizations were brought under an apex body called the All Manipur Nupi Maanbi Association (AMANA), headed by Santa Khurai.

With various health initiatives in place, SAATHII began to move into trans rights and advocacy in 2011, Randhoni would tell me in her Imphal office. Transwomen were part of the organization, but even they did not know of the transmen in Manipur until after the NALSA judgment.

'That's how low the visibility is,' she said. 'Even those of us in the field thought "transgender" and "transwomen" were synonymous. Only around 2013–14, we came to know of this community and started searching for them in Manipur. Santa would go meet them one-on-one, first Hemabati and through him, some others. She would urge them to come out so they could all ask for their rights. Eventually, they formed the collective ETA. And you know, when the Transgender

Welfare Board for the state of Manipur was finally formed, in August 2016, it had a representative from AMANA, one from ETA, and one from SAATHII among its members, which really empowers us, when we're talking about rights.'

The most important outcome of the NALSA judgment, she said, was the entitlement to a legal identity document through the Gender Identity Change (GIC) affidavit. The affidavit needs to be published in two local newspapers and then in the state gazette. Once that was done, all legal identity documents could be changed, so that transpeople could access the government's welfare schemes.

'The problem is, some people have different genders on different identity cards,' she said. 'You need to make sure your GIC, Aadhaar card and bank account have the same name as well as (the) same gender. Only then can you apply for schemes like the Pradhan Mantri Awas Yojana (a housing scheme for the urban poor). And that is important because typically, the son inherits the property, since the daughter will be married off to someone else, who inherits from *his* parents. In the case of transmen, such a thing is not possible. So both the transman and his partner have no property. We've been negotiating with the families to make (such a) provision. Of course, legally, daughters and female-born children are entitled to property, but we try to settle it with the family instead of taking it to court and causing a rift.'

Various trans rights groups have been pushing for schemes that specifically benefit transgender citizens. Randhoni told me they *are* given priority under certain housing schemes such as the Indira Awas Yojana (IAY) and Priority Household Ration Cards, but no single scheme that caters exclusively to transpeople has materialized.

With so many claimants to so few schemes, there was such high demand for allocation of land that the government could not possibly approve all applications. It would be easy for them to reject applications from transmen if there was even the slightest mismatch in name or gender on any document. Money for building a house would only be allocated if the applicant had land in his or her name.

～

My translator, who went by BD, was a chatty twenty-two-year-old with opinions on everything from Irom Sharmila and the Ima Protest to the adoption of the Meitei script and the insurgents' stance against the screening of Hindi films in Manipur—'They did not even allow the shooting of the film on Mary Kom here; they did all the shooting in Shimla side, because the faces are similar there'—down to the right times of the day for having breakfast, lunch, tea, and dinner.

Accompanying him was his friend Aily, also a transman, Hemabati, and the latter's partner Nanao. As we headed to the house of the first couple I was to interview, we passed several open spaces that had been improvised into football fields. 'Youth clubs are very active here, sister,' BD said.

He had just returned from Chandigarh after graduating with a degree in engineering. His mother knew he wanted to transition, and was supportive; his father hadn't spoken about it.

'I'm trying to get a government job first,' he told me. 'Once I have independent means of income, I will tell them. I know they will accept me, but I want to prove they did a good job of raising me. Otherwise they will get depressed. So first I'll apply and find a position, and then tell them.'

Twenty-one-year-old Aily had told his parents, and they were supportive, he said. He did not talk much. To most questions, he would grin and answer in a word or two.

Hemabati smiled a lot, and seemed cheerful most of the time. 'My English is not good, my Hindi is not good,' he said, apologetically. 'So I don't speak a lot.'

'That's okay, my Meitei is pretty bad,' I said.

Nanao laughed and high-fived me. Hemabati smiled again, 'My brain has become a bit slow. I'm a literate person, but because of my suicide attempt, I was in hospital, unconscious for five days. So now I have to try very hard to do things I could do easily before.'

The casualness with which my interviewees spoke about suicide had almost ceased to unnerve me. Some even spoke of multiple suicide attempts as if they were so many trifles. 'My first suicide attempt failed because my sister found me,' someone would say, or, 'No, no, I was hospitalized only after the third suicide attempt.'

Often, they seemed so happy when I met them, laughing and joking with others from the community, that I would think of the depression as something in their pasts, something so irrelevant it was forgotten. But then, their partners would say, 'That day, he was so depressed, he told me to forget him and get married to somebody and have children; he said he would commit suicide', or they would mention antidepressants that they had been taking. And then suicide seemed like the snake in the Garden of Eden, constantly lurking, tempting, threatening.

In Memoriam

November 20 is observed the world over as Transgender Day of Remembrance, a commemoration that began in 1999 following the murder of American transwoman Rita Hester in her apartment on 28 November 1998. She was murdered with such venom that forensic reports said she had been stabbed at least twenty times. Her assailant remains unidentified and at large. His or her motive remains a mystery. Since there was no theft, it is assumed to be hate.

Each year, there are tens of transpeople in every city whose names are added to the list of losses. Typically, there is a march, followed by a candlelight vigil and a reading of the names of transpeople who died that year—from suicide, from homicide, from disease, from despair.

From: All about our Famila
Directed by: Chalam Bennurkar
Interview with Sumathi Murthy

'Last year, when we did her memorial programme, two days later another transperson as radical as her is killed by her parents.'

Shaking her head, she adds, 'I don't know how much more strength I will have to deal with all these things. And I don't think I can take any more deaths of these people. I can't. I mean, like, even I'm getting tired. I don't want to see another friend dying in front of me. So young. How much, how much more? And these are not natural deaths. These are *not* natural deaths. These are deaths because . . . because of the society that we have. Because of the people that are around that they cannot provide space for people who are not like them. How much more? How many more people will die just because they don't get space to live? And why? I don't think Famila is dead at all; I don't think that she is dead. If she was dead, it means activism is dead. I mean, even now I am very critical about this sexuality movement; it is not a movement. It is *very* NGO-ized. Bloody, it's so NGO-ized that the movement actually started with funding. Thankfully, there were people like Famila who have managed to make it into a movement. But (it) failed miserably, because (of) all kinds of politics, not just society outside, but within the movement, within the NGO-ized circles. Where's that space? How can activists grow if you close all the doors? And how many more activists will die? You don't know. You and I actually don't know. Tomorrow, because of this kind of frustration, because of this kind of depression, of not being able to do something, or of not being recognized for what you have done, and of not being . . . and survival issues. You and I might get jobs outside, but what about transpeople? How much . . . how . . . I don't know, I don't know, I feel like if there is no radical change in this country, we're going to lose more Familas. There *has* to be radical change in this country. Otherwise, definitely we're going to lose more Familas, and I don't think I would want to see that. I would have no strength. I have no strength.'

And she shakes her head.

On the day of our meeting, 30 June 2017, Sumathi Murthy had become Rumi Harish. I asked which pronoun I should use—'they' or 'he' or 's/he'.

'No he-she,' Rumi said. 'Just call me Rumi.'

'No, I mean while referring to you.'

'Rumi.'

'The pronoun?'

'Don't use pronoun. Don't use pronoun. Let it get repetitive. I'd rather be genderless.'

'Not even "they"? Because I can't say, like, "Rumi and I sat in Rumi's office" or . . .'

'No, not "they". You just use the name, how many ever times. So what? The question of pronoun is also problematic. It's such a patriarchal thing. Why, because you have a universal pronoun which is so patriarchal—"he" for everything. Why use that?'

Author's note: While I do respect Rumi's stance on pronouns, I am concerned that the unusual sentence structure I was requested to use might make this section farcical and take away from the importance of Rumi's statements. In lieu of a pronoun, I will use 'R' for Rumi.

Rumi was sitting outside Alternative Law Forum in Bangalore. R looked different from the last time I had seen R. It was the first time I was meeting Rumi, but in videos of music and theatre performances, R had shoulder-length hair, usually tied into a ponytail or bun, and wore salwar-kameez, or a T-shirt with jeans. That day, Rumi had R's hair cropped short, and was wearing a formal shirt with jeans. Something about R—and until we sat down to an interview, I did not know Sumathi had changed her gender identity—carried a masculine vibe.

R and Sunil are involved with LesBiT, of which Karthik Bittu Kondaiah is also part. Rumi had started working with the NGO Sangama in the year 2000.

'This idea, the concept of transmen, was not evolved to that extent. At that point of time, I was actually feeling that I'm a transman,' R said.

'Oh!'

'But (I) didn't have enough courage and guts to say it out (loud), because I've been trained as a classical musician for thirty-odd years and if I have to change in this manner, I would lose my concerts. As it is, I had lost my concerts because they didn't like anybody going out of this whole morality background. So I was very worried about changing my image, changing my dressing, whatever. And I just kept quiet. I was working on (a) project (for) lesbian and bisexual women at that point of time, but it didn't really speak about transmen.'

Rumi did not see R-self as lesbian or bisexual. Sangama was involved in crisis intervention with lesbians, hijras, kothis, and other sections of the queer community. They would speak to people who were clinically depressed and those who were suicidal or had attempted suicide; in the case of runaway couples, they would intercede with the family and the police. It was around this time that Rumi began to work with Famila, mainly for 'male-born community people'— transwomen, kothis, hijras.

Their female-born counterparts—lesbians, bisexual women and transmen—rarely contacted Sangama. Rumi and Famila would look for articles in magazines about couples in trouble, and try to reach out to them. Among the couples they met were Charupriyan and Gayathri, and Kiran and Kavya.

By 2005, there was a small group of about ten people, who felt the need for a space separate from the transwoman, gay, male bisexual and intersex communities. None of them could relate to terms like 'lesbian', 'bisexual woman', 'cis' or 'trans'. The words belonged to a foreign language, alien to them. And they could not find regional equivalents in any of the southern languages at the time. LesBiT evolved organically, within a Sangama project that provided space for lesbian, bisexual women, female-to-male transpeople and their partners—cis or trans—to meet.

'(Sangama was) making us go to the regular meetings with the other community people, where everybody would be there. And we never found it comfortable to speak in front of others because they were not sensitive, they would always pass comments, especially on the female-to-male transpeople, saying how can you become a man, how can you call yourself a man, how can we treat you as a man, especially between 2005 and 2010, when we could not even think of surgeries.'

They wanted a space to debate gender and argue about the understanding of gender, but without the toxicity. They decided they would keep the group open to partners of transmen who were transwomen, and to other supportive transwomen, as well as to sex workers who identified as lesbian. Their only conditions were that there should be no conflict, and people's self-identification should be respected. Some of the transmen in LesBiT saw themselves as heterosexual husbands, and their partners called themselves 'heterosexual wives', and their identity was accepted without question.

The members of LesBiT were mostly working class, often Dalit, and came from various states of south India, with one or two from other parts of India. They had various adjustments to make.

'We did not have the language or the discourse of queer politics like how we have now,' Rumi said. 'We evolved our own understanding of gender, our own understanding of sexuality, our own understanding of relationships, and we struggled hard in terms of trying to understand ourselves in the regional context.'

The migrants had to adjust themselves to Bangalore, 'which demands a certain English language competency'. The cosmopolitan nature of a city that was quickly being recognized as the country's fifth metropolis gave them the freedom to dress the way they wanted and live the way they wanted. There were times when they had trouble finding houses to rent, and Rumi and others would have to negotiate with the landlords. It was usually easy to negotiate, because they lived in far-off, suburban areas, which were just beginning to develop, and the rental transactions were in cash, without formal agreements. Their salaries were in the range of Rs 3000–4000, and most of them could not afford more than Rs 800 as rent. Many of them lived in a little community of houses owned by hijras. R asked me not to reveal the name of the settlement, since the safety of its residents could be compromised.

But, even as other things settled down, they found little frictions among themselves—for instance, caste was a factor. Some people denied their own caste privilege, and others subtly—even unconsciously—betrayed casteist prejudice. Over time, they began to become conscious of it, and have open discussions.

Which brought them to the other problem—they did not have a single, common language. Some of their members could only interact with an interpreter.

Somehow, a group that had been formed because of the need to create a safe, private space, also became the cynosure of all eyes, a vehicle for awareness.

'Basically, there was this constant pressure from everybody saying come out and tell your story, come out, come out, tell your story, come out, tell your story, come out, tell your story,' Rumi said. 'So we wanted to break that somehow. So Sunil said, why am I being forced to come out like this, and why should I tell the story in a way that you're expecting me to tell the story? Why can't I have my own creative way of telling the story? And telling my story not just because you're asking. You're in a very comfortable situation, that's why you're asking me for the story. So then, (for the) very first time, we thought instead of coming out, we said we will do a cultural programme. And our idea was to present the *issue*, not our own stories.'

Rumi had recently begun to compose music for theatre in Bangalore. And R thought it would be a good idea to use theatre as the medium for presenting the issues they had in mind. Their first play was called 'Typical Indian Woman'.

'The way we showed it was: there was this Indian woman, who would constantly come and go back, and in between there are different kinds of female-born people showing that there is no *one* image of the typical Indian woman. A female-bodied person can be anything. It was a wide range that we wanted to show and that would be through snippets: of a love story, of a conversation between a transman and his brother, maybe parents of a runaway couple. So we did that. But the biggest hindrance for this was that we could never converse in any one language. Most of us did not speak English. And there was no other common language either. So we started learning each other's language(s).'

Everyone now spoke a smattering of Malayalam, Kannada, Hindi, Tamil and Telugu. Language was not really a barrier within the group, and so they thought it could work with an audience too—they could do multilingual plays.

'We did this thing where, in the same skit, the father will speak in Kannada, the son will speak in Malayalam, the brother will speak in Telugu, the mother will speak in Tamil. We did this. And it worked. All the way back in 2007.'

Their second play, 'Colours of Love', addressed abuse and bullying on college campuses. The characters had various identities—lesbian, female-to-male transsexual, bisexual—and the play explored how scared they were to come out.

Their next play was 'Love Letters'. 'So, basically, there are different kinds of couples. Each one of them will start reading letters to each other, and again it was in different languages. So if there was one letter in Malayalam, the response to it will be in Tamil. Okay? And after reading one letter to each other, they will go back. Then there is another story. After they read, they'll go back. Then there is another story. After *they* read, they'll go back. So then again, when these people come back, they would read out the next love letter where the story continues. So you have almost five stories happening simultaneously. In different languages.'

It was an interesting and empowering exercise. There was no director as such. There was no scriptwriter. Everyone wrote his or her segments. They evolved their own methods of working, their own theatre exercises, their own ways of syncing the tone of their respective dialogues with the whole.

'The whole idea was that people should not see us as guinea pigs, specimen pieces. The response should not be, "Oh, you're so special", "Oh, really, what all you've been through" types.'

Their other plays looked at issues that were pertinent to the community, that outsiders may not know—the difficulty of finding employment, the issue of 'corrective' rape, how caste compounded discrimination against transpeople.

'If I asked you right now, like one particular line, or one particular scene that you remember, one skit which is most memorable to you from all the work you did . . .' I began.

Rumi's eyes lit up at once, and R began to laugh. 'Ah! There is this *Musical Chairs* that we did.'

'Oh, I've seen that!'

'So you must have seen Deepu's act in it. It was a transman who did a transwoman's role . . .?' I nodded, and R continued, 'Deepu, who . . . you know, he passed away, he committed suicide . . .'

'I know.'

'I mean, that role, you should *see* the *way* he has done, you know, his skills of *acting* . . . and he being this transman, *so* different, my god, it's stunning. That play really broke us also, but really brought us also together.'

Rumi was laughing, but R's eyes were sparkling a little too much. 'Mangai directed it for us. And she got involved with *all* of us then.'

'She . . . yeah, we spoke about Deepu.'

Rumi shook R's head. 'I can't.' R smiled, defeated.

'We don't have to.'

'No, there's lots of deaths that . . . I'm like, very . . . just day before yesterday was one year after her death. She used to be a woman, the first woman cab driver of Uber. She was a very close friend, Bharti, who was part of LesBiT. She passed away last year, 27 June. So . . . there's lots of people who died like that. I have seen transwomen, transmen, both of them. So it feels like I'm . . . sometimes I feel why I'm living so long, why these young people are dying . . .'

~

I met him at a party for transmen and their partners. He told me he was suicidal. Counselling didn't help. Two days earlier, he had gone to the terrace of his apartment complex. He had stood on the parapet, holding on to the water tank. For a few exhilarating seconds, he felt he was flying. He would count up to thirty, he decided. If someone happened to walk into his view, it would mean someone was listening. It would mean he mattered. He would climb back down. If no one walked into his view, it would mean the world didn't care about him. Seconds before he would have jumped, the watchman blew his whistle. A stray dog shot out of the gate, followed by the watchman. He did not jump. If the watchman had looked up, he would have seen a girl in tears, not a boy in depression. Did he decide not to jump because the watchman and the dog were signals from god? Or had he latched on to a whistle and a canine because he didn't want to jump? When he stepped off the parapet, he was not sure whether he was grateful or resentful. He was still breathing. In a body he saw as a trap. 'Next time, if there's nobody,' he said, and made a gesture, swiping his hand past his throat. He smiled.

"And what are you looking at, huh?
What are you looking at?
You're checking me out, aren't you?
Checking out my beauty?
My marvellous breasts...
Compared to that...
hmmphhh...
Aishwarya Rai...
...aren't I the hotter chick?

A Boy Called Deepu

Musical Chairs
Devised by: LesBiT
Directed by: A. Mangai
*With everyone else out of the game, only one ciswoman and one transwoman
are left in competition. They begin to run around the lone chair, singing:*
Paattu naarkaali potti
Naarkaaliyai neeyum pidi
Oduvadhu vetri alla
Utkaarnthaal vetri
Odu Odu Odu O!

The musical chairs contest is on
Hurry up and find a seat
You can't win by running
Victory comes once you sit,
Run, run, run, run!

*The ciswoman pushes the transwoman away and grabs the chair. The
transwoman walks seductively around the chair, grinning at the audience.
She laughs and adjusts her dupatta.*

TRANSWOMAN: What are you looking at? (*Giggles and wags a
finger*) Do you see me? Am I not a beauty? Hmm? My figure and my long,
long hair? The anklets whose music enchants you when I dance? (*Sticks a
leg out and moves it in delicate paces along the floor*) My marvellous breasts?
Isn't that what you're thinking? Compared to that . . . hmph . . . Aishwarya

Rai, am I not the hotter chick? (*Strikes a statuesque pose*) But then . . . the people at home, society, the public, they believe that if you've got breasts, you're a woman and if you have a penis, you're a man. But . . . isn't there such a thing as the mind, the heart, in the middle?

Who could play a transwoman who would have the audience in splits one second, and stunned into silence the next? Who could tease them and shame them? Who could flirt with and chide and reason with and draw empathy from an audience of laypeople? Who could do this without offending transwomen?

'Deepu was the only one who could do it,' Mangai told me, with a smile. 'You know, he had just started transitioning, so his feminine qualities were not entirely gone. And the way he did it . . . the way he could hold the audience. My god! We wanted to get him to NSD (National School of Drama) or some place where he could really shine . . .' She trailed off, and began to blink rapidly. 'He moved to Kerala, and we heard he was doing well.' After a long pause, she had to wipe her eyes. 'I feel responsible. I *am* responsible. All of us are.'

Grief, a word that carries the viscerality of a vivisection and the silence of a scream in vacuum, pain so much beyond the comprehension of others that it can only fold into itself. There was a boy called Deepu, whom everyone loved. So ethereal a singer that his voice brought tears to people's eyes. So incorrigible a joker, with such perfect timing and such charm, that everyone whom he annoyed would be doubling up with laughter in moments. Now, his name brings tears to people's eyes, helpless yet accountable.

Facebook event (Public)
28 July 2012
Condolence Meeting and Film screening for Deepu
Details

```
Dear all,
Our good friend Deepu, a working class FTM from
Kerala, committed suicide late last night. We
```

will mourn this huge loss to our community by screening the film Kalvettukal in which Deepu shares some of his own history and music along with other FTM transpersons. Additionally, we will also share some videos of Deepu singing. Please join us to mourn and rage against this world which gives little to no space for transpeople, particularly FTM transmen.

Thank you for your time,
Rituparna, Aryan, Satya and Tanmay.
Date: Saturday, 28 July 2012; 6 p.m.
Venue: Sarai Basement, 29, Rajpur Road, Civil Lines. Please check the page for the directions.

About the film:
Kalvettukal (Sculptures)
Directed by: Gee Ameena Suleiman
33 minutes/India/ Malayalam, Tamil, Hindi (with English subtitles)

Kalvettukal is a multilingual docu-fiction film about transgender men in south India. The film, through its three chapters, explores the lives, desires and issues of transgender men. The first chapter of the film, 'Our Stories', fictionalizes the real-life story of Tintu and Swapna and how they fled from Kerala to find freedom to live and love in a less oppressive space. The second chapter, 'Our Desires', through a dream sequence, explores one of the expressions of erotic desires of the community. The third chapter, 'Our Voices', captures the voices, issues and politics of three transgender men

through interviews. The transgender men in
the film emerge as strongly political people
who radically challenge society's notions of
gender, love and freedom.

Kalvettukal is an attempt at writing our own
histories in stone so that they can never be
erased. The film was made using a fellowship
grant given to Gee Ameena Suleiman (who himself
identifies as a transgender man) by the South
Asian Network to Address Masculinities. The film
was made almost entirely by the LBT community
with very little support from outside.

50 went, 6 interested

'Kerala has a way of killing people,' Mangai said. 'Deepu . . . he was . . .
he was just . . . I haven't reconciled myself to that loss.'

His friends remember his pranks. They remember how he would
not stop smoking even in hospital, with intravenous drips attached
to his body, how he would disarm the nurses who smelled the
cigarettes in the toilet. His friends remember how he would make
up impromptu songs and render them with a comical expression. His
friends remember how he would phone them to sing the Sufi songs
he and they loved, improvising for lyrics he did not know with vocal
acrobatics. Deepu in a juice shop. Deepu in a petrol station. Deepu
giving them missed call after missed call because he had run out of
balance from calling everyone he knew to announce that his hormones
were working, that hair was sprouting on his smooth face.

'*Loose-u maadhiri* suicide *pannikuttaan* (he committed suicide like
a "loose-u"),' a friend of his said with a sigh, sounding more annoyed
than bereaved, as if Deepu had got caught cheating in an exam, and
not jumped off the train, leaving behind a mobile phone that carried
recordings of his songs. To acknowledge a bereavement is to surrender
to depression. The only way to stave it off is to deny it happened.
What a *silly* thing to do, suicide. How *silly* of him . . .

The boy who could make people laugh has now made them cry forever. The boy who was such a vital presence everywhere he went is now a memory. He grins out of photographs, and sings out of videos, his posts are still up on Facebook, but the struggles that drove him to his final act remain invisible.

His friends would begin talking about him, and not complete their sentences.

'We used to laugh so much during rehearsal because . . .'

'I pulled up by the side of the road because my phone would not stop ringing, because I had seven missed calls in the space of two minutes (and called back) to ask what the emergency was, and he told me he had found the beginning of a moustache, and I told him to . . .'

'Once he sent me a message about how it was . . .'

They shake their heads and stop. They reach for tissues, try to talk, and then break down. How can they bear to remember Deepu?

I had seen him in video recordings of three plays, one film, and in an uploaded video of one song, his eyes closed. And when I saw him in an old video of the Bangalore Pride, dancing and laughing with one of his friends, I felt my vision blur and realized I was in tears.

You were so loved, by so many people, I wanted to shout to the boy whose mouth is all teeth, whose body is all music. *Why could you only see the hate?*

I feel the grief of his loss even without knowing him. How do his friends find the strength to wake up in the morning?

Home Truths

21 April 2017

'I'm taking part in a fashion show,' Selvam had told me on the phone. 'Come and see us all if you can.'

It was part of an event for the launch of a documentary on transpeople. For the first time in history, one of the organizers told me, there was a fashion show for transmen alone.

In the dressing room, seven transmen, including Selvam and Jovin, were trying on various fluorescent shirts over white dhotis.

'Look at this pimple.' Selvam sighed, squeezing the skin around a tiny zit. 'It will be in all the photographs of the function.' He looked at me. 'Don't laugh. I swear, I've never had a pimple ever before, not even when people were in love with me.'

'You get pimples when people are in love with you?'

'That's what they say. But I never had them, even when I was a "ladies". My older sister used to rage at me. She would pick fights with me. She would ask how my skin was so perfect. But now, two days without the medicines, and my eyes are sunken, I can barely sleep, and everything around my face feels stretched.'

'Why haven't you gone to the endocrinologist?'

'Where's the time? And the money? First there's this fashion show, and then I have to go to my village because my sister's baby's first birthday is being celebrated. There are things I need to do for the baby, so I'm saving up the money. I'm the thaimaaman, after all.' He sighed. 'I have such big problems. My wife didn't want me to go to the village. We had a big fight, and I've deleted all her photos from my phone. Now I miss her face.'

The term 'wife' was used loosely, I had noticed. It could mean live-in partner; it could mean recent girlfriend. Several of my gay and trans friends seemed to take particular pleasure in saying 'my husband' or 'my wife' in a tone of proprietorship, not over the person but over the relationship, the word, perhaps because they had had to fight so hard for the right to use the label. Even years into their partnership, even years after the formalization of marriage, they said it with the delight of newly-weds, as if tasting the word for how it felt in their mouths, and what it meant to them.

'Maybe look at her WhatsApp photo,' I said.

'She doesn't look too great in that one. She hasn't worn make-up.' Suddenly, he looked up and frowned. 'You're teasing me.' He sighed. 'You can delete all the photos you want, but can you erase someone from your heart?'

'Oh, she'll be back. You guys fight all the time.'

'I don't fight. She does.'

He was going to meet his parents in the meanwhile, he said. 'Now that we've broken up, I don't have to ask her permission. My father hasn't been well. He has some problem with his legs. He's over sixty, you know, and his work is very taxing. He has to carry cement bags, and each of those weighs 50 kg. When I go, I step in for him, and he can rest. You have to carry up to eight bags of cement up several storeys. That's what construction is. I would have gone already, but then there's this fashion show, and they're giving me an achievement award.' He slumped his shoulders. 'My wife said she would come with me to see me get the award. She had even bought a sari for the occasion. And now she's gone and had a fight with me. Love is the biggest headache anyone has. The only medicine for a broken heart is friendship. So after I return from my parents' house, I'm going to go to Bangalore and Kerala and meet all my friends and stop thinking about my wife. She used to get jealous when I travelled. Let her feel jealous now.'

∼

18 May 2017

There had been several changes in Selvam's life. His 'wife' was back home. He had quit his job at the terrace gardening company. The work was too difficult, and they did not pay him on time, he said.

'I'm going to be a tailor,' he announced. 'My sewing classes are going well. Now I know how to cut cloth for churidhar, blouse piece, trousers, shirts, everything. See, I stitched this myself. Now I'm going to my parents' house to get the sewing machine back.'

His sisters had unexpectedly arrived at his parents'. His brother Mani had been staying with his parents to help his father out.

'I just want to make enough money to settle my parents down, back in the village.' Selvam sighed. 'I brought them here thinking our life would be better. But my father works from six in the morning till midnight. He gets Rs 1500 a month for "watchman duty". And then Rs 400 a day for labour. If I could make that much money, he could retire and go to the village. My brother works hard too, poor thing. He can't stay long with them. He works for one of his former teachers at the music college, and then takes classes for kids in a school, and also accompanies musicians across the state. He hasn't asked me for money since he finished college. He even bought me a watch.'

'You showed me. As a New Year's gift.'

'No, he bought me another one after that. Our older brother is not like that. He's got a family of his own, and he thinks his duties to his parents are over.' Selvam shook his head. 'Your duties to your parents are never over. I'm in love. So is my younger brother. But we're their sons first. Now, I have to start saving for my younger brother's wedding.'

'Why have a grand wedding?'

'Because people are stupid,' Selvam grumbled. 'To maintain our dignity in the village, we have to do certain things. My brother's wedding will cost us more than a lakh. And god knows how much the girl's family will spend. For my sister, we gave ten sovereigns in gold, vessels worth Rs 1 lakh, and then there were wedding expenses. My older sister only wore three sovereigns' worth of jewellery, but now everyone's spending more on weddings, so we had to. It's not a

question of how much you have, or how much you can. It's all about
how much you show.'

~

We drove into the factory where his father worked. Their home was a
two-room concrete structure in a corner of the compound.

'Selvam mama!' a child's voice cried.

'Selvam mama has come!' another said.

A boy and a girl ran out to embrace him, and a third—the one who
had spotted him first, and was too small to walk without help—began
to wail.

'All of them know you as a man?' I asked, softly.

'All of them. They believe it happened naturally.'

His mother was making dosais for us on a wood stove. They were
used to meeting his friends, he said. The family was 'a social type'.
They liked having guests over. His younger siblings were chatty.

'Selvam, you promised to buy me a fairness cream,' his sister said.

'What are you going to do with it, you're married anyway, and he's
stuck with you however dark you are,' his brother Mani said, with a laugh.

She threw a blade of grass at him.

'Let me show you how everything in the factory works,' Selvam
said, and the four of us set off. As he took me around the gardens,
where his father grew his own vegetables, and then showed me how
the cement mixer was operated, his brother and sister began to argue
about how old they were. She insisted she was twenty-two, twenty-
three at the most. Mani was twenty-eight, and said she was two years
younger than he. They agreed that he had been born in 1989, and she
in 1991.

'Madam, you please calculate our ages in your own time,' Mani
said. 'If you speak to her about maths for more than two minutes,
you'll forget even one-plus-one. My entire family is like that. My
mother has been saying she is forty years old for twenty years.'

'Your mother looks the same as she did when I first met her,'
I said.

'I think she's been looking this way since she was fourteen,' Mani said, with a laugh.

The family did not seem keen to talk about Selvam's transition. They brushed aside my references to it. Selvam had told me I could ask them how he had been as a girl. When I did, Mani shrugged. 'Oh, he used to tease our older sister a lot. He would play pranks on her. He'd fold paper into insect-like shapes and put it in our sister's ear, and she would scream and scream. It was hilarious. They were always arguing and fighting.'

'He used to sleep in our room when he was a girl,' his younger sister said. 'Once he became a guy, he went and slept outside, with the other two boys.'

'He is the only one of the boys who wasn't beaten up,' Mani added. 'He escaped it. He has only been beaten once by my father. Our father dotes on the girls. He used to buy mixture packets for them. He said it was because they would have hard lives once they got married. Their lives are pretty smooth after marriage. Wasn't worth our sacrificing the mixture.'

'You want us to get beaten up by our husbands or what?' his sister asked, and punched him for good measure.

'Well, as long as you don't beat your husbands up.'

'I used to hit her a lot,' their mother called. We had circled back to the house, and she had been listening. 'I didn't hit the boys, and my older daughter is fine, but the younger one gives too much lip. I've whacked her, I've scalded her, I tried everything.'

I sat by her, and asked her about Selvam's transition. She widened her eyes and made a 'hush' gesture, though I had spoken softly. 'No one knows,' she whispered. 'We haven't told anyone here. Sometimes, when the other labourers come by, they say they heard a girl's voice, and ask whether one of our daughters has come home. And I tell them our son has. Then they say they heard a female voice, and I say they need to clean their ears.'

'Were *you* confused when he told you?'

'I don't understand such things. He says he's changed. I have to believe him, right? It's not like I can make him strip and check. Everyone has a right to dignity.'

I looked at Selvam, standing out of earshot, with a niece on his shoulders.

'Your haircut looks stupid, Mani,' he was telling his brother. 'I'll get you a good one once we return to Madras.'

'I want to ride on Mani mama's shoulder now!' the child said.

His mother was smiling at them, the two sons playing piggyback with their sister's child.

～

'Your family's fun,' I said, as we drove back.

'My family doesn't know I've been taking hormones. Or that I've had surgery. I did tell you I don't like fooling people, but sometimes you don't have a choice. It's hard to explain to people who won't understand. I'd rather lie to my parents than break their hearts.' Selvam looked at me, and added, 'But don't worry about me. I have another family. My friends. I had grown up thinking I was a freak, that there was no one like me in the world. Meeting them has given me my life back. And then there was my Paatti. She's the one who started *Kannaadi Kalaikkuzhu* for us.'

'Are you talking about . . . Mangai?'

'No, no. Her name is Mina.'

'Mina Swaminathan?'

Selvam looked at me in surprise. 'You know her?'

I did, as did most people involved in theatre. She has been an innovator in the dramatic arts for years, even taking theatre to kindergarten children as an educator. She is also the wife of geneticist and agricultural scientist M.S. Swaminathan, the architect of India's Green Revolution.

'I have to take you to meet her,' Selvam said, delighted. 'She'll be thrilled that you're my friend. I introduce all my friends to her. Sometimes, I think I take them along because her experience and her insight will tell her whether they are good people or bad, and she will tell me what she thinks. At other times, when I feel particularly confident about my judgement, I think I take them along so that she will be reassured I am in good company. I'd like her to be proud of me.'

～

My Paatti

Our plays would trouble people, make them feel ashamed, make them think differently about us. But we were also reliving our worst experiences. Each time we enacted those stories, in rehearsals leading up to the performance, some of us would break down.

I was a man, and I pretended I did not cry.

But then Paatti—who had not only started the group for us, but got us a grant so that each of us was given a salary—saw me blinking back the tears. She came and hugged me. It was the first time someone had hugged me. I had never let my mother or father or brothers or sisters, or anyone else for that matter, hold me close. I did not do hugs. But when my Paatti hugged me, something broke inside me. The tears I had held back all these years began to fall out of my eyes, on to her shoulder.

'Don't worry,' she told me. 'Your Paatti will be there for you, always.'

And she has been. She was the one who insisted I take money from her for my surgery. I know her family is a prominent one. I don't know what each of them does, but many of them live abroad and they all speak English. We have this prejudice that people who speak only English think no end of themselves. But they are all very kind. She has nothing to gain from me. People like that are usually wary of the world, worried that everyone is looking to take advantage. But my Paatti is not like that.

I told you I was going to Gujarat to have the surgery. She asked me to get her the name of the doctor. She vets everyone for me.

~

Blessings

'Do I look smart?' Selvam asked, as he climbed into my car. 'I have to look smart. This is the first time I'm going to meet Paatti after my surgery.'

'Hasn't it been a year and a half?'

'Yes, but I wanted to make sure I looked healthy. And by the time I got my health back, it had been six months. And then I felt it had been too long. I'm only able to go now because you're coming with me. Otherwise, I'd be too ashamed.'

Mina Swaminathan had been waiting to receive us. When she saw Selvam, her face melted into a smile, and she drew him into a long, warm hug. He grinned, and mouthed to me, 'Didn't I tell you?'

'He doesn't have a choice,' she said to me. 'When he sees me, he has to be hugged.' She sat him down and touched his chest lightly, 'Has hair grown here? Are you able to keep your shirt off like you wanted?'

'I have been off hormones for a while,' he said, shyly. 'There was a problem with my blood count.'

'What kind of problem? Is it too low?'

'I'll be all right. I've been eating well.'

'Have you started saving money for the surgeries you'll need?'

'I have . . .' Selvam hesitated.

'How much?'

'About . . . ten thousand.'

We stayed for an hour and a half. Selvam was loath to leave. 'I'll come see you soon, Paatti,' he said. 'When this book about me comes out, you must be there for the launch.'

As we left, his Paatti gave him a little card. 'Your Paatti's *aasirvaadham*,' she said. Blessings.

In the car, Selvam said, 'Did you notice she smiled in a certain, knowing way when I told her I had saved money? She knows I lied. I feel ashamed now.' He opened the card. A smaller envelope had been taped to the inside. There were several crisp notes in it, which he held out to me.

'See? I knew she would do something like this. I'm not going to spend this. I will keep them with me forever. They will be reminders of my Paatti's generosity and her love for me.'

Voicing Silence

Mina Swaminathan and A. Mangai had met in 1992, when the former moved from Delhi to Madras. Mangai had been involved in theatre over the past decade, and Mina quickly became part of the theatre scene in Madras. She would conduct workshops in Alliance Française and Max Mueller Bhavan regularly. Mangai was part of the Left movement, and had been asked to produce a play for a conference of the All India Democratic Women's Association (AIDWA). The AIDWA's rules mandated that the actors would have to be delegates of the conference. And so she requested Mina to conduct a workshop for them.

'We chose a play called "Manalur Maniamma", later renamed "Chuvadugal", which I'd adapted based on the novel by Rajam Krishnan,' Mangai said. 'I didn't feel confident enough to direct it, so I asked Mina to come on board.'

Their first play was strangely prophetic of the work they would do much later. It tells the story of a child widow, who refuses to be defined by her widowhood, cuts her hair into a stylish crop, wears dhoti and *bunyan* (vest) with a red towel on her shoulders, and rides a cycle to go out and work. Through long and often exhausting journeys from home to the rehearsal space, Mangai would tell Mina how there was a need for more women to take to the stage. They discussed new, experimental forms of storytelling. Why did the main character have to be played by one person? What if they had various women playing her? Their conversations evolved into the Preamble for a theatre group they would start together, Voicing Silence. Mina urged Mangai to make a presentation for prospective funders, whom she arranged to meet.

'We got the funding. It was some insane amount like Rs 2 lakh a year, at *that* time, in the early '90s, can you imagine?' Mangai laughed.

They worked with Dalit women, with construction workers, with students, with various marginalized groups, producing at least a play a year from 1992 to 2003. Many of these plays were professionally recorded, and the scripts published. They tackled issues including caste, female infanticide and foeticide, and exploitation of labour.

Around 2000, Mangai began working on the story of Amba and Shikhandi. She did not see it as gender transition, so much as the construction of gender into femininity or masculinity. One aspect of the story was the idea of moulding the male body into a masculine body. The other was desire. Amba was driven by anger, but the basis of her anger was desire, Mangai pointed out—desire for her lover Salva, desire for marriage to a man, which prompted her to ask Bhishma to do the honourable thing and marry her. So there was Amba's longing for sexual fulfilment on the one hand, and Bhishma's glorified celibacy on the other. He believed curtailing his desires was a virtue, almost a religion. Amba, however, saw it as yet another curse, yet another curb on the life of a single woman, this frustration of her libido.

'It was new in feminist discourse in India at the time,' Mangai said. 'We've never talked about sexuality and desire. The discourse was more about violence, about being a victim. It's the year 2000, we're discussing HIV and AIDS, and it's clear that people are not having monogamous relationships. We began to explore desire, and when you're looking at sexuality, you can't restrict yourself to heterosexuality.'

Around this time, two transwomen activists—Shabeena Saveri and Priya Babu—were considering options for a cultural programme around the Koovagam Festival, which had suddenly become famous after interest by international television channels. A common friend introduced them to Mangai. Shabeena was based in Bombay and Priya in Trichy. They came to Madras to meet her.

It was Voicing Silence's first interaction with transpeople. Despite being progressives, both Mangai and Mina had several preconceived notions about transpeople and recall their reservations. They had seen only two avatars of transwomen—they either begged on the streets, or sold their bodies for sex. On Priya Babu's invitation, they travelled to the jama'at to meet her 'sisters' and 'mother', Mohanamma. To their surprise, Mohanamma and her chelas were involved in a small business enterprise.

'They were selling this hair oil,' Mangai said, with a smile. 'And Priya had long, lovely hair, so she was the model.'

They met a small group of transwomen, and found six–seven people who were interested in working on a play. They could dance, they could sing to some extent, but they were not sure they could act or deliver dialogue.

Mina and Mangai asked them to think about it. Voicing Silence was happy to produce a play and train them. 'Let them take the initiative and approach us,' Mina told Mangai, as they left. 'We'll need to rehearse for weeks, and we can't keep coming here if they're not interested.'

Eight months passed before Priya contacted them again. At the time, she had filed a case at the Madurai High Court, demanding election identity cards that had a 'Transgender' category under 'Sex', so that transpeople could vote. Priya was keen on using theatre as a campaign vehicle to draw attention to transwomen, to make the world see them as people with jobs and aspirations and talent and dreams.

The play was called 'Manasin Azhaippu (Call of the Heart)'. The story was that a kingdom is ruled by a queen. It was a cheeky parallel to the situation in Tamil Nadu, where Jayalalithaa had won the election in 2001. In the play, the citizens approach the queen to ask for identity cards. When the queen looks at their certificates and then at them, she begins to laugh—what are these women doing with certificates that bear male names? Each of them begins to tell the queen her story—birth, upbringing, the teasing at school, the trauma at home. The queen was played by Diana.

I had met Diana briefly more than a decade ago, a couple of years after the play was staged. She was weak, and her once-beautiful features had been ravaged by HIV. We bonded over our crushes on Kamal Haasan. I told her I only dated men who at least vaguely resembled

Kamal Haasan in *Sathya*, and she laughed and held her hand up for a high-five. Then she hesitated, as if she was not sure I would touch her. When I high-fived her, she held and squeezed my hand.

'I keep thinking, if I were a woman like you, I would have got married and had children, and perhaps my daughter would have been sitting with us and laughing too,' she said, wistfully. 'I would not have had to do sex work, and I would not have got AIDS.'

'Diana was so beautiful,' I said to Mangai.

'She was. And she did such a brilliant job.'

The rehearsals came with challenges. Mina and Mangai asked them to wear loose clothes, preferably T-shirt and pyjamas, or kurta and pyjamas, but they refused.

'They said they can even do somersaults in saris, but they would not wear anything but (the) sari, because they had fought so much to wear it,' Mangai said. 'It was a fascinating experience.'

For the first time, they had an insight into the problems of transpeople, beyond transition alone. Housing was a challenge. The rent was always doubled when transwomen wanted the house. People assumed they would turn their houses into sex dens, and did not believe they were doing other work to support themselves.

'I thought this was a *civic* responsibility. The Kerala government's Kochi Metro employment initiative failed because they didn't have support from society, and these women couldn't find accommodation. How do you survive? You *need* to create a discourse in the society. It's not just enough to talk about the right and the wrong and to ask for political rights. It's important to educate the rest of the society,' Mangai said.

The songs in the script had been penned by playwright Inquilab. The play ends with a chorus of the line: 'If our identity rests on that single organ, we stamp our feet on this civilization and walk away.'

The backdrop was a wall of false hair, about three and a half feet long. In the final scene, the transwomen would move through the false hair, and plait it as they spoke.

The play travelled across the state, was performed at various festivals and even in public spaces, and documented by Tamil writer

Ambai for her women's collective SPARROW. The play even aired on the Tamil channel Win TV.

The court's judgment on the voter identity cards was favourable. The transwomen then approached the collector of Kanchipuram district to ask for land in Bukkathurai, and the Natarajapuram settlement was granted.

Mangai left on a Fulbright scholarship soon after. When she returned and got back in touch with Priya, she found the group in disarray. Several of them were depressed. They had been given land, but not enough money to construct houses. They had borrowed money, and literally built them with their own hands. Several had lost some of that most precious asset—their hair—from bearing vats of sand and stones on their heads.

They wanted a distraction from their trauma. And thus began the conception of 'Urayaadha Niniaivugal (Unsettling Memories)'.

This time, there was an addition to the group—Selvam was the first transman both Mina and Mangai had met. He lived with the group of transwomen, who worked with Sudar Foundation. Mina and Mangai were used to transwomen and their sensitivities by now. But they had to change their vocabulary for Selvam. If someone were to use the female pronouns in referring to him by accident, he would throw tantrums. It was a challenge even for the transwomen in the group, who tended to use male pronouns mainly as insults.

The story was this: a 'Best Family' contest was announced; contestants would have to send in photographs of their families, with a story, and the best would win. The transwomen in the jama'at and Selvam begin to talk about their birth families, showing photographs. Since the actors would find it too painful to narrate their own stories, the directors devised a way out—they would enact each other's stories. But in Selvam's case, this was impossible. None of the transwomen wanted to play a transman. And both Mina and Mangai felt the poignancy and humiliation of having to wear female clothes or having a period could not be conveyed by a transwoman, who longed for both.

They held several discussions on how to handle Selvam and his story. During rehearsals, he got his period for the first time in months and bled heavily. But he refused to wear sanitary pads. Each time he had to pull on the skirt, he would break down.

Once, when he crumpled up and lay down on stage, sobbing, Mina held him for several minutes.

'Do you want to remove this piece?' Mangai asked him. 'We don't have to include your story if you don't want to.'

He looked at Mina. 'What do you think, madam?'

'Call me "Paatti",' she said. 'I think people should know about these problems. None of us knew before we met you.'

'My Paatti wants me to do this,' Selvam said, drying his eyes. 'I will do it. Other people should know we exist.'

Mangai told me, 'I still remember this performance, where we had taken them to LesBiT in Bangalore. And for the first time he met other transmen—Sunil, Sonu, Charupriyan . . . and that day, he just couldn't pull on the skirt. He broke down, like that, on stage. He couldn't do it. Everyone in the audience began to cry too. Some of them said we shouldn't have made him enact the story. But that day seemed to change him. That was the last time he cried. We travelled to Delhi, and he wanted to enact the story, and he could go the distance.' She paused, 'I think . . . sometimes, I think, in theatre, because you're doing it live and opening your wounds in public, it's huge, you know. I still haven't figured out how to deal with accountability. Someone trusts you with their story. And you want to show it on stage. But what impact does it have on the actor?'

'I always knew he could do it,' Mina said. 'He is strong. And it is an important story to tell. People like him, they are rare. They are hidden. Unlike male-to-female, they can't come out and form a group. It's too risky, too dangerous. Selvam has taken a lot of risks in his life. He worked as a construction labourer. You know, if he'd been caught . . . if he'd been found out, then . . . you never know.'

'I remember him telling me, "*Vera vazhi illaame naan ivunga kooda irukkavendi irukku* (I have to stay with them because I have no choice),"' Mangai said. 'Because there is no jama'at for a transman and there's no guarantee of safety.'

Selvam would often tell me his Paatti gave him the courage to tell his story.

'He always wanted to act,' Mina said. 'And he had a story to tell. I met a few other transmen later—very few. But they would come for a short while and then leave. Selvam somehow stayed on. There are fewer restrictions on transwomen, because there's a tradition. There's an acceptability about them. Of course, you're divorced from the rest of the social world, you live in their world. But whatever it is, you're accepted *somewhere*. His was an interesting case because he was this biological woman, surrounded by aravanis who were very protective, who looked after him, who saw his plight as worse than theirs. But they used to wonder how long they could keep him with them. They're not well-off. It was hard for him to find a job too. And there are so many expenses. He needed to save up too.'

They received a windfall through the theatre grant. They were increasingly enthusiastic about the play, and no longer seemed like amateurs.

'It wasn't hard to make them tell their stories,' Mina said. 'The material was all their own. I think, when you feel strongly about it, it's coming from you, then the feelings are already there. It's not that you're learning a play and acting. But it would vary a lot, from performance to performance. And every flash of improvisation would elicit responses from the others. They were never rattled.'

The gig seemed promising. Their performances were received well, and the grant was extended.

'People found it interesting that a group of transgender women and men were doing theatre. They were invited to a lot of places,' Mina said. 'Various NGOs called us. But then they weren't able to sustain it. For one, not all of them are equally talented. And then there's a lot of movement. Many of them go back to their villages. We were hoping to find a leader within the group, someone who could source plays, and then help them develop the play . . . but then, they lead such fragile lives, they would not always find the time to commit. And there were tensions within the group—people would fight with each other and then not be able to work together. Someone would suddenly walk out. It was a floating group. I wish it could have lasted. Theatre is a powerful tool. You can get anything through to the audience using it.'

The group disbanded organically, but some of them stayed in touch with Mangai, and others with Mina. Both of them went out of their way to stay in touch with Selvam, because they worried about him.

'One very nice thing about his family is that they have been so supportive, they have helped him,' Mina said. 'His parents took care of him, they lived with him, they kept house for him. So he is able to survive. Without a group, without somebody around you, without people with whom you can live and work, it's difficult to survive. That's why it was so important for him to get his surgery. He would be less vulnerable.' She touched my arm. 'Do you know if he's earning well now?'

'Not very well, ma'am.'

'Because the other surgery, the bottom surgery, is very expensive.'

'I believe it would cost at least six lakh rupees.'

'And he doesn't have that kind of money.' She looked grim. 'There is no other way but to get the surgery to protect yourself. So that you can get on with the business of living. You can survive, do some work, earn a living, make friends, live, eat, try to lead a life. For all of this, you need to be working. So you have to really survive in the working world. So the kind of clothes that you wear, the kind of job that you choose . . . all these are factors. And what he was doing, the construction—it needs a lot of skill and practice and determination and courage.'

Validation

24 May 2017

Keerth was happy that day.

He had gone with two of his friends from the group, a gay couple, to a village an hour and a half's drive from Madras.

'It was so beautiful,' he said. 'There were these baby goats who came to suckle our fingers. The mother had three, and there was not enough milk to feed more than two.'

After the long ride and a walk in the fields, they had had a heavy lunch and Keerth had fallen asleep across the bonnet of their car.

A watchman had struck up a conversation in Tamil with the couple, of whom one was not a Tamil speaker and—tired from the journey and lunch—decided it was simpler to nod in agreement than try and understand and respond.

'How much do you earn?' the watchman asked. He nodded.

'Fifteen–twenty thousand?' the watchman asked. He nodded.

'I thought it would be twenty–thirty?' the watchman asked. He nodded.

'Or thirty to thirty-five?' the watchman asked. He nodded.

'*Unga payyanaa* (Your son)?' the watchman asked, gesturing at the sleeping Keerth. He nodded.

His partner began to laugh. Keerth woke up, and was told the story. The validation of his gender left him so happy he couldn't stop smiling all the way back to Madras.

26 May 2017

We were sitting in the canteen at IIT. Keerth kept grinning on and off.

'You know, a very interesting thing happened,' he said, and then smiled enigmatically.

'You and your build-up.'

He laughed. 'Build-up is very important.'

'Oh, spill it.'

He had received family support from an unexpected source. His uncle had recently found him on Facebook, under his assumed name.

'Suddenly, he "Like"-ed one picture. I freaked out. How did he find me?'

He checked their list of mutual friends. There was only one—a transman whom he knew.

'I asked him how he knew my uncle, and he told me he'd been renting a room from my uncle and aunt for ten years, and they were very supportive. This guy told me I should come out to my uncle, he would be sure to understand. But you never know—what people can accept in tenants or neighbours, they may not with relatives.'

He did not speak to his uncle, but his aunt called him one day and after making insipid conversation for a while, blurted out, 'Do you have some hormone problem?'

He didn't know what to say.

She went on, 'You've cut your hair?'

'I told her I would explain everything to her when we met, but these ladies can't take suspense, no?' he said, and then suddenly looked sheepish. 'Sorry, no offence to you. I didn't mean to generalize. Anyway, finally I told her I've been having some hormone trouble for two–three years. And then she said, "I remember, even as a child, you used to speak about pretty girls all the time." It's funny, you know. My dad and I used to check out girls all the time. I used to brighten up when I saw pretty women, and I'd tell him I wanted to make friends with them.'

'And he didn't think it was strange?'

'I don't know. I think it just didn't strike him,' Keerth said, with a shrug.

His uncle and aunt began to call him by his male name. But once, his uncle had accidentally used his feminine name, and it upset Keerth enormously.

'I was wondering why. For twenty years, people only called me by that name. Why does it hurt so much now? But it does. I try to rationalize, and say it's not a big deal, but I feel that twinge.'

He wasn't sure he could handle working at a company where people would address him by his female name. He did want a job immediately after college, so he could save money to transition, but perhaps it would be more sensible to freelance, he said. The pay would not be as good, and it would be harder to find a job outside campus recruitment, but he would rather join a company with a complete male identity, in all his documents. He had friends who were transitioning while working, and they invariably had a hard time.

~

18 June 2017

My wonder woman . . .
To the girl who made me smile
#mybaby

#எனதழகியே
என் உதடுகளுக்கொரு புதுவளைவு கொடுத்தவளே
உன் சுவாசத்தை மறக்க மறுக்கிறேன்...
என் அர்த்தமில்லா மின்கலத்தின் எரிபொருளாய் வந்தவளே
உன் சிந்தனைக்குரியவன் நானாய் உலாவுகிறேன்...
என் அவள் உன் அவன் நாம் புதுவிந்தைக்காவியமாவோம்!

To the girl who made me love
To the girl who made me live

To the girl who makes me complete♥♥

'Love-aa? ;-)' I texted.

'Aama,' Keerth texted back, 'I'll tell you in person when I meet you at Pride.'

The Taste of Prejudice

'He's a character,' a mutual friend who was going to introduce us had told me. 'Either he will love you or he will hate you.'

He was lying on a hospital bed, a sheet drawn up to his waist, when our friend led me in. She was his card-carrying attendant, and she gave me a suspicious look when I entered. He did not seem to hate me. He smiled, and when I told him I'd just come to see him and wish him luck with the recovery, he said, 'You came to see a patient without (bringing) even sweets?'

'You're not allowed to eat outside food,' she interjected.

'At least sit with me for some time. I'm so bored.' He smiled.

He had had a mastectomy a few months earlier, a car accident a few weeks earlier—he showed me pictures of the crash with some triumph—and had just had the first of his uro-genital reconstruction surgeries. He had also brought a friend along to the hospital—a friend who had opted for a free SRS through the Kerala state government's scheme, which had been terribly botched and caused him severe, even debilitating, discomfort and infection.

'But our friend will not give any interview,' she said.

It was pointless to explain that I wasn't hoping to wheedle an interview, but that I wanted to meet the friend because I was worried about his health after what I had read. And perhaps I wanted to reassure him that strangers cared. She wasn't inclined to believe anything but the worst of anyone.

'He doesn't want to *meet* anyone either,' she said shortly.

'(The) last time media people met my friend, (they said) it was just an informal chat, and then put up his details and pictures from Facebook without his permission,' he explained.

'Like all of us, our friend also has his privacy settings,' she added, unnecessarily, I thought. 'And everyone misquotes us. When I came out . . .'

'Came out as in . . .?'

'As trans.'

'Oh! I thought you were cis,' I said. She was small and wiry, with sharp features and a feminine voice. She pursed her lips, and I wasn't sure whether she was flattered or contemptuous.

He told me he had heard about the book I was writing.

'Why exactly are you writing the book?' she asked.

'Well, I guess a lot of people don't kn—'

That was as far as I would get.

She interrupted, with an exasperated sigh, 'Everyone says they're writing so that people will know about the community. They know everything about the community. They just don't want to accept.'

He smiled as I tried to explain that the community to which I was referring was transmen, not transwomen.

Our mutual friend, who had been silent for some time, suddenly asked, 'Do you think transmen are softer because we are born female?'

'I've been wondering about that,' he said, with a smile. 'Right now, I'm doing research. I'll tell you in six months.'

Her face reminded me of a meme I had seen on 9gag: 'I may look calm, but in my head I've just punched you 99 times.'

Aloud, she said, 'We won't say anything on record. We have got multiple death threats for speaking about the surgery that went wrong. I have spoken about transwomen's issues and got death threats.'

It appeared they had enemies both within and outside the community. She spoke about various things on which I was not to quote her, and dismissed most of what I said as 'conspiracy theory', including the much-reported culling of street dogs in Kerala.

'But Jose Maveli . . .' I began, referring to a politician-priest who prided himself on killing street dogs.

'Pffft,' she said, and turned to him. 'Look, she's an intellectual and she believes whatever she reads in the papers.'

In response, he said, 'I *hate* Kerala.'

'I love Kerala,' she said staunchly.

'Because you don't live there, my dear,' he said, grinning. 'But I was outside Kerala for twenty-five years. I still hate it.'

'Twenty-five years? How old *are* you?' I asked.

He smiled. 'Guess.'

I had thought he was in the vicinity of thirty. It turned out he was forty-six.

'I have fought so much in life,' he said, with a sigh. 'Now I just want to get married and settle down. I'm looking for a wife.' A nurse came in to give him his soup. He said something to her in Malayalam and she giggled.

'You should marry one of them,' our friend said after the nurse had left. 'They will even take care of you, change your bandages, they know everything.'

'Are you married, Nandini?' he asked me with a wink.

'No.'

'But she has a boyfriend,' our friend said. 'Right?'

'Then I'm *very* tired.' He leaned back with a dramatic sigh. 'I need heart surgery also now.' He then gave me his number. 'Call me when you break up with him.'

I did not dare look at her, but asked, 'Aren't you guys a couple?'

He laughed.

'How?!' She gave me a bewildered look. 'I'm twenty-one, he's forty-six. We're just friends.'

As is typical, that statement was proved false by a series of tabloids, which they contacted to break the news of their engagement. 'Man who became a woman weds woman who became a man,' screamed *Mid-Day*, in a headline riddled with misgendering. They had told me they became friends because both of them used to write for the same Malayalam weekly, but in the tabloid version, they had fallen in love during three hours spent in a doctor's waiting room.

The piece would detail how they shared common altruistic desires—to counsel parents of transpeople—and how they planned to adopt a child. It also went into details of their personal histories, his delight at being shouted at by co-passengers when he boarded the ladies' compartment of the Mumbai local even pre-transition, her ambitions to meet the prime minister to explain the ramifications of transphobia, and before-and-after pictures to sensationalize what hormones and surgery had achieved.

And so it was that when I called him, it was not to announce my break-up but to congratulate him on his engagement.

'I knew you were too intelligent not to find out,' he said, with a laugh. I explained that it wasn't quite rocket science. The only person who had received a more enraged glare from her than I had was the young doctor who came in to change his bandages. 'Everyone get out,' the doctor had said with a genial smile, and as she began to fluff the pillows, 'You also. Only *I'm* allowed.'

The story would go international, with the *Daily Mail* picking it up in the UK.

This time, the narrative included death threats. In its succinct style, the *Mail* headlined it, 'Transgender couple who met in hospital while awaiting surgery get DEATH threats after news of their wedding plans went viral—but they insist bullies won't stop them marrying.'

This piece said the 'love-struck' couple had been 'bombarded with threatening messages' since news of their engagement 'went viral on social media'. She had also apparently received a personal phone call, cautioning her against giving interviews, or else.

He told me I could write about them and their plans to adopt a child, as long as I didn't name either of them. He also told me people within the trans community were threatening them. 'They're saying we have spread a fake news about our marriage, to make money,' he said. 'None of our trans brothers or sisters is supporting us.' He asked me how much I would pay to write about them. They were happy to come to Madras and be available for interviews if local channels and newspapers—and national dailies headquartered there—wanted to interview them. Could I arrange this for them?

Not long after, one of my friends belatedly shared the first tabloid article. The comments below it read:

'Basically, a man and a woman got married . . . *yeh kya* news *hai* (what news is this)?'

'Pen apply pineapple apple pen.'

'More like face swap on snapchat.'

~

I had often seen ugly comments in response to stories on transpeople, particularly pre-operative transpeople. A story about a British transman, twenty-one-year-old Hayden Cross, who had paused his hormone therapy and put off his mastectomy in order to have a biological child, had several hate comments in response.

'Patriarchy will never allow sex, sexuality, gender identity and expression to be liberated,' Satya said. 'No amount of NGO-ization is going to do it for us. What we need is to work towards a public culture where these are issues questioned, reconstituted and owned by the public—not the state, not the law, not the media.'

Satya had often voiced his concern about the 'NGO-ization' of the trans rights movement. The transmasculine groups on Facebook and WhatsApp have formed a 'life-giving' support network, he acknowledged, particularly in the absence of other social support and absolute lack of familial support, in addition to state apathy. The NALSA judgment had barely been implemented and the Transgender Bill had been consistently distorted in each subsequent version. It was important to fight; but with any fight came the threat of hijacking by vested interests.

'Just like what happened with the women's movement, the radical potential of such spaces will be diluted, career activists will be instated, and the community divided against each other,' he said. 'It will be crucial to see whether any of these spaces will finally hold out or be sold out, in the sense that, will they remain political at their core, or be reduced to just service provision—again, something that in my opinion took the steam out of a potential gay movement in the wake of the HIV/AIDS crisis. I hope we are not going to be reduced to sponsored pride marches, coming out on TV, subjects of sensational "before and after stories" for print and online media, and that the trans discourse can be brought into a life-world of its own and is part of a reality we call "everyday life".'

While doing my interviews, I saw how much emphasis there was across transmasculine networks on 'telling one's story'. It was often obvious to me which of my interviewees had already done media interviews and 'come out'. They had particular ways of narrating their stories, structured and neat, without ambiguities, without vulnerability. It would take several conversations before they began to let me into their lives, let me see beyond the manufactured-for-media version of their 'struggle'.

When I was confronted with the tabloid-friendly version of their stories, I would wonder whether I was falling into a trap with the book. Was I combing their lives for stories, stripping them naked so people could see their wounds? How did one distinguish trans discourse and raising awareness from these coming-out stories, which are increasingly in demand, complete with before and after pictures?

I put the question to Satya, and he told me this could be seen in the context of 'transmasculinities currently being practised in India'.

'Raising awareness with coming-out stories is a "product" of the idea that neo-liberal capital needs to keep churning "identity politics", so that it continuously fragments and reproduces, without ever really raising the questions of historical distribution and ownership of resources in our societies. They are rarely self-aware of these frameworks they land up serving, and it's interesting to see the degree of individualization that they stand for and promote. It's all about "me, my individual struggle for transition", my heroic journey since I "was male/female" and now "am female/male". The coterminous status of the very idea of "coming out" with the emergence of media is so conspicuous. "Coming out" is always "coming out in media", a coming-out which is therefore supremely valued, and which makes "coming out" to family, friends and communities "of a lower status" and "not heroic enough". It mimics the values that have come to inhabit our media-dominated lives. If you are not "out *in* media of *a* certain kind", you are "not out", you are "not a hero", you are "not that valuable" and therefore, you are a lesser human being. It stands on, and perpetuates, a competitive representation within identity politics and remains largely self-serving.'

In such a context, the 'NGO-ization' to which he referred was a peculiar institutionalization of the political, in which it was stripped of its radical potential and aligned with the flow of the movement in media, within the framework of the 'neo-liberal capital'.

It also struck me how formulaic media coverage of LGBTQIA issues had become, a dance between reporter and interviewee with choreographed movements to guide the story arc—confusion and misunderstanding, followed by resolution to face things head-on, followed by professional success and reconciliation with family, followed by self- and societal interrogation. Having imposed a superstructure on every story, could we make space for the truly personal and the truly political?

Closest to a Man

The two transmen had been laughing and joking about their experiences with doctors.

'How old are you both?' a lesbian activist asked.

When they told her, she said, 'Hmm . . . a little young for me, but who's going to say no to tender meat?' They laughed, and she said, smiling, 'I like flirting with F-to-Ms. I think it's the closest I will come to being attracted to men.'

Their mouths were still drawn into laughs, but their faces fell.

Most lesbian support groups have had a quibble—though they see the problems that confront them and the transmasculine community as similar and perpetuated mainly by patriarchy, transmen often go out of their way to distance themselves from lesbians. There have been efforts to form collectives of 'female-born' or 'assigned-female-at-birth' queer people, but there are very few such groups. They include LesBiT in Bangalore, LABIA in Bombay, Sappho in Calcutta and Qashti in Delhi, but other than LesBiT, their membership of lesbians largely outnumbers those of transmen. Do transmen prefer not to associate themselves with lesbian groups to ensure that there is no confusion of their identity, no misgendering?

Karthik Bittu Kondaiah, who is a member of LesBiT, said, 'In some sense, they have a certain founder-effect because of a strong, predominant lesbian identity. Whereas, in LesBiT, the numbers are different, with considerably more transmen than lesbians, and that gives you a different perspective.'

Bittu doesn't think it's fundamentally about a distinction from lesbians, and points out that the converse dynamic can also be problematic. 'I know certainly (of) several transmen, whose lesbian partners have been part of a circle that has made them feel like they shouldn't transition—who have either discouraged their transition or have essentially told them that they find it difficult to be with them post transition.

'And from the question of lesbian interest in transmen, some transmen understandably feel it's a violation of their gender identity to have someone identifying as lesbian to be interested in them. So those experiences also shape the way in which transmen view lesbian identity.'

I remembered how angry Zubair had been when he said, 'Lesbos hit on you.' At the time, I had seen it as evidence of his prejudice against homosexuality; I had not thought about the erasure of his own identity that the romantic interest from lesbian women symbolized.

That said, some transmen—like Rumi Harish—have identified as lesbian at certain points in their lives. It is important not to seek to fit people into neat boxes, Bittu said.

～

Maya Sharma and Indira Pathak from Vikalp (Women's Group) work on queer issues in Gujarat. They call themselves a feminist group that seeks to protect the rights of same-sex-loving women. They have also been working with transmen, particularly in crisis intervention, and intersex people.

The crises with which they deal include 'corrective rape' and forced marriages, transpeople with cis or trans partners who want to elope, and legal obstacles that intrude on the fundamental rights of transmen and lesbian, bisexual or intersex women.

When I eventually met Maya Sharma, I would be struck by her kind eyes, lovely smile, and brilliant comic timing. On the phone, her voice was reassuringly soft but firm.

A long-time activist, Maya has written a book which is considered a seminal work in queer research in India. Her *Loving Women: Being Lesbian in Unprivileged India* (Yoda Press, 2006) tells the stories of several couples and single women who identify as lesbian. It focuses on anecdotal accounts of working-class lesbian women in India— Maya wanted to look at an alternative narrative to that of the urban, Westernized, middle-to-upper-class Indian lesbian. Her interviewees are those who would typically be seen as lacking agency, and she explores how they negotiate space for the expression of their sexuality.

In her introduction to the book, she speaks of a story she came across during her research—a Hindi biography of a woman born in 1925, Narayan Chitravali (Shri Nirmal Narayan Mahaprabhu), published in 1999. The description of the person indicates they could have been trans, but it seemed to me that Maya viewed Narayan as lesbian since she used the female pronoun. Maya writes in the introduction: 'She is described as being of andro-gynous appearance, performing male tasks and rejecting women's gender roles outright. She had been engaged to be married in Nepal but could not go through with the wedding ceremony and fainted before garlanding the groom—her mother had to complete the ritual. She became so traumatized by the prospect of marrying that she was taken to north India to recuperate. She had a tense relationship with her family after this.'

This person was known to have had a partner, from whom they were inseparable.

'I did not see her as lesbian,' Maya would tell me later. 'She was one of the many that made me deeply uncomfortable in painting everyone "lesbian", but in the context at that time—of going back to history to find ourselves, to name those who got lost, to find the spaces that were taken then—I felt "lesbian" was the word that got shunned, perhaps abhorred; and I was "reacting" even through what I wrote. Besides, the vocabulary, or the word "trans", was not what was so prevalent (at the time). It has been a long, long journey in a short time from "lesbian" to including the word "trans" in our vocabulary and in our understanding.'

Maya feels the HIV/AIDS control programmes created the idea of 'MSM'—Men having Sex with Men—as a category, turning a verb into a noun and giving it an identity. But perhaps the word 'male' and the AIDS control programmes that specifically targeted male-born people from the community, had played a part in marginalizing female-to-male transpeople, Maya said, 'once again creating an invisibility of female-bodied persons who identified as men'.

Maya points out in the introduction to her book: 'Indian culture and society have generally viewed the female body as a site for all kinds of action and reaction, but not as a legitimate site for sexual autonomy or personal agency. Women's sexual experiences are generally understood solely within the established parameters of reproduction.'

When we met, she spoke contemplatively of the fact that the literature around women's homosexuality in India is focused on violence—rape and humiliation—and that the pleasure narrative has not found a place in discourse. In the book, she also speaks of her own discovery of her sexual orientation, after marriage to a man followed by childbirth.

While doing interviews for the book, Maya found that some of her subjects did not identify as women and used masculine pronouns 'to define themselves'. But even the discourse around lesbians was fairly new—she had been effectively researching the book since the late '90s, when she had come to terms with her own sexuality. Maya would tell me that she was aware of having a crush on a female adult when she was in her early teens, but she had not had the vocabulary or awareness to root the emotion in orientation. When she did understand her own orientation, she began 'in coded disclosures' to find other women like her. Many of her interviewees had not heard the word 'lesbian', and asked to which language it belonged. She began to wonder: Did they know of transmen? They were led by instinct, but did they find the vocabulary to place that instinct? And was the vocabulary true to their identities?

Maya told me the word 'lesbian' was being used infrequently even among people of a privileged class.

Having been involved in the women's movement and labour movement since the mid-'80s, Maya joined Vikalp (Women's Group) because she saw a need to bring together women facing various kinds of oppression in isolated areas, alone and without support.

She had not been thinking of researching or writing a book. Around the turn of the millennium, the global themes of violence against women and the absence of literature on women loving women had prompted her to look particularly at working-class lesbians, 'as evidence to prove our existence beyond class boundaries'. She had been writing 'in the spirit of activism', compelled by 'the frustration and the deeper feelings the subjects evoke'. The notion of writing a book only came when a publisher asked her.

Maya told me that, in the course of her work, she found that any couple which defied heteronormativity, whether it was two women or a trans- and cisperson, or two transpeople, faced particular kinds of oppression.

In the case of transpeople, there was yet another challenge: jobs were hard to find, and unemployment made someone easier for the family to disown, since s/he made no indispensable contribution. There was societal prejudice. There was no legal recognition. She feels that much work needs to be done at the grassroots level, in rural areas, from finding people who need help, to raising awareness, down to negotiating with the government.

As far as trans rights are concerned, Vikalp has been trying to get the NALSA judgment implemented in Gujarat. An enquiry filed under the Right to Information Act showed that transpeople were not getting any of the benefits to which they were entitled, and barely any of the rights.

For instance, the judgment says transpeople should be granted a pension, but this is yet to be announced by the government, and none of the benefit schemes has been implemented. 'It is a process,' Maya said, tiredly.

We were discussing whether there was any point in expecting the state to make provisions when the almost ironically titled Transgender Rights Bill, 2016 was drafted as callously as it was—'utterly shameless',

Maya called it—and how class and caste played into alternative
sexuality and gender, when she pointed out something that would be
repeated by others in the following months: transmen were visible,
but what about their partners?

'My concern is that there's a lot being written about transmen,
which is very good, but then their partners, somehow, are being
overlooked. Because the tendency is to go towards something that is
very visible. Transmen, in *that* sense, are visible and their violations are
finding articulation very clearly. Even the state's approach is towards
transgender. And so we're looking, I feel, more outward, because it
makes sense, to what the state can give; and not what is happening
within relationships and intimacy.'

She had sensed that transmen, for all their problems, had been able
to negotiate a space for themselves, 'however fragile, however small'.
But their partners remained invisible, less accepted than the transmen,
and she had always wondered why. Did it have to do with the notion of
gender, of women having to be controlled, whereas someone who had
transitioned from female to male was allowed to set his own terms, to
some extent? And did the idea that a woman must be controlled ring
true both to her own family and to her transmale partner?

'It would be interesting to examine the situation of the women
partners,' she said. It would be hard to generalize. There are transmen
who have been forced into marriage to cismen and raped, sometimes
even impregnated. When they walked out of those marriages and
found female partners, both trans and cis, how did they behave with
their partners? What were their ideas of the male–female dynamic?
And what did having a male appearance without 'the baggage of
masculinity' do to the psyche of the transman? 'I think it's important
not to reduce them to a he-ness to be politically correct,' she said. 'It's
a lot more nuanced.'

Transmen have often experienced the difficulties of being a girl
child, because they have been perceived as girls in childhood. They
have experienced the vulnerabilities of the female body. The idea of
being trapped in that body was related to the extent of one's gender
dysphoria—there were those who did not want surgery, there were

those who desired particular surgeries, and there were those who could not feel content or complete until they had gone the whole hog.

'Sometimes, I think it's very crucial to recognize this feeling of being trapped, but also there is this other side, where an opportunity is given to someone to choose, to not be so stereotypically bound in two boxes, of, you know, the male needs the moustache, the aggression and whatever; and that you can be a man irrespective of those. And with such an opportunity, your perspective can perhaps change, and change with age, change with circumstances. I think that gender is as much a changing thing as any other reality of life. Because we often get very fixed. In so overarchingly stating that most people do not change, we forget those who actually change. And then if we talk of rural, tribal people who have not been exposed to the possibility of change, can we then safely draw a conclusion that there is only one reality, one goal?' Maya asked.

Every time I met partners of transmen, I would look for nuances in their reactions—did they betray discontent? Were they happy to play the extreme gender roles their partners typically assigned them because of their own need to feel masculine? And what about the transmen who shared chores, who were keen to establish an equal relationship? How were they seen by the community? How important was surgery to the transman and to his partner? In what ways did surgery change the relationship?

From This Day Forward

'There's this very interesting person called Charupriyan. He's a writer and poet. He drives a cab in Bangalore. Have you spoken to him?'

The house was on the top floor of an apartment complex. Potted plants lining the corridor sprouted flowers and vegetables, and I could smell sambar as I walked into the house.

Charupriyan, solid in trousers and shirt, carrying a whiff of tobacco, greeted me.

'Papa, she has come!' he called.

'Hi!' Gayathri said, waving from the kitchen. She was wearing a nightie that looked new. 'You're joining us for lunch.'

The paintings and needlework wall hangings that decorated the house were Gayathri's handiwork. The furniture was cosy, the place spotless. In the bedroom, two single cots straddled a double bed.

'Sometimes the kids come, sometimes relatives,' Charupriyan said, by way of explanation. I didn't know who the 'kids' were. 'So, do you want to know about my life, personally? Or the lives of thirunambis in general, their sexuality, a woman's attraction to them and so on? Because the thirunangai community is a majority. We are very, very small, and scattered, and people don't know much about us. Right?'

He was quite the orator, and had a way of laying out things simply and clearly, like a schoolteacher. 'The reason for this is simple,' he continued. 'The life of a woman as circumscribed by society and our culture is that a girl should be like "this". So female-borns who want to change into men or live as men, we continue to be dominated.

Whereas male-borns, even if they transition to female, are transitioning from a point of authority. So they set their own rules. That is the main difference between the two communities, and it's important to keep it in mind, though all of us face common problems of prejudice and health issues and all of that.'

He believed the problems with society, with the police, with criminals, with employment, were in some way relieved for transwomen because they could leave home and find a quasi-family in a jama'at that worked as a support system. A chela's guru was obligated to look after her and protect her. In old age, her chelas were expected to provide for and serve her. Transmen had no such support system. They had to rely on themselves. Sometimes, their partners too relied on them.

The lives of all thirunambis were the same until puberty, he said. 'I was always interested in sports. From Classes 5 to 10, whatever rank I got in my studies, I would always win the first prize in every sport. You know, we have made this distinction between male and female sports—what men play and what women play. They were happy when I won at hopscotch or kho-kho or *pallanguzhi*, but they wouldn't like it when I played cricket or football. "They" being family as well as society. So even at the time, this thing of playing with *pasanga* (boys) was all the same. Every transman, as a child, does the same thing: secretly taking our father's or brother's clothes to school or play, changing into those, and so on. The "matter" is in how they have overcome their trials in life after puberty.'

Charupriyan was the last of four children—he had two brothers and a sister. His family was not well-off. His parents had had an inter-caste marriage—his father was Gounder, and mother of a lower caste—and there was some prejudice against them in the village. It was when he began to like Gayathri that he became aware of the problems caste caused. Gayathri was Chettiar, and her mother did not like the idea of her being friends with an inter-caste child.

'You've been a couple since childhood?' I asked.

'Oh, yes, we were in the same class from sixth standard. By ninth, we were in a committed relationship.'

Until Class 5, he had gone to a government school in a village near Erode, established under Tamil Nadu's Ooratchi Onriya Thuvakkappalli (Panchayat Union Elementary School) scheme. The main purpose of the school's existence was to provide a free noon meal for children. He would have to walk six kilometres to the city because he could not afford the bus ticket. His school encouraged him to play sports. For three years, Gayathri and he were friends. When they were in their early teens, he began to sense his attraction for her.

'I didn't have any close friends other than Gayathri, so I didn't know whom to speak to about it. So I told her I liked her. Back then, I remember thinking it was wrong for this thought to be in my head, for me to like a woman; my mind should not go this way. But when I told Gayathri, she asked me for some time to think it over. And within three months, we were writing love letters to each other, slipping them into each other's school bags. We had both filled our diaries with thoughts of each other.'

பட்டுக் கூந்தலில் முத்தமிட ஆசை
சந்தன நெற்றியில் முத்தமிட ஆசை
மீன் போன்ற கண்களில் முத்தமிட ஆசை
ஆப்பிள் கன்னத்தில் முத்தமிட ஆசை
ரோஜா இதழ்களில் முத்தமிட ஆசை
சங்கு கழுத்தில் முத்தமிட ஆசை
கொடி இடையில் முத்தமிட ஆசை
பூப்போன்ற பாதங்களில் முத்தமிட ஆசை

To kiss the silken hair
To kiss the sandal-smeared forehead
To kiss the fish-shaped eyes
To kiss the apple cheeks
To kiss the rosebud lips
To kiss the conch-like neck
To kiss the narrow waist
To kiss the flower-soft feet
I yearn

Charupriyan would visit Gayathri's home after school, but didn't feel welcome. 'She's from a rich family. My father was a coolie. Her mother would make sure I understood the difference in social status.'

But it didn't occur to their families that the relationship was not platonic until, on Gayathri's birthday, Charupriyan gave her a gift. His father would give him Rs 10 a week for pocket money, as would his oldest brother. He had saved Rs 170 over two months, and bought her a night lamp. Their classmates were not used to celebrating birthdays or buying presents. So it became something of a sensation. The teachers learnt about the gift. The students as well as staff began to gossip about the two girls who behaved like a couple. Gayathri's mother stormed into class with the night lamp the next day, shouted at Charupriyan, and then went to the principal to complain.

'The principal summoned me, and asked whether I had bought my father a vest, or my mother a sari. What was the need to spend so much money on a gift for a friend? Back home, my diary had been found. So both of us were caught,' Charupriyan said, with a smile. 'And our letters to each other were rather explicit. In a co-ed school, people are usually worried that boys will ruin their girls. They were bewildered by the idea of these two girls ruining each other. Our parents set rules and made security arrangements. We were not to talk to, look at, or sit anywhere close to each other. As soon as we finished our Class 10 exams, we were shifted to different schools.'

Over the next two years, each attempted suicide several times. 'We were not very good at it,' Charupriyan said, with the same sense of irony that peppers his poetry and essays.

Once they had graduated from school, Gayathri was forced into marriage. Her father had died early, and her maternal grandparents were supporting them financially. Her mother wanted her married off quickly, before the income dried up.

'I went and made this "dialogue delivery",' Charupriyan said. 'I said I don't want all this, I want you, I'm blind, I can't do anything without you, I know nothing else. I felt like I was going crazy. But Gayathri had begun to feel guilty. She said what we were doing was wrong. We had to go our separate ways.'

Her mother—whom he refers to as '*bayangaramana villi* character', a forbidding female villain—had ensured he would not be able to see an invitation, so that he could not land up at the venue and trigger a dramatic turn of events.

Charupriyan considered diverting his mind by studying further. But his family could not afford it. He began to work as a saleswoman in shops. He worked in a readymade clothes shop, 'ever-silver'—local idiom for 'stainless steel'—vessel shop, sari shop, audio cassette shop—'the only one I liked, I could listen to music all day'—and tried to distract himself. He knew Gayathri lived in Erode, but did not know where. 'For two years, I would spend the entire lunch break wandering the streets on a borrowed scooter, looking for a glimpse of her. Erode was not a big city. I had to see her *somewhere*. But for two years, I didn't. And then I found her by coincidence. Of all things, a common friend of ours—who was a neighbour of her mother's—told me that she had come to her mother's house one day, and written something in a chit for her paternal grandmother, who lived next door. What had she written? This girl didn't know. She saw her throw it to her grandmother as she was leaving.'

Charupriyan hatched a plan. He knew her grandmother's phone number. He called from a public telephone, pretending he was Gayathri. 'So I asked her if she got the paper I had left for her. She said she had. I asked her if she had understood what I had written on it. She said, "Yes, your phone number, right?" So she'd written her home landline number for her grandmother, without her mother's knowledge, because those two women didn't get along. I asked, "Did you note it down correctly? Read it out, let me check."'

I gasped, and Charupriyan said, 'Yes, your mind works like a criminal's when you're desperate, no? So her grandmother read out the number, and I noted it down. My entire body was shivering when I dialled her number from the public telephone. It had been more than two years since we had spoken. I could feel my heartbeat becoming irregular. Who would pick up, who would pick up? Gayathri did. She answered, and said, "Hello?" And it had been so long. My throat went dry. I told her who I was. She got a shock. She began to yell, "Why are you calling me? Keep the phone down!" and she slammed down the receiver. But I could not stop my hand. It kept dialling her number, though she kept slamming down the phone. And then suddenly, her mother-the-villi picked up. She began to scream at me, and said nasty things. Gross things. She said, "Her life is going well, stop trying to ruin it. You're a prostitute. Go to a park. You'll find clients."'

Charupriyan could not let go. 'I thought of everything we had been through together, the problems in school, our families quarrelling with each other, the neighbours peeping out of their homes . . . there had to be an explanation. Had she lost her memory? If that was the case, I had to make her remember. And the only way to do that was by calling over and over again.'

And so he did, persistently, until one day Gayathri broke down and said she had a child. Her family was important to her, and these calls could make everyone suspicious. Charupriyan should marry a man too, she said.

முடிந்தால் நான்
இறந்த
மூன்றாம் நாள் வா
காதல் சாம்பலோடு என்னை சேர்த்து அள்ளலாம்
எதுவுமே நிலை இல்லை
நிலையானது எதுவும் எனக்கில்லை
பாசம் வைத்தே பறிபோகுது என் உயிர்
ஆயுள் முழுவதும் உனக்காக காத்திருக்கத் தயார்!
மரணம் போல் நீ நிச்சயமாய் வருவதாயிருந்தால்
காலம் எனக்குக் கற்றுத் தந்த பாடமாய்
கண்ணோரம் துளிர்க்கும்
கண்ணீர் துளிகளோடு
நானும்
கையசைத்து விடைபெறுகிறேன்

If it's not too much trouble
Come visit me on
The third day after my death
Scoop me up along with the ashes of our love
Nothing lasts forever
And I have nothing that lasts
My life slips out of me in measures of love
I would wait my entire life for you
If you intend to come, with the certainty of Death
With the lessons time has taught me
That shimmer as tears from
The corners of my eyes
I too
Wave farewell and leave

'That was the first time I took to alcohol. I would drink in secret, all the time,' Charupriyan said. 'At home, people began to pressure me about marriage. My mother would cry each time a proposal of marriage came. She said it was hard enough that I was inter-caste. I should latch on to someone quickly. I ran out of options. I said yes. So I got engaged to a man.'

On the day of the engagement, one of Charupriyan's neighbours, who had a phone, came running to the house and whispered to him. Gayathri had called that morning. She wanted Charupriyan to call her back. It was urgent. He was thrilled. Surely, it was of some significance that Gayathri had chosen *that* day to call? Surely, it was a sign that the engagement should be broken and they should run away together?

He called Gayathri back, from his neighbour's house. He was willing to leave home. Would she run away with him? No, she could not leave her child, she said. But she needed him in her life. Could they talk on the phone every now and again?

They stole conversations even as preparations for Charupriyan's wedding were under way. He couldn't call off the wedding. It could trigger a series of suicides in the family. And with Gayathri not willing to run away, there was no point. But they could lead double lives together.

'On the day of my wedding, a "thrilling" thing happened,' Charupriyan told me. 'So they took me home, and asked me to step over the threshold with the right foot after the *aarti*, like they ask brides to. So there I am, still garlanded, when the phone rings. And my father-in-law says, "You're the lady of the house now. The moment you stepped in, a bell rang. That is an auspicious sign. Go answer the phone." And I was totally bewildered. I had no idea who it was. It must be a relative of theirs. What would they say? So I picked up the phone and said, "Hello?" And it was Gayathri. She'd got the number from my wedding invitation and called. I jumped out of my skin. My in-laws asked who it was. I said it was a friend who could not make it to the wedding and wanted to wish me.'

Charupriyan's nuptial home was in Tiruppur. Calls to Erode were long distance. As he and Gayathri spoke to each other, the telephone bills began to go up. Their husbands had become suspicious. One day, Charupriyan's husband had pressed the redial button, and spoken to Gayathri's husband. They decided they had to bring their wives 'under control'. The next time Charupriyan called, Gayathri's husband answered the phone. He asked Charupriyan never to call again.

'In the meanwhile, there were major problems between me and my husband,' Charupriyan said. 'I couldn't . . . how do I say it, *be a good wife to him*. You know? My "mindset" was different. We didn't have a "first night". Each time he came to me with the intention of . . . *that*, I was horrified. I was a man, how could I sleep with another man? I can't blame him for approaching me. He didn't know my gender. Gayathri would tell me, though, that there was a masculinity to me, a strong notion of being male. Why could my husband not sense it?' He paused. 'In the end, it happened . . . very . . . with a lot of force. He went and told his mother, directly, that I was not behaving as a wife should at night. So they called a small panchayat. And then . . . there was nothing I could do. It can only be called rape. Rape. Those nights. It was. . . it went on till I "conceived".'

It was the beginning of another nightmare. Charupriyan and the husband had never seen eye to eye. 'My mind was all Gayathri, Gayathri, Gayathri. And his mind was family, family, family.'

Charupriyan was expected to do all the housework, even while pregnant. They had a large house, with no maids. It fell to Charupriyan to sweep and swab the entire house, with a cloth and bucket of water. They had a mop, but insisted on the floor being cleaned with a rag. They had an electric blender at home, but would make Charupriyan grind flour and chutney on a manual churner operated with a heavy stone. The phone was locked so that he could not call home.

'I was biding my time. When I was seven months pregnant, I had a window, when they had all gone out. I slipped out to a public telephone and called my mother. I asked her to advance my *valaikaappu*'—a function where a pregnant woman is given glass bangles, and eventually sent to her maternal home—'and to take me back. I didn't think either I or the baby would survive another two months of this torture.'

When his family arrived, on the morning of the function, they found Charupriyan bent almost double at the manual churner, grinding chutney. Charupriyan's sister was in tears. They could not wait to take him home.

In the last stages of Charupriyan's pregnancy, he faced a terrible dilemma. Gayathri was visiting her friend one street away from Charupriyan's mother's home. She asked him to come over. It would be their first meeting in years. But Charupriyan could not bring himself to go. 'We had been boyfriend and girlfriend. She saw me as a man. And now, here I was, pregnant from another man. It would be too humiliating. I felt tense, guilty, disgusted with myself. I can never forget that moment.'

He was under severe physical strain too. A medical examination showed that the baby was in a precarious position. A natural birth would not be possible. Charupriyan had a caesarean section and was advised three months' bed rest. The slightest strain could cause the stitches to unravel.

But within forty-five days of childbirth, Charupriyan's husband arrived. He was expanding his business, and needed help at home. He had a garment factory, and said he needed someone to count the money to pay the workers—he had had to employ more people.

It was a ruse.

'You know what the work was? You know these panties for children? The ribs have to be sewed on to the holes for the child's legs. So I would have to place the rib on the panties and pass it on to the workers. You had to do this sitting on the floor. And there's no break. Your hands have to literally fly to keep up with the workers' pace. He didn't want to pay someone to do this, and so he made me do it for free. I could almost feel the stitches in my abdomen split, one by one. I had to wake up at 5 a.m., prepare breakfast, feed the baby, and be at the factory by 8.30. I would have a half-hour lunch break at 12.30. At 3 p.m., there would be a tea break. I had to make the tea for everyone. And then I would have to work till 6 p.m. In the meanwhile, of course, I'd have to do the housework, wait on him, sort out the baby's feeds, and everything else. And I had no money, not even to buy shampoo. You know these old movies and the TV mega serials, where the daughter-in-law is tortured, her family humiliated when they visit? This was the real-life version of that.'

After months of this, Charupriyan decided he had had enough, and said the only way the marriage could be sustained was that they moved out of his in-laws' place and lived as a nuclear family. And Charupriyan would no longer work at the factory. A long, intense, angry debate followed. Finally, the husband consented, on the condition that Charupriyan's family did not visit and broke off all contact. Charupriyan agreed. The new house was right behind his in-laws'. There was no telephone and no television. Charupriyan would sit at home with the baby all day, cooking and crying. He would make secret calls from public telephones to Gayathri when he went out to buy vegetables.

'I had no money, so I said I could not call her often. She asked me for my home address, and promised to send money. Each month, she would steal some money from her husband and send me Rs 1000 by post. Just the notes in an envelope, so that I could call her. Hidden inside a letter. I don't know how it reached me every month without getting stolen.'

Once, Charupriyan overslept in the afternoon and did not hear the postman call. He heard his husband come home, and went out to lay the table for lunch. He froze. His husband was fingering an envelope, with the address in Gayathri's handwriting.

'This came by post,' he said.

'My heart stopped,' Charupriyan told me now. 'The letters she would write. If he read it, that would be the end of everything. But that was the day I discovered he could not read. They had hidden it from me, just as they had hidden the fact that he was prone to epilepsy. Imagine. He's holding the letter, and then he passes it to me and asks what it is. I said it was the wrong address, and went and kept it back in the letter box. Only then I realized how useful it was to have an illiterate husband.'

In one of her letters, Gayathri begged Charupriyan to come see her. She missed him.

Charupriyan worked out a ploy. His cousin lived nearby. 'So I spoke to my husband and asked him permission to visit her. I said I'm always at home, alone with the baby. My cousin wants to see the baby, so let me go when you're at work. He fussed at first, but I kept at it till he agreed.'

Charupriyan told his cousin that his husband was not letting him visit home. He wanted to see his mother. Could she look after the baby for a few hours, while he slipped off on a bus and returned? The cousin agreed.

It was an elaborate scheme. Charupriyan would pack lunch for his husband, and ask to be allowed to spend the entire day at the cousin's. He would wear a nightie because the neighbours would find it strange for a woman to wear a sari to walk a couple of streets. He would carry a sari and blouse in a bag, hidden under the baby's blanket, sometimes under the baby. He would change at his cousin's, take an auto to the bus stand, take the bus to Erode, and another bus to go to Gayathri's house. It was a two-hour journey each way, longer when there was traffic. Charupriyan made two such visits. He did not go to see his mother. There would not be enough time.

'The third time I did it, it was almost the last day of my life.'

The husband was annoyed that Charupriyan wanted to visit the cousin yet again. Charupriyan promised it would be the last time in a while. He went to Gayathri's house without event. As they were cuddled together and talking, Gayathri's husband came home for lunch, unexpectedly. Charupriyan rushed to hide in the storeroom.

'He rarely came home for lunch, and when he did, he would eat quickly and leave. But that day, of all days, he settled down to sleep in the hall right after lunch. Not even in the bedroom. There was no way for me to slip out. The time dragged on and on. And I, without making a sound, stood in the storeroom. I had to stand all the time. If I sat, I would be visible. It had no door, only a partition. It was five o'clock.'

'And your husband would come home by six!'

'No. It was Saturday. He would come back only at 8.30. That was my excuse for wanting to go to my sister's. But then it became six o'clock, and Gayathri's husband was still asleep. The thing was, even if I'd left right then, I would not make it back on time. It was seven. This man showed no signs of leaving. Finally, he staggered out. As soon as he left, I began to run. I ran to an auto, went to the bus stand, ran after the bus that was leaving. I finally reached my street at 9 p.m. The baby was in my cousin's house. And I was in a sari. He would ask how I had left in a nightie and returned in a sari. But I had to see whether he was back.'

Charupriyan slipped into his house. His husband was in the kitchen, making dosai. Charupriyan tiptoed back down the stairs. Perhaps the husband had just come home. Perhaps he had been too hungry to go to the cousin's house and demand that Charupriyan come back and make dosai. Perhaps Charupriyan had enough time to go to his cousin's, change clothes, and bring the baby back. He would think of an excuse. He could say the baby had taken ill.

Just as Charupriyan reached the bottom step, his husband called, calmly, 'One minute. Go inside. I'll go to your sister's house and come back.'

'Why, what . . .' Charupriyan stammered.

'Nothing, go on in. I'll be back.'

He strode past Charupriyan, who followed him, panicking.

'I don't know for how long you people have been fucking with me, but it ends today,' the husband said.

Charupriyan was terrified he would create a scene. His cousin would try to negotiate, saying Charupriyan had only gone to meet his mother, surely he could not be blamed? The husband would call a 'panchayat', and Charupriyan's mother would say she had not seen Charupriyan. His mother would also guess he had been to see Gayathri.

'I was caught in the centre of a spider's web. I was stuck every which way,' Charupriyan said.

The husband stormed into Charupriyan's cousin's house and began to shout at the cousin's husband. Charupriyan managed to get a couple of minutes alone with his cousin, and learnt of the events of the day. Apparently, the husband had shut the factory in the afternoon and come to the house, asking where Charupriyan was.

'I didn't know what to say, so I said you've gone to the temple with my brother,' the cousin said.

Charupriyan was relieved. He went and joined the husbands in argument.

'I just went to the temple with my brother. And we dropped in on his mother on the way back. That's all.'

'So where is your brother?' the husband demanded.

'He saw me into a bus and stayed behind with his mother,' Charupriyan said.

The husband wordlessly got on his motorcycle.

'I knew he was going to my aunt's place. It's a forty-minute ride. So I called my mother and said I need my aunt's number urgently. Of course, the first thing she asks is, "What's the problem?" And my tension is rising. I had to call my neighbour to call my mother, and then wait for the number. And then I had to call my aunt's neighbour and ask them to fetch my aunt. And all this is late at night, when people would be asleep. I finally got through, and told her there's a problem, my husband is coming, please tell him I came home with your son after going to the temple and left at 8 p.m. And then I spoke to her son too.'

When Charupriyan's husband reached, the aunt and her son corroborated Charupriyan's story. He wasn't convinced. He swore he would get to the bottom of it, rode back, and went straight to his parents' home. Charupriyan lay awake all night.

In the middle of the night, his husband came home, dragged him out of the bedroom, through the hall, and then across the threshold even as the baby wailed. He locked the front door, leaving Charupriyan on the steps. It had begun to rain. Charupriyan sat, shivering in the rain, hoping none of the neighbours would see him. At 4.30 a.m., the husband opened the door to let the sodden Charupriyan in.

A panchayat had been called. Charupriyan was to pack all his things and prepare to leave the house. His mother had been asked to come to the panchayat.

'I realized that was the day my "case closes". My life had to end. So I doused myself in kerosene.'

'What!'

'Yeah, there was no other way. There was no escape. I'd been locked in, my fate sealed. Under such tension, I didn't know what to do. I was only afraid I would be humiliated in front of the entire extended family. So would my mother. Gayathri's life could be ruined too. So I set myself on fire. My husband came running with buckets of water and put it out. The neighbours came in, made me bathe, and took me to the panchayat.

'They asked me gross things at the panchayat. They said do you prefer *pombala sugam* to *aambala sugam*—intimacy with a woman to a man. In the end, my husband picked up this huge stone, and came running towards me. I ducked just as he threw it. Or it would have been "Govinda. Case closed."

'I don't know where I found the guts, but I had had enough. I said, "Okay, I'm going to accept the truth. I like Gayathri. I want to live with her, I love her. I'm *going* to live with her. Do what you can." My mother was right there. I said this in front of everyone. Because people had got to know. Even if I lied, I would be caught out. There was no point. Then they asked my family to return whatever had been spent on me since the wedding, and all my jewellery.'

Charupriyan refused. 'Your son has not treated me like a woman, leave alone a wife,' he said to the mother-in-law. 'He's used me like a machine. Even when I had no interest, even when I couldn't. Ask him how much he has tortured me. He's a demon.'

Their solution was to dissolve the marriage by breaking the thaali, the gold necklace which symbolized Charupriyan's marital status.

Charupriyan refused. 'Whatever has to be done must be done legally,' he said. 'I'm keeping my son, and I need property for him. I need alimony.'

His mother had been howling and beating her breasts. 'How could you talk to elders like this?' she sobbed to Charupriyan.

The husband grabbed the child and carried him off, asking Charupriyan to fight for custody.

'I ran right behind him,' Charupriyan told me. 'I found the strength to prise my son away from his arms and said, "How do you know he's your son?"'

'Charu!' I gasped.

'There's a reason for that. When I "conceived", my husband asked me for the time and date of intercourse. He insisted we hadn't been together after I had last got my period. He was sitting down with maths that he could not wrap his head around, and would ask me disgusting questions, right until I left for my mother's place for my delivery. And then he said he would not acknowledge the child as his unless he looked like him. So when I said this, and grabbed my son, my mother-in-law said, "Let it go. Like you can't have another child." With another woman, of course.'

'But where did you find the gumption?'

'From knowing I would never see him again. And that was the last time I saw him. I haven't seen him since. Not till this moment.'

Charupriyan then went to his mother's place with the baby. He made a call to Gayathri. She did not ask him if things had turned out all right. Had she not been worried about him? No, she said, she had been at hospital. It turned out Gayathri was pregnant for the second time.

'It felt like someone had punched me in the gut,' Charupriyan said. 'She was all I had left. And now she was pregnant, again.'

Charupriyan decided he had to return to work. He told his family he needed money for his son. They did not object. The job was in Erode, and Charupriyan was able to meet Gayathri often. He explained to her husband that there were problems in his marriage and he had come away to his mother's house. It was not unusual.

'He was a violent man, too, Gayathri's husband,' Charupriyan said. 'A wife-beater. When he was drunk, he would hit her with his belt. So on the one side, she and I were able to meet every day. But then we would spend these sessions talking about how awful our lives were. This went on for two years. My family began to broach the subject of reconciliation with my husband. My son needed a father, they said.'

At this time, Charupriyan came across an interview with a runaway couple in the Tamil weekly *Kumudham*. Nandu and Sheela were from Kerala, and they were being helped by an organization called Snehapoorvam. Charupriyan thought he might find a solution if he spoke to them. But how would he get their number?

'I found the number of *Kumudham* from the telephone directory,' he told me. 'And I knew that I had to speak a certain way. I said I'm calling from the Lions Club and I want to register my protest against these perverse women, who were living in a way that contradicted the laws of nature. I said society would not accept this, and we had to correct their morals, and I was part of a ladies' club that wanted to bring these young women to their senses. They gave me the reporter's number. I gave him the same spiel. He claimed he didn't have their personal numbers, but gave me the organization's.'

Charupriyan felt like he had been thrown a lifeline. He kept trying the number for a week. Finally, someone picked up and spoke Malayalam. Between the speaker's Malayalam and Charupriyan's Tamil, they managed to figure out the situation. They put him in

touch with Sangama. He called Sangama's office in Bangalore, but
the staff could only speak Kannada and English, neither of which
Charupriyan understood. Finally, a Tamil speaker got on the phone,
and put him in touch with a friend of the organization, Shekhar, in
Coimbatore. If there was an emergency, a threat to their safety, he
could help. Shekhar put them in touch with a couple in Palakkad, a
transman and his ciswoman partner. They told Charupriyan that he
and Gayathri were welcome to stay with them. Coimbatore wasn't far
away, and they could travel for work.

Now that they had a way out, Gayathri agreed to run away. They
would leave their three children behind. Charupriyan made Rs 3000 a
month, and had saved most of his earnings. Gayathri was a housewife,
but she had gold jewellery and Rs 2 lakh in the bank account she shared
with her husband. They hatched a plan, over a month. One day, when
her husband was away in Bangalore on business, Gayathri went with
Charupriyan to the bank.

'She said she had to withdraw the entire amount. We lied that
there had been an emergency and her husband needed the money.
The clerk said you can't do that with a joint account. She had to at least
ask her husband to give them the go-ahead over the phone. We said
the husband has a medical emergency, and we're rushing to Bangalore.
We needed the money.'

A combination of tears and pleas and lies worked. They took the
money, packed their clothes, and left the suitcases in Charupriyan's
office. Fortunately for them, Charupriyan had been entrusted with the
keys. Gayathri's husband returned that night. Early in the morning,
Gayathri slipped out of their home, leaving her children behind.

'It was the hardest thing we had done. Her second one was still
nursing. She had fed her, put her in the cradle, and then come out,'
Charupriyan said. 'And that morning, when I was putting my sari in a
cover, my hands were trembling so much I kept dropping it. My four-
year-old son came to me, and said, "Amma, let me hold it for you,"
and held the cover open, smiling, with no idea that I was about to
leave him behind forever. It felt like a stab in my heart. This child had
no father, and now he was losing his mother. I impulsively took him to

a shop nearby, at 6 a.m., bought him his favourite snacks, and brought him back home. Then I told my mother I was going to the temple, and left, with only my purse.'

Gayathri was waiting outside the office. They were both in tears. They went straight to Palakkad, in silence, to the address the couple had given them. The couple got a shock when they arrived. They had not informed them of their arrival in advance. They did not know Charupriyan and Gayathri had children and husbands. It could become a police case. They called up Sangama and said there was a crisis. Charupriyan and Gayathri boarded a bus to Bangalore.

The police were already on their trail. When Gayathri had disappeared, her husband had waited till afternoon, and then gone to Charupriyan's house. Accompanied by Charupriyan's relatives, he went to the police station and said two women had disappeared. The police traced Charupriyan's mobile phone. They saw it had last been used in Kerala.

'So the Tamil Nadu, Kerala and Karnataka police came and found us in Bangalore,' Charupriyan said. 'I don't think so many forces have been deployed even for terrorists. But the despair was mixed with some relief. Both of us were broken at having had to choose between each other and our children.'

They ran away several more times, and left a trail of bread crumbs each time, perhaps consciously. Every time, the police would find them and then wash their hands of a family matter. Gayathri and Charupriyan would be under a house arrest of sorts for a few weeks. As soon as their families trusted them not to run away, they would.

'Finally, I gave Gayathri an ultimatum,' Charupriyan said. 'She had to let me know. We couldn't keep running and returning. We had to choose. She said she couldn't. She couldn't live without me, and she couldn't live without her children. And I knew exactly how that felt. But then, finally, we did run away. And we haven't gone back.'

'The children?'

Charupriyan and Gayathri had forced themselves not to get in touch with their children for a year. Once they were in Bangalore and settled and untraceable, they made calls home. Gayathri's husband had divorced her in absentia and left their children with her mother. He had remarried. Charupriyan's son was with his grandmother too.

'I began to speak to him on the phone, but it would be four years before I saw him,' Charupriyan said. 'In the meanwhile, I'd cut my hair and begun to dress like a man. My mother did not want me coming home. But she would bring my son to the railway station. We would have a meal together and talk. It was worse for Gayathri. For five–six years, her mother would not let her see the children. Then, one fine day, her mother decided she could no longer look after them, and sent the two girls here.'

Their family was complete, in a sense. A couple of years earlier, Charupriyan had brought his son, who was then in Class 8, to Bangalore. Things had improved back home too. Charupriyan's family invited him and Gayathri to family functions.

A couple of years ago, Gayathri's younger daughter had moved back in with her father's family. That was a long story, Charupriyan said. His son had gone back to his grandmother's to finish his schooling. He would likely be back in Bangalore for college. Gayathri's older daughter lived with them.

And how did the children take their relationship?

All of them knew the truth, Charupriyan said. His son hadn't spoken about it. He does get along with Gayathri, whom he calls 'Akka'. He has met Charupriyan's transman friends, and seen them undergo medical transition.

'I told him I too want to change like they have,' Charupriyan said. 'And he told me that's none of his business. He said I should make that decision myself. He hasn't questioned why I'm like this, why I like Gayathri . . . but the thing is, even if I'm a man, I'm his mother. I worry that transitioning will spoil his future. It's all right for us to live here; no one can ask us personal questions. But then if my son were to fall in love with a girl, if he wants to get married, I need to speak to her family as his mother. I don't want problems for him with the in-laws. I don't want them to deride him. Of course, I do want to transition medically.' Charupriyan smiled.

~

Gayathri and I were chatting in the kitchen. She had shown me her plants. *Roja* was playing on TV, and was interrupted by an ad for *Bigg Boss Tamil*. We began to discuss the show, and how bizarre it was for people to lie despite so many cameras being on them, recording their words and actions. One of the contestants struggled to speak Tamil, and Gayathri laughed.

'This reminds me of our initial days here,' she said. 'We didn't know Kannada. We didn't know English. We must have sounded as silly as that girl.' She turned to me. 'We moved to Bangalore in 2005.'

'I just told her the whole story,' Charupriyan said, with a laugh.

'Was it a "deep interview", papa?' Gayathri asked.

'No, no.'

What did they mean, 'deep interview'?

Gayathri laughed. 'So there are all these questions, right? We've learnt to classify interviews, depending on what purpose it's for. For books and articles, they look at an overview, the main points—how did you come into the community, what kind of crisis did you have, how did the family know, what are the problems outside, and how are you now. A "deep interview" is the kind where they want to look at the emotions we underwent during each stage—when you crossed each situation, did you have that "emotional knowledge"? Did you have information or support from the people in your surroundings at that time with regard to your sexuality? How did you feel when *this* happened, when *that* happened? Those are the questions they ask.'

'Doesn't it trouble you to relive it?' I asked.

'We're used to it now. But, yeah, sometimes it can take a toll. How's the food?'

'It's awesome. I particularly like the *keerai* (spinach).'

'I made that,' Gayathri said. 'Charupriyan made the *poriyal* (vegetable).'

I was surprised he cooked. Most transmen, particularly those with partners, tended not to.

'The thing is, we might have had some hesitation in talking to you if we'd been back in Erode, away from this NGO circle,' Charupriyan said. 'But now, we're so used to speaking freely, at events, to the media, on YouTube. You can ask us anything about which you need clarity—I get the sense you're hesitating. You can be *free* and *open*.'

'Also, you're a lady,' Gayathri said. 'Sometimes, men ask questions that seem intrusive. And they themselves are uncomfortable with us.'

Her daughter stepped out of the bathroom and waved to me.

'I think you should interview our children also,' Charupriyan said. Gayathri's daughter looked mortified. When I asked if she would speak, she giggled and shook her head.

'Oh, come on, tell her what you feel. Does it disturb you?' Charupriyan asked. She shook her head. Charupriyan sighed. 'Okay, give me two minutes to smoke.'

Gayathri and I chatted as we cleaned up after lunch. I was struck by how similar her voice and inflections were to Charupriyan's. When I complimented her on the house, she smiled. 'Oh, we're just about comfortable now. He bought the car a year and a half ago. He makes decent money now. For as long as we were working with NGOs, we didn't make much money. We used to have one-room apartments, with a small bathroom. The bedroom, dining, sitting, kitchen would all be in that one room. We could barely keep our kids with us, you know. The ups and downs I've seen in thirty-five years . . .'

'You're thirty-five?'

'Yes. I'm thirty-five. Charupriyan's thirty-four.'

'And your kids are finishing school?!'

Gayathri laughed. 'Yeah, well, eighteen is considered a late marriage where we're from. He must have told you about all the drama.'

'He told me about when he first called you. How you freaked out.'

'Oh, I had completely closed that chapter in my mind, at the time. I thought the relationship was wrong. I'd always felt that way. We can only accept a relationship as "normal", when we have seen it either in the movies or in the family, happening to people like us. But when you don't see anyone like that, the thought persists that it must be wrong if no one else feels this way. And when you're that young, you're impressionable. My mother said, how can a woman love a woman? It is against nature, against society. And I accepted it. I'd forced myself to lose interest in him, to forget him. But when he wouldn't stop calling, I couldn't stop the flashbacks. I remembered how much in love I was. And I fell in love again.'

Charupriyan had finished his cigarette, and we joined him in the bedroom. My teeth had begun to chatter in the cold. Gayathri laughed. 'The weather here is different, huh? Remember, papa, everything was so strange, the place, the weather, the language?'

When they had first moved to Bangalore, the staff at Sangama had told them what they could do to help. They would mediate with the police and their families. They could give them accommodation for three months, and reimburse travel expenses incurred while searching for jobs. They could also fund skill development classes in a field of their choice—basic computer knowledge, driving, or language. And they could give one of the partners a job at Sangama. After three months, they were expected to be relatively independent. There would be other couples in crisis who needed financial and logistical support.

Gayathri took up the job in Sangama. Charupriyan worked with an agency that liaised between domestic help and employers, finding maids and cooks for a commission. He picked up some Kannada on the job, but it was hard to communicate with as rudimentary a grasp of the language as he had. Besides, he wasn't sure how his employer would take to his switching his sari and long hair for the look he wanted—masculine clothes and short hair. So he moved to the NGO sector, first as an office assistant and slowly working his way up to data entry operator.

Around this time, LesBiT had begun to come together. This small group would meet at the Sangama office every Sunday.

'It was fun, wasn't it, papa?' Gayathri smiled. 'We'd talk about our happiness, our problems. And then we began to work on street theatre for awareness.'

'We scripted and rehearsed the plays all by ourselves,' Charupriyan said. 'And they were big successes.'

Rumi had told me, I said.

'We actually got paid for it. Can you believe it? We would perform, and then do a hat collection at the end, and divide the money among ourselves. Mangai madam got involved, and she made sure we were invited to a lot of places. Sometimes, all the money would go to one person who needed it. Like Kiran—you know Kiran?'

'The disability rights activist?'

'Yes, yes. We once put the money into buying a wheelchair for him. At other times, there were other people with emergencies. And we were so successful that we registered LesBiT as a separate organization and came out of Sangama.'

For several years, both Charupriyan and Gayathri worked within the NGO circle. They enjoyed most of the work, particularly crisis intervention.

'Bringing lovebirds together, that's what we like to do,' Gayathri said. 'But the thing with NGOs is, there is always politics. Someone is bitching about you, someone wants to get grants, someone is looking to exploit you, someone wants you to say nice things to the media . . . you can't spend your entire life in the NGO sector. And Charupriyan found it even more irritating than I did.'

Charupriyan took over the narrative, 'So she told me I had to move out of this field. I had to find something about which I was passionate. I've always wanted to drive. I like the idea of driving. But I was scared. But she gave me this encouragement, this support, and it's only because of Gayathri that I realized driving could be a career. And this way, you're independent.'

Charupriyan took driving lessons, got his licence, and then registered for a women's cab service. The hours were long, the workload heavy, and the income was not proportionate to the demands of the job. Almost worse than all this was the fact that the cab was painted a bright pink, to mark itself as a women-for-women taxi. Charupriyan resented being addressed in the female gender, and a pink gender marker was exasperating. But he needed the experience. A cab without a yellow number plate was useless, and he could not apply for a yellow number plate until he had clocked a certain number of hours as a cab driver. A year and a half ago, he had finally saved enough money to make an initial payment on a car, and take a loan for the rest.

He had run it as a cab for a while, working with various call taxi services. The pressure was too much. A driver needed a certain number of peak hour rides, he had targets to achieve, and incentives were dependent on criteria that were almost impossible to meet. Eventually, he attached himself to an IT company. He would be given a fixed salary. He had to ferry employees back and forth from office for particular shifts.

The work was hard. He had to be at the office by 5 a.m. He usually returned home around 9, sometimes 9.30 p.m.

The other drivers at the company appeared to see him as a woman, Charupriyan said. He didn't hang out with them. The uniform is white-and-white, but Charupriyan prefers to wear coloured trousers with a white T-shirt. He is often stopped by the traffic police for random checks, but there is a silver lining.

'They say, *"Ili, appa"*. Get down, man. Which makes me happy. It's the thing most cab drivers dread, because they're going to fine you, but you fine me as a man, I'm happy.'

'But you do look like a man,' I said. 'There's something about you, the way you walk . . . your gestures . . .'

'Yeah, you need to observe closely to figure out he's not a cisman,' Gayathri added.

'The voice and the chest will give me away,' Charupriyan said.

'Oh, please, I've met cismen with bigger breasts than a lot of women,' I said.

'Are you a journalist or a comedian?' Gayathri laughed.

'Both, actually.'

'You know, I always wanted to be a journalist,' Gayathri said.

'And I a policeman,' Charupriyan added. 'I did apply. You know, I even got the interview card. But then we decided to run off to Palakkad, so I threw it away.'

'He didn't tell me at the time,' Gayathri said.

'It was hard enough to persuade you to run away when you were weighing me against our kids.' Charupriyan winked. 'If you added a government job to the mix, we'd never have left Erode.'

'Do you know Prithika Yashini?' Gayathri asked.

I didn't know her personally, but I did know of her. She was the first transwoman to join the police force.

'In her case, she had to show them a surgery certificate and everything. My situation is not like that,' Charupriyan said. Every time we spoke about surgery, his eyes would flicker, as if he was visualizing himself with a flat chest. 'The surgery is far less expensive now. Earlier, it would cost around Rs 80,000. Now, it's come down to between Rs 25,000 and Rs 30,000. This is the top surgery. Even the bottom surgery is being done in India now. Earlier, there were no facilities. I met a transguy from Bombay, and he showed me how they had removed skin from his back to graft a penis. It cost him Rs 20 lakh. I guess you want to brag after you've spent that kind of money. But then, the situation is getting weird now. We'd seen this among transwomen. The ones who have had surgery would call the ones who haven't "kothi" or "pottai". Usually, "pottai" is used by senior transwomen on their juniors. But once you do the operation, there's this promotion of sorts, where you treat others as inferior. I don't want that prejudice to come into our community, but it seems to be slowly seeping in.'

An acquaintance with whom he had discussed it said it was natural. The acquaintance had finished some of his surgeries and was on hormones; Charupriyan wasn't.

'He said, "How can we both be equally male?"' Charupriyan told me, and paused. 'To my face. Earlier, no one questioned things like this. At meetings, when we were asked who was F-to-M, we would all raise our hands. Now I'm the only one. It seems they're all "man", not even "male", they've become *man*.' Charupriyan laughed.

'I keep doing research into all this, in case he wants to make the change at some point,' Gayathri said. 'And there are *so* many complications. You need to make sure your doctor can be trusted, that your body can take it. There are many factors. People are so keen to have the surgery done, they're rushing in as soon as they have the money. Working-class people are spending money they don't have on the bottom surgery. What's the use? The only thing is people can see a bulge when you wear trousers. For that small thing, why take such a big risk?'

'You can't call it a "small thing", papa,' Charupriyan said. 'I may not have such ambitions, but those who want to change really want to. Desperately. Look at the hijra community. They go for so many sittings to get laser hair removal. They change their voices. Get the silicone implants, and do the bottom surgery. It's all cosmetic, but they need it. So it's not an ordinary thing.'

'I didn't mean it was an ordinary thing,' Gayathri said. 'People have various opinions on various subjects. I think there are some aspects to me that are male and some that are female. I feel gender is unnecessary in 75 per cent of the places where it is used. But we bring it into everything.'

'But . . .' Charupriyan began.

'I'm only saying it's *my* opinion.'

I found it admirable, the way they negotiated their way around misunderstandings and disagreement, debating without argument. I had rarely seen such equality and respect in romantic relationships, irrespective of gender or sexual orientation.

'Look,' Charupriyan said. 'You say gender is unnecessary most of the time. But if we don't bring in gender, can relationships work? Could you live with a male? Someone who has a man's body?'

'Attraction to me is not about the body,' Gayathri said. 'I do see you as male. And if you chose to have surgery at some point, I would be perfectly all right with that. I would still love you. You would still be the same person. Attraction, to me, comes from affection, from love, from instinct.'

'Enough "dialogue", papa,' Charupriyan said. 'Gender *is* an important issue. That's why we had trouble with our families, right? I mean, you said just yesterday . . .'

He smiled, and Gayathri began to laugh. She turned to me. 'It's a bit of an adult joke. What I said was . . .'—they exchanged a private laugh—'So I said the penis is not important just for the relationship, but for the society. I mean, the penis can overcome caste, but not gender. You can say your daughter ran away with a man of the lower caste, not with a transman. The first question is, "But *what* will you do?" As in, for sex. Everyone wants to know how we have sex. Both gender and sexuality, in my opinion, are private matters, the individual's or couple's concern. And this longing for the binary, even within the community, is subscribing to the prejudices of a heteronormative society. The very same prejudices and the very same society we wanted to escape. This obsession with our stories, our sexuality, our gender . . . fine, I see that the personal is political. But your politics can't be built around your personal life alone. Why identify someone like that? Fine, it *is* a part of my identity. So is my voter ID card. No one asks me to produce it every day. If you come to speak at a meeting, they won't introduce you as "Heterosexual Nandini", right? So why am I "Lesbian Gayathri"? I didn't like that. My identity is not "lesbian". My partner is male. I've seen that with hijras too. You see them being interviewed on TV, their names are prefixed by "thirunangai". So you're looking at just this label, not the person.'

Because the discussion on trans rights has somehow veered largely towards gender and sexuality, governments believe the only help transpeople need is financial aid for surgery, Gayathri surmised. Gender change on certificates without surgery is almost impossible, despite the NALSA judgment. Discrimination at the workplace is not punishable by law. Unisex toilets are rare. There are problems with housing. And free SRS will not solve any of it. A government cannot be called 'trans-friendly' simply because a free SRS scheme exists, Gayathri said.

'We need to negotiate with the government on other fronts too,' she added. 'Not just SRS. Because the centrality of surgery to everything has made all transgender issues revolve around whether they have had surgery or not.'

The NGO-ization of the movement has left people disillusioned. Even within the trans movement, transwomen are far more prominent than their female-born counterparts.

'When something happens to someone from our community, it's only F-to-Ms who show up,' Charupriyan said. 'But when there's a protest over the arrest or suicide of a hijra, we all go. And when the cops come to chase us off, the M-to-Fs run faster and *we're* caught and arrested and fined and detained. This is NGO politics. That's why it's so easy to get funding for HIV/AIDS projects, it's why everyone is into healthcare for sex workers. People think the trans community is entirely into sex work. Because particular interests dominate the discourse. So when we go ask for rights, everyone says, "What more do you want? We have done *so much* for transpeople." Look at the problems transmen have. What are they?'

Gayathri counted them off on her fingers. 'Job opportunities, language problems, forced marriage, rape, relationship trouble, depression, suicide. Have I left anything out?'

They snorted with laughter.

~

'Hi! I'm Kiran from Chikballapur,' said the voice on Charupriyan's phone. '*Bolo ji.*'

'Dei, you dog, now you speak English and Hindi, huh?' Charupriyan laughed. He would later tell me Kiran usually spoke a mix of Telugu and Kannada, and now clearly Hindi and English had been added to the mix.

'Am I on speaker mode?' Kiran's voice laughed, in Kannada, and then continued in English. 'Okay, you all come to my home tomorrow. You can meet my partner.'

Charupriyan would drive us there, and Gayathri would translate.

'Good, Gayathri, you're doing a part-time job now,' Charupriyan said, with a grin. 'Maybe interpreter madam can do her eyebrows with the money. And facial.'

நான் பிறந்தவுடன்
என்னை ஒரு பெண்ணாய்
அடையாள படுத்தியது
இந்த உலகம்

பட்டாடை உடுத்தி
அழகு பார்த்தாள்
என் அன்னை

உனக்கெதற்கு கார் பொம்மை
பிடி பல்லாங்குழி பெட்டி
என்றாள் அண்ணன்

வீட்டில் கடைக்குட்டிப் பெண்
என்று பாசம் பொழிந்தார் அப்பா

இத்தனைக்கும் நடுவில்
என்னை என்னவாக
அடையாளப்படுத்துவதென்று
குழப்பத்தில் நான்

வயது ஆக ஆக
என் ஈர்ப்புகளும்
உணர்ச்சிகளும்
வேறாக தோன்ற

இந்த சமூகத்தின்
கோட்பாடுகள் என்னை
அடக்கி ஆள்வது போல்
ஒரு மரண வலி

ஆண்களைப்பார்த்து
வெட்கித் தலைகுனிந்து
ரகசியமாய் புன்னகைக்கும்
என் வயது பெண்களைப்போல்
நானில்லை

காதல் கல்யாணமென்று
மற்ற பெண்களின்
வயது ஒத்த பால் உணர்ச்சிகள் இல்லை
மாறாக

பெண்களை இரசிக்கிறேன்
ஒரு பெண்ணென மணக்கத் துடிக்கிறேன்

ஆண் போல் ஆடையணிய
நினைக்கிறேன் ஆனால்
நடந்தது வேறு நடத்தியது வேறு
ஆம்
என் திருமணம் வேறு ஒரு ஆண்மகனோடு

உடம்பளவில் பெண்ணாக இருந்தாலும்
மனதளவில் நான் ஒரு ஆண்
எப்படி

மனதளவில் ஆணாக இருக்கும் என்னை
இன்னொரு ஆணுடன் சேர்த்து வைத்தார்கள்

பெற்றோர்களின் சந்தோஷத்திற்காகவும்
கௌரவத்திற்கும் என்னை
எதற்கு பலியாக்கினார்கள்

இனி வரும் இராத்திரிகளை
எப்படி எதிர்கொள்வேன்
என் பயம் பிரதிபலித்தது

ஒவ்வொரு இராத்திரியும்
ஒவ்வொரு நிமிஷமும்
விஷமாகி போனது எனக்கு
தெரியுமா உங்களுக்கு?

தாலி என்ற அங்கீகாரத்தை
வைத்துக் கொண்டு
புருஷன் என்ற பிசாசின்
காம வெறிக்கு ஆளானேன் நான்

தினம் நித்திய இராத்திரி
தாம்பத்தியம் என்ற சம்பிரதாயத்தை
என்னுள் புகுந்தி
விருப்பம் இல்லாமல் என் தேகங்களை
உணர்வுகளை
சில சில ஆக உடைத்தானே

இதுதானா உங்கள்
கலாச்சாரத்தின் அடையாளம்?

தாலி என்ற அங்கீகாரத்துடன்
கலாச்சாரத்தின் அனுமதி பெற்று
என்னை அணு அணுவாக
கற்பழிப்புச் செய்யப்பட்டது

இதற்கு உங்கள் சட்டத்தில் இடமுண்டா?

பெற்றோர்களே
திருமணம் என்பது அவரவர்களின் விருப்பம்
நீங்கள் பெற்று விட்டீர்கள் என்பதற்காக
எங்களை விற்று விட அதிர்கள்

The moment I was born
This world
Identified me as female

My mother
Wrapped me in silk
And admired its effect

Why do you want cars?
Take the pallanguzhi box
Said my brother

For the baby girl of the house
My father reserved all his love

In the midst of this
I stand dithering
Without knowing what I am,
As what I identify

As I grew older
As my desires, my emotions
Seemed out of place

I felt the mortal pain
Of societal norms
Hounding me, binding me
In a dictatorship

I was not like the
Girls of my age, who
Blushed and hurried away
But smiled in secret
When they saw men.

I did not succumb
To the dreams appropriate
For a woman of my age,
Of love, of marriage to a man
Instead,

I drink in the beauty of women
I ache to marry a woman

I long to wear
The clothes of a man.
And yet what happened
What was set in motion
Was different.
Yes,
My marriage was
To another man.

My body alone is female
In my mind I am a man.
How,

Did they marry off this male-in-mind me
To another man?

For the happiness
And pride
Of my parents
Why was I sacrificed?

How will I counter
The nights that await me?

My fears dawned.

Every minute
Of every night
Turned into poison
In my throat.
Did you know?

For the rights sanctioned
By my nuptial chain
The monster who was my husband
Subjected me to his ravaging lust

Every night
He thrust
The traditions of a relationship
Into an unwilling me
And broke my body,
My emotions
Into bits

Are these the markers,
Of your culture?

With the sanctions of my nuptial chain
With the acquiescence of culture
Atom by atom,
I was raped.

Do your laws make place for this?

To all parents:
Marriage is a personal choice
The privilege of birthing us
Should not license you to sell us

For Better, For Worse

Charupriyan was cleaning his car.

'Gayathri's upstairs, I'll come in a bit,' he called, when I arrived.

Gayathri's daughter was sitting by the plants, studying. 'Amma!' she said, when Gayathri came out to greet me, and then frowned at her. 'Why are you in a sari?'

'We're going to meet a politician, that's why,' Gayathri replied, with a laugh, and then turned to me. 'You'll see when you meet Kiran.' She looked at her daughter, 'Do you want to come?'

'I have to study,' she said.

'Have you seen a girl like this, studying on Sunday, when her mother asks her to come out for a road trip?' Gayathri shook her head. She was unabashedly proud of the girl. Her daughter spoke fluent English, and her Tamil accent had the slight affectation of those who cannot speak the language too well. She wanted to be a doctor, and her grades had been consistently high. There was a good chance she would get into medical college on merit.

'We can't afford capitation fees and things like that. That's why Charu's son had to go back, you know. The fees were Rs 60,000. Back home, it's nowhere close to that,' she told me. 'So we decided to send him back to finish his twelfth. He hates studies. He's a clever kid, he does amazing things with PhotoShop, he repairs all our mobile phones when anything goes wrong. He wants to start working as soon as possible; he would keep pestering Charupriyan to let him drive when he was here. He'll do well as a technician, in anything, mobiles or computers. We want him to finish his twelfth, so he can do some vocational course and then start working.' She smiled suddenly. 'My daughter's marks are high enough to get aid, so we're able to keep her here. I don't know why schools are getting so expensive. It's basic education, right? And if you want to send your children to college . . . it's not easy. We look comfortable now. To a large extent, we are. But there are times when we panic about the future.'

The rent for the apartment had been going up over the last couple of years. They now paid Rs 7000. There were nights when they broke down and cried, worried about how they would make the rent and their children's fees and . . . and . . .

She began to tell me about her younger daughter.

A couple of years ago, she had been hit by a Bangalore Municipal Transport Corporation (BMTC) bus on her way to school. Her leg was fractured in several places. Charupriyan and Gayathri rushed her to hospital, but they would not begin treatment without an initial payment of Rs 30,000. They begged the staff to administer first aid, and promised they would bring the money. But the girl was left lying on a gurney from 8.15 a.m. to 3.30 p.m. In despair, Gayathri called her ex-husband to ask him for money. They had to file a police case because it was an accident.

'The doctor actually told me that unless I made arrangements for money immediately, her legs would have to be amputated,' Gayathri said. 'I went crazy. I screamed and cried in the hospital. Then I literally ran to the police station and began to shout outside. All the NGOs helped us, and there was media coverage. People started questioning the hospital, and then journalists went to the BMTC office, and they were forced to do something.'

They filed a case against the BMTC, and were awarded damages— enough to pay for the surgeries the child would need.

'For all this, her father came and gave us one thousand rupees,' Gayathri said.

'But he demanded that you send the child back with him?'

'He said he should have at least one child. And I felt guilty because I felt I had failed in looking after her. I've always asked the children what they want to do. I don't think it's right for parents to make decisions without their consent. My younger daughter has a soft corner for her father. He spoils her, buys her ice creams, never asks her to study. She's not very ambitious. She wants to get married once she's done with school, and he'll make sure that happens,' Gayathri said, with a wry smile.

Charupriyan had joined us by now, and added, 'Her leg is perfectly fine now. But Gayathri still gets drunk calls from that man, and he screams abuses about the accident.'

'Just yesterday, he called,' Gayathri said. 'We were speaking about you, and we were looking forward to meeting Kiran and Kavya today. And this guy called some four–five times, first on my phone, then Charu's. Because the child is with him, I thought it might be an emergency, and picked it up the fifth time he called. There was a torrent of abuse. Such ugly words, I couldn't sleep all night. He's got another wife now, another child, and then ours too. He's got a family. If he must scream at someone, why me?'

The fact that her husband continued to make appearances in her life was stressful. 'As if we aren't under enough stress,' Gayathri said. 'It takes so much effort to raise our children under such a unique partnership. My older daughter says this is *my* life, and she doesn't know whether she has a problem with our relationship or not, but it is not her decision to make. She goes to visit her father during annual holidays, but she's more attached to me. The younger one was practically a baby, with no understanding of what a typical family structure is and why we're different. She's only thirteen now.'

Charupriyan laughed. 'She used to call me "Appa". I quite liked it. When we'd go shopping, she'd hold up a dress and ask me, in front of the salespeople, "Appa, does this look good?" And Gayathri herself would try to shut her up, but she wouldn't care. She wanted to call me "Appa", so "Appa" it was. And then my son would call me "Amma". And her older daughter calls me "Charu". My son calls Gayathri "Akka", though I tried to make him say "Amma" or "Periamma". With her daughters, I said, "Please don't call me Akka-Lokka. I just want to be called by my name."'

His son is a bit harder to fathom. 'Boys don't really talk openly about these things, right?' Gayathri said. 'Even with friends, their conversations are about music and sports and girls. Not about things that trouble them. So he doesn't interfere in our lives, and he's very friendly to me. I'm often his confidante, and he tells me things he wants kept secret from his mother . . .'

'. . . because he knows I will whack him if he does something irresponsible,' Charupriyan said.

'. . . and he's okay with Charu's short hair and dressing style.'

'Except to functions,' Charupriyan said. 'When I wear a pant and shirt, he shakes his head and says, "Amma, seriously? This is what you're wearing to a wedding?"'

They have begun to come out to their families. Charupriyan recently told his nieces, who found it strange that Gayathri's daughter called him by name, that his life was a little different from those they had seen. 'I said, "This is how I am. Gayathri is my wife. You're old enough to know." I don't know if they will ever switch from calling me *"chiththi"* (mother's sister) to *"mama"* (mother's brother). But for now, respect and acceptance are enough.'

They still felt guilty over running away without their children. What had the little ones felt back then? What had they been told?

'We had been longing for that moment when we would finally be together,' Charupriyan said. 'And yet, we found we couldn't enjoy it. The kids are a very, very big deal. We would be sitting together, holding hands, crying for them. They were the only things on our minds. There was so much guilt.'

It was time to leave. Charupriyan went to an alcove in the wall, which held several small idols—an improvised temple of sorts—and prayed. Gayathri lit the lamp. Her daughter waved to us as we left.

Something about their life filled me with mixed emotions— it was somehow uplifting and heartbreaking at the same time. As Charupriyan kicked a stone aside and got into the car, keeping his legs slightly parted as men do, I had a sudden image of him in a sari, with long hair, pregnant and grinding chutney in the morning. All I wanted for this little family is that they should be happy and safe, I thought.

~

Charupriyan loved driving, particularly on interstate highways, where people mostly followed the rules. 'Back in our village, people cross the highways as they wish and then swear at the cars,' he told me, with a laugh. He would often take Gayathri on road trips. They went to Kerala, where they had several friends. He wanted to take her to Coorg sometime, perhaps Ooty.

'Do you mind if I ask you a personal question?' Gayathri asked.

'It's only fair, since I'm practically writing your biography.'

'How come your parents didn't harass you about marriage? They're okay with your not wanting kids? They don't try emotional blackmail on you?'

'Oh, they married "late" themselves,' I said, making air quotes. 'And a bunch of my friends are divorced. So . . .'

'I think a lot of people get married from pressure. Even love marriages,' Gayathri mused. 'As in, heterosexual people. But if you look at the community, I feel the love is genuine, you know? Because there are no other considerations. It is about the person alone. It's not like, "I make Rs 30,000, you make Rs 50,000, let's get married." Our love is our lifeline.'

Her words reminded me of a discussion from Plato's *Symposium*. Aristodemus has gone to a banquet in Agathon's house, and as a group of philosophically and hedonistically inclined men wonder how to entertain themselves, since they're too hung over from the previous banquet to douse themselves in alcohol again, they arrive at an agreeable solution: instead of 'listening to the flute-girl and her noise', each will make a speech in honour of love.

Of these, I was tremendously moved by Aristophanes' speech the first time I encountered the theory. Professing to 'open a new vein of discourse', he proposes that there were originally three sexes—men, women, and an androgynous union of the two. We were round, with four hands, four feet, and two faces on a round neck. As we rolled about on our eight limbs, we had 'terrible' strength and swiftness, even plotting to climb to the heavens and attack the gods. This left the celestial councils in doubt—they could, of course, destroy our species along with our pride and other follies, but this would entail forfeiting forever the sacrifices we periodically offered to keep them in good humour. Reluctant to sacrifice the sacrifices, Zeus hit upon an idea—they would cut each of us in two, so that we would have only half our strength and the gods would have twice as many sacrifices. He then split us 'as you might split an egg with an hair'.

So that we would remember this lesson, Apollo was ordered to twist our faces so we had to look down upon the gash where we had been cut. So we would not bleed to death, our loose skin was pulled taut and tied into a knot around the navel. We were also warned that if we did not behave ourselves this time, we would be cut into half yet again, and would 'hop about with half a nose and face in basso relievo'.

The two halves of each of us went searching for the other, seeking nothing else, ready to die of hunger in each other's arms. Either feeling sorry for us, or—more likely—worried we may die out naturally and stop offering sacrifices, Zeus then had our genitalia repositioned, so we could go forth and multiply, where possible.

Aristophanes then posited that 'the characters of men differ accordingly as they are derived from the original man or the original woman, or the original man-woman'. In what may be indicative of Plato's own sexual orientation, he suggests: 'Those who come from the man-woman are lascivious and adulterous; those who come from the woman form female attachments; those who are a section of the male follow the male and embrace him, and in him all their desires centre. The pair are inseparable and live together in pure and manly affection; yet they cannot tell what they want of one another. But if Hephaestus were to come to them with his instruments and propose that they should be melted into one and remain one here and hereafter, they would acknowledge that this was the very expression of their want. For love is the desire of the whole, and the pursuit of the whole is called love.'

Aristophanes' theory shook me because it spoke to me of a love that transcended sexual desire, which is often considered either the purest or basest expression of love. This love was not bereft of sexual desire, but the desire was simply an intrinsic part of the various ways in which we longed to be with someone. This love was so powerful and so pure that we wanted to belong to each other, to be close to each other, in every possible way—emotionally, intellectually, spiritually, physically, verbally, philosophically, in thought, word, action, deed.

So often, we wonder about 'The One'. Does that person exist? Could that person make a sudden entry into the life of someone who has been cynical all of his or her life, and throw it out of balance? Could Aristophanes' theory explain why a first meeting with someone does not feel like a first meeting, why within only weeks of knowing each other, that person becomes the first we turn to in crisis, why we're willing to break all our relationship rules for that person, why we feel so secure in a particular relationship when we have been clingy or nervous or possessive or suffocated in others?

Aristophanes concludes his little speech with, 'Wherefore let us exhort all men to piety, that we may obtain the goods of which love is the author, and be reconciled to God, and find our own true loves, which rarely happens in this world.'

If such love is so rare, what happens if we don't find those halves? Do we simply reconcile ourselves to the halves we find, wrong halves that are something of a fit because we have the right projections and receptacles in our bodies? And what happens when, having joined other halves that did not truly belong to us in our desperation to become whole, having had Hephaestus stitch us together, we meet those original other halves of us? Is it inevitable that we will meet them, because destiny and our instincts are constantly leading us to them, constantly ensuring we don't move too far away from each other at any point, or when we do, ensuring that we somehow find ourselves in the same geographical space? When we wrench ourselves away from our wrong halves, either upon meeting our right halves or before, surely we leave some of our skin behind and carry some of the wrong half's? Surely this dead tissue leaves part of our skin wrinkled? Surely we bear scars from where we lost our own skin?

When we have only parted with scars to show for our time together with the wrong halves, we could perhaps be healed simply by our encounter with our original other halves. Perhaps a few adjustments must be made, a few tissues torn and the skin cauterized, a few memories blown off, but we will fit together, seamlessly, *almost* as if we were never parted, over time.

But what if we're not left with just scars? What if we're left with children, forever tying us in some way to those wrong-halves? How do we fit them into a union with the right halves? Can space be made for them? What if one half of a man-man or a woman-woman was joined with the wrong half of a man-woman? Is too much skin lost and too much dead tissue carried for that half to ever become whole again, even after meeting its right half? Or did the universe feel so sorry for us, so sorry for our loneliness and longings and scars and separations and tears and trauma, that it conspired to make us whole, somehow accommodating the children, somehow exorcizing the ghosts of wrong-halves past?

Charu and Gayathri seemed to have found balm for their wounds, not just in each other, but in an entire system of support, in a network of halves separated from wrong-halves or searching for the right-halves.

'We kind of form these quasi-families,' Gayathri told me. 'Like Sonu says he's my brother. And that Charupriyan is his son. So my daughters call him "Sonu mama". And then Charupriyan asks his son to call him *"thatha"*. So now, everyone calls him "Thatha-mama".'

The Targaryens had nothing on these guys, I thought.

Gayathri laughed. 'In a way, even these relationships are like falling in love. Just as lovers look at each other, and feel this connection, you feel by instinct that someone is your brother or sister or child or whatever.' She sat up. 'I'm very interested in relationships, you know. In interactions.'

'Madam has made a movie about it,' Charupriyan said. 'It's on YouTube. She even won an award.'

Gayathri laughed. Some years earlier, they had attended a workshop during the Bangalore Queer Film Festival. Gayathri's film was about two women in love, but she could not remember what she had called it. Charupriyan snorted, and asked me to watch his short film. It was called *En Aasai, En Kanavu* (My Desires, My Dreams). He had told his story on film.

En Aasai, En Kanavu
A dream not deferred
Bangalore Pride 2010
1:52 mins

I only began to wear 'pant-shirt' once I moved to Bangalore, after I met my friend Sonu. When I saw him, I had a vision of what I could be. I had first thought he was a cisboy—his spectacles, cigarette, 'boy cut, pant-shirt'. I would be questioned when I wore 'pant-shirt' to work. The day I got a job with an NGO, I asked my friend Christy to take me for a haircut. The barber asked what cut I wanted. I said, 'Boy cut'. He looked me up and down, and then cut off all my hair. I felt like a weight had been lifted off my shoulders, literally.

4:41 mins

When I see my child, I don't know whether I'm playing the role of a mother or a father to him. I'm not able to bring myself to tell him not to call me Amma, to call me Appa.

5:02 mins

There is no space for my desires, my dreams, in my own life. I have had to live in accordance with their wishes. Who are they? We first live for our parents; then for our husbands; then for our children; when do we get to live for ourselves? I lived for them all this while. Now I want to live for me. And that's why I dusted everything off myself and came away.

'Papa, you're driving too fast,' Gayathri said.

'For god's sake,' mumbled Charupriyan, but slowed down.

'Everyone drives rashly, papa, I'm worried about accidents.'

He ignored her, and she turned to me. 'You know, we make it sound all hunky-dory, right? That we have this family now, our friends are family and so on. Yes, there *is* a lot of love. We make it a point to celebrate birthdays in a grand way. And because we've known each other so well and so long, we tease each other all the time. But then, when I watch *Bigg Boss*, I think we're not so different, you know. There *is* a lot of bitching. A lot of gossip and raking up personal stuff. NGO politics. And it comes to such a pass that sometimes you cannot say "hi-'bye" without sounding false. These ugly fights crop up. And we save only the positives in our minds and feel we've overcome some baser human quality. But we're not always like that. I think it would be a lot better for all of us if we were open, if we spoke about things. Otherwise, it becomes toxic. We're creating another version of the society from which we withdrew.'

Till Death Do Us Part

We had been driving for a long time. Kiran was on the phone, giving us directions. We were to look for a church.

'Where is this church? We've passed a temple, a mosque, everything but a church,' Charupriyan grumbled.

'*Alle iru, alle iru* (Stay right there, stay right there)!' Kiran called over the speaker. 'I can see you!'

'This guy lives so much in "outer",' Gayathri marvelled. 'How does he do it? And he has to come to Bangalore all the time to lobby with the government.' She turned to me. 'I had to come somewhere near here for a meeting once. He insisted on bringing me home. It started raining, but he took me to the market to buy fish, made Kavya cook it for us, and then dropped me all the way back. He's a lovely guy. "Very helping nature". That's what I like about him.'

I recognized Kiran from the newspaper clippings and videos I had seen online. He was in a customized mobility scooter. 'Welcome, welcome!' he called to us, and then drove off down a series of narrow lanes.

'Yo, politician!' Charupriyan called. 'Why don't you get the government to widen the roads?'

'This is Nisarga, the NGO I started,' Kiran said once we had disembarked, pointing to a little office with a board.

He had recently got Rs 75 lakh sanctioned to distribute scooters to 100 people with special needs, he said. The modification of the scooter would cost Rs 22,000, and so each scooter cost Rs 75,000.

'We also have KVS—Karnataka Vikalachetana Sangathane—with 4000 members, and Nisarga has 2000. We chose 100 people on the basis of their needs for work and education,' Kiran said.

A monkey leapt down from the roof, and Gayathri gasped. 'There are monkeys here?'

'His kids,' Charupriyan said, and Kiran punched him lightly.

Kiran got off the scooter. He had had polio as a child, and his legs were folded under him. But he manoeuvred himself nimbly on his hands. He tried the door of his house. It was locked. 'Wife bathing,' he told me, in English. 'Ladies doing make-up for long-long time. Already half an hour for bathing.'

When Kavya finally emerged and let us in, we noticed that the shelves were stacked with awards. Citations hung from the walls. Pride of place had been given to a Karnataka State Government award, with a citation that began 'Viswa Vikalachetana Dinadare (World Disability Day) . . .' I could not read any further because the top of another award protruded in front of the letters.

'He treats awards like so much waste,' Gayathri said, pointing at a shelf where several statues and plaques were piled on top of each other.

'How much did they cost?' Charupriyan grinned. 'Twenty-five rupees or fifty? You got them all from some sports store, no?'

'Wait. You open my cupboard and see my albums,' Kiran said in English, and brought out several thick photo albums.

'You spend your entire salary on albums, huh?' Gayathri looked on as he reached for more albums from another shelf.

'He asks for an "album subsidy" from the government,' Charupriyan said.

I asked if I could take a picture of him with the albums, not for publication, I said, but perhaps for a sketch.

'He'll be even happier if you're publishing it, preferably on the cover page,' Charupriyan smirked.

'I don't think I can photograph his awards. This needs a video,' I said.

There were pictures of Kiran with everyone—Andhra Pradesh Chief Minister Chandrababu Naidu, Karnataka Chief Minister

Siddaramaiah, actors Mahesh Babu and Vishnu Vardhan, several ministers, members of the Legislative Assembly (MLA), senior police officers, groups of transmen, groups of differently abled people, commercial sex workers, children . . . He seemed to have printed out practically every picture taken anywhere, at conferences, meetings, celebrations, rangoli competitions, home visits, even hospital visits.

The albums dated back to when Kiran and Kavya had first moved to Bangalore. There were old pictures of the entire gang.

'Look how thin Charu was!' Gayathri laughed.

'*Kandraavi-a irukku* (It looks terrible), *chee*,' Charupriyan said. 'I look like a school kid.'

'And Sonu!' Gayathri hooted with laughter. 'Just look at him, pre-transition!'

'This F-to-M is cute,' she added, pointing, and Kavya and I bent over to look.

'Look at our wives, checking out other dudes in front of us,' Charupriyan said.

'My daughter and I check men out all the time,' Gayathri said. 'I like checking men out. I think (actor) Vikram is handsome. And then (actor) Kamal Haasan in the *Bigg Boss* ads. Both of you can flirt with Nandini if you want.' Kavya laughed.

'When did you get this shirt?' Gayathri asked Charupriyan suddenly, pointing at a photograph.

'Who's this girl?'

'He looks like a pucca criminal!'

'Where was this?'

'Why do you have this jerkin on in all your photographs? Couldn't find the zip or what?'

'You should get a Guinness Record for the most protest rallies attended.'

'These are not all rallies,' Kiran said, and began pointing to various photographs. 'This was at the protest in 2012, after the Nirbhaya gang rape. This is at a sixty-six-day protest against the water problem. This was at a handicrafts workshop. This was a protest with the corpse of an HIV-positive person. They refused to do a post-mortem, so we sat with the body for a day until they relented. This was at the state awards ceremony. This was when we got the scooters distributed. This was the inauguration of Nisarga. This was . . .'

'How the fuck do you have so many pictures?'

'I've printed very few,' Kiran sounded smug. 'There are many more in the "system" (computer).'

'Uff, politician, show us family pictures!' Gayathri sighed.

'Hey, hey, is that Chandni?' I thought I recognized a transwoman I had met at Sangama about a decade earlier.

'Yes. You know her?'

'She had adopted a baby, right?'

'Yes, her daughter's come of age now. This was at the function,' Kiran told me.

I was suddenly overwhelmed. I had interviewed Chandni for a documentary, and remembered her daughter as a baby. I had videos of her playing with the cord of my microphone. Chandni had been worried at the time that the baby would be taken away from her. It had not been easy for her to adopt a child. Each time she had visited orphanages, asking to adopt, she had been asked why she wanted a child. How could they be sure she wouldn't sell the child into prostitution? Chandni had begun to cry as she told me the story, and I remembered that her daughter, less than two years old, had begun to cry too, looking at Chandni. Knowing that more than a decade later, they were together, safe and happy, made me well up.

Kiran had retrieved an album of family pictures. 'This is my mother. This was from a trip to Mahabalipuram. This is Kavya's niece. This is my sister's son. This is . . .'

It was a while before we repaired to the bedroom. Kavya had begun to cook, and Charupriyan offered to help her, since Gayathri was going to translate.

'See you, goodnight,' Kiran said, as Charupriyan closed the door.

'Goodnight-aa? Hello, I've brought her for an interview and nothing else,' Charupriyan popped back in. 'Hey, Kavya, did you hear what your husband said? And with Gayathri also in the room!'

We had been laughing for so long that I expected it would be a while before we could settle down to the interview. But Kiran was a seasoned interviewee, and he switched modes right away.

His full name was Usha Kiran Nayak, he declared, and he made sure he used all three parts of it. Usha was the name given to him at birth. Kiran was the name he had chosen. Nayak was a caste name that indicated he was adivasi. He was particular about identifying himself by his caste. His nickname was Badri. Among adivasis, nicknames such as 'Badri', 'Badru' and 'Badra' were the norm, he said, because it is the name of their god.

'Growing up, I knew about casteism, I knew about the problems of adivasis, and I knew about disability rights,' he said. 'But I didn't know anything about gender.'

Kiran had an older sister, a younger brother and a younger sister. Until he was nine years old, it hadn't occurred to his family to send him to school. They lived in a remote, forested area, and the school was some distance away. It wasn't important for girls to study, they thought, and for a girl with a disability, who would need help to even board a bus, it was out of the question. But a teacher who lived nearby and worked at a government school heard about the girl who was reported to be bright, funny and talkative, but was not allowed to attend school.

'That teacher was a "turning point" in my life,' Kiran said. 'He used to come home on his bike and pick me up every day. He even supported me financially till I finished the seventh standard. He gave me special coaching so I could get double promotions and study in a more age-appropriate class. And then he got me admitted into a ladies' hostel so that I could graduate from Class 10.'

Hostel left him lonely. He wasn't used to talking to girls, and felt nervous around them. His childhood friends had all been boys. Then he met a girl with whom he had something in common—they were both victims of polio. Saritha and he became good friends. He had almost given up. He had been so depressed that he had wanted to drop out, but Saritha convinced him to stay on. They both passed their Class 10 matriculation examinations.

They would need scholarships to study further. Kiran had done well in his exams, and would qualify for both caste-based and disability-based aid. But he needed certificates to prove he was indeed an adivasi with polio, though his name and appearance should have sufficed. His family went from office to office for three years, trying to get the certificates. They couldn't. Neither could Saritha. They found that seven people who had also qualified for a scholarship were studying in the first year of pre-university in 2003, but had not received the aid to which they were entitled.

'We thought, if we had fought so hard and not got scholarships, it would be impossible for others to do it,' he said. 'So Saritha and I decided we had to start a public struggle. Seven of us got together and organized it.'

They chose 3 December 2003, World Disability Day, to hold a meeting. They spoke to the concerned MLA and invited him to the meeting. They went to the taluk office—which oversaw local administration—for a list of people with disabilities. There were more than 14,000 in the district. They went to the *gram panchayats* (village councils) and district post offices and collected the addresses of 2600 people, whom they invited to the meeting.

They did not know they needed police permission to assemble in such large numbers. They hadn't made arrangements for food or water. They had invited the MLA and submitted a letter speaking about their grievances: the difficulty of obtaining certificates, problems of accessibility in educational institutions, requests for pension and wheelchairs for those whose income was below poverty line.

By 9 a.m., the park was teeming with people. More than 3000 had come, including the families of the students with special needs. Police vehicles arrived and a superintendent of police asked them to leave. Kiran said the MLA had given them permission. Where was the letter? He did not have one.

Luckily for him, word of the commotion in the park had spread and the media had arrived before the police. There were about twenty police personnel, outnumbered by the media. There were

3000-odd attendees for an event that showed no signs of starting. The superintendent called the MLA.

'That man got into a panic,' Kiran grinned. 'This is 3000 votes, right? So he asked them to arrange for food, water, chairs, and tents. He said he would come to address us.'

When the party workers whom the MLA had sent arrived with the chairs and tents, Kiran began to lead chants, saying they did not need chairs, they needed wheelchairs; they did not need tents, they needed pension; they did not need food, they needed education; they did not need water, they needed buildings with ramps.

The MLA arrived at 3.30 p.m., by which time the chants had become more sophisticated and demanding. He had intended to make a quick speech, promising to look into their needs. Before he could speak, the attendees began to fire questions at him. Where could they get medical certificates? What about a bus pass? What about a railway pass? Where could they apply for pension? When would these be delivered?

He stared at them in confusion for some time, and then announced that a camp would be held. He called the district collector (DC), and announced a date. They took a picture to commemorate the meeting. When Kiran showed me this photograph, I noticed that the seven organizers of the meeting, all with disabilities, were smiling, while the MLA looked about as confused as Kiran had described.

'We had been fighting for this for three years. And now one meeting, one phone call, had ensured we could get everything done,' Kiran said. 'This was the next "turning point". The media had covered the event. As soon as it was over, some thirty-three of us came together and decided to start a voluntary organization to work for the rights of the disabled. So we called it Prajwala Vikkalamoola Sankshema Sangam (PVSS). And after the media coverage, we got a lot of support. The Students' Federation of India, women's organizations, farmers, everyone began to support us.'

'So you're a "by-birth politician",' Gayathri said.

A Dalit leader from the Madiga Reservation Porata Samiti, Manda Krishna Madiga, got in touch with Kiran. PVSS, with the help of the various support groups who had offered their help, began to organize awareness programmes, where they would tell differently abled people about the rights to which they were entitled, collect signatures on petitions, and ensure media coverage.

'Within a month of the first meeting, Chandrababu Naidu had invited us, for the first time, to Hyderabad. We ourselves got a shock,' Kiran said, and brandished a photograph of the meeting. 'We told him we were fighting for basic needs and basic rights—education, pension, travel passes, accessibility, employment opportunities. We asked for an office.'

It was granted. Chairs, tables, computers, office supplies, and cupboards were donated to them by various organizations.

'We were all students, and we had no salaries,' Kiran said. 'But we had a place to meet during weekends, even while we continued our education. My family was supportive. As for Saritha . . . well, that's a different topic.' He grinned.

'Oh! You had a love story back then!' Gayathri whistled.

'Hello, hello, hello, calm down, Aunty,' Kiran said in English, holding up a hand. 'Saritha is Kavya's sister.'

Charupriyan and Kavya joined us as Kiran told us how they had met. Saritha's and his families had got to know each other well, and Kiran would often stay over at Saritha's place, since it was closer to the college and office.

'I don't know how Kavya perceived me,' Kiran said. 'I'd always felt like a boy. My family didn't object to my short hair or boys' clothes. And I was busy with work. Then in 2004, around the time Saritha and I were studying for our exams, Kavya came and proposed to me.'

'At the time, Kavya became "mentally disabled",' Charupriyan said, and they all laughed.

'Don't mind us, we keep teasing each other like this,' Gayathri told me unnecessarily.

Kiran had always been attracted to Kavya, but he felt it would be unfair on a woman to deprive her of biological children, which he knew by now he could not provide. He said they could be good friends, and take things as they came. Kavya insisted she was in love with him. They were still in school at the time, and Kiran figured there was no harm in a little romance. In 2007, Kavya had to be rushed to hospital with severe pain in her appendix. The doctors said they had to operate immediately, but she refused to undergo surgery unless Kiran was with her. He was out of town on a meeting. Saritha made a frantic call to him, and he rushed back. While the appendix surgery was on, Kiran sat in tears, with Saritha comforting him. The families began to sense that there was more to the 'friendship' than met the eye.

'Then, of course, they threw all their energies into searching for a groom for Kavya,' Kiran said. 'All this while I was practically living in their house.'

One day, Kavya led him to a river and gave him an ultimatum. He had to find a way to elope before her family arranged a marriage for her, or she would jump into the river.

He promised to find a way out.

'Once, we saw an advertisement in a newspaper, saying there was going to be a "free marriage ceremony" at the Tirupati temple,' he said. 'We were joking about how it would be a good idea to run away there. Then, we began to seriously consider it. I called the number given in the newspaper, and told them our families were opposed to it because I had a physical disability. They said family was not a problem. We needed a government ID proof, which said she was over eighteen and I was over twenty-one.'

Kavya was twenty, Kiran was twenty-two. But his voter ID card had him down as 'Usha Kiran Nayak'. He took a photocopy, in which he used whitener to remove the 'Usha' and change his gender to male. At the temple, they did not even check the IDs. They simply filed them away, and asked Kiran and Kavya to get in line. Theirs was one of 125 matches formalized that day—9 March 2008.

Unknown to Kiran, Kavya had written a twenty-six-page letter to her father, apologizing for what she was about to do. In the letter, she declared that she loved Kiran and could no longer live with her family. She thanked them for all that they had done for her over the years, but she could no longer be in touch. She was going to Tirupati to get married, and they would not see her again. She left behind all her jewellery. She wore a sari that Kiran had gifted her on her last birthday.

They had gone to the house of a relative of Kiran's, who was supportive of their relationship, in Nizamabad.

'The only thing my cousin said was, because we had got married at the temple away from the family, we should get married once more, in her presence. So we got married for the second time in two days.'

They had switched off their phones, but after the second ceremony, Kavya called her father to tell him she was married, and there was nothing he could do to end her relationship with Kiran.

Her father had, however, already approached the police and filed a complaint against a twenty-two-year-old woman called Usha Kiran Nayak for kidnapping his daughter. The police had been trying to trace the phone, and when Kavya switched it on, they figured out where the two were. In their absence, Kavya's father had also gone on a rampage, ransacking the office of PVSS and getting into a fight with Kiran's family. It had turned into a brawl involving some neighbours, and several people were hospitalized.

When Kavya spoke to her father, he said he was going to find them and drag them back home. He would bring the police with him. Kiran told his cousin, who called up the media and asked them to come to her house. The police were threatening a runaway couple, she said.

After they had made the calls, Kiran thought it might be better for everyone if the newly-weds went back home, to Warangal, and confronted their families.

So the police and media turned up at the house in Nizamabad, and found that the runaway couple was missing. The police figured out that they must have returned to Warangal, and alerted their counterparts there.

'Even as we reached, the police and media were waiting for us,' Kiran said. 'We had made a big mistake.'

They could identify him because he had to lever himself on to the floor. Cameras rushed in to capture the faces of the two "women" who had got married. The images were being aired live on television. Autorickshaw drivers and locals began to shout at them, asking how they intended to have sex. Reporters were screaming questions at them. What name would Kavya put under 'Husband's name' if she took out an insurance policy? Didn't she want children?

'You should have seen Kavya that day,' Kiran said. 'She suddenly stood straight and said, "What happens in the privacy of our bedroom has nothing to do with you. I don't ask any of you about your marriage and children, and you have no reason to ask me. The only people involved in our decisions are me and him. We need each other. Neither of us needs you." I was shocked. I was supposed to be a leader and demonstrator and all of that. And this girl, who had barely spoken even to me, was standing up and saying this. I was both proud and shocked. I was worried they would start physically attacking us.'

A television reporter whom Kiran knew from his work with PVSS had arrived. He managed to get them away from the commotion, under the pretext of interviewing them, and rushed them to his office. They were asked to stay in a room on the third floor. No one in the office knew they were there.

'We stayed for hours. The police was looking for us. So were our families. And the media. We felt the whole world was against us, and no one would support us. So we made this final decision. Kavya was wearing glass bangles. We decided we should crush them, mix the shards into water and drink them. We would commit suicide. But we wanted to talk to our parents one last time. So I switched on my phone to call my mother.'

As he narrated this, Kiran's voice began to shake. He stopped and smiled. Then he wiped his eyes furiously. Gayathri passed him a water bottle, which he took. He screwed and unscrewed the cap, without drinking from it.

'Drink, drink,' Gayathri said.

'No, I'm fine.'

'Shit, man, you've been through so much,' Charupriyan said.

'You know how you said you were scared by our story yesterday?' Gayathri said to me. 'That's how I feel now. My hands are trembling.'

Kiran drank some water, smiled, and took Kavya's hand. 'Because of this live show on TV, Manohar of Sangama had seen us. Then he called some friends of his in Hyderabad and asked them to trace us and help us. They had been looking for us everywhere. A lot of people knew my number because of PVSS. So they'd found my phone number and were trying to contact us non-stop. But our phones were off. When I switched mine on to speak to my mother, before I could dial, it rang. This man spoke to us in Telugu and said they were coming to help us, where were we. I told him we were going to kill ourselves. He said please don't do any such thing, our crisis team will come and get you, we will help you. He hung up, and then Manohar called and spoke to us. He knows Telugu. He was on the phone with us for half an hour, talking us out of the idea of suicide. He said there were a lot of couples like us whom they had helped. They would help us too.'

Kiran was so suspicious, he asked his reporter friend to verify that the calls were authentic. They were. The crisis team reached the office at 2 a.m., and took them to Hyderabad.

When they walked into the office, everyone clapped. A group of transwomen had come to show their support for them.

'We were terrified,' Kiran said. 'We saw all these transwomen. And then there were boxes and boxes of condoms. We thought we had been conned and brought into some sort of sex ring.'

Charupriyan and Gayathri collapsed with laughter, and Charupriyan held out his hand to Kiran for a high-five. 'Same, da. We thought the same thing when we came to the Sangama office. Only later did we realize NGOs have these HIV/AIDS prevention programmes.'

Manohar was already on his way to the office and reached soon after they arrived. He told them Sangama and their allies would support them. They could come to Bangalore and meet other transmen if they wished, or they could stay on in Hyderabad. They would not be in any danger. Kiran and Kavya decided it would be best to move away, at least for a while.

'So it was decided we would move to Bangalore. But then the hijras said they had seen us on TV, and they had wanted to help us, and so we were part of their family. And now they brought garlands and said we should get married in front of them, before we left.'

'Wow, you got married thrice in a week,' I said.

'And to the same girl,' Gayathri said, laughing.

Two of the hijras temporarily adopted Kiran and Kavya, and solemnized the marriage for a third time.

On 17 March 2008, they arrived in Bangalore.

It was a revelation. They met Sunil, Rumi, Christy, Charupriyan and Gayathri. Manohar took Kiran to Philomena Hospital for a series of check-ups, to see whether corrective surgery could be done on his legs. Kavya began to work as a volunteer in Sangama's library. She made friends and found a support system. Kiran was deemed fit for surgery. It was scheduled for six months later. There was a 50 per cent chance of improvement, the doctor said.

He got a job as a data entry operator with Suraksha, the same NGO where Charupriyan was employed. They became good friends.

When he was admitted to hospital, Kiran was hopeful. He would require three surgeries over a year. As a special case, Sangama had removed the three-month restriction on accommodation and support for him. The first surgery was to use a splint and Plaster of Paris to try and straighten his backbone. The second and third would be performed on his legs. Eventually, the doctors decided the curvature on his spine was too advanced to be corrected. It could have been done when he was still growing. But twenty-two was too late an age for success.

Kiran took it on the chin. He began to learn Kannada. He attended meetings, and realized there were various categories of transpeople, of alternative sexual expression and orientation. His interaction with the community made him aware of his own disillusionment—he didn't draw fulfilment from his day job. He had liked the work he was doing in Hyderabad. He wanted to continue to work for disability rights.

Manohar suggested that he apply for a fellowship programme, which was open to disability rights activists, sex workers, and transgender and intersex people. He was given some seed money to start a project in a place of his choice. Kiran decided on Chikballapur. It was an hour's journey from Bangalore, and it was close to Karnataka's border with Andhra Pradesh, so most people spoke Telugu as well as Kannada.

He planned to work for transpeople and those with special needs. He learnt of a non-governmental organization for transwomen sex workers, and began to make enquiries. Kiran went to their cruising spots and tried to make conversation about their problems. They shooed him away. He was costing them clients, and they didn't think he could help. No one had been able to do much for them. He spent six months of the year-long fellowship trying to make friends in the trans community. No one seemed interested in what he had to say.

He had an idea. He began to sit at the railway station all day, with a packed lunch. Transpeople who begged on trains would get off at lunch break. He got to know some of them. They had lunch together. They told him the sex workers among them were terrified of harassment and wouldn't come out. They would try and convince them to meet him, provided he had a concrete plan for fighting for their rights.

Over time, he got to know transpeople, both men and women, in the district. Eventually, they had a meeting during which they debated whether an organization catering specifically to trans rights was needed, and voted yes. They named it Nisarga, and elected thirteen office-bearers. Kiran was made president. They wanted to register Nisarga as a charitable organization. But they ran into problems.

'The registrar's office said there were no transgender people in the district,' Kiran said. 'I told them I could give them the names of 3000 people. But they did not want us to form an organization. There were local politicians who were afraid of any form of unionizing. And they were worried about what transpeople could do. They threatened us. They made us run around from office to office. Finally, we had to get a lawyer and register the organization.'

The first item on their agenda was to look for alternative means of employment, so that transwomen did not have to depend on begging and sex work for income. Transmen, of course, had no real means of income. They usually posed as teenage boys and were paid miserable wages for hard labour. Kiran got a grant from the state's ministry for women and child development. Nisarga held a workshop in which transpeople were trained in various handicrafts—weaving mats,

making baskets, flower decoration, sewing, pottery and other skills—
and given seed money of Rs 20,000 to start their own self-help groups.

'We got various other funds sanctioned, so now Nisarga can
run independently. I've stepped down as office-bearer, and am just a
member,' Kiran said. 'I want to focus more on disability rights.'

'Listen, man,' Charupriyan said suddenly. 'We've been teasing you
about being a politician and lobbying and posting stuff about yourself
all the time. I just want to tell you, openly, that I'm sorry. I had no idea
you've been through all this. It's such a big achievement, da.'

Kiran laughed, 'Oh, it's okay, it's okay.'

They shook hands.

Kavya and Gayathri rolled their eyes.

Kiran's first high-profile case with disability rights activism took
him to Gudibande taluk, a little over 30 km away from Chikballapur.
In 2010, a fourteen-year-old girl with multiple disabilities, including
mental retardation, had complained of severe stomach pain. When her
mother took her to hospital, they learnt she was six months pregnant.

Kiran had put up posters with his mobile number across most of
the district, in public places as well as outside police stations, hospitals
and schools. The girl's mother called him. Kiran went to meet her
with a team. 'The girl told us three men used to visit her home in
the afternoons, when she was alone, make her lift her skirt, and hurt
her. When we approached the police station, they wanted the names
of the three men. The girl identified them, but they were politicians
and had clout. The police tried to ask us to back off; then they began
to threaten us. But I called the media, and we protested. Finally, they
arrested the three men and a woman who was their lookout, a pimp
of sorts.'

He told me the case was high profile, but I could not find reports
in English language newspapers, or independently in other languages.
Kiran did show me a cutting he had kept, from a Kannada newspaper.

'This girl was about eight months pregnant by then. She couldn't
abort. Her parents told us to sort out her life for her. Kavya and I
stayed in hospital with her for fourteen days. When she delivered the
baby, it turned out to have multiple disabilities as well. We had to help

them approach the children's court and give up the baby, relinquish rights, so that it could be looked after in a government home. In the meanwhile, her rapists came out on bail within a month. They used to threaten and blackmail us, asking us to withdraw the case. Finally, they offered the girl an out-of-court settlement—Rs 2 lakh from each of them, and an acre of land.'

Three years after the case was first filed, the girl accepted the settlement.

The media attention that the case received pitched Kiran into the public eye. Several people began to approach him with similar cases. People with disabilities wanted to register with his organization. He decided to start Karnataka Vikalachetana Sangathane (KVS) to cater to people with disabilities who also belonged to disadvantaged groups—HIV-positive people with disabilities, transpeople with disabilities, sex workers with disabilities, people who belonged to scheduled castes or tribes and had disabilities. Their membership has now expanded to nearly 5000, he said. He calculated that with the MLAs' and MPs' quota for disability funding, as well as government pension schemes, they could potentially have funding worth Rs 1 crore a year, to look after their health and education.

'The facilities are so bad, and they're blind to the irony. We had been trying to meet the DC. When we finally managed to get an appointment, we found the meeting was on the third floor, and there was no lift or ramp. All of us had disabilities. Obviously, we protested outside.'

Their demands included D-group postings in government jobs for transpeople, 3 per cent reservation in educational institutions for people with disabilities over and above all other categories under which they were eligible for reservation, and the same demands they had made in Andhra Pradesh—for accessibility, bus and railway passes, pension, medical certificates, and medical check-ups.

Eventually, the DC recommended his name for a Gaurava Award by the Karnataka state government in 2016. Kiran won the state award the same year. 'Uff, they needed so many verifications for that. You have to show them your passport, you need witness signatures to every declaration—which includes a letter confirming you're not a Naxalite—and then you have to give your family photo to them . . . every document that you have ever encountered in your life, you have to submit.' He didn't seem particularly bothered by it, though. It made him feel rather special. He was being given an award, so prestigious and at a ceremony that would be attended by people so important that his entire life had to be audited and vetted before he could be cleared to attend the function.

His work, which had led to his selection for the award, was reported widely in the vernacular media in both Karnataka and Andhra Pradesh.

'Sakshi TV did a programme on us,' Kiran said. 'And that's how our families accepted us. Kavya was very close to her family, especially her father. And things got so bad our families had actually held a ceremony to declare us dead, and had hung up our garlanded photographs on their walls. They basically thought we had gone the wrong way, begging or doing sex work, because they think that's what transpeople do. So once Sakshi TV told our story, they accepted us. Now, they consult us before organizing any function, arranging marriages and so on.'

At this point, Kavya clutched her stomach and groaned.

'Pregnant?' Gayathri asked.

'Five months,' she replied.

They all laughed, and Gayathri sang, '*Namba mudiyavillai* (I can't believe it)!' I noticed, quite often, that partners of transmen would joke about pregnancy or look fondly at other children. They made light of it, but I wondered about their yearning for biological children with their lovers—were these little fictions more than jokes, a bubble that lasted for a few seconds, a reprieve where they could imagine different lives? When I was making my documentary on transwomen, one of them had told me she liked going to pharmacies and asking for sanitary pads. If they handed them to her nonchalantly, it was validation of her identity as a woman. If they stared, she would snap, 'What are you looking at?' She enjoyed their confusion.

Looking at Kavya holding her stomach, almost caressingly, I felt suddenly sad.

Kiran took her hand. 'Kavya is everything to me,' he said. 'She never stops me or gets anxious about my going for meetings, despite my problem. Her confidence in me gives me confidence in myself. Her support is essential to the work I do. I'm this leader outside, but when I come back, I want to be a child.'

He is open about his gender identity, he said, but he would prefer to be known for his work in disability rights.

'But there is something I have to say,' Kiran said. 'Something important for the trans community. One of our friends in the community, a transwoman called Bharti, committed suicide. It's been a year and fifteen days.' Rumi had mentioned her too. 'Her death has laid all of us low. We've begun to feel that whatever work we do, whatever rights we fight for, we are not able to save people like us. And we ask ourselves: why? The reason we can't save each other is that we haven't got our basic rights; our basic needs are not secured. Just as the basic needs for people with disabilities are wheelchairs and ramps, in this case, it is ID cards—voter ID, ration cards, driving licence. I have twenty-two ID cards. I know so many VIPs, so many politicians, and yet I'm not able to stop people from my community from committing suicide. We're asking for a camp to be held so people can get their documents sorted. And then we can apply for everything else—pension, housing, land, everything. The first thing they want is three different ID cards. You could spend your lifetime going in and out of the doors of government offices, and get nothing done. But in a camp which is dedicated to giving you your ID cards, you can get five done in a day.'

~

The boys wanted some alcohol to go with the food. They set off on Kiran's scooter, and suddenly, it was just us girls.

'Phew,' Gayathri said, slumping back against the wall. 'I feel like I've seen a big movie. And some ten continuous shows a day. Your life is so dramatic!'

Kavya laughed.

'Have you thought about the fact that . . .' Gayathri seemed to be struggling to phrase it, '. . . you know, there's no organization for partners of transmen?'

Kavya shrugged. 'We're there for each other, no? As in, we and our husbands?'

'Yes, but then when I talk to *you*, there's something else there, right? We understand each other,' Gayathri said. 'You know, Nandini, we all come from heterosexual families, right? So some things are internalized, like gender roles—with respect to one's partner or husband, whether it's (sexual) "satisfaction", or the respect you command, or chores, we have this expectation of what you get from him. This causes a lot of problems between couples like us, because you cannot fulfil these expectations as a transperson. Because . . . whatever you say, a man and woman can go out at midnight, without fear; but if Charu and I go out, there is a certain fear that we have internally. When your partner is trans, you become the privileged one in a way, because the society sees us as women, fulfilling a woman's role. The transperson is seen as an aberration. So we need to protect ourselves as well as that person. *And* we need to move forward in life.

'It's important to have these discussions, but we cannot even have them in front of our men, because they might not understand where it's coming from. They will react to it. They will be hurt. I've been in LesBiT for ten years. But not many of us can talk about this openly. In the group, we brush aside a lot of things. Because not everyone can relate. But when we femme partners meet, the things we talk about are different. These issues don't seem like a big deal to our male partners, or to lesbian women, but then these are things that need to be "cleared". A lot of femmes won't give their partners up, won't speak of their violations. I'm a feminist. I speak for myself, I use my voice. I won't expect support from others. But I don't think I should be consigned to a role so that my partner can have validation in his role. You know?

'Slowly, femmes have begun to speak about these things. That their partners were different before surgery. That they have become more chauvinist, that the male ego is presenting itself in a bigger way after. These things are just beginning to come out, and that too behind closed doors. Many of them won't speak even in private. They hide it. That's why we need a support group.'

There were other things ciswomen partners wanted to discuss, but couldn't, she said, like the desire for biological children. Gayathri and Charupriyan were exceptions, since they happened to have biological children, albeit with men they despised. But not having the choice of bearing a biological child with one's partner could be depressing.'

'And then there is the issue of family acceptance. In most cases, even when they seem to accept you, even when they know the truth, they pretend you're a friend of your partner's. They call him by his female name, and they won't acknowledge you as his wife. They may treat you as an important member of the household, but then they refuse to acknowledge that you're a daughter-in-law or sister-in-law. That hurts.'

She told me she had questioned everything, all her life—untouchability, which was observed in her house; the idea of marriage; a woman's right to say no; why love should be dependent on gender and caste. 'I like (poet Subramaniya) Bharathiyaar a lot. Reading him made me question everything. And I think, having interrogated the norms set by the family into which I was born, I must also interrogate the norms here, within the network I have chosen. For everything, people will give you three–four kinds of answers—"scientific reason, social reason, family-culture-based reason". And is any of these a true "reason", or is it an "excuse"? Who is making assumptions, and how? If a cismale husband sees you as property and blames societal conditioning, it's unacceptable; when a transman, who has been through this crap himself, sees you as his property, why should we accept it?'

I turned to Kavya, who smiled uncomfortably.

The boys returned then, empty-handed. It was a Sunday, and all the liquor shops were shut.

'No business sense,' Kiran grumbled.

Kavya had made quite a spread—rice, two vegan dishes for me, fish curry and egg for the others. I wondered if she went all out every time someone came home to interview Kiran, which was fairly often. When they had first moved to Chikballapur, she had taken up work in the kitchen of a hotel. She would have twelve-hour shifts, and she had to cook so much she permanently lost her appetite, she said giggling. She spoke to Gayathri in a mix of Telugu and Kannada, asking after her children, sighing over the increasing prices of vegetables and meat.

'We've decided to go on holiday,' Kiran announced. 'We'll rent a bus. Only F-to-Ms and partners!' He reeled off the names of about seven couples. He and Charupriyan began to plan the logistics of seating. Then, they began to analyse which couples were likely to fight and ruin the holiday.

'We'll tell _____ not to bring her, or to keep her under control. Two-day camp and picnic.'

~

As we drove away, waving goodbye to Kiran and Kavya, I remembered being administered the polio vaccine orally. My last dose had been when I was five years old. It was bitter. It was not a mandatory vaccine at the time, and there were educated people in metropolises who did not bother vaccinating their children. I thought of Kiran, growing up on the outskirts of a forest, running and playing in childhood, before his legs were rendered limp by his parents' failure to administer six bitter spoonfuls of vaccine. How hopeful he must have felt that this could be corrected by surgery. How much the doctor's final diagnosis must have hurt.

'Is this Kiran's NGO?' Charupriyan said as we passed a bar called Nisarga. 'Take a picture, Gayathri. Let's WhatsApp it to him. Ask him if this is how he's conned people into giving funds.'

'This one is open,' Gayathri said as she took the picture. 'Didn't you guys come this far? You were gone a long time.'

'No, we just went to the bars in that area, and all of them were closed,' Charupriyan said. 'What did you girls speak about when we were gone?'

'Male chauvinism,' Gayathri said.

'Bitched me out, huh?' Charupriyan grinned.

'But you *do* share chores,' I said. 'I haven't seen that in a lot of couples. I mean, you made the keerai yesterday.'

Charupriyan exchanged a smile with Gayathri. 'No, it wasn't always like this. We had the same problems. We've been through a lot, Gayathri and I. We've changed now. It hasn't been an unbroken relationship, you know? There were such terrible misunderstandings in the middle that we even broke up. It was my fault. I have made a lot of mistakes. I was different when we were back home. But once I got my "boy cut" and changed my dressing style, my attitude changed. I *was* chauvinistic. I would refuse to do chores around the house. I felt she had done all this for her ex-husband, why was I different? It's taken us these ten years to reach this stage.'

'Yes,' Gayathri said. 'I was telling her how, in heterosexual relationships, there are discrete boxes. Duties each of you is assigned. Like my husband will be my guardian and there's no need for me to work. I am given a position of respect as the daughter-in-law, the lady of the house. Here, I have to come to terms with the fact that I will not be given that respect, both by his family and by society. A lot of girls think about it, but they don't say it out loud.'

~

When we were nearly at Christy's—he lived in the settlement Rumi had mentioned—Charupriyan turned to Gayathri, 'I've found a shortcut. Do you recognize this place?'

Gayathri squinted. 'It's been so long . . . hey! There's that Café Coffee Day. And the chicken shop. That was the way to Anand sir's office, no? Oh, this was where you guys got the beer every day?'

'Not *every* day,' Charupriyan said, with a sheepish laugh.

'This was a jolly time,' Gayathri told me. 'We had just come to Bangalore. Almost every week, a new runaway couple would be here. That's how I learnt Kannada, Telugu, even Hindi. I used to go straight to the couple and ask them for their story. I would speak in Tamil, they would speak in their language, and somehow we began to understand each other at some point. Everyone here has had a fraught life. But everyone here is happy.'

A Safe Place

Even as Charupriyan was parking the car, we were surrounded.

'Oh my god, look who has come!'

'Long time! Where have you been?'

'How is _____? Is she still with her father, or back with you?'

'Has _____ finished school?'

A group of transwomen had crowded around Gayathri and Charupriyan, hugging and kissing them.

Christy Raj was the only transman living there at the time. He came over to greet us, smiling.

'Your haircut is different,' Gayathri said.

'Style,' Christy said, winking.

'*Aiyo . . .*'

We went into his house. Watching the television was a transwoman. Sowmya was Christy's partner, and a long-time resident of the settlement. She spoke fluent English, Kannada, Tamil and Hindi. She worked with Payana, a community-managed NGO that supports people with alternative sexualities.

'How is Kiran?' she asked.

Gayathri was telling her about the vacation Kiran was planning, when a young transwoman, with hair just beginning to grow down to her neck and an awkwardly hitched sari, popped in.

'Mummy!' she called, 'Shall I bring tea?' She spoke in halting Kannada. Sowmya nodded.

'Hi!' the young transwoman said, turning to Gayathri.

'What's your name?' Gayathri asked.

The transwoman looked at Sowmya, giggled, and said, 'Subbu.'
'Stands for?'
'Subbalakshmi.'
'Nice name,' Gayathri said, and Subbu laughed and ran out of the house.

Christy's mainstay was video editing. He freelanced on television, ad and photo shoots. He was also a community correspondent with Video Volunteers, an NGO founded by TED fellow Jessica Mayberry and documentary film-maker Stalin K. They experimented with various models of storytelling by the community. I was familiar with some of their work through India Unheard, a YouTube channel that features people from marginalized societies or communities, reporting on the problems they face.

'What I liked most about them was they had an "Other" option under gender,' Christy said. 'Kalki Subramaniam (a well-known transwoman activist) had also been working with them. I wanted a job in the mainstream, as a community representative, and so I applied.'

His first report was a walk-through, in which he spoke about his own life.

He did not know his birth family, he said, and had been adopted by a transwoman in Bombay, hinting his biological mother was a commercial sex worker. 'In that place, if a baby was born, they would either dispose of it or give it to someone who wanted a child,' he told me when we met. 'So I don't know my birth mother. I only know the Amma who raised me.'

Christy was one of three children the transwoman had adopted—two girls and a boy. She had plans of raising them and educating them well. When it was time to send them to school, she left them with her relatives in Bangalore, so that they would be raised in a family, and travelled back and forth between Bangalore and Bombay, where she had her 'business'. The children would go to Bombay for the holidays.

By the time Christy was in Class 6, there were several indicators that he was not the girl his adoptive mother wanted him to be. He would write love letters to girls in his class, sometimes even to the teachers. There were complaints about him, and his mother would beat him up. Over the next few years, he would refuse to wear tight-fitting shirts and skirts. He insisted on cutting his hair, and would wear his shirt collars lifted.

'The influence of patriarchy will automatically come for everyone,' Sowmya said. She spoke to me in English, while Christy employed a mix of Tamil and Hindi, with a smattering of English. Sowmya continued, 'So his mother felt a girl should listen to her. Though she was a transwoman herself, she didn't understand when he felt he was in the wrong gender.'

'I can't even say it was her fault,' Christy said. 'She saw only three "pictures"—male, female, transwoman. Transman was a new "concept", a new name. Because of the "patriarchal world", a girl cannot become a man. She also had that "mindset".'

Christy's adoptive mother took him to temples and astrologers, hoping they could 'cure' him. She would not let him cut his hair. Eventually, she announced that she was going to arrange a marriage for him. Christy decided to run away, in 2003.

'I got caught. She beat me up, she and some others, and left me to die on the pavement,' Christy said.

He doesn't recall who helped him or dressed his wounds. But he did have some jewellery on him, and his brother's clothes. He pawned the gold, got his hair cut, and tried to figure out what to do. He didn't know there were organizations and support groups for transmen.

'I met Sheetal and Nandu from Kerala,' he said, 'and they introduced me to Sangama. I already knew (trans activist) Revathi Amma from when I was with my Amma. She convinced me that I was too young to make the transition, that I was just confused, and sent me back home. Again, I was "under house arrest". My Amma let me keep the short hair, but I knew she would get me married off. So I called Revathi Amma and said I had to get out of there.'

Revathi asked him to come along with her for a programme she was attending in Bombay. It was a meeting of the World Social Forum, held from 16 to 21 January, 2004. Christy met several other transmen, and realized he could transition too.

Sowmya cut in, 'This was about fifteen years back. There was no knowledge of or exposure to transmen. We transgenders ourselves didn't know about them, how they were different from lesbians. We were only able to accept the two boxes society has got—male and female. Once we do our complete sex change, we're female. When you don't have the knowledge, you can't accept an identity which is different from these.'

Revathi introduced him to Sowmya, who was involved in the trans movement. She took him into her home.

'His mother and her chelas came and beat me up very badly,' Sowmya said. 'They attacked me and said he would have come back home if I was not there. She caught me by my hair and hit me and kicked me. She said I had ruined him. As a senior transwoman, she was commanding me to get out of his life. I said, "I can't chase out someone who comes and asks for support. When I left home and came, no one in my community rejected me; so this is the same situation. How can I not offer him shelter? As a senior in the community, you should understand we are all human beings. You didn't accept him. He needs support. What can I do?" I couldn't hit her back because she was my senior. But I could refuse.'

He was under Sowmya's protection from 2004 to 2008. Several transmen had begun to move into the settlement. It wasn't easy to keep them safe, Sowmya said. This was not cosmopolitan Bangalore. This was an area in the outskirts, where women didn't wear trousers and shorts and shirts.

'People could see that they had breasts, but wore their hair short. They would ask questions. When they see transwomen, they assume we are sex workers. They think they can accost us any time and demand sex. And now they saw a lot of people whom they thought were cross-dressers, and assumed they were also involved in sex work,' Sowmya said. 'A lot of crises would come up then. We could not sleep a wink. People would harass them when they went to shops. If we let it go once, it would become the norm. So we would have to rush to intervene, to negotiate. Sometimes, we would get calls for help in the middle of the night, and we would have to run. *So* many problems!'

The counselling was not very good back then, Christy said, even in NIMHANS (National Institute of Mental Health and Neuro Sciences). 'They used to speak with a "patriarchal mindset"—like why do you want to become a guy, you will have a child, those are the ways in which they would counsel us. The doctors themselves didn't understand us. At the time, Dr Shekar Seshadri was on the board of Sangama. So we spoke to them and began to sensitize NIMHANS. They formed a team to counsel transmen specifically. It took a while. Around 2008-09, the team began to function.'

Getting a psychiatrist's certificate to start hormone therapy became easier. Earlier, a transman had to undergo two years of counselling, followed by a year in male clothes, to give him a chance to change his mind.

'But we told them we have already struggled for fifteen years,' Christy said. 'Why should we struggle for three more years, how can we deal with it? If we could change our minds, we would have done so already.'

'Forget visibility,' Sowmya said. 'Just look at safety. To be born female and to show oneself outside as male. It's a big risk.'

One could not undergo surgery without the psychiatrist's certificate. And one could not feel safe presenting as male until one's breasts had been removed, Christy said. Earlier, self-identification on bond paper was enough for endocrinologists to administer hormones. But, ironically, after the NALSA judgment, they had begun to insist on a counselling certificate. It took Christy only three months to get his certificate, because the doctors knew him well from his work with NGOs.

'But the surgery is like a trial,' he said. 'However much money you pay, they "experiment" on you. Senior doctors ask their students to do it. For experience. You heard about the botched penis reconstruction in Kerala? It's fine if you're rich. But we're from the working class. We collect donations and get surgeries done. Now I need corrective surgery. Where do I get the money? The government offers free surgeries, but you need a ration card and voter ID card. It's not easy to get those, because they won't change your gender without an SRS certificate. And you can't get that certificate without doing surgery. We can't use old ID cards, because most of us run away from home very young, and often without our documents.

'And to get that rejection, after going through the humiliation of showing our bodies to doctors to certify, it's cruel. Doctors believe you can't become a male if you don't have the "bottom surgery". According to the NALSA judgment, if we claim to be male, we're male; if female, we're female. But it hasn't been implemented anywhere.'

When even the state could not validate the existence of transmen, how could their own families, Christy asked. Most of them were not aware of transgenderism; they did not even know it was not an intersex variant. His mother, who *was* transgender herself, began to come around only after transwomen activists spoke to her and she met other transmen. She eventually accepted Christy as her son, before her death in 2010.

As an activist, what does he want to see?

'Mainly, toilets, shelter, and SRS,' Christy said. 'We've been asking for unisex toilets. Now, they've come up with the concept of "Transgender toilet". That's supposed to be a victory. Tell me, would anyone who is trying to pass off as a man go into a toilet marked "Transgender"? I've grown a moustache and beard, and everyone thinks I'm a cisguy, and then I go into this toilet, and there will be questions, I will be outed in public. I heard of cases in Mysore, where they have one such toilet. All the F-to-Ms who used it were sexually harassed after.'

'And then shelter is important,' Sowmya said. 'Because I was here, all of us M-to-Fs were here, these guys could come and feel relatively safe. We had to work through a lot of prejudices. Transwomen believe the surgery is very important for you to fit into the binary. The thing is, we have a support system which helps us get our surgery. These guys don't. It's nil. Zero. And they can't take up house together, because if people suddenly see five young guys, with a feminine appearance but masculine behaviour, living together, they're going to talk. They might even threaten. Just looking at them closely will give them away. And whatever lies they have said to get the house will be exposed.'

'Shelter is *the* biggest challenge for the working-class community,' Christy said. 'I never talk about upper-class transpeople because they have education, if nothing else. Even if your parents disown you, as long as they have put you through college, you can get a job, you can survive. Migrants with no education, no money, no support, and no home . . . where will they go?'

'But even those well-educated F-to-Ms have trouble, Christy,' Gayathri interjected. 'Yes, they'll get jobs for as long as they hide under the assigned gender. But the moment they start expressing their "original gender", they lose their jobs, just like working-class people.'

The vocabulary used in the community could be eye-opening. Gayathri used the word 'original', as if the gender of a transperson were hidden behind external appearance even at birth, and I found it interesting. I would have confused 'original gender' with 'assigned gender' if she had not phrased her sentence as she did. In such a context, was the phrase 'gender transition' itself offensive, I wondered. One can't transition into something that one already is. Should we call it 'gender affirmation' instead? Which phrase would be appropriate?

'Even among transwomen we know, the ones we speak to, raise awareness, and so on, about 25 per cent are so tuned into the patriarchal mindset that they believe a girl cannot become a guy,' Sowmya said. 'So a settlement like this is the exception, not the norm. You need support during crises, you need a place to stay, you need a job to support yourself, and you need facilities for surgery. That's what we're asking for.'

'And healthcare for transpeople,' Christy said. 'Not just surgery. Many of us have to fight depression. We need competent mental health professionals. And we need trans-friendly doctors.'

⌒

As we were about to leave, Christy asked for a photograph with all of us. A transwoman took it for us, and Gayathri asked her name.

'Subbalakshmi,' she said. 'Subbu.'

'Oh, both of you are called Subbu?!' she looked, puzzled, at the other Subbu.

'Oh, that one gives herself a new name every day,' Photographer Subbu said, and the other Subbu giggled. 'She uses all our names, and sees which one people like best. She's not yet decided on her name.'

Charupriyan and Gayathri dropped me off at Sunil's house. As we hugged goodbye, Gayathri touched my shoulder. 'Please convey a big "hi" and "thank you" to your parents on behalf of us. For not forcing you into marriage. For treating a daughter like a human being.'

Saviour

23 August 2017

Respected Nandani-ji,
Namaste. i am 57 yrs old transmen. i had thrown out in my home because i am smthng wrng.
i can tell to u my story. i did all surgery and hrmne change with guidness of my freind who give shelter, and now blessing of our spiritual guruji Matashri.
my freind is transgender lady ie hijra. she take care me since i got thrown out.
my phone no. _____
blessings of Matashri always.
Mukesh

28 October 2017

They lived together as brother and sister, they said. The transman asked for their location not to be identified. The chelas of his 'sister' Sitadevi believed he was her biological younger brother. His 'sister' spoke Hindi, which he only spoke with difficulty. But they were not happy I had brought an interpreter with me. 'I could have translated, humm,' Sitadevi grumbled. As the four of us sat on the portico of the traditional home where the 'sister' lived with her posse of chelas, neighbours would pass by, greet them, and give me curious looks.

'Ram, Ram,' said one to Mukesh, who nodded back and then extended his hand for a man-to-man shake. The two began to speak about the impending visit of a relative of the neighbour. The chat went on for a while, and ended with an invitation for the brother and sister to visit their home. Suddenly—to my surprise—the neighbour bent down and touched the feet of Sitadevi, who smiled and grazed her palm against his head, murmuring blessings.

'You must come with your daughters and bless my grandson,' the neighbour said.

Sitadevi assured him she would, and he left, bowing his head.

'There is a lot of respect for us here, humm,' she said, smiling at me. 'Everyone knows how much power we have. If we curse them, their lives are ruined. Humm. But we don't curse. It's wrong. You should not curse people. If we bless them, it will come true. So we try to give our blessing. Hummm.'

'Sometimes, they curse,' Mukesh said. 'The curse of the hijra is very powerful. It will stay with you for seven generations.'

'We don't curse, though.'

'Seven generations of the family will have problems,' Mukesh insisted.

'You should not curse unnecessarily,' Sitadevi said. 'When there is a need, you must teach people a lesson. Hummm. But not abuse power just because you have it.' She punctuated the more profound of her pronouncements with 'hummm', something between a sigh and snort. Everything about her seemed to ride on ambiguity. Even the colour of the sari she wore—which was also the shade of the kurta and salwar Mukesh wore—was ambiguous. It was the uniform of the ashram of their 'spiritual guru mataji'. It was an odd pastel colour, which could have been anything from grey to beige to cream to peach, quite like Richie Benaud's suits.

'For everything, we take advice from our Matashri,' Mukesh said. 'I even asked her about whether I should talk to you. She did *dhyaan* (meditation), and told me I can. Then she asked one of her devotees to write an email for me. I don't know English. Nothing at all.'

'Should we go inside?' I asked, as a middle-aged couple passed us, giving me and the interpreter curious looks.

'Our nephew and his wife,' Sitadevi called. My interpreter blushed. The couple stopped and smiled at us. The woman called out what sounded like an obligatory compliment about me. Then, she asked me a question. I turned to my interpreter, who was smiling and would not make eye contact.

'She's from outside,' Sitadevi said. 'She doesn't know Hindi, _____, anything. Only English. Hummm.'

The middle-aged couple seemed to approve.

'How about him?' the man asked, pointing to my interpreter.

'He's our nephew, of course he speaks _____,' Sitadevi said. 'Go, get their blessings.' She nudged him with her foot. My interpreter got off the steps and touched their feet. They looked at me, as if surprised I hadn't followed my husband. 'She's from abroad,' Sitadevi placated them. They nodded.

'Love marriage?' the woman ruffled my interpreter's hair.

Sitadevi grumbled a reply, which my interpreter later told me was, 'As if the kids listen to us these days.'

Once they had passed, and my interpreter had returned and resettled himself a little farther from me than before, Sitadevi winked at me. 'It's a nice evening. We can sit outside. Did you like my story for you?' I laughed. My interpreter seemed to relax a tad. 'See, our entire lives are about getting out of uncomfortable situations. We need to come up with stories all the time.'

One of her chelas brought glasses of tea.

'Now, go inside and ask everyone to stay in their rooms,' Sitadevi ordered. 'Don't disturb us for a while.' The chela rushed off, looking chastened. Sitadevi sipped her tea delicately, the glass tinkling against her many rings and bangles. Mukesh slurped his and made an odd smacking noise with his lips as he swallowed. 'Tell her your story,' Sitadevi told him.

'They wanted me to get married when I was sixteen,' Mukesh said. 'I used to be very depressed, but I didn't know why. I wanted short hair like my brother. I wanted to play with the boys. But they would never let me play with the boys, even when I was a child. They used to give me and my sisters dolls. I broke all of them. My sisters would cry. And my mother would beat me. I was never allowed to live like a man; people in villages are that way, right? So they got me married to a boy from the next village. Then I ran away from that home after a month, and came to my parents and cried. They got very angry and sent me back. Then again, I ran away, and this time my in-laws would not take me back. My father disowned me and told me I was dead to them.'

'But he never did anything wrong with his *aadmi* (husband),' Sitadevi said. She used the Hindi phrase '*galat kaam*', euphemism for sex—particularly illicit relationships or prostitution.

'Yes, yes, I never did anything. He anyway did not want anything to do with me. I'm fat and ugly, right. He used to go to hookers all the time. My family was rich, so he married me only for the money,' Mukesh said. 'He had lots of "girlfriends" too. His character was not good.'

'The aadmi was very handsome. Fair. This one is so dark. And doesn't look nice. As a man, it's okay. But girls have to be beautiful. This one wasn't. So, obviously, the aadmi married for money,' Sitadevi added.

When he was asked to leave home, Mukesh went straight to Sitadevi. Sitadevi had been his brother's classmate in school. As the only transwoman from the village, she was also its biggest scandal before Mukesh had disgraced both his families—the one into which he had been born, and the one into which he had been married.

'We always kept in touch,' Sitadevi said, 'because both of us knew there was something wrong with us. I used to wonder why he was trying to be a man when I so badly wanted to be a woman. And I still don't understand completely why a woman would want to become a man. But then maybe that's how he feels about me.' She laughed, and Mukesh smiled. 'So I took him to my mother'—by which she meant the senior transwoman who had accepted her as a chela—'and told her that he is my sister, and something must have gone wrong with God's plans, because he is a boy and I am a girl, but we got the wrong bodies.' It was a matter of great curiosity in the household. But eventually, they found a quack who could supply them with hormones which would have the opposite effect of those the transwomen took.

'My period stopped soon after that, and hair began to grow here,' Mukesh gestured at his face and chin. 'But I wanted to get surgery done, and I was wondering how to do it.' Sitadevi and her 'sisters' used various gels to enhance their breasts. But they had no idea what could reduce them. They had a set of rituals which would culminate in their 'nirvana', the removal of their male genitalia and their transition to womanhood. But how could someone want those parts they were so keen to discard? And how could they be fixed on a woman? They did not know.

'Then our Matashri came to do a darshan in ____,' Sitadevi said.

Mukesh had seen a poster with 'Matashri's' face on it and details about her visit. Something about her face had given him a sense of peace, he told me. Sitadevi and he went to the gathering, and when it was his turn to touch her feet, he had held on to them and begun to weep.

'She touched my shoulders and kissed my forehead and asked me to come to the ashram with her,' he said. 'I didn't have to tell her anything. She just knew.'

Sitadevi said, 'Hummm.' It seemed to me she was less devoted to Matashri than Mukesh was. Nevertheless, they had relocated to a town close to the ashram. Sitadevi had eventually joined a jama'at of transwomen in the town. Now, she was the most senior and de facto head of the jama'at. Mukesh had always been introduced as her brother. He had eventually been operated upon, for free, at a hospital run by the ashram.

'There was no pain,' he said. 'Matashri blessed me.'

Did he think 'Matashri' might be willing to talk to me?

'Matashri will talk to everyone, but only when the time is right,' he said, looking into the distance. 'When she wants to talk to you, you will feel it.'

'Hummm,' Sitadevi said.

She snapped her fingers, and one of her chelas hurried outside to pick up the three empty glasses.

The 'Network' before the Network

In many ways, the period of the early '90s, a time without mobile phones and internet, was indescribably frustrating. The biggest challenge for me was not, not having transmasculine support, but not having the financial resources, and, not having access to information and medical professionals. When the latter began to be available, it was something (of an ordeal) to deal with the fact that one's condition was seen as (the effect) of a 'mental disorder'. Being a student of biology, who 'swore by science' at the time, it was not easy to come to terms with this verdict of medicine. Overall, the experience was of increasingly being made a 'non-person' and evaporated from various places in the fabric of social life, and the resulting sense of isolation was extreme, with many moments of wanting to end the unbearableness.

—Satya Rai Nagpaul

Most of the transmen I met had found a label for themselves and made friends within the community through social networks. What was life like before Google? I barely remembered. What had it been like before mobile phones, before Facebook and WhatsApp groups, when transpeople were not visible to each other, when they'd had no source of information for medical or legal help?

'When did things resolve themselves for you?' I asked Satya.

'Things have still not resolved (themselves),' he said, with a smile. 'Being trans, as with any other gender practice that is not "the norm", is a lifetime's engagement with the questions that are thrown up from the experience. Serious struggles remain. Of legit medical assistance.

Of societal and state support. Of engaging with "gender" as a domain of questions, not only to "others", but to "oneself", and of fighting the menace of the fetishizing media.'

In the final book of Doris Lessing's *Children of Violence* series, *The Four-Gated City*, she speaks of a chilling psychiatric label: 'a nothing-but'. You're nothing-but your problem, whatever it is at any point of time. You're nothing-but a depression, an Electra, an Oedipus, a schizophrenic, a bipolar. It terrified me to think of people reduced to a single word, to the networks of nerves reduced to a few syllables that encompassed all that those people had been, were, and could be: nothing-buts to be medicated and pharmaceutically corrected. For weeks after reading the book, I would find myself freezing at points of the day and thinking what I was, depending on my roles and moods and appearance to others: nothing-but an anxiety, nothing-but a medium, nothing-but a paycheque, nothing-but a tantrum, nothing-but a sob, nothing-but a peal of laughter. When I went out and did stories, it seemed to me that my interviewees were nothing-but a sound bite, mixed faces and genders and ages to constitute an acceptable vox populi.

When Satya spoke of media fetishization, I thought of the boxes into which so many of my interviews for the book could fit: nothing-but a student, nothing-but a disabled, nothing-but a rape victim, nothing-but a crisis, nothing-but a lesbian, nothing-but a dysphoria, nothing-but, nothing-but, nothing-but. How did one escape the slotting of people? How did one escape the labels? And once one had been slotted and labelled, how did one escape that perception of oneself? When Charu and Gayathri had begun reeling off types of interviews, and asked me what kind I wanted, I had felt almost panicky. Was I part of a group that was reducing people to anecdotes? How did a story transcend the anecdote? What did a story sound like before it had been polished in NGO settings? How would people who had never been interviewed earlier respond to my questions?

~

Hemabati had the day all planned out. We would criss-cross Imphal and its outskirts, meeting various couples and halves of couples, transmen from Manipur who had agreed to speak to me. He, Nanao, BD and Aily squeezed into the back seat of a box car, driven by a man Hemabati called his 'Jamaai Raja (son-in-law)'. He was the son-in-law of Nanao's cousin.

As we drove to our first meeting, Hemabati began to tell me about Empowering Trans Ability (ETA).

'We chose the name because in Meitei, 'eta' means best friend,' he said. 'It is used among girls, but since we are born as female, we don't mind.'

'That means,' BD added, 'if both of us are best friends, sister, I will say, "You are my eta."'

'And what is the male equivalent?' I asked.

They all looked at each other and then laughed. 'It's not common. We don't remember.' The taxi driver didn't know either, and seemed somewhat embarrassed about it.

'Men don't talk sentimentally like that, no?' he smiled.

We arrived at a little corner shop. A woman smiled in welcome as we entered. A door in a nook led to a small room with soft carpets and a generously sized single bed.

Meme was the ciswoman partner of Thoibi. Most transmen in Manipur went by their given names. The younger among them, those in their twenties, had either modified their names or taken on new ones. Meme was fifty-one, and Thoibi fifty. As Thoibi wrapped up some work in the store, we settled down in the room. Nanao began to roll some paan.

'See, this is the Manipuri language,' BD showed me a newspaper. 'There are more than thirty-five tribes here, with languages of their own. Now, the kids are learning Meitei. This state is very troubled, no? India doesn't even know where we are. In my fourth year, my teachers used to think I was from Nepal. You feel bad to hear such things, na? Sometimes, it's like they don't have any general knowledge. You ask even a first-standard child here, "Where is Pondicherry, where is Goa, Punjab, Srinagar, Jammu," they will show you on a map. You ask,

"What is Telangana," they will tell you it's a new state. But mainland India is not like that. The only northeastern city people know is Guwahati. So they will ask, "How far from Guwahati?" It's actually 500 kilometres, but we just say, "Oh, very near". They expect us to speak Hindi to prove we are Indian. Because of all this, the militancy started, and because of the militancy, the Assam Rifles are here, and because of that, there are so many problems.'

There were particular problems for transmen. Military and police presence in the state was high, and security checks were common. Vehicles could be stopped and searched anywhere. People could be frisked anywhere.

~

The biggest celebration in Manipur is the Yaoshang Festival, which marks the harvest every year. It is a five-day celebration, of which the highlight is Thabal Chongba, the moonlight dancing. Just hearing the rhythm of the drum could make a Manipuri want to dance. It is also the season for courtship, because the circular dance comprises men and women standing next to each other, holding hands. The boys would travel from village to village in the district. The Thabal Chongba was held at a different village each night. When a boy met someone particularly interesting, he would contrive to pick her up the next day and take her dancing in the next village.

A group of cousins was returning from a night of moonlight dancing. They were boasting happily about the girls they had met, the ones they had invited to the dance in the next village, the ones they would see the next day, and who had scored the hottest of the lot.

Suddenly, their motorcycles were waved down by servicemen.

They asked them to get off their bikes for a body search.

'This one is a girl, sir,' one of the cousins said.

The policemen looked at each other, at the cousin who was squirming, and then laughed.

'Yeah, right. Stop fucking with us and line up,' they said.

'No, sir, she really is a girl.'

'Really? Then ask her to remove her shirt and prove it.'

There was no woman among the security personnel, and the boys were
pleading with them to let the girl go without touching her, when a senior
officer's jeep drove by. The driver rolled down the window to ask what the
commotion was.

Hands folded in obsequiousness, one of the cousins explained to the
senior officer, who waved them on impatiently. They clambered on to their
motorcycles and rushed off before the jeep had passed, so that the leering
security personnel could not stop them again.

~

'Even now, we have problems at security checks,' BD said. 'Sometimes
they say, "Hey, you're a boy, why are you coming in this line?" And
then we tell them, "No, no, we're girls, we look like this because we
are sportspersons. That's why we have short hair." I don't like saying
I'm a girl, but I don't have a choice.'

Hemabati often looked amused when the younger transmen
spoke about their dysphoria, about wanting to have surgery.

'There are no facilities now,' he said, 'and most of us are not well-off.
But when I was growing up, even thinking about surgery was impossible.'

Hemabati and Nanao had been together for fifteen years, they said.
Nanao spoke almost constantly, and gestured every time her hands
were free, which wasn't often—she was making paan from betel leaves
faster than she could chew. Her lips and most of her teeth were stained
red. Her hair reached down to her hips, and she had a lot to say.

'My English and Hindi are both not very good,' she told me in
broken Hindi. 'But that's the least of my problems.' She laughed and
held up a palm for a high-five.

Most of ETA's members called Hemabati 'Yambung'—Meitei for
'brother'—and Nanao was 'Bhabhi'. The Meitei word for 'sister-in-
law' was '*inamma*' or '*ittaima*', depending on the gender of the person
addressing her, but they were not commonly used and the Hindi word
'bhabhi' was the norm.

The two had met when Hemabati's cousin married Nanao's sister.
Nanao said, laughing, that she used to be a 'jolly, fancy type girl' with

lots of boyfriends. She and Hemabati spoke often, and he liked her, but he hadn't dared approach her. She had several cismale suitors helping her father in the fields in the hope of impressing her.

When Nanao's mother passed away, she sank into depression.

'Then Yambung came and looked after her like a mother,' BD said. 'She didn't feel the absence of her mother because he supported her so much.'

There was something comforting, almost maternal, about Hemabati's presence, but he didn't seem female, Nanao said. She had not thought of herself as lesbian, but began to feel an attraction for Hemabati that she could not explain. When she was twenty and he was twenty-two, they decided to get married.

I noticed that in Manipur, the partners of transmen referred to themselves as 'lesbian', even though they had never been attracted to women. All of them said they were heterosexual, and couldn't explain why they called themselves lesbian except with, 'because he was also female by birth'. Everywhere else in India, the partners referred to themselves as 'femme', unless they did identify as lesbian by inclination.

Hemabati said Nanao was the first person to understand him. He was allowed to wear trousers to school until he was in Class 6. But after puberty, the family wanted him to grow his hair. He cut it off himself, with scissors, one day, and tried speaking about it to his brother. He tried negotiating for permission to maintain his short hair until he finished school. It didn't work.

'Every year, I will cut my hair and come home. Family war will start,' Hemabati said in English, smiling. The last time he did it, in Class 10, his family disowned him. He moved to his maternal uncle's home, a few doors away, and attended college.

'So, so hard,' he said. 'I was selected to take part in an international karate tournament, but I was so depressed, I did not go. I attempted suicide twice.'

'If we had been together then, I would have given him the firepower to go and participate in the tournament,' Nanao said. 'All he needed was someone to encourage him.'

I thought again of Aristophanes' halves. In finding each other, in finding those right halves and fusing into a unit, they found again the terrible strength and swiftness to roll around the roughest terrain and even challenge the gods.

It wasn't easy to convince their families. Nanao's two brothers and sister are still trying to convince her to marry a cisman, she said.

'But my father-in-law is my best friend,' Hemabati softly said in English, and smiled. 'It's so good.'

'He knows I'm very strong,' Nanao said. 'Once I've made up my mind, there's no point trying to change it.'

Hemabati's family is still not willing to accept them. He and Nanao had moved into a rented room, which cost Rs 110 a month, in the early days of their relationship. Once Hemabati's brother got married and his wife moved in, Nanao decided they should live with his parents too. His parents were not happy with the arrangement, but Nanao was insistent. She was a married woman, she said, and she belonged with her husband's family. Finally, the family built a little annexe for Hemabati and Nanao.

'But they won't sign over any of their property to us,' Hemabati said.

'And they don't treat me like a daughter-in-law,' Nanao added.

She spoke fast and animatedly, often clapping her hands for emphasis.

There was a family shrine in every Manipuri house, she said, where everyone would gather to pray. It was customary for the women of the house to take turns leading the prayer—they would cook a rice pudding as offering, and light the lamp and incense sticks. It was never Nanao's turn.

'My mother-in-law is the "Number One Gangster Villain",' Nanao said, raising her index finger to underscore her point, and Hemabati began to laugh. 'She never says anything to my face, but bitches about me to everyone in the neighbourhood. And then she tells my husband that I've ruined him. Because he won't listen to her, she goes and tells everyone in every house nearby, "Ohhhhh, look, my daughter has got spoilt after marrying that girl. She has turned her into a male . . ."'—

she imitated her mother-in-law, complete with a bent back— '. . . all this, even if a guest comes to the house for tea.'

But their younger relatives accorded them respect, Nanao said. They made it a point to visit the annexe when they came home, and treated her like the bhabhi she was.

'My mother-in-law doesn't allow me to welcome guests, so I just stay in our room. I can't go there and behave like another guest.' Nanao snorted. 'And the older relatives expect me to go and greet them, but I won't. Let them come to my house if they want. I'll be the hostess there.'

They celebrate their functions independently—Yaoshang and Cheiraoba, the New Year. Typically, families have a grand feast and then climb the hill to pray at a temple. It hurts Nanao that they are not part of the ritual, that a divided family sets out from the same house.

'I don't want their property—they have land and fields, let them keep it. All I want is respect.' She turned to Meme. 'Am I right?'

Meme shook her head. 'They don't give us respect. We moved away from home. Long ago.'

Thoibi came in from the shop and dusted his hands. He introduced himself as the secretary of ETA. He had always been a sportsman, playing kabaddi, football and karate. Being a sportsperson allowed him a degree of freedom—he was allowed to wear his hair short, and his family didn't object to his male clothes.

'I even participated in an international karate competition, in Kerala,' he said, 'in 1993. After I finished my BA.' He was now an instructor, and had coached many students. The fact that the youth sports clubs in Manipur were so active gave most sportspeople a source of income as coaches after their playing days were over.

He and Meme had been neighbours, and 'childhood best friends'. Their families assumed it was a friendship between girls, until Meme told her brother and sister she wanted to marry Thoibi.

'They locked me up, like it happens in the movies,' Meme said. 'And they said they would arrange a marriage for me the next day. They even told me whom I was to marry. But in the middle of the night, I packed a few things and escaped through the window.' She went to an aunt's house, and sent word to Thoibi to meet her there.

They eloped the next morning, and haven't been in touch with their families since. It has been twenty-four years, Thoibi told me, smiling. He didn't have strong ties to his family. He had lost his mother when he was a child.

He and Meme had initially lived in a little shack, but found out how dangerous it could be for two 'women' to live alone.

'One night, some drunk people came that way, and told me they could do anything to me,' Meme said. 'Thoibi had gone to the market. They said they could take my hand and take me to the fields, and there was nothing I could do.'

They closed in on her, but left when they heard footsteps. A neighbour was returning from the fields. When Thoibi came home, only minutes later, he found Meme in tears. She told him how scared she had been, and he ran after the drunk men, caught up with them, and beat them up.

'I smashed all their faces. One of them broke a tooth,' he said.

It caused a furore in the village. A council of elders sent for Thoibi and told him that girls ought not to chase after men and draw them into fights. When Thoibi said they had harassed his wife, the village council asked him how he, a woman, had a wife.

'Brother Thoibi knew they would not help,' BD translated for me. 'They even sent some goonda types (thugs) at night to frighten them. But, actually, the goondas were better than the village elders. When Brother Thoibi and Sister Meme explained the situation, they said they would look into it, and they didn't come back.'

This was only one example of the problems they faced, Meme said; twenty-four years is a long time, enough time for harassment on several fronts. They worked odd jobs until they had enough money to start a small shop, which eventually expanded into the two-room shack it is today.

'Everything is a problem,' she said. 'We can't get below poverty line cards, food security cards, we can't even get our address registered because they say we're two women and can't be married to each other. We should have our names in our families' ration list. It's like we live in a different world, where we can't access anything. And, of course, our families don't accept us. Both our relatives and government officials ask us how we can have children. There are so many childless heterosexual couples. They are not denied basic rights, are they? We have made this sacrifice, we have given up our chances of having children, to be with each other. We're not asking for special allowances. We're only asking for the subsidies due to us.'

They're beginning to worry about the choice now, Thoibi said. They are getting old, and worry about who will take care of them. Their families knew where they lived, but hadn't bothered getting in touch. They couldn't depend on their nieces and nephews. They had considered adopting a child, but they would not pass the house checks.

'Can we put me down as the father, and her as the mother?' Thoibi asked. 'They may allow single women to adopt, but we only hear of rich single women adopting. We're not rich. But we have enough money and love to raise a child. That's why we have joined this organization, ETA, to ask for our rights and to ask the government to allow adoption for transgender people.'

'We can represent our cases to the government through an organisation,' Hemabati added. 'Because there *are* some rules which will allow us basic rights. The problem is, in some districts, people don't follow the rules. They don't even know the rules.'

The state government had announced that there would be job reservations for transpeople. The only documents required, other than photographic identity proof, were the gender identity change (GIC) certificate and an affidavit from the Transgender Rights Board. Surgery is not required for the GIC, and several of ETA's members have the certificate. But since ration cards and job applications are processed in small government offices, each transman had a different experience, Hemabati said, and was subject to the whims of the people sitting at those desks.

'We're asking the government to make a pucca announcement,' BD told me. 'Because they have said the forms will allow you to apply as Male, Female, or Transgender, but there's no option for transgender people in the form. If they make an announcement in the newspapers, we can show (officials) the clipping, and say the government has passed this order. If we go to the office and show our GIC, they ask, "What is GIC?" When we say it's our gender identity change certificate, they ask, "What is gender identity?"'

That was why it was so important to form a group. When one person was turned away from a government office, he brought representatives of the organization back with him to liaise with officials. It was hard work forming ETA, Hemabati said, but he had found that every transman he met knew a few others. Even before social media networks had made it possible for people to find each other, practically every village had its own little network of transmen.

'Maybe only two or three, but most people knew others like them,' Hemabati said. 'Many of us got into sports because we felt like men, so we met each other. We would speak about how we were uncomfortable with other girls, but comfortable with each other. And then we liked girls, but we wanted them for wives, not friends.'

'But at least they have an organization,' Nanao said suddenly. 'We lesbian partners don't.'

She said there were unique problems the partners of transmen faced. Years, even decades into partnership, they could be harassed over their 'failure to find a husband'. Arranged marriages were not the norm in Manipur, but when a woman was in her thirties or forties, her family might encourage her to enter a marriage of convenience with a cisman.

They were considered inauspicious at family weddings.

'Married women wear different clothes from unmarried women,' Nanao said. 'Our traditional dress is different. I'm a married woman, but when I wear the clothes of a married woman, they pass snide remarks.' She snorted. 'We can do no right. When we're with our partners, they say we're ruining their lives. If we leave them because their families want us out, they tell our partners, "See, didn't we tell you she was a bitch? She was stringing you along, and she's dumped you now. That's how women are. Now *you* should also marry a man." And if we marry cismen because of the pressure, the husbands won't respect us anyway, because we'll be seen as hand-me-downs. We've lived with someone else, and we're with them only because we need financial support.'

To give up the prospect of having biological children was a sacrifice, Nanao said, and Meme smiled in agreement. 'When we meet our childhood friends, and we see them with children, we sometimes feel jealous. And there are some rituals a woman whose firstborn is a son can perform, as a matron, at weddings. So the women who don't have sons get pitying glances from the others. And we get pitying glances from *them*.' She laughed and slapped her thigh. 'We give up so much, we build a life together. And we don't get respect. We should at least have a forum to talk about such things, with each other. We haven't even thought about the rights we ought to have as partners of transmen.'

~

I noticed that there was only one picture of Thoibi and Meme, faded with age, in the house. I offered to take some photographs for them. BD and Hemabati scouted for a spot, and settled on a bridge with fields on one side, and a widening river on the other. Thoibi and Meme stood awkwardly, looking into the distance. I asked Thoibi to face the camera. He turned his head in the opposite direction, and Meme gently took his chin to correct the angle. He suddenly kissed her cheek, and Meme's eyes lit up.

An older woman passing by let out a gasp of delighted laughter and drew her hands over her mouth. Meme blushed, and Thoibi kissed her again. Only when I looked at my photographs later did I notice a mistletoe-like plant hanging down from a branch above them.

The Thirunangais' Ramayana

When a transwoman joins a jama'at—a household with her adoptive mother and a network of other relatives—she inherits its folklore. And the tale that sustains thirunangais, giving them a place in history and mythology, is a story from the Ramayana. This story cannot be found in most versions of the Ramayana—not Valmiki's, not Kambar's, not Tulsidas's—but it is sacred to the thirunangai tradition.

When the Crown Prince of Ayodhya, Rama, was banished to the forest after a series of misunderstandings and machinations, his bride Sita and his brother Lakshmana insisted on accompanying him. So did the entire kingdom of Ayodhya. Finally, as they were about to enter the forest, Rama turned to the subjects of the kingdom and said: 'Please walk no further with me.'

The people of Ayodhya obeyed. But they refused to leave the spot. They would wait right there for his return, due thirteen years later.

'No,' said Rama. 'Every man, woman, and child who loves me must return home.'

Every man, woman and child returned home. As the crowd began to disperse, Rama, Lakshmana and Sita walked into the forest. They did not notice that some people stayed behind. They saw them again, thirteen years later, still waiting.

They loved Rama, but they did not consider themselves men, women or children. They were the hijras of Ayodhya.

Had Rama known of their devotion, known that they would not be able to choose between their love for him and their obligation to obey his commands, because he knew their loyalty was greater than that of other humans?

Or had he too, this paragon of virtue and justice and deference to the rule of law, forgotten they existed?

As they waited by the forest through thirteen long years for his return, what did those transwomen feel—elation, pride, rejection, despondency, or resignation to invisibility?

The legend goes that when Rama returned, he was stricken with guilt, and rushed to embrace them, that he promised he would look after their ilk for all time, and told them they would always have a special place in his heart.

Were there only transwomen in Ayodhya, who were not-men-not-women? Or were they themselves guilty of the same oversight, to atone for which Rama swore he would protect them for eternity? In fostering this story down the generations, had they forgotten about another category of neither-man-nor-woman? Were there no transmen in Ayodhya? Or did they stand waiting too, ghosts to the very people who were ghosts to Rama?

'Stop Transgender Bill 2016'

This bill is not just a watered-down version of the Trichy Siva Bill. It has poison added.

—Delfina, member of Nirangal

When the people whose rights a Bill is supposed to guarantee begin an agitation against it, it's fair to suppose it must have got something rather wrong.

For the first time in Indian history, a Bill had been introduced that could have decriminalized partnerships and marriage among transpeople, which are not recognized under Section 377 of the Indian Penal Code. The Bill, informally known as the Trichy Siva Bill, after the name of the Rajya Sabha MP who proposed it, offered various other rights, including reservation in educational institutes and companies, the right to self-identification of gender, and pension.

So great was the hope riding on it that trans and intersex people, as well as their allies, liaised with Trichy Siva. Mina Swaminathan was among those who approached him to include a clause about medical assistance. When the Bill was passed into law, there could be no loophole which would allow the government to deny financial, infrastructural or logistical assistance to transpeople.

In April 2016, it would become the first private member's Bill to be passed by the House in forty-five years. But soon after its passage in the Rajya Sabha (Upper House), and while it was pending for discussion in the Lok Sabha (Lower House), the government said it would table its own version of the Bill, and did so in August 2016 in the Lok Sabha.

Ever since the NALSA judgment, various groups and individuals from the community had been interfacing with the ministry of social justice and empowerment (MoSJE), Satya had told me. The last few years had been a 'roller-coaster, in terms of how the Bill has gone from one Parliament session to another'.

To the disappointment of everyone involved, the Transgender Persons (Protection of Rights) Bill, 2016, as the new document was known, omitted several of the provisions in the Trichy Siva Bill, and even contradicted the NALSA verdict.

Among the provisions of the Trichy Siva Bill that were discarded as 'impractical' were employment exchanges and exclusive courts in each district for transgender people, national- and state-level commissions to monitor trans rights, and protection of the children of transpeople.

The Bill was immediately opposed by various sections of the trans community. The Lok Sabha Speaker referred it to a Standing Committee of the social justice ministry, seeking a report within three months. The eighteen-member committee liaised with various non-governmental organizations fighting for trans rights. When it did finally submit its report in July 2017, the recommendations included recognition of marriage, divorce, and adoption rights for transpeople, quotas in government colleges and universities as well as in government companies, and the right of any person to identify as female, male or a third gender irrespective of medical intervention, including surgery.

However, the ministry decided to ignore all the requests for amendments and said it would reintroduce the original version in the winter session of Parliament.

The trans community, shocked by this decision, has been organizing protests since November 2016, highlighting the problems in the Bill.

For one, the Bill has limited the gender options for transpeople to 'transgender', and to even change one's gender from that assigned at birth, the applicant will have to seek approval from a screening committee and submit proof of surgery.

This screening committee will consist of a chief medical officer, a district social welfare officer, a psychologist or psychiatrist, a representative of the transgender community and a government-nominated officer.

Trans rights groups which were involved in communication with the Parliamentary Standing Committee pointed out that the right to self-identify one's gender without medical intervention or certification has had international precedent. Argentina, Denmark, Italy, Ireland, Ecuador, Malta, and Colombia recognise the right, and the US has made a start with New York. So why, in India, did 'experts' have to attest that a person was transgender when the Supreme Court has ruled in favour of the right to self-identification?

When the committee put this question to the ministry, the latter replied that cismen might misuse the provision to claim benefits. The trans community has pointed out that the Bill ensures there are no real benefits to being trans. Besides, the single seat for a person from the trans community would make that person something of a gatekeeper, and this could lead to various forms of lobbying and power play within the community.

The demand for a sex reassignment surgery certificate will affect many people on the gender spectrum, including pre-operative and non-operative transpeople and those who identify as gender-fluid and gender-neutral, to say nothing of intersex people.

Since the NALSA judgment deems gender tests unnecessary and intrusive, legislation that violates the judgment can be challenged in court. But this would be a long process, and groups fighting for trans rights would rather 'give the government a chance to chisel the Bill' through a collaborative process, Satya told me.

One of the provisions of the Bill is that no transperson will be separated from his or her immediate family on the grounds of being a transperson, unless the family is unable to take care of the person, under which circumstances 'the competent court shall by an order direct such person to be placed in rehabilitation centre'.

Since many young transpeople face hostility and even violence from their natal families, the committee recommended—as the

Trichy Siva Bill had—that adoptive families such as the hijra jama'at be recognized as 'families'. The ministry replied that 'parallel systems' could not be allowed to exist, and that they would only 'increase the chances of his physical and sexual abuse' (sic).

Even more troubling is the provision that a transperson whose family is 'unable' to take care of him or her must be placed in a 'rehabilitation centre', with no clarification as to why 'rehabilitation' is necessary or for how long this period will last.

Another provision, which criminalizes, 'Whoever compels or entices a transgender person to indulge in the act of begging or other similar forms of forced or bonded labour other than any compulsory service for public purposes imposed by Government', has also upset the trans community. Begging has traditionally been one of the ways in which young transwomen make money for their jama'ats.

Several states have already criminalized begging, and transwomen have been picked up by the police and either arrested or held in detention centres. But this new provision would essentially dismantle the entire structure of livelihood of the jama'at.

On 28 December 2017, Gee posted on his Facebook page:

transwomen going back after rehearsing for a dance programme to be hosted by social justice dept in kozhikode brutally beaten up by police at 2.30 a.m. Jasmine and Sushmita are admitted in Beach hospital. One has a broken hand and the other has serious injuries due to lathi blows on her back. While beating them, the cops said "It's dangerous for people like you to be allowed to live". Kerala model of development and inclusion.

Images of their injuries accompanied news reports. One of the comments under a report read, 'If cops don't beat who will? They harassed me for money on a train . . . there must be some reason the cops hit them.' (sic)

Many transpeople question the motives behind the government insisting on introducing its own Bill, despite a private member having started the process. The difference between the two versions is marked, and some of the provisions in the Trichy Siva Bill, which could lead to the legislative decriminalization of Section 377, are missing from the government's version.

While the Bill has vague provisions for punishment of anyone guilty of physical or sexual harassment or assault of transpeople, it has not detailed the punishment or mentioned specific laws that will prevent such harassment or assault. The existing laws in the Indian Penal Code are not gender-neutral, and assume that the victim is a woman and the perpetrator a man.

In August 2017, this loophole allowed four people to escape conviction for the rape of a transwoman.

A nineteen-year-old transwoman was gang-raped in the Wadgaon Budruk area of Pune. Section 377 would have ensured the rapists' culpability if they had violated a 'man, woman, or animal'. But since the victim's gender in the medical report was listed as 'other', the section could not be used. Section 376, which deals with punishment for rape, could not be applied either since it only applies to the rape of a woman. The court approved the bail application of the four accused. The victim told the media she had chosen not to appeal, because she felt 'broken emotionally, physically and mentally'.

But Section 377 can be, and usually is, used against transgender sex workers.

Another provision of the Bill reads, 'Every establishment consisting of one hundred or more persons shall designate a person to be a complaint officer to deal with the complaints relating to violation of the provisions of this Act.'

When the committee asked why organizations with fewer than hundred employees had been exempted, the ministry replied: 'It is not practically feasible for small establishments to designate a Complaint Officer. However, the mechanism of police system is robust in India for taking care of such grievances.'

In a letter to the ministry signed by several organizations, including Nirangal, Orinam, Sampoorna Working Group, and Telangana Hijra Intersex Transgender Samiti, the definition of 'establishment' was questioned. Not only were transpeople working in organizations with fewer than hundred employees left out, but so was everyone working in the unorganized sector. They pointed out that the Sexual Harassment of Women at Workplace (Prevention, Prohibition and Redressal) Act, 2013, had broad definitions of 'employee' and 'workplace', specified that workplace harassment committees should be headed by women, and that there was provision for women working in organizations with fewer than ten people, in the unorganized sector, or as domestic workers, to approach a local complaints committee. Why had no such provision been made in the Transgender Bill, 2016? Why did transpeople working in the unorganized sector have no safety net? Transpeople have little faith in the police, and there is little the best-intentioned police officers can do when the law has no provisions for justice, they pointed out.

The Bill also ignores demands for 'penal action against abortions of intersex foetuses and forced surgical assignment of sex of intersex infants', punishment for medical negligence, and the provision of separate wards in jails and juvenile justice shelters for transpeople, which would be supervised only by female police officials, provision of separate wards in hospitals, as well as a Transgender Persons' Welfare Commission to look into human rights violations against trans communities. Instead, it suggests the creation of a National Council that will only be empowered to advise the central government on transgender policies.

In response to the protests, the standing committee tried to liaise with the ministry again. The objections began right with the name of the Bill.

In its interactions with the standing committee, Sampoorna had specifically asked that the Bill also include intersex people and distinguish them from transpeople.

The committee recommended the renaming of the Bill as 'The Transgender and Intersex Persons (Protection of Rights) Bill, 2016', to which the ministry replied: 'Transgender is an umbrella term which includes intersex persons also. Re-wording the title of the Bill would not serve any purpose.'

Karthik Bittu believes the confusion of transgender with intersex could be an impression fostered by the community itself: 'I think some transpeople have portrayed themselves as intersex. And that's part of what has influenced the Bill to go in this direction. The perception of transpeople as intersex is an erroneous perception and it doesn't do anything to help intersex people; it's a disservice to both the communities, in fact.'

Further dialogue between the committee and the ministry ended in farce. Part of the blame for this lies with the committee itself, which seems to have very little understanding of trans issues.

In its report, the committee uses the derogatory term 'eunuch' to refer to transpeople, and the report is riddled with other errors, including such bizarre observations as: 'Intersexual people are not visibly distinguishable in the West. In marked contrast, eunuchs in the Indian subcontinent are found to dress and behave differently, in addition to living apart in bands and groups. India and other South Asian countries are the only places where the tradition of eunuchs is prevalent today.'

This not only conflates 'intersex' with 'transgender', but also leaves out transmen and those assigned female at birth, equating 'transgender' with 'transwoman'.

'Given the government's rejection of the Parliamentary Standing Committee's recommendation as of the last session, I am not very hopeful about what will unfold,' Satya told me, in early 2018. 'Trans, and not intersex people, are going to be visible in the "law". Even the Parliamentary Standing Committee has made the grave mistake of clubbing "intersex" within "transgender" and we are far from a critical mass of intersex people for that to be taken up now.'

The committee's report goes on to blame British colonialism for the abolition of kingdoms and the loss of livelihood of transwomen, who were patronized by kingly courts.

Such conclusions lacking any sociological or historical basis wouldn't pass muster even in the term paper of an undergraduate student in any of the universities in India. But clearly, the Ministry believes that the golden period of trans- and intersex people in the subcontinent was destroyed by the British, instead of our collective disempowerment being the result of various factors like caste, patriarchy, state apathy, transphobia, lack of awareness, public prejudices etc. in addition to the criminalizing laws of the colonial empire and the nation state.

—Gee Imaan Semmalar, *First as Apathy, Then as Farce: The Transgender Persons (Protection of Rights) Bill, 2016*, Orinam

Soon after the budget session of Parliament ended without the Bill coming up for discussion, I emailed Satya, asking, 'What do you think the most important provisions in law should be? What is crucial for transpeople, specifically transmasculine people?'

His reply illustrated his disillusionment:

> The law must address the question of 'full citizenship' of trans, intersex and gender non-conforming (GNC) persons. The questions of 'full citizenship' have to be addressed from the point of view of historical disenfranchisement, as well as what we know today about trans-intersex-GNC self-hood. If these perspectives do not inform the attempts of the legislative and the executive, we will be yet another constituency which will be just another 'tick-mark' via the already problematic category called 'third gender'.
>
> The saddest aspect for me about this moment is that even the Parliamentary Standing Committee on the TG Bill, constituted by members across political parties, has not put out a 'good enough' recommendations report. The moments of learnings about trans-intersex-GNC lives, which they had the opportunity to witness through various state visits, as well as the depositions held in New Delhi, should have given rise to deep (reflection) regarding the 'real' questions about gender and sex, but (they did) not. There is not one place in the report that has held the cis communities responsible for the current state of affairs and asked for accountability in this regard. The report is constantly underlined with 'pity' and the one consistent emotion running through its pages is one of 'we should do something for *them*'.

It took me some time to work out what first struck me as a contradiction—if cispeople were responsible for the current state of affairs and should be held accountable, did the cis community not owe reparations? Was the cis community not obliged to do something for the trans community? When I re-read Satya's email, I understood that he took issue with the fact that the cis community, led by the Parliament, saw these reparations not as obligatory, but as charity.

The notion of 'us' doing something for 'them' came from the position of privilege that allowed one to feel sympathy, even pity.

'Transmasculine people will continue to be the marginalized of the marginalized,' Satya wrote. 'The "traditional" bias of the government is already apparent in various places. A stark recent example of such a narrow vision is their attempt to replace the mention of the word *"hijra"* by the word *"kinnar"* in a recent film that came up for certification to the CBFC! There is the great possibility that transmasculine-intersex-GNC people are going to be the "default riders" on this bus for trans rights.' In other words, they would have no say. The bus would be driven by cispeople.

On 18 March 2018, the Bill was sent to the Cabinet after an inter-ministerial consultation followed by vetting by the ministry of law. Nine amendments were finalised, keeping in mind the recommendations of the Parliamentary Standing Committee.

The definition of 'transgender' had been changed. The initial version had stated that the term referred to someone who was 'neither wholly male nor female, a combination of female or male, or neither female nor male and whose sense of gender does not match with the gender assigned to that person at the time of birth'. It had been replaced by 'a person whose gender does not match with the gender assigned to that person at birth and includes trans-man or trans-women (whether or not such persons has undergone sex reassignment surgery or hormone therapy or laser therapy or such other therapy). It also includes person with intersex variations, gender-queer and person having such socio-cultural identities such as "kinnar", "hijra", "aravani" and "jogta".' (sic)

While transpeople who have undergone surgery will not need to be examined by a district screening committee to avail 'benefits', provided they have medical certificates to prove they have transitioned, it is not clear what these 'benefits' are; and it is not clear what sort of tests or screening those who have not had surgery will have to submit to. Even those who *have* had surgery will have to get another certificate from a medical superintendent or chief medical officer in order to apply for a gender change to the district magistrate's office.

The committee's request that every establishment, irrespective of the number of employees, would have to designate an officer to deal with complaints of discrimination or harassment, has also been accommodated. But there is no word on the options for redress in the case of transpeople working in the unorganized sector.

Most importantly, it has not exempted transpeople from Section 377.

It has not included them in the 'Other Backward Classes' category, which would have allowed them the benefit of reservation in government jobs.

There *are* contradictory opinions on the Bill.

'How can you simply self-identify without a certificate?' an activist who asked not to be named said. 'Or how can you identify within the binary and then ask for reservation as trans? It's like wanting reservation under the Scheduled Castes or Tribes category, but refusing to divulge your caste or producing a caste certificate. Or like asking for concession for HIV-positive people on trains, but refusing to carry your identification to prove your condition.'

'I think the objection is to do with being screened for the certificate, rather than getting the certificate itself, no?' I asked.

'It depends. There are those who question the intrusive screening, and in that case, we can start a dialogue about non-intrusive screening. But you can't simply certify yourself, right? You can talk about who is on the committee. You can talk about the process. You can get into the "how", but not the "why". If you want concessions and benefits, you need to produce some identity that merits those.'

Again, because concessions and benefits could be issued by the centre as well as the state, the logistics involved in formulating an identity card would be a nightmare. Some states, such as Tamil Nadu and Manipur, have already issued transgender cards that will allow transpeople to avail of benefits. The Kerala model, though, has received some flak over the last couple of years.

'As someone who served actively in the District Transgender Justice Board of Ernakulam for a year, I would like to convey my sheer disappointment at how the Kerala government and Social Justice

Department still do not show the basic understanding of the policy which they are supposed to implement,' Vihaan wrote in a Facebook post. 'They continue to push transpeople to go along with their whims and fancies on the threats—if you question/don't cooperate, things will move even more (slowly). A good example of this kind of ignorance and bullying is evident in the Transgender ID cards to be produced and distributed by 31st of March this year.'

The idea behind issuing transgender identity cards was that people who self-identify as trans, regardless of surgery, could avail benefits provided by the government, which had set aside an annual budget of Rs 10 crore for trans welfare.

The first template of the transgender card did not have the Kerala government's logo and only carried the logo of the Social Justice Department, making it unacceptable as a legal proof of identity. The transgender and intersex symbols had been mixed up in the card. There were other issues with the card: it allowed no space for a transperson to identify within the binary.

The card was ready to be issued in August 2017. By March 2018, the Social Justice Department announced that the budget would lapse if transpeople did not avail of the benefits within the financial year. The department hastily constituted a board comprising a psychologist, psychiatrist, district medical officer (DMO), and three members of the transgender community to review applications for the card, decide whether any applicants should be asked further questions, and then issue cards where they saw fit.

When trans rights activists asked why there was no option to choose one of the binary genders, they were told it was to ensure that cispeople did not apply for the card and avail benefits that were not due to them.

'What a bizarre logic,' Vihaan wrote. 'The TG card has been designed for "transpeople". Anyone who carries this card is obviously going to be identified as transgender or transsexual (someone who has undergone a transitional experience) by the state. This is validated by the screening process where you show required documentation. How difficult is this to comprehend and monitor?'

Timeline

14 April 2014: The Supreme Court delivers its landmark verdict on the right to self-determination of gender identity, which comes to be known as the NALSA judgment, and gives the Centre six months to implement it. The Central goverment, through MoSJE, files a petition asking for clarifications pertaining to the timeline of implementation and the inclusion of transpeople under the Other Backward Classes category.

December 2015: The MoSJE puts out a draft of the Transgender Rights Bill and invites feedback from organizations and individuals. The Bill is called 'a very diluted and distorted version' of Trichy Siva's Bill by Sampoorna Working Group. Various groups send in their responses.

August 2016: The MoSJE tables the Transgender (Protection of Rights) Bill 2016 in the Lok Sabha. The trans community says it is 'further regressed' from even the draft bill.

August 2016–July 2017: Parliamentary Standing Committee is set up, and various networks and groups of transgender people write critiques and responses and even depose in front of the committee.

20 October 2016: A letter addressed to the MoSJE, signed by thirty-three organizations and 105 individuals, asks for a month's time to collate responses to the Bill from the trans and intersex communities, saying the new Bill has moved away from the previous provisions 'to such an extent that we strongly believe that it will result in further discrimination and violence towards the transgender community'.

1 November 2016: An addendum to the previous letter addressed to the MoSJE, and signed by twelve organizations and forty individuals, demands fifteen changes and insists on face-to-face meetings with stakeholders.

4 November 2016: A conference titled 'UNAIDS Consultation with Transgender and Hijra Community and Experts' is organized in New Delhi. A Charter of Demands is drafted, asking for specific revisions in the Bill. It makes the point that subgroups such as jogappas, jogtis, aravanis, kinnars and others have been left out of the Bill.

21 July 2017: The Standing Committee on Social Justice collates and presents the 43rd Report on the Transgender Bill to the MoSJE and then to the government.

16 November 2017: MoSJE announces that it has rejected all recommendations made by the Standing Committee and will instead reintroduce its original Bill of August 2016 without any changes.

18 March 2018: Bill is sent to the Cabinet after an inter-ministerial consultation followed by vetting by the ministry of law.

Indian Transman

HOME ▾   RESOURCES ▾   POEMS ▾   ABOUT   CONTACT AND CONTRIBUTE

FEMALE TO MALE LIFE OF A TRANSMAN, TRANSGENDER MAN

FTM Passing Tips

Posted by JAMAL SIDDIQUI on AUGUST 4, 2017

Being a pre-operated transman is exhausting. Most of the time people don't acknowledge your gender, you do not look your age (like a teenage boy), misgendering by saying, "Oh sorry mam I thought you are a boy" and haunting gender dysphoria.

Here are few tips with you which you can pass as a male and lower down your dysphoria.

1. Identify where your dysphoria lies: Identify what are the things that give this distress and dysphoria. Is it the feminine clothes, the haircut, the way people treat you, your body (chest, what you have in your pants, feminine skin, no or lack of facial hair)? To not get traumatized and by identifying your dysphoria...

Follow

▶ YouTube

VIDEOS

Uploads

Questions and Answers, Transman India, FTM mukul

7 months on T/FTM,Transman

How to start transition from Female to

Update on T shoab/Indian Transman

On Shoib Indian Transman/FTM

Tea servan India-introduction/FTM

'I Used to Think My Penis Would Grow One Day'

Got up with red eyes again. Praying to God that everything will be alright by tomorrow! But deep down I know that tomorrow will be just like today or any other day.

Everyday I struggle to look at the mirror because I don't recognize the person whose reflection I see. Everyday I struggle to get out of the house or to face people. Their curious gazes disturb me a lot.

When there is no one in the house, I take out my mother's dupatta and tie it around my chest to make it look flat. Of course, this is not as easy as it sounds because then I can barely breathe. I steal my sister's kohl and make a moustache on my face, and when I had long hair, I would wear a cap to hide my hair. It feels good.

But could I go out like that? Of course not! What would people think? 'Who is this freak? Are you a boy or a girl? Have you joined a circus, weirdo?' I was scared to face these questions, so I would let my desire to dress up like a boy just lie.

—Blog entry by Jamal Siddiqui, 25

I met Jamal at Chez Jerome in Lado Sarai in Delhi, an LGBTQI-friendly place where the bathroom had the androgyne symbol and a sign that said, 'We don't care'. I had read Jamal's blog earlier. When we met, I was rather surprised by how soft his voice was, and how reserved he seemed. 'It's better you ask me questions. I won't know what to tell you otherwise,' he said.

'Perhaps we can start with childhood?' I said.

His account was a little different from the others I had heard. The story arc itself was similar, but he would pause at distinct places and reflect on his life at that point, why he had made certain decisions, how he had earned certain freedoms, and what relevance his life had to the larger community of transmen.

Jamal's father was in the air force, and he had grown up across several cities—Madras, Delhi, Ahmedabad. He was made to wear the girls' uniform when he was a child, but when they moved cities and he was admitted into a different school, in Class 4, he insisted on wearing shorts as the boys did. His father relented. His given name was not a common one in India, and his teachers did not realize it was a girl's name. Things were fine for as long as everyone thought he was a boy.

But a few months into his time at the school, a family friend told one of the teachers he was a girl. Word spread in the staff room. Every day, he says, every class, his teacher used to make him stand at his desk and ask him why he was not in a skirt. Did he not respect the school's rules? How could a girl wear the boys' uniform? He was to wear a skirt the next day.

When he refused to comply, they would take him to the senior staff, including the principal, and try to coax him. Some tried to reason with him, and some were harsh. His sister and parents were called to class and humiliated, he said. He was ordered not to sit with the boys or play with them, and to make friends with the girls instead. He began to dread the sports hour. He loved playing cricket and football, but only the boys were given the equipment. The girls were to play volleyball or kabaddi. He opted for painting instead of sports, but missed playing the games he liked. And his classmates, the very ones he had considered friends, began to bully him. It left him anxious and diffident, but he was determined not to change the clothes he wore.

At home, though he had a sister, older by three years, his parents gave up on trying to dress them identically. He would refuse to wear frocks, and that was that. 'I think there's an advantage for women that . . . and I don't know whether it's an advantage or not, but it's okay for a girl to be a tomboy when young. People believe it's a phase.'

As he grew older, the pressure to wear female clothes, to grow his hair, was immense. His father was increasingly aggressive, even beating him when he refused to change out of the clothes in which he was comfortable. He stuck to his guns, even when they refused to buy him male clothes. At one point of time, he had literally nothing to wear. His mother finally went out and bought him a collared shirt.

His first period was 'devastating', he said. He had hoped puberty would be heralded by the sudden appearance of a penis. Now, he was turning into the very opposite of what he wanted to be. As his secondary sexual characteristics developed, his dysphoria intensified. He was in severe distress. He thought it would pass, but as his chest began to bulge, as facial hair refused to sprout, he found himself in deep depression. He had no friends. He tried to convince his school authorities to allow him to wear trousers, but they were not receptive. He was convinced he was the only one in the world with this problem, and he had no one to talk to about it.

'That's when I stopped believing in religion, when I was around fourteen,' he said. 'Because I used to feel like *aisa kyun*? Why? If Allah loves you, then why this suffering? I always knew that I was different. But I was also a biology student. So I don't know, I always had this curiosity—I wanted to know. And then (the) internet came into the picture. Then I started reading and stuff. And then I got to know.'

He figured out he was transgender. And now he wanted to know why. But the internet being the leviathan it was, he chanced upon an article which called it a 'condition' that may have been caused by a complication in pregnancy, or possibly a head injury as an infant, which had led to 'mental imbalance'. It could also have been caused by one's parents treating one as a boy, the article said. He asked his father why he had been given male clothes. His father said he had insisted he would wear nothing else.

Perhaps he was going against nature? Perhaps he must align his gender identity to his body? He tried being a girl. He began to wear women's clothing, he grew his hair, he even had a boyfriend.

'But the more I pushed myself to be feminine, the more I lost my self-worth. Eventually, I got suffocated. I dropped out of college. And then I started doing some jobs. I was desperate at that time, to go through surgery and all. And so, yeah, I started my first job. I used to earn around Rs 3000.'

Growing up, he had never had space. And he had never had money.

So when he began to earn, he would spend on clothes, on fancy dinners, on haircuts, on anything to distract himself from the constant depression and pain.

He was twenty-two when he first heard the term 'gender dysphoria'. He searched for NGOs working for transpeople in Delhi, contacted a helpline, and spoke to a counsellor who pointed him to research material and told him about sex reassignment surgery.

He was desperate to have surgery, but he knew it would take him a long time to save enough money.

'The other thing is, I never had (the) courage to do it. But I think once you *decide* to do it, you never look back.'

And so he got himself a bachelor's degree in information technology through distance education. His job prospects improved, and he began to earn a 'decent salary'.

In early 2016, he met the woman with whom he would fall in love—Rituparna Borah, director of the NGO Nazariya and a lesbian activist. They moved in together in February 2017, and he began his hormone therapy soon after. He also started his YouTube channel to document it live. His partner's identity as a lesbian does not bother him.

'She accepts my identity,' he told someone who asked him about it, in my presence, 'so I should accept hers, right? It's *her* identity.'

'See? See? This is why I'm with *this* guy!' Rituparna laughed at the time. 'Otherwise I'd have kicked him out of my house!'

Now, he told me, 'She was very supportive. She is still very supportive. She always gives me that space and understanding. She's the first person who understands this dysphoria thing and all these issues. I had girlfriends before, but they were not very understanding. So I feel very comfortable (with her).'

His family has begun to come to terms with his identity. Jamal hasn't had a conversation with his father about his gender dysphoria, but he does visit him and his father hasn't brought up the changes in his appearance. He has spoken to his sister about the hormone therapy and his plans for surgery, and she has met Rituparna. His mother passed away last year, before he had begun his medical transition. Jamal told me his chief support system was the community.

'The transmen *might* be invisible, but they *are* very supportive. I think people have become more active. The NALSA judgment also gives that freedom or space, the right, to come out and say this is your identity.'

But there were problems at the workplace. In the first company in which he worked, a security guard noticed he was wearing a chest binder and began to ask questions he found 'extremely offensive'. He registered a formal complaint against her with the HR team, and she stopped harassing him.

Transmen could face sexual harassment from female security guards, he said. On a visit to the Red Fort, he was 'dumbfounded' when a policewoman at the security check thrust her hands into his trousers to check whether he was male or female. He was too shocked and scared to talk to anyone about it. And even if he wanted to report the incident, where could he register a complaint? He did not know.

His next job was with a technical BPO (Business Process Outsourcing) company. During his training period, they would have 'intervention' sessions, at which people could ask each other questions. He was usually asked about his clothes, which he didn't think was anyone's business, but he was polite until it crossed a line.

'Like, when we went on the floor, after the training period, there was this guy who used to keep asking me "Do you like girls? Do you like boys?" It went on for two–three months, and it was becoming too much. His questions were offensive. "Are you a lesbian?" "How do you like to have sex?" "Do you find guys attractive?"'

The norm was that new employees would have to sit with a slightly senior colleague after the training period, so that they could learn the ropes.

'If I was sitting with a woman, this guy would come and ask me, "Look at this girl, do you find her sexy?" and she would be right next to me, you know? So it was really shitty. I complained against him to HR, but then things turned against me. I sort of had this "lesbian" tag to deal with at work. I was there for a year and a half, and eventually I had to leave. Because there was this other thing. We had a system where, if women were working at nights, they would have to be picked up and dropped back with a guard in the car. And for me, because I look like this, the guard would get in and say, "Are you a girl? Are you a girl?" Every time, for a year and a half. This was a rule, that a guard should go with women, and our gender was mentioned in the sheet. So there was nothing I could do about it.'

He was set to join a new place, as a networks trainer, the following week.

'Let's see how it goes,' he said. 'The last job, it got too much.'

Jamal Siddiqui's YouTube Channel
Video 2
Posted on 25 April 2017
4th Shot Indian Transman FTM

Day before was my fourth shot. It's been two months. So if you look at the journey from the first shot to the fourth shot, there's a certain amount of pain. Because if our body is not (used) to this, there is pain.

I think we should also talk about pain too, which is there. Apart from that, my voice has also started to change. It goes from 'uh-hhhhh' (imitates) . . . like this, it goes like this. So that's the only change I've noticed till now. There's a small amount of facial hair; not much.

Apart from that, I have also noticed that my smell, my body smell, has also grown strong, which was not there. Yeah.

Someone who had come across one of Jamal's videos got in touch with him. He seemed out of sorts, and Jamal offered to share his mobile number so they could talk. But the transman who had got in touch said he couldn't talk. The sound of his own voice upset him so much that he avoided conversations. Another transman was willing to speak on the phone, but when Jamal invited him to a meet-up of transmen, he refused. His body was too feminine, he said.

They had several closed WhatsApp groups, some for lesbian and bisexual women as well as transmen, and some exclusively for transmen. It was important to find spaces for transmen to discuss issues because they were such a small minority that even LGBTQI collectives tended to ignore them, he said. Indian actor Aamir Khan's show *Satyamev Jayate* had made an episode about the LGBTQI community, but not one transman was on the panel.

A few weeks earlier, Jamal had held an event at the same cafe where we were meeting. In order to organize the event, he started a WhatsApp group and Facebook page called 'Transmen Collective'. Members could add other transmen they knew, and the event became bigger than they had expected. Many of them became good friends in the course of planning it. A group of transmen had even driven in from Haryana.

After introductions, they had an open mic session—people could share their stories, sing, perform stand-up comedy, read poetry, and dance. They spent most of the evening dancing and taking turns at the DJ console. Slowly, they began to break off into little groups, and talk about themselves.

There was a special energy, he said, in meeting each other. It did not feel like the first time they were meeting. They could discuss 'life beyond gender and sexuality'.

Jamal Siddiqui's YouTube Channel
Video 3
Posted on 28 June 2017
Update on T shots Indian Transman

Hi, everyone. It's been six months. I have some growth here (touches his moustache). *And* yahaan pe *(here), if you can see it* (rolls his finger down to his chin and tilts it up). *Also there is some growth* yahaan pe, *then there is* yahaan pe . . . (finger round to his ear and then down again towards his neck)

*Also, my voice has changed a lot. And yeah, it's been a good journey.
People have been identifying me and recognize me and acknowledging
me as a male. So it's been a great journey.*

Was he still an atheist, I asked.

'I'm not an atheist. I'm inclined towards spirituality. To be very
honest, I'm not the Q'uran-reading type, I don't do namaz. But I can't
remove that Muslim identity from me. That's also a part of me. So I go
to the dargah. And I pray there.'

Dargahs don't allow women to go right inside the sanctum. Jamal
had never had any trouble passing off as a man, he said with a smile.

We could see the Qutb Minar from where we were sitting. In old
pictures of the tower, it stood on empty land, aloof, almost desolate.
Now, like most monuments in Delhi, it rose above smoke-filled
highways, pitching visitors into history the moment they walked into
the complex. It had been built over two centuries, with several failed
experiments delaying construction. Restoration work was done after
earthquakes, and modifications made on impulse, until 1848. There
was something beautiful about it, this odd structure with storeys
belonging to different eras, its oldest parts having weathered 656
more years than the newest. We think of monuments as permanent
structures, but the truth is that they only outlast us, humans and most
animals and perhaps some trees. Are they any more permanent than
we are, any less flawed, with their additions and scars and patches and
restorations?

Suddenly, we heard a loud voice, getting louder as it reached
the door, '*Haan, haan*, he must be here only . . . he's doing some
interview . . .'

Jamal stood up.

Rituparna swept in, followed by almost everyone I had planned
to interview in person over the next weeks—Maya Sharma, Vihaan
Peethambar, L. Ramakrishnan.

I was trying to reconcile myself to the surreal fact of three
interviewees based in three different parts of India showing up at a
cafe between 1000 and 2000 kilometres from each of their homes, and

mine, when Rituparna said, 'Cigarette *dedo* (Give me a cigarette),' and picked a pack from Jamal's shirt.

She is the kind of woman who makes the entire room take notice. Tall, with a carelessly worn handloom sari, and large bindi and accessories to accentuate an exquisite face, she has a commanding voice and the articulateness of speech characteristic of those who have a lot of theories and don't like to put them down in writing.

The newcomers had been attending a conference on the economic inclusion of gender and sexuality minorities. It was the first time Jamal and Vihaan were meeting, and they began to chat in low voices. 'By the way, I love your writing,' Vihaan said to Jamal, who replied, 'I read your piece on the Kerala model, was it? I was going to . . .'

'Yaar, order your drinks and then start your *bhaichara* (bromance, in this context),' Rituparna said.

Over several mojitos, we broke off into smaller groups to chat.

'He's been eating my head with his blog-vlog,' Rituparna said. 'Every day it's like, what shall I talk about, what shall I talk about? He's written about love and romance now.'

'Next step is erotica,' someone else said.

'Good time for erotica. Orgasm, desire, pleasure,' Rituparna said. 'That's why we want to start a group, to talk about these things. These guys can all have their secret groups. But lesbian and bisexual women are not allowed to have them.'

'I know,' Maya said.

'Why not? Who objects?' I asked.

'Many people, including transmen,' Rituparna said. 'They only want trans-inclusive. I said trans-exclusive. Because there are so many queer women's issues—queer ciswomen's issues—to discuss. They shot me down. I'm "transphobic".'

'You should say it's open to lesbian and bisexual transwomen,' Maya said. 'There are lots of queer transwomen too.'

'Yeah, yeah, I know,' Rituparna said. 'But I think there are many issues specific to queer ciswomen that we don't talk about. Like how it plays out, being female assigned at birth and also having the identity of queer.'

'But why not transwomen?' I asked.

'Because may be there are some issues specific to queer ciswomen, right?' Rituparna replied. 'Can't there be? If there are none, then we might as well not have another such event ever. But surely we should have the right to just discuss these issues? And also, can we talk about issues without talking about violence? Just by using the pleasure discourse or by using the desire discourse. I was talking about that with Maya earlier. We have been so focused on the violence that we forget all other interactions.'

'Yes, there's no discourse in India around pleasure for women,' Maya said. 'As an affirmative emotion. Our discourse has been entirely about rights and the public space. What about personal space, what about what happens between two women with each other, as opposed to with men?'

'We need discourse that looks at the politics of pleasure,' Rituparna said. 'We are queer people not because we have faced violence, no? We're queer people because our lives are different. And how different is it? It challenges patriarchy, it challenges so many different things. So it's something that needs to be celebrated. Queer relationships can also challenge heteronormative family discourse. It's only after the queer feminist discourse that the challenge to marriage happened. The critique of marriage, the critique of coupledom, the critique of so many things. It's because of the queer discourse. And this queer discourse is not celebrated. How can you talk, then, about alternative discourse? We're again falling down into the same binaries of man and woman and marriage and children and all the other things.'

She added, 'Most guys, when they meet any bisexual or lesbian woman, they say, "Can we do a threesome?"' She rolled her eyes. 'Thank god, Jamal never asked me that.' She smiled. 'You know, I've dated transmen before, but he's the first guy who's actually transitioning medically. This is going to be interesting.'

'But you identify as queer?' I asked.

'Yeah.'

'So it's more about the person than gender?'

Rituparna began to laugh. 'So I had a huge crush on him when I saw him.'

'I was very shy,' Jamal said. 'I mean, she's *the* Ritu, man.' Rituparna had been involved in LGBTQI activism for more than twelve years, and was well known in the circles.

She had always been attracted to masculine people, and had only had butch women, transmen, or genderqueer people for partners.

'There *are* transmen I've dated who were hyper masculine and very violent and aggressive, and I couldn't sustain such a relationship because I identify as a feminist,' she said. 'It *is* true that they can have that (tendency) . . . but see, that masculinity also comes from the fact that they have to perform, no, in certain ways? Like transwomen are also more feminine than ciswomen. And there are some ciswomen who would be okay with that kind of gendered relationship, because that comes with socialization. Luckily, with Jamal, that has not happened.'

To be lesbian, and to call oneself 'lesbian', she felt, was a political identity, 'in this invisibilized world of female sexuality'.

'My identifying as a queer feminist, while I'm in a committed relationship with a transman, has been questioned by some people in the transmen's collective. I have been told directly also that I should be calling myself straight now that I'm in this relationship. So my identity has been questioned. My answer to them has been that Jamal knew before getting into a relationship with me that I'm queer, I'm not straight. So when he didn't change his identity, why should I change my identity? I'm still attracted to women. And it doesn't mean that I'll change my identity to calling myself straight just because I'm in a committed relationship with a transman.

'This identity politics is something I was quite unhappy about. My identity is important to my being. If I say I'm straight, my whole identity vanishes. I'm not a cis heterosexual person per se. If I was heterosexual, I wouldn't have faced so much trouble with my family. My parents would have been happy that I'm heterosexual and not queer.'

But she feels her attraction to masculine people of various genders within the spectrum is rooted in the challenge they represent to gender normativity and gender heteronormativity.

'A lot of people have told me how there's no support system for partners of transmen,' I said.

'No support. No support.'

'Is that something you miss?'

Rituparna considered. 'Hmm. For me, I have not *missed* it, because I have also been part of the movement and I have a lot of friends. But there is a . . . a sort of invisibility of feminine queer women in the entire discourse. There is a strong invisibility of feminine partners, feminine ciswomen, feminine lesbians, feminine queer women partners of transmen—there is no support system. And I don't know if partners of transmen want to be part of such groups or not. But I see that sometimes, people are not even sure of their own identity. Sometimes, I see transmen whose partners are cis and they will call themselves 'lesbian', but they are not attracted to women. I think it's lack of information, lack of discourse. So, yes, there *is* a need for a support system, a huge need. And these conversations, about domestic chores and things, they're conversations we *need* to have.' She smiled suddenly, 'I don't know how he feels about having a feminist, outgoing . . .'

'I think it's amazing,' Jamal said, before she could finish. 'I've learnt so many things from her. Feminism, I've learnt from her. She's the one who gave me that perspective; she moulded me towards feminism. And even with my writing, she's helped me a lot. I have learnt a lot from her. That's how I feel.'

5 Things To Know About Dating Transmen In India
By Jamal Siddiqui
6 August 2017

- *Every transman is different—some may be macho, some may be feminine in their gender expression, and some may just be your boy-next-door. People generally assume every transman will be into women. Transmen can be straight, gay, bisexual, queer or of any other orientation. Our identity is an integral part of our lives and loving us would mean loving and accepting it too.*

- *In trans discourse, language is important. Language is not just words but also body language or how you acknowledge the gender of a transperson in their presence and absence. Some questions are insensitive. For example, asking, 'Would you be able to be a father after surgery?', asking about assigned names, or misgendering in any form, is never acceptable. When dating a transperson, people should use trans sensitive language.*

- *If you're dating a transman, you need to understand gender dysphoria. Every transman experiences different levels of dysphoria. It can give us a lot of distress, and make us angry, anxious, or depressed. We might want to talk about it or we might not. Give us that space. Dysphoria is already disturbing and a heartbreak can add to the distress.*

- *We are often compared to cisgender men by our partners, or by society. Socially accepted marriages and having biological children are seen as important and often many transmen feel that since they are not cisgender, they won't be able to meet these expectations. This comparison creates vulnerability which in turn leads to the fear of rejection, and inhibition in their love lives. But because we are not cisgender, it is not right to assume that we won't be able to satisfy our partners sexually or emotionally.*

- *Many women assume that just because we were assigned female at birth, we will be able to understand women's issues and their lives better. But that is not always true.*

  Being in a relationship with a transman in India can be difficult at times. But with a little understanding and patience from both sides, love and romance can be wonderful. Exceptions aside, we are amazing boyfriends, husbands, partners, fathers, companions and sons-in-law.

In a video on his channel, Jamal said he wanted to make a vlog with Rituparna, so she could speak about the challenges involved in dating a transman, the sensitivities of which laypeople were not aware. The slightest accidental misgendering could trigger severe anxiety and depression in a transperson.

We go through intense gender dysphoria, and with dysphoria comes stress, anxiety, panic attacks, and other mental health conditions.

Apart from all these mental health issues, in India, doctors still treat gender transgression as a disorder. The Diagnostic and Statistical Manual of Mental Disorders IV (DSM-IV) uses the term Gender Identity Disorder (GID). In DSM-V, it has been reclassified as Gender Dysphoria. According to some transgender persons, GID reinforces the binary model of gender, and pathologizes gender. Its being reclassified as Gender Dysphoria might help resolve some of these issues because it refers to discontent experienced by transpeople. I am, however, still carrying the Gender Identity Disorder certificate even though I don't believe transmen have a disorder; it's just that we are different and transgress gender norms.

It is high time we talked about the mental health of transmen. Some transmen are undergoing therapy for mental health issues caused by an unempathetic society. Some transmen have also committed suicide because of it. How many more lives?

—Blog entry by Jamal Siddiqui

'No one talks about mental health, no?' Rituparna looked at Jamal. 'Everywhere, they only discuss dysphoria, dysphoria. But everyday mental health is a big issue for queer people. All of us struggle with it. And (discussion on) mental health is only limited to dysphoria when it comes to transmen, and lesbian-bisexual women don't exist only.'

Various violations of transmen, often unintentional, happen even within the community.

In a blog titled 'How Queer Spaces can be Transphobic', published on 20 May 2017 by the website Gaylaxy Mag, Jamal wrote about a 'micro aggression'—a violation not easily recognizable but as valid as overtly manifested physical, mental, social, and economic violence—that had occurred at an event to mark International Day Against Homophobia, Transphobia and Bi-Phobia (IDAHOBiT), organized by the American Centre with Humsafar Trust, Harmless Hugs and other groups.

A WhatsApp invitation to the event asked for a 'valid photo ID proof', which was required for entry.

SWEEKAR- TOWARDS LGBTQ ACCEPTANCE
For the first time in Delhi, The Humsafar Trust - Project DIVA with support from 'Save the Children' is organizing an event on occasion of International Day against Homophobia and Transphobia (IDAHOT).

Sweekar is an open platform for LGBTQ and allies to exchange viewpoints and intermingle.

Event details are as follows :
Date: 20th May 2017 (Saturday)
Time: 1.30 pm to 4.00 pm
Venue: The American Centre, Delhi.
RSVP ONLY: https.//goo.gl/forms/ F8D6 SooL rp9x 3HQU2
PLEASE CARRY VALID PHOTO ID PROOF

Asking for a valid photo ID from people who did not have legal documents that had their chosen names and genders was a violation, he said, and it was shocking that organizations working on LGBTQI issues should be unaware of this. It is hard enough to use legal documents identifying one by the wrong gender in non-LGBTQI spaces. When he and some others objected, he was told it was for reasons of security. Finally, the organizers said those who did not possess legal documents could meet a representative of Humsafar trust, one of the organizers, who would escort them into the American centre.

Jamal was not happy. He felt they should have thought things through before choosing a venue which required a photo ID. He was also upset that when he registered his protest, the organizers said some transpeople had been to the embassy earlier and had no objection to using documents that identified them by their old names and genders. The level of dysphoria for each transperson is different, and one could not compare them and say a regulation is not transphobic because some transpeople did not feel violated by it, he said. To ask transpeople to report to a representative, which cispeople were not required to do—however valid the reason may appear to some—was discriminatory because they demanded 'equal rights', not 'special rights', not exemptions.

Jamal was among the first people who got his gender identity changed on all his legal documents, without having undergone sex reassignment surgery prior to it. If the new Bill were to pass into law as it is, it would be impossible for anyone else to do it.

In June 2017, Jamal and Rituparna had approached the gazette office in Delhi. Rituparna told me the staff had been rather friendly. They had even apologized to Jamal for not being aware of the law regarding gender change when he had shown them the NALSA judgment.

'I was about to scream,' she laughed. 'Remember, Jamal? I was like *ta-ra-da*, then (the official) said, "Relax, ma'am, come after lunch. I will sit with you properly and I will explain the entire process. It will take time. Please, please come after lunch." I was like okay, fine. Because I always fight. At the Aadhaar office also.'

'But we *have* to fight there,' Jamal said.

The gazette officer, though, was helpful. Since they did not have an SRS certificate, he told them he did not need one, and gave them forms through which they could make their case. They did not need a lawyer or endorsement from doctors. They were given the format for 'Self-Declaration for Change of Name/Gender', of which they had to submit two printed copies.

SELF DECLARATION FOR CHANGE OF NAME/GENDER
PUBLIC NOTICE

1. I.........................Daughter/Son/Transgender   of ....residing at .... hereby undertake that I, ...want to change my name to ....and gender as Male/Female
2. I, ...henceforth be known as ....S/O or D/O of ....
3. The above statement made by me is true and correct to the best of my knowledge and belief. If any legal issue arises in this regard at any stage I will be responsible for the same and, The Department of Publication will not be liable for any consequences arising therefrom.

Name and Signature
(Previous name)

Witness No. 1
Full Name: _____
Signature: _____
Address:_____
Phone no./Mobile no. _____

Witness No. 2
Full Name: _____
Signature: _____
Address:_____
Phone no./Mobile no. _____

It would take between two and three weeks for the gazette to publish the notification, and the fee in Delhi was Rs 1400, to be paid in cash.

PUBLIC NOTICE

1. I,   JAMAL SIDDIQUI Daughter of   .
, residing at .   4,
Rohini, Rithala, North West Delhi, Delhi-110085, hereby
undertake that I, ...   JAMAL SIDDIQUI want to change
my name to SAHIL JAMAL SIDDIQUI and gender as Male.
2. I,   SIDDIQUI henceforth be known as
SAHIL JAMAL SIDDIQUI S/o of .....—. .

3. The above statement made by me is true and correct
to the best of my knowledge and belief. If any legal issue
arises in this regard at any stage I will be responsible for
the same and, The Department of Publication will not be
liable for any consequences arising therefrom.

JAMAL SIDDIQUI
[Signature]

One is also required to put out an advertisement notifying the public of name and gender change in a national newspaper.

PUBLIC NOTICE

It is for general information that I was previously known as.............., D/O of.................., R/O, ...and after undergoing Gender Transition therapy under the supervision of registered medical practitioner in Delhi, have changed my gender as male. I henceforth be known as................., S/O................, R/O, . It is certified that I have complied with other legal requirements in the connection.

'Giving the ad in the newspaper was a problem,' Jamal said.

They had first approached *The Hindu*, and the advertising department had made a booking 'and acknowledged it with the code "CHENHOB-0617000294"' to Jamal.

On 26 June 2017, at 12.21 p.m., the Classifieds office had sent the advertisement content to senior staff for approval. This was then forwarded to the legal department. At 5.14 p.m., the legal department sent an email, which asked for 'gender transformation proof from hospital or any other document'. At 5.18 p.m., the Classifieds office forwarded the mail trail to Jamal, urging him to send the documents immediately, since it was to be published on 28 June. On 27 June 2017, at 8.47 a.m., Jamal sent a Gender Identity letter.

The Classifieds team forwarded this to the legal department, saying, 'Hope this is sufficient for us to proceed publishing the advertisement.' At 12.56 p.m., the lawyer replied, saying, 'This does not prove anything.' 'The certificate of undergoing treatment given by the Regd Medical Practitioner as per your guidelines matches with the advt contents,' a representative of the ads team wrote. 'Shall we proceed publication of the advt now?' (sic)

At 2 p.m., the lawyer wrote, 'You cannot. Speak to me.' At 2.23 p.m., the representative wrote to the rest of the Classifieds team: as per legal advice, the advertisement could not be accepted for publication and the client was to be informed. At 2.47 p.m., the team forwarded Jamal the mail trail, and said they could not publish his advertisement and would initiate a refund.

In response, at 11.20 a.m. on 28 June 2017, Jamal sent an affidavit provided by his lawyer, who was also copied on the email, and modified the advertisement to say he was undergoing gender transition therapy under the supervision of a registered medical practitioner in Delhi.

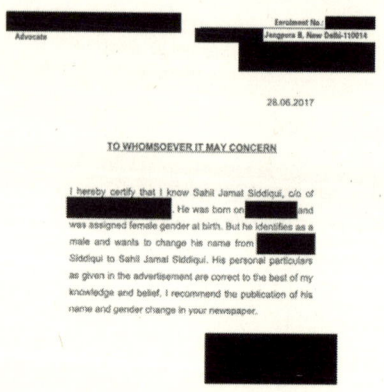

At 2.21 p.m., he received a short email: 'Sorry for the inconvenience, we can't process your advertisement because the supporting documents which are submitted by you are not meeting with our requirement.' (sic) The booking was cancelled and a refund initiated.

'I had a fight with them. And I tried to explain to them there's NALSA and everything. But then they said no, we can't do it,' Jamal told me.

'Like I wrote a letter, as Nazariya director also, saying that this is what it is, and we CC-ed the lawyer,' Rituparna added. 'And we submitted another letter from a lawyer, explaining why the NALSA judgment made (the) SRS certificate unnecessary.'

Finally, they had gone with *Sikh Times*, which charged Rs 1500 for the advertisement.

They needed the Gender Identity Disorder or Gender Dysphoria letter from the psychiatrist, the Self-Declaration in 2007 word format, copied in a CD, two recent passport size photos, a printout of the NALSA judgment, and a copy of the applicant's Aadhaar card.

I wrote to the legal department of *The Hindu* as well as the Classifieds team several times, over many months, asking for the specifics of the law that prohibited publication of Jamal's advertisement. I did not receive a reply.

When even getting an advertisement published in a newspaper could be such a challenge, with so many resources at hand—education, community support, access to lawyers and doctors—could one imagine the life of a transperson who was underprivileged in every sense, Jamal said.

Jamal Siddiqui's YouTube Channel
Video 6
Posted on 22 October 2017
Nine months on Testosterone
Few bad experience
FTMTransmanIndia

The reason I started this YouTube channel was that when I started searching for videos myself, I saw that there were a whole lot of foreign videos, from US, UK, everywhere. But there was nothing from India, and so I started a transition vlog. I accept that my videos are not regular. At times, I'm busy with stuff. So let's talk about my transition update.

I had a check-up last month, and my results showed a swelling in my lungs, because of which the doctor refused to increase the dose of testosterone. But he said he could reduce the interval, and so from fifteen days, I now take a shot every ten days.

They've called me for a check-up after another month. Let's see what happens. He's also given me some precautions (to follow), saying things like no oily food, need to exercise and everything. I'm keeping this in mind too.

Apart from that, last week I had a wrong injection, due to some negligence.

9 October 2017

In his blog post 'Nine Months on Testosterone: A Rough Patch', Jamal details the complications he has had of late. A terrible stomach upset left him feeling weak and fatigued. His liver function test revealed a swelling in his liver. Jamal's doctor did not prescribe any pills, but outlined dietary restrictions. He also lowered his dosage of testosterone from 250 mg every fifteen days to 100 mg every ten days. It upset him, but he visits a psychiatrist once a month—transition can take a toll on one's emotions—and was able to reconcile himself to the lowered dosage.

He had been working particularly long hours at his new job, and was too tired to go to his regular pharmacy to buy his shots. He went to the neighbourhood pharmacist to check whether he had the shots he needed. The pharmacist gave him a box with five shots. Jamal took it to a nurse, 'without really checking the box'. As she opened it, he noticed that the shape of the container was different. The name was different from the usual shot, and he decided to Google it later.

When he did look it up, he realized that instead of Sustanon 100 mg, which is for female-to-male transpeople, he had been given Susten 100 mg, which is an oestrogen shot for male-to-female transpeople. He called up the pharmacist to complain. The latter claimed he had only given him the injection specified in Jamal's prescription. He did not appear sorry.

At times I wonder what would (have happened) if I (had) been illiterate and couldn't read at all what was written on the box. It is so irresponsible of him and also, it put my transition in danger. I called the Endo(crinologist) immediately, explaining (to) him what has happened, and he said that it is dangerous, and please do not take any shots till next fifteen days.

—Blog entry by Jamal Siddiqui

A few days later, Jamal began to experience mood swings. On 9 October, he got his period for the first time in six months. It broke his heart. It would have been easier to accept the occurrence if the period had been a natural consequence of the adjusted dosage, but it had been triggered by the wrong hormones. He was furious at the pharmacist, and at himself for not checking the name on the box.

Happy Pride

Keerth could not wait for Pride. He was going to wear a veshti for the first time, he said excitedly.

'I'll wear sunglasses or something, because this might get covered on TV, and if some relative recognizes me and talks to my parents, it will become a big headache. I'm also thinking . . .' he said, with an eager smile. 'I can get a fake *meesai-daadhi* (moustache and beard), and I can see how I will look post-transition!'

Being part of the community had made him think about a lot of things of late, he said.

'There *is* some pressure on people to come out during Pride. If you don't want to come out, some people think it's the social conditioning your parents or family has given you. That's not always the case. People could have various reasons, sometimes even personal safety, in some cases. There are layers to it. You know, this transwoman who is a friend of mine, when you wrote that article about me, she sent me a text saying, "Oh, good you have come out. I will never come out in my lifetime. I will never have the guts to come out in my lifetime." Everyone has gone through a lot. They get harassed sometimes. I know another transwoman who likes women—she wants muscles and all that, like a six-pack, and she goes to martial arts classes, she's attracted to women, and some people in the community itself can't understand why she wants to transition in that case. I myself found it very absurd. Then a friend explained to

me that everyone need not stick to the norms, trans or cis. I'm still
working through all these things.'

~

25 June 2017

It was the day of the Pride Parade in Madras. The Pride march would
start at the T.N. Rajarathinam Stadium, and wind around it for a
couple of kilometres before circling back. It was a Sunday, but the
street was full of cars.

'See my pansexual flag!' one of my friends yelled to me.

Someone wearing a psychedelic wig waved at me, and it took me
a while to recognize her as another of my friends.

'Happy Pride!' everyone was saying to everyone else.

Passers-by stopped to stare at the colourful procession, complete
with glitter make-up, gigantic balloons and placards that voiced their
objection to everything, including a ban on the murder of animals,
which the holders of the placards believed was Brahminical.

I had noticed, particularly in recent times and particularly after
the Bharatiya Janata Party's election victory in 2014, that various other
issues were being raised by transpeople, against oppression of various
kinds—against oppression of Dalits, against oppression of Muslims,
against oppression of ciswomen and homosexuals. Was the movement
looking towards intersectionality?

'Intersectionality has been the buzzword for some time now,
but it's easiest on the lips,' Satya told me, wryly. 'At a recent national
meeting, called by a prominent transwoman, during the discussion
on reservation for transpeople, it was only two of us transmasculine
persons who insisted on including the category of caste within the
category of trans. It was unbelievable to witness the blanket opposition
by all transwomen in the room as well as the transmen there.'

One of the challenges with legislation in India is that certain issues,
such as reservation in particular categories for education or jobs, are
considered state subjects, while reservation in other categories would

be a federal subject. Telangana, for instance, promised 'Backward Classes' status for all transpeople, irrespective of their caste by birth.

'I don't know of anybody who has actually gotten something out of the BC status,' Bittu told me. 'Some people have, for example, applied for housing rights, and they have been promised some, but I don't know whether they have gotten it. There are only two transmen I knew from rural Telangana when I lived in Hyderabad. One is OBC (Other Backward Classes) (by birth), and the other is Dalit. And they both would certainly benefit from such a scheme, but we currently don't have documents that we can use; I don't even have a clear idea of (which) documents we will need to push for those rights.'

In a media interview, Bittu had mentioned that the elite LGBT movement focuses limitedly on issues like Section 377 and marriage rights in a way that Bittu found was 'insensitive to serious issues faced by working-class and Dalit-Bahujan minorities among LGBT people'. What were these serious issues, I asked them.

'Homelessness, no employment options, police brutality, physical and sexual assault, murder,' Bittu said, without hesitation. 'I am not placing issues in a hierarchy, but just claiming that we can address all these issues together instead of focusing on just some.'

Satya had stronger words for the elite LGBT movement. 'Lesbian, bisexual and queer women's spaces have historically been extremely dehumanizing of transpersons. A lot of this has started to shift in the last few years, years that have seen the coming in of the funding on trans issues. The NGOs serving the gay population on HIV / AIDS are undergoing a similar shift now.

'Working politically with intersectionality requires a common minimum understanding of what it actually is. The foremost of these, in my opinion, are two ideas—that all of us are constituted *at* intersectionalities; and secondly, that when working with its specificities, we not only know that which brings us together, but also our "differences".'

It would be a major point of difference for me with my friends from the community who asked the government to keep out of their bedrooms and their kitchens. The two could not be equated, I felt.

Yes, the government could not tell you whether to cook cabbage or brinjal. It could equally not tell you whether to cook cows or goats, but it could tell you to cook neither, and I spend most of my spare time wondering why the murder of any animal is legal. Surely, those who opposed the oppression of humans should also oppose the oppression of animals? Perhaps even more so, since animals are far more helpless against the might of the meat and dairy industries, than the average human is against the prejudices of his fellows?

'How can you be against one form of oppression and support another?' another animal rights activist had said to me, and the sentence had become something of a mantra in my head.

At both the Madras and Bangalore Pride parades, I was disturbed by the number of banners which carried messages against the beef ban. I did not think cows were any holier than goats or chickens or dogs or cats or ducks or parrots or fish, but I was relieved that one species of animal received some kind of protection, however misguided the source.

I wondered whether this 'intersectionality', which in practice seemed to be the adoption of all purportedly liberal causes in the course of standing for an entirely different cause, had something to do with the NGO-ization of the movement. Was the fight becoming a march for television airtime?

Someone began to beat a drum, I could hear whistles, and a group of transwomen broke into dance. Press photographers rushed to zoom in on them.

Two of the transwomen twirled rainbow umbrellas and batted mascara-laden eyelashes for the cameras. Reporters were fluttering about with recorders, mobile phones, notebooks, and videographers. Everyone was being interviewed.

'Are you a journalist?' several people asked me, noticing my camera.

'No, just here as an ally,' I replied.

Most looked grateful, and some called out 'Thanks'. Others looked disappointed, occasionally disbelieving.

The drama of the march, its televisation and the stilted photography, focusing on the most colourful sections rather than the people who had fought the fight for so long—older transwomen, commercial sex workers, and the parents of queer, non-binary, or transgender children—was getting to me. Why were three white women and a couple in dreadlocks being interviewed about a Pride march at which they were tourists? Why was a group being exhorted to dance by a cameraman, and why were they obliging him?

I moved to the rear of the march, to look for Keerth. Was he wearing his veshti and false beard and moustache? We were on the phone for several minutes. 'Turn around, turn around, look . . . in front of you, there! Near the car!' he kept saying, and finally gave up and shouted my name.

'Dude, I thought you were some *guy*,' I said.

'I *am* some *guy* only,' he said, laughing, and pulled me into a hug. His hair was shorter than ever, something between a tonsure and a crew cut. 'Come, come, I want you to meet my friends.'

We walked with the parade for a while. Some of the organizers were worried that the march had started on time. Many people from the community had not yet shown up, because it was usually delayed by about an hour. Would the visuals make it seem like it had clocked lower attendance than the previous years?

I encountered a bearded man wearing a nine-yard sari.

'Can I take a picture?' I asked.

'Sure. Can I hold my mom's picture up too?' he asked, and posed with a black-and-white picture of his mother.

I took several pictures of him, and didn't notice that Keerth and his friends had walked ahead. When I was done with the photographs and searching for Keerth, two policemen cleared their throats.

'Madam,' one said, '*Yaaru avaru? Appadi irundhavaru ippadi maarittaara* (What is his story? Did the person in the photograph become this bearded man)?'

The question was a pleasant surprise. I had not expected policemen to fathom that someone might want to grow a beard and moustache. The transman narrative was not well known. For someone from the force to ignore the most obvious conclusion—that the woman in the photograph was the man's mother—and assume a gender transition was remarkable. It was a welcome change from the security guard at the stadium, who came running from his post each time someone strayed anywhere near its gates, wagging his baton and yelling, 'No allowed! No allowed! *Manaa hai*. No come.'

I finally found Keerth, striking manly poses on a bike with a couple of other young transmen. When they were done, we rejoined the parade.

'Oye, tell me the love story,' I nudged Keerth.

He grinned. 'Nethra and I have been talking more often. I'm hoping things might work out.' He had started writing poems to her again.

In front of us, two policewomen walked hand in hand, as did so many of the couples.

To Have and to Hold

When word spread through the transmasculine networks that I was working on a book about transmen, several members of these groups reached out to me. I didn't have to go through a process of selection—everyone had important stories to tell. But Aashish Arora[1] would become something of a golden goose—he had been through various forms of discrimination, from workplace problems to peer bullying, was engaged to be married, was in the process of 'completing his surgeries', had bribed his way through government offices to get his documents changed, and was about to start an entrepreneurial enterprise.

Aashish Arora had the rest of his life planned out. He had been on testosterone for just over a year. His mastectomy and hysterectomy were completed in May 2017. He was planning to have his phalloplasty done by the end of the year, so that he could marry his girlfriend of eleven years in January 2018.

He had never had to fight his parents. He was born with hypospadia, a congenital mutation which frequently presented with uro-genital sinus and hermaphroditism. In his case, he had an enlarged clitoris and higher than normal production of testosterone. He was assigned female at birth, but the doctors could not be entirely sure. By the time he was eight years old, it was clear he was not inclined towards femininity.

---

[1] This person's name has been changed on request.

'General acceptance in the family was good, but yes, outside it was very bad, very, very, *very* bad. Very bad,' he told me. 'Through my childhood and teens, I wondered what my future would be. I'd think: "Will I become a bread-earner or will I be married off to someone, and become somebody's wife? And what will happen then? Because I don't fit into that at all."'

He never showed any interest in dolls, and liked playing with cars and swords and bow-and-arrow sets. He was being trained in classical singing, with his music teacher encouraging him to explore higher pitches. But after school, he was always playing football, officially for the girls' team but most often with the boys. He would go on to represent the city, and eventually the state, in the women's team. His sports skills ensured he was popular in childhood. During his teens, though, the boys whom he saw as his mates began to see him as a girl. They would bully him. He felt humiliated representing the girls' team. He only ever had one female friend in school. Everyone else on the team and in school seemed to think he was a freak.

He tried to switch to the boys' team. His father even spoke to the coach, explaining his congenital condition. He was not successful. Aashish started acting out, and began to have problems in school— he told me he was increasingly aggressive, getting into physical fights with schoolmates. He spoke rudely to his teachers, and was nearly expelled from school.

'So my parents sat me down and told me one thing,' he said. 'Get yourself educated. It lifts you to a socio-economic stratum, you can get out of this mess. And I love giving exams, you know? I *love* it. I have this itch to study. I don't ever want to stop. Because it's been instilled in me that once you go ahead and get yourself on the right track, nothing can beat you.'

He went abroad after his graduation, got himself a master's degree in Business Administration, and eventually a PhD from the London School of Economics. There was an active LGBTQI group on campus, but he didn't meet any transmen and stopped going to meetings.

Through his teenage years, his parents had been trying to make enquiries about surgery, but very little information was available.

'My dad even explored options abroad, to see how we could get me operated. But nothing came of it then. So I decided I should just throw myself into studies. A lot of transmen don't, you know. Many of them have other pressures too—there's the internal pressure and societal pressure already, and then you add to it parental pressure.'

Even with education, finding a job post-transition is not easy. Aashish had no trouble being recruited as a woman, but his problems began when he started speaking about wanting to transition. His first job after getting his doctorate was with a private bank. He remained silent about his gender identity.

'But the ladies actually screwed my happiness over there,' he said. 'They'd keep asking, "Why are you not like this? Why don't you just dress up? Why are you cutting your hair? Why are you doing this?" And then they used to have this Traditional Day, where you had to wear a sari. And I never did. And then they would say I'm not being a team player.'

None of his superiors questioned him, but there was constant pressure, he said. He eventually decided to quit and joined another private bank.

He had decided to transition by then, and came out to his supervisor and the human resources team at the new workplace.

'They initially tried to be all activist about it, but then there was some pressure,' he told me. 'One of the managers there started making my life miserable, and finally they asked me to put in my papers. It was the same thing—that I have to dress formally in a sari sometimes, or I'm not being a team player (because I'm) refusing to comply with the dress code. And when I said I wanted to take time off to do surgeries, it was like no, put in your papers.'

I wrote to the bank, mentioning the manager in question by name, and asking about their gender discrimination policy as well as their guidelines for medical leave. Multiple emails to the human resources team, senior general manager and head of human resources as well as the managing director, with reminders for a response over several months, went unanswered.

Aashish told me he considered fighting the bank over gender-based discrimination, but decided it wasn't worth the effort. His next job was with an Indo-Italian joint venture headquartered in Delhi. Right after his recruitment, he spoke to his colleagues and the HR about his plans of transitioning, and asked to be called by his chosen male name.

'It was a nightmare,' he said. 'All these years, I was desperate to get closer to what my reality was. But they made my life miserable. Like catcalls and teases and writing on my desk. And I would come back to find my things scattered around my cabin. I actually fought it for six–seven months. I had a very rough 2013–14, and it's something which I'm not able to come out of till date. I'd have gone completely bonkers if my family hadn't been so supportive.'

'But you could have sued them if you had evidence?'

'No, I didn't catch anyone red-handed, na? I would see these ugly notes to me, my things thrown about, and I would hear someone catcalling. Where was the evidence? People would not pay attention when I was speaking at meetings. They would start laughing and giggling among themselves. So then my leadership was called into question. It broke me down. That's how they got rid of me. They couldn't terminate me without adequate reason, but they made life so difficult I decided to quit.'

I wrote to the human resources team at the company's headquarters in Italy as well as the one Indian contact listed on their website, asking if they could confirm or deny Aashish's account, and provide their side of the story, as well as supply me with their guidelines regarding gender discrimination. I received no reply.

Aashish spoke to his parents about his problems in the workplace. They asked him to take time off, have his surgeries, and perhaps start his own company. He didn't know any other transmen at the time, and there wasn't much literature available on gender transition. He spent most of his newly acquired spare time on the internet, searching for other transmen. He found videos posted by transmen from Western countries, and began to email them. Eventually, someone put him in touch with Sampoorna India.

'Satya was the first transman I ever met,' he said. 'And when I saw him, I was so excited, I was like oh god, he doesn't look *anything* like a woman. And I think the first thing I asked him was, "Can I touch you?

Like, please don't misunderstand, but I have to make sure you're real."
And he started laughing. I mean, he's got this grizzly beard, and I was
like I *want* to become this, because this was the physical appearance
that I *first* wanted, because the first thing you realize when you look
in the mirror is, "Oh, I don't look like a man", however you behave.
You know?'

Satya added Aashish to various social media groups and mailing
lists. It was 'wonderful' to be in touch with other people like him.
There were local groups that would hang out together. 'It's different
from your other regular friendships. I have friends who think I'm a
cismale, who aren't aware of my transition. And there are other friends
who support me, but don't understand. Here, every one of these guys
is actually going through the same thing.'

The group would also help each other out with research on which
doctors were trans-friendly and reliable.

It took him only a couple of days to get the psychiatrist's certificate,
which would allow him to begin his medical transition. He started his
hormone replacement therapy.

'The first three months, I didn't realize anything, except that the fat
was shifting from my hips and thighs to the belly. But after six–seven
months, my voice began to drop. It's completely below my previous
bass. I can't sing any more. And my physical appearance is beginning to
change, slowly, very slowly. Sometimes, people still say "ma'am", and
I don't get offended, you know. A lot of people get very upset, but I've
decided I can't put that pressure on myself, to prove my masculinity
every minute. I'm going to meet my surgeon in August to talk about
the phalloplasty. That's usually done in three stages, but because the
clitoris is already enlarged, I think one of the segments of the surgery
will be unnecessary.'

Before starting hormone therapy, he had his oocyte stored.

'My partner is super-supportive, and her family knows about me,'
Aashish said. 'But my in-laws don't want me to come out, which is
fine. We've been family friends from childhood and all that. We're
planning to get donor sperms and have one kid from each of us, you
know?'

He has recently opened a restaurant, and has considered starting a talent management agency.

'I want to do something for transmen. I've been working for eight–nine years, so I know which companies are trans-friendly. IBM hires, Wipro hires. The cost of surgery is very high. So I'm looking at getting transguys lucrative jobs, so they can make money quickly. In India itself, the minimum cost of surgery is about Rs 9 lakh, without your medicines and room charges and so on. If you go abroad, it's Rs 30–40 lakh. So I'm planning to negotiate with these companies to include this in their medical insurance policy for employees, so they get some relief. And then I want to negotiate with hospitals also, because what they do is, when you have medical insurance, they hike up the bill and then the 60 per cent you have to pay out of your own pocket becomes almost the same as what you would pay at the regular rate without insurance.'

He knows several transmen who are suicidal because they cannot afford their surgeries. No one who doesn't go through the pain of being in a despised body with despised functions can understand how urgent the need to change that body is, he said. The pain could be far worse in the absence of familial support.

And there are pressures even within the community, to present oneself as a certain kind of macho man.

'We have to acknowledge that any man, cis or trans, has some softness in him. There are times when he needs a hug, there are times when he wants to cry, there are times when he doesn't want to be all independent and fierce. But then even within the community, people will say, "Oh, you still have a streak of woman, that's why you're crying." If that's how you think, I can't help you. I can't change people's mindset as a whole. But I think it's important to talk about these things with other transmen. The pressures we put on ourselves, you know. Being a man doesn't mean you have to pull up your collar and roll up your cuffs and walk like a rogue.'

He also believes the conversation about heteronormativity needs to find currency among transpeople.

'There are so many sexual combinations that you *cannot* get it. I know people who are open to both the sexes. Like dating women and also having sex with men. I don't understand that part of being a transman, actually. Because as a cisman, you wouldn't, right? You can't have sex in that way, vaginally. But then, I guess everyone has their preferences. And even if you can't understand it, it's all right. To each his own. As long as they've had their psychiatric evaluations, and know what they're doing, it's fine.'

He had had his documents changed a few months earlier. The official route was 'too much effort'. Each time he tried to explain the NALSA judgment in the gazette office, the person in charge would stare blankly, look at the text of the judgment which he brandished, and ask him to come back with a lawyer. 'And then they look at you like "third community" is basically some alien invasion,' he said.

Finally, he decided to pay a bribe.

'That's it. Ten days. That's all it took. I didn't even have to go to any office. They sent me all my documents home—name change, gender change, everything. And this was my birth certificate, okay? I got myself a brand new one. No one questioned me. Thankfully, I was born in '86, when you had hand written records. So I paid this guy Rs 15,000, and said please give me this record, and backdate it. And then I applied for a new passport. Then I went to the Aadhaar centre, and got my certificate with my new name and gender and everything. Then, you get your PAN card sorted according to your Aadhaar. Once your papers are sorted, that's most of the problem solved, because everywhere, that's what they want.'

He got his degree certificates reissued, claiming a name change.

Could I mention all this in the book?

'Please do. And send your book to the human resources development ministry also,' he said. 'Let them know how irritating their system is. Let them know what all we have to do to just live. I mean, they're treating us like cattle, you know—"Oh, these guys are creating a problem, okay, give them some subsidy." I don't know where those funds are going. We can't get certificates, and so we can't get jobs. Instead of allocating these phantom funds, if they just issued a notice saying any company discriminating against transpeople can face sanctions, that would change the entire lives of people from the third community.'

Live and Let Die

8 July 2017

'You look different,' I said, as Rommel Mohammad waved to me from my computer screen.

'Yeah, I was about to shave, then I thought I'll show you how I look before that,' he said, with a bashful laugh.

'And you've cut your hair.'

'Does it look good?' He smiled when I nodded. 'I feel so sad when I have to shave. But I have very good growth. Some of the other chaps who started hormones with me, they don't have this kind of growth. It depends on genetic factors, age, and things like that.'

He was excited. He had registered for a workshop organized by the Asia Pacific Transgender Network in Thailand. When he spoke about the network, he would speak short, adjective-filled sentences, like a child. He had 'many friends' in Thailand. The community was his 'entire support system'. There were 'ten transmen in Bangladesh', most of whom were younger than he. He 'liked giving them advice'. He liked knowing he wasn't the only one.

'How have you been otherwise?'

Rommel sighed. 'Not so good. Risks are there, every day.' He laughed.

He had considered migrating, and was weighing his options. Returning to Bangladesh wasn't safe, he said. Across South Asia, the governments seemed to be regressing, even as people appeared to be more accepting. He had told some of his former colleagues in Dhaka about his transition, and all of them had lauded him on the decision. It was brave, they said. But 'brave' is an ominous word, particularly in the subcontinent.

He had considered working in Thailand, and his friends had helped him look for jobs. He was happy to work even as an assistant in the clinic; but the requirements for a business to sponsor a work visa were stringent. They needed a minimum number of staff to qualify, and had to show a formidable bank balance.

He could look at doing his postgraduation in a developed country, and then hope for a job that would allow him to get a visa and settle down. But he would have to spend at least $10,000 on tuition fees alone, aside from living expenses. The entrance exam for Australia, which was an option, would cost him 2,00,000 taka for the first part, and 5,00,000 taka for the second—to write which he would also have to travel to Australia.

The only places that were actively looking for doctors who had qualifications from other countries were Islamic states. And he could not bear the thought of wearing a burkha. The country in which he worked at the time did not impose the burkha, but people he knew would casually ask him why he didn't wear it. Back home, he could wear the unisex salwar-kameez. Some of the other transmen he knew in Bangladesh wore their hair short, and even pre-transition, had an androgynous appearance.

But he did not want to go back. His family would create problems, as would 'society'. He knew a doctor from Bangladesh who was a transman, but this doctor had agreed to marriage to a man in order to migrate.

'His husband knows everything. I don't know how they live, what arrangement they have. Maybe they are living like a gay couple. I don't pry. He hasn't started his transition yet. He's six years older than me, and he kept telling me I should wait, I will throw away my career by hurrying this. He is planning to write exams and settle (down) in the US. He will start his transition only after sorting out everything else. I'm impatient. I'm very stubborn like that. I can't wait. If this career goes, let it go.'

'But you do like medicine, right? You want to specialize in surgery?'

'Yeah, my father wanted me to become a doctor, and I also liked it. But then, I don't know whether it will be possible to do my post-graduation after transition, you know? And I can't stop this now. If you have to choose between your profession and your life, what do you choose?'

There had been various little pressures even in medical college. Some of his professors said his short hair made him look rebellious, even impolite. 'They were not letting me pass the viva,' he said. 'They feel a doctor should look formal, wear certain kinds of clothes. So I had to grow my hair a little. And, of course, my family was also asking me to stop cutting my hair. I got tired of fighting. How long can you fight? I thought I'd just finish my graduation, I'd act until then. But now, I can't be like that again.'

Of the group of ten transmen he knows in Dhaka, only three have begun their transition. They had depended on him to administer their hormone injections and adjust the dosage, until he moved. His oldest patient was forty-eight years of age. 'He has been suppressed all his life,' Rommel said. 'Until we met. And he finds so much freedom in starting hormone therapy. I feel so sorry for him. I started HRT at twenty-eight, and I feel I wasted so much of my life. What must he feel? I mean, in our country, people live for something like fifty-eight to sixty-two years. He's already forty-eight.'

Rommel's contract at work would expire at the end of the year. It would be a relief to get out alive, he said with a laugh, but he was worried about clearing immigration. On his last trip to Sri Lanka, he had been stopped because he looked different from his photograph. They asked him several questions, and he believes the only reason he was allowed to pass through was that he was attending a conference at the invitation of the Sri Lanka Human Rights Commission. When he was leaving the country, he made sure he wrapped a shawl around his head. Each time he had to travel, he stopped his hormone injections for a couple of weeks. That could cause severe depression.

'I don't know what I'll do.' Rommel shrugged, and smiled at me.

'Surely things have to improve back home? I mean, Bangladesh did give legal recognition to transgender people sometime ago, right?' I asked.

'In 2015. November. But that's only transwomen. As in, hijra. They think they're born like that. Once, they announced some job quota. And they had to get a physical examination and medical certificate. For the certificate, they tested the blood hormone level and found it consistent with cismale. So their applications were rejected; they said they were acting like hijras to get jobs, and they were actually male. For the medical certificate, they only have blood test and physical examination. No psychiatrist. And there is no policy to change your gender (on identity documents).'

He was planning to coordinate a meeting with the Bangladesh Human Rights Commission to speak about the rights of transmen. A lawyer whom he knew was helping them with advocacy.

Rights activists had held a meeting to draft a petition to the government, asking for a clear policy on transgender rights, about a month earlier. He had got very involved in advocacy after the workshop in Sri Lanka.

'I came to know about how people work for human rights. Sri Lankan transmen were telling us how they came out of a really bad situation, how they fought for the right to change their names and all that. This was done through the Human Rights Commission. One of them said you just can't stop putting pressure. So I'm coordinating with the other transmen. We all take turns calling and following up with the Bangladesh Human Rights Commission. It's tiring work. Every day, I spend four–five hours just speaking to the other transguys, making sure all of us are on the same page, all of us are willing to put pressure. And then we all spend some time emailing various people, various organizations working for human rights. Sometimes, I say if I put this much effort into any relationship, the girlfriend would think I am amazing.' Rommel laughed. 'I don't know how long it will take, but Inshallah, it should be okay . . . it *has* to be okay, right?'

I did not know what to say. 'Even Pakistan has a law for transgender people,' I offered, lamely.

'Yeah . . . so I think it will be okay. But the thing is, even if there's a law, if someone thinks it's against the religion, they can come to your house and kill you, like they did with Xulhaz Mannan. And we're all so worried about our lives, we sometimes decide to keep quiet. Because nothing is more important than being alive, right?' He laughed.

But they did keep the pressure up. One of the transmen who had attended the last advocacy meeting gave Rommel the name of a woman from the Human Rights Commission who had seemed keen on fighting for transgender rights. He had looked up the website, found three women with the same name, and then looked up their photographs and asked his friend which one of them she was.

'This is the kind of work I have to do,' he said, with a laugh. 'First you have to send them an email. And make sure you CC it to their superior or someone in the International Human Rights Commission, and also all the other transmen, so that they will have to reply to avoid looking bad.' He began to laugh.

'Don't you get angry? And frustrated?'

'Of course. But nothing comes out of that. You have to try and be positive. You have to laugh when you're irritated.' He smiled again. 'Can I ask you something?' I nodded and he paused. Then, with another smile he said, 'Are you very busy, or can I send you a text sometime? I feel like talking now and again. I feel like you understand.' He looked at me and laughed. 'Didi, you look as if you're going to cry. Don't worry so much about me.'

'You can send me a text whenever you want, and we can Skype. Unless there's a cricket or football match on. Nothing is more important than cricket and football.'

'Yes, I agree with you,' Rommel said, with a grin.

It would be the last time I spoke to Rommel on Skype for as long as he was in that country. A diarrhoea epidemic was sweeping through the region where he was based, and as the only doctor for hundreds of miles, he was working long hours without leave. Worse, even adults had begun to ask whether he was a man or a woman. 'In such a small place, people have hardly any work other than gossip,' he wrote in a frantic email on 24 July 2017.

He was contemplating a move to India. It was not easy to register as a medical practitioner in the country. One had to clear examinations set by the Medical Council of India, or secure the Diplomate in National Board, in order to qualify for private practice. The Indian government is yet to decide whether doctors who are not Indian citizens are eligible for medical licences.

29 July 2017

Dear Nandini,

Its not a kids matter anymore. This week I came to know there is a group of boys , who don't believe that I am a girl. So since I came here they were following me. Observing my activities: Where I am going, to whom I am talking. Even if I am at room they are tried to hear from outside.

Here I have good friendship with a girl. Later they started following both of us. One day they asked that girl what relationship we have. Later I came to know about all of this.

This is not the safe way, to start Hormone. But u know how long I have waited for this. Still now thinking, trying to convince myself

Regards,
Rommel.

He could not complain about the harassment he was facing from the group that was stalking him. In a country where transitioning was illegal, making himself conspicuous in any way to any authority could get him in trouble. He could, technically, pause his transition, but it was too hard on him to do so, even for the briefest period.

A friend of mine put him in touch with several trans rights groups in India, which posted alerts about jobs for transpeople and inclusive workspaces. Rommel was hopeful that once his contract term ended, he would find the time to study and write the requisite exams. He would switch careers, if that was what it took to migrate.

'I Have No Story'

'I haven't met any boy like him.'
'He's a really wonderful transman who realizes how patriarchal and male chauvinist the attitudes his community has imbibed are, and he's very strongly feminist, very strongly calling fellow transmen out on their sexist behaviour.'
'You have to speak to Sunil. He was a state-level cricket champion back in Kerala.'

Every time I spoke about gender, patriarchy, non-conformity, or prejudice within the community, I would usually be asked, 'Have you spoken to Sunil?' And when I said I hadn't, I would be told how unique Sunil was. I have lost count of the times I've been told, 'You *must* speak to Sunil.'

I had read practically everything Sunil had written on the issue of gender transition, and I'd rarely encountered such clarity and originality of thought in any gender-related discourse.

In my own experience, I played cricket so I thought I could handle my expression of gender identity in terms of my masculinity in the name of sports. But that also came under fire though my father is a sportsperson. He tore my shirt, snatched away my cricket uniform and burnt it in front of me because I was not behaving like a woman. My father would beat me black and blue because of my gender expression. For me, the biggest question always was, why did I have to receive so much physical and emotional violence? I was wondering if I could ever file a legal case against my father and family.

What becomes evident from these instances and others is that female-born sexual minorities also experience public violence, but the violence in private spaces is built into the system. Private space is in the family or within relationships, where you do not go public or to the police stations to lodge complaints. It is where you cannot go public in the name of family honour. It is a situation where police refuse to register the complaint in the name of 'family honour'. While State officials may come in to 'help', they are often more concerned with morally policing LGBT people and women.

Though male-born sexual and gender minorities have restrictions and norms of heteromasculinity, they still have access to a space, no matter how small it might be. Sometimes male-born (homo)sexuality and gender expressions get cultural sanction by religion. For this community, there is a history, there are mythologies. For female-born sexual and gender minorities, there is no such space—we are always under (the) control of the system. Our sexuality and gender expressions are regulated according to a system that denies our existence. This system punishes female-born (people)/women at every step and also has the power to block the outside world entirely. Moreover, female-born gender and sexual minorities are often not in a position to run away from an environment because they have been conditioned to be dependent (especially economically). While male-born sexual minorities might have economic mobility to escape from their families, female-born persons are often discouraged from education due to the context of poverty.

We believe that the time has come to develop a legal and political agenda that addresses these instances of interpersonal and structural violence that female-born sexual minorities face in India.

—**From *Towards Gender Inclusivity: A Study on Contemporary Concerns around Gender*, by Sunil Mohan assisted by Sumathi Murthy (now Rumi Harish)**

Though the idea of relative privilege between transmen and transwomen has been the subject of some debate, few people are willing to voice their opinions publicly. I wanted to speak to Sunil about privilege among the powerless—transwomen and ciswomen, transmen and transwomen, transmen and ciswomen.

'I have no story,' Sunil told me, with a smile.

'But I know one about you,' I said.

Vihaan had told me he, Sunil, and Sonu used to play for the same cricket team in Kerala. When Vihaan had begun to transition, people often asked him if he had met Sunil.

'Everyone was like, you should meet Sunil, you should meet Sunil,' Vihaan said. 'And I had no idea who this Sunil was. So I went to the Sangama office, and suddenly this person walks in and says, "You?!" and I'm like, "You?!" and then Sonu walks in and he's like, "You?!" Obviously, I'd known Sunil only by his given name, and then I find that this guy was my old teammate.'

Sunil laughed when I narrated it. Like Rumi, Sunil would prefer that I did not use a pronoun. I decided to use 'S' instead of the pronoun.

Sunil does not plan to take hormones or have surgery, and yet I sensed no femininity in S. I would often encounter that among interviewees who had not opted for medical transition, and I wondered whether the hormones made any difference except in terms of external appearance. There was certainly no difference in vibe.

'The first thing is, I don't identify as a transman,' Sunil said. 'Why should I be seen as a third?'

S had a way of speaking that transfixed the listener's attention. Sunil's voice was soft but firm, S's words seemed to fall into place of their own accord, and there was something artistically beautiful about the gestures S's hands made, a mastery of stillness and movement one sees mostly in the limbs of dancers.

'I think the concept of defining certain things, like when you start defining identities, it (ensures) that people *will* fall out from that. Society made two, we're making ten, but even from that ten, people will be left out. Because it's uncomfortable for certain people to kind of be stuck to that framework of this thing. For me, you can say gender is not an identity. It's an expression and we can't define that. People express gender in different manners. And what we are seeing as identity is not actually gender. It's certain roles that we have fixed and we say you have to perform this, and so we perform it. Even to make these categories, even NALSA's man–woman–whatever choice is, like . . . see, my question is, why should I become a third or a trans? It's (for) the convenience of the existing system to be sustained in the same manner. The existing system is a power structure. To sustain that power structure, you're putting certain people—whoever is disturbing your system—aside, saying okay, you are this. I have not chosen to become a trans or third. You have given it to me, for *your* convenience.'

In that sense, it was removing power from the people who didn't fit in. And unless we question the basis of creating binaries and tertiaries, we are only reinforcing a problematic system, S said earnestly.

Sunil felt this question could have been raised earlier, along with the first wave of feminism. It was this issue that had made a movement for women necessary, S said, and while that movement had its achievements, and while it should be respected because it was the movement which had created platforms for S to ask this question, it could have been asked decades ago.

'So you're saying the binary itself should be questioned—not why they are not equal, but why they are two separate categories?' I asked.

S nodded.

The binary made no sense, even biologically, even in the most rudimentary understanding of science, because it made no space for intersex people—a chromosomal variant, which cannot possibly fit into the binary.

'It's just lazy,' S said. 'You're just finding reasons to reject these things (like the existence of intersex people). That's why this whole argument of natural, unnatural, even the question of marriage . . . the talk was around reproductive biology. But if the purpose of a sexual relationship is reproduction, why is the condom being used? The government itself has supplied condoms. It's obvious, no, the double standards? By using condoms, you're admitting you know that sexual relationship is for pleasure. So why is it that certain people, one set of people, can have sex for pleasure, while others cannot?

'We live in an assumed world. There is an assumption that everyone is a man or a woman, and all of those men and women are heterosexual. No one will ask you, "Why are you heterosexual? How did you know? When did you realize? How do you get attracted to a man?" By assuming a majority, we are forcing people into that majority. Even with the Section 377 judgment, with the re-criminalization, you're saying the majority are heterosexual. Then you're saying it's democracy. Where is the democracy? Even if it's one person, that person's needs and rights should be protected; that is a democracy. If you're working only for the majority, that's not a democracy.'

But instead of questioning the notions of binary and the understanding of gender-as-category versus gender-as-spectrum, the community itself had subscribed to the binary, S felt. In reinforcing the binary that had initially cast them out of society, or at best adapting it, the community might be creating a hierarchy of its own, which largely revolved around medical transition—hormones and surgery. Did someone qualify as trans if his or her or their dysphoria was milder than those of others in the community? The NALSA judgment is hailed as a milestone in the community's struggle for equal rights. But was the community truly using it to create an alternative to the norm, or was the judgment in fact creating fissures within the community by clubbing identity with benefits? Calling oneself 'trans' could allow a person to avail of certain benefits. Fitting into the binary would provide other benefits. And in slotting people into boxes, were we imposing an artificial discreteness on gender, which could be a range of things depending on whom it concerned?

Perhaps we needed to interrogate the issue of gender itself. Did a voter ID card or driving licence or ration card or Aadhaar card or passport need to contain a person's gender? How was that more relevant, I thought, than a note on whether one was right-handed or left-handed, whether one was gay or straight or bisexual or asexual? If we began to think of gender as performative and not biological, how was one's gender anyone's business? Could we envision a time, a society, in which it would seem absurd to have one's gender written on an identity card?

To take the question a little further, could the demand for benefits as a necessary salve to fix the wrongs, the prejudice that society holds, spur a vicious cycle, where people were keen to get the benefits rather than fight the system that created the need for those benefits? It is the question that haunts India where reservation based on caste and gender is concerned. It is a question that haunts the world in the context of colonialism—must the leaders of former colonial powers apologize to former colonies, must the perceived holders of inherited privilege apologize to the perceived losers of that privilege, and if so, on whose behalf? What reparations are due to the descendants of those who were tormented by the ancestors of others? How long do the reparations go on? And what does it do to maintaining the power structures?

Where the community is concerned, people often speak of 'celebrities'—activists who have become spokespersons for the community, and who might not represent various sections of the community accurately. Often, these spokespersons have also become gatekeepers, deciding who is authentically part of the community and who does not qualify. They also set standards for language, deciding which phrases are offensive, and which topics taboo. This, I thought, may be part of the reason so many transmen were hesitant to discuss relative privilege; the question of 'privilege' was becoming increasingly problematic.

When I discussed 'cis privilege' with Rumi, in the context of Chimamanda Ngozi Adichie's comments, R made a nuanced point.

'Somebody like Adichie talking about the privileges of a transwoman and privileges of Adichie is very different from a sex worker Dalit ciswoman and a trans Dalit woman, both of whom stand in the same place for *dhandha* (soliciting), talking about their privileges, being cis or being trans. It is entirely different. So you have to recognize the (relevance) of which ciswoman is talking. You cannot put all the ciswomen together. I don't feel (like) a woman. But at the same time, if I go to the dhandha area, I don't look like a man, how much ever I try to bind my breasts and how much ever I try to walk like a man. My face by itself is so feminine, and I can't take hormones, and now I don't know how my body will change and if I'm ready for such a change. I *am*, I *want* the change, but I may not be ready for such a change for health reasons. There are all these factors.

'But me going and standing there with them, even to like sort out a crisis or whatever it is, I am assuming a threat there. Okay? I'm just assuming a threat. But they know they really *have* the threat, a bigger threat than me. Because if the police come, they will be chased out. And looking at me, the police will not chase me out. So I am assuming a threat. They are not assuming. They know.

'So there are different kinds of women, which includes transwomen. And of course, there are different kinds of privileges. Like, for example, when the police is chasing, if you compare the three of us, I will not even be chased; while a female sex worker—if she is having periods or if she is having some other problem, like a gynaecological issue—and a transwoman, and if they are chasing and these people are running, what kind of problem will it be for a ciswoman and what kind of a problem will it be for a transwoman? Just look at it. There's not much difference. Okay?

'The question is not just about periods and the question is not just about giving birth to a child, whatever fuck nonsense it is. The question is how you're trained to respond, how much of gendering is done inside you.' R paused. 'And what is the reminiscence of the old gender that you carry along with you. Because even I am assuming a threat based on my old gender—on the assigned gender, not the taken gender. By the taken gender, I'm really very cool there, as a man, and a man with power because I'm going there as a person who is going to talk to the police. But at the same time, I am also trans.

'Yet, for me, there's this whole cis privilege which even if I want to fully give up, I cannot. Because all my identity proofs are in my cis name. And even if I want to change those things, my parents will create unnecessary problems.

'Sometimes, you know . . . for fifteen–twenty years, I have fought for other people's rights, other people's changes, negotiating with their parents and everything. Now I feel like I'm too tired to do the same thing all over again when it comes to me. Somehow, after all this struggle and fight, there's this fatigue inside.'

But perhaps it was important to discuss the relative privileges of the transmale child and the transfemale child, as it was to discuss the relative privileges of the transmale adult and the cismale adult.

Living Smile Vidya, in her memoir *Naan Saravanan Vidya*, examines the idea of gender privilege. She speaks of her father's fondness for his last-born and only son—a pre-transition Vidya, who was named Saravanan. While Saravanan's sisters cooked, kept house, and got Saravanan and themselves ready for school in the absence of their mother—who would leave early for work—Saravanan's only task was to study. His father was thrilled for as long as he got the first rank. But when Saravanan slipped to second in an exam, his father pulled off his belt and whipped the boy, kicking his stomach in a rage. As Saravanan's femininity began to manifest, he had to endure bullying in school and anger at home. When Saravanan became Vidya, she could no longer stay at home or continue her studies. Her family's support was conditional on her dressing and behaving as a man, even after her surgery. And so the student who had won scholarships throughout school and excelled in college, emerging as the topper in her MA Linguistics course, had to join a jama'at in Pune and support herself by begging on trains.

The transmale child's trauma begins mainly at puberty, since 'tomboys' are considered amusing, even a source of pride—'my daughter plays better cricket than my son!'—and there are various restrictions on them, including their parents' reluctance to send a 'daughter' out of town to work or study, to allow a daughter to remain single when she should be married off, their keenness to 'protect' a daughter until she can be handed over to a 'protector' husband, in a society where female virginity is treasured and male virginity is irrelevant. But, occasionally, transmen would tell me their parents were secretly pleased to have a son, particularly when they had no siblings, or no male siblings.

It was important to speak of the freedom and mobility at different phases for different transpeople, or we could be portraying them solely as victims, Sunil told me now, just creating sympathy. But it might be considered politically incorrect, even transphobic, to articulate such concerns.

The idea of sympathy is an offshoot of power structures, Sunil said. 'That's why I say I don't have a story. I have certain things to say, which are experiences: how I got through the journey of my life, and what thoughts and things have emerged from it. I don't want to give you a story and create sympathy. I don't want to make myself a victim for you. But people love to hear that story and feel sympathetic. To *give* sympathy. Who are you to give something or deny something to me? It is a position of power which has been created. To call someone "subaltern" is to call yourself superior. And in dumping such identities on people, you're pushing them away from the mainstream. We also need to critique this idea of "victim", where instead of speaking of injustice alone, you reclaim what you are, your right to choose your identity.'

And the idea of victimization, S pointed out, was not restricted to the community. It was *la mode* to have a victim finding empowerment through the storification of a lived reality—in cases of domestic violence, in cases of dowry harassment, in the case of prostitution. What if someone *chose* a career in commercial sex work or pornography? Would society not see it as transgressive? Would society not prefer for someone to have been forced into these careers, to be a victim? And unless we started having such conversations openly, interrogating privilege and victimization, how could we change the power structures?

Perhaps it was the existing power structure, the understanding of gender roles as they exist in the heterosexual norm, that fostered male chauvinism among transmen and submissiveness among transwomen, S said.

'When you choose what kind of man or woman you want to become, why do you choose the same models you have seen earlier? You become the kind of man you did not want to marry; you become the kind of woman whom you have seen victimized by cismen. We didn't have models for our gender identity or sexual orientation. So why do we choose models for our performance of gender?' S asked.

The invisibility of transmen both in life and literature made it particularly hard for their families to accept them, but it had often caused some transmen themselves to be confused about their identities for a long time. Among them was Rumi.

'My gender was always a question to me,' R had told me. It was only a couple of months before we met that R had begun to identify as transgender queer, and no longer as a woman.

I had read an interview with Rumi when R identified as Sumathi, about coming out to R's parents at the dining table. It took them about ten years to reconcile themselves to the idea that their daughter was lesbian. Now, R had to go back to them and fight to be addressed with a new identity—as a son, not daughter.

Several transpeople had told me they felt a sense of guilt in coming out to their parents, as if they had let down the hopes and love with which they had raised them. Rumi told me R felt no such guilt.

'I *understand* them, from where they're coming. That's extremely important. It's important for us to understand where they are coming from. They're coming from the same patriarchal society which is Brahminical, which is heterosexual, heterosexist in nature, which cannot understand beyond binary genders, which is also based on biological sex. So they come from the same system. And when I am different—unfortunately, I'm forced to call myself different because the system is that way, the system has codified everything—I understand, but I don't feel guilty when they are feeling sad about me. I want them to recover from the sadness. Like very recently, my mother said, "You claim to be a feminist, why do you want to become a man? Are you feeling ashamed to be a woman?" I said it's a question of comfort. My mother is a sculptor. So I said, "If I forced you not to do sculpture in a day and only cook or do some puja the whole day, would you feel comfortable?" And she said no. I said that's exactly what I feel if I'm forced to be a woman. And she's like, "Oh . . . now I understand." So, basically, you need to explain to them in a manner that they will start understanding. Most of the time what we do is, we're emotional, they're emotional, there's no point in explaining to them . . . But there, I've taken it as my responsibility to explain, because fortunately or unfortunately, they're parents. They've raised us. So we do have a responsibility towards them. So I need to *explain* it to them. But I don't feel guilty about it.'

The other fight Rumi has is with R's voice. R is not worried about R's voice changing texture, because R can adapt to it. But R's voice could lose the dexterity and power of decades of training. 'For me, this concept of oh-your-voice-should-be-beautiful-and-melodious doesn't apply at all. I don't believe in that kind of melody nonsense. According to me, the most beautiful voice I have heard till now, the one I'm most fascinated with and the kind of voice I want, is that of M.D. Ramanathan. Can you call M.D. Ramanathan's voice melodious?'

'I don't know . . . I haven't analysed it. I just know I love his voice.'

'Ah! That's exactly, that's exactly what I'm saying. A real singing voice, you don't analyse. There's no gender to voice, okay? And you say beautiful voice, melodious voice, there is *gendering* in it, in terms of male voice, female voice. For voices like Gangubai Hangal, for voices like M.D. Ramanathan, for voices like Siddheshwari Devi, Begum Akhtar, for somebody like Zohrabai Agrewali, there was no gender in their voices. They were just singing the way they wanted. I believe in singing like that. It's not a question of how the sound hits you. The question is of how I'm able to make a space in your heart. So *that's* my voice, where I am present in my voice, not the artificiality.'

But Rumi does want to try hormones for a few months, and see if R is able to retain the technical speed and power and malleability of R's voice.

'There is this pressure of being a good person, good woman, good musician, which means morally correct, for which I was struggling for twenty years. At some point, when I really felt this is all *bakwaas* (nonsense), that's when I gave it up. I started questioning the tenets and the gender restrictions *within* music. I had not thought of sexuality so much, but I definitely thought about caste and gender, quite a lot . . . in terms of who plays what, who sings what, what is devadasi music, why only (a) certain kind of women sing thumris. And why is it called "semi-classical"? I really don't understand in what way it is "semi". So there are a lot of internal questions that I used to bring up.

And so I was bringing changes in my music, which other musicians did not like.'

Rumi could not recall a time when R didn't have a sense of discomfort within R-self, in R's own body, even in childhood.

'One doesn't have the choice of thinking beyond gender because it is assigned on the basis of external physical appearance. But now I felt it was important to change that appearance, to change that notion.'

Rumi, even as Sumathi, began to change the way R dressed over time. First, R discarded the dupatta, and then women's attire entirely, to wear a male kurta-pyjama, and eventually trousers and shirt at concerts.

As I was writing about my interviews with R, I found myself listening to the musicians R had spoken of as voices free of gender. And in the straining of the chords, in the lack of vocal acrobatics, I began to sense a faith and trust in music, a certain love for music itself that transcended genre and gender. All the categories we have found for music—orchestral, symphonic, polyphonic, Western, Hindustani, Carnatic, folk, ballad, thumri, ghazal, pop, rock, metal, rap—are artificial, imposed. In the end, music is sound waves. And in wanting to slot music into boxes, in wanting to analyse the singer's capabilities rather than the effect of the sound, of that particular combination of sound, the rousing of the heart, the inexplicable sadness and joy and tears and smiles, how much we lose.

Hierarchy

A conference of autonomous women's groups was taking place in Calcutta. Mangai had been invited to stage a show. She wrote to the organizers, saying she would like to bring Manasin Azhaippu.

She received a letter of regret. While they would love to have her over, there might be logistical issues, since the actors were all transwomen. Which toilet would they use? Could she think of another play to stage, with cisgender actors?

'Even autonomous women's groups, which are far better than many other organized left women's groups and other bourgeois, NGO-style groups, were not ready to accept this issue,' Mangai told me. 'What can we expect from anyone else? One would expect the marginal to understand another marginal. Which I don't think is a given, not with gender, not with caste.'

~

Transwomen were more visible than transmen, but also dealt with various kinds of prejudice. Transmen may be seen as aberrant, but their anatomies made them harmless in the popular imagination. How did the two communities interact? And was there reason to believe transmen may be imbibing some of the prejudices in the transwoman community, particularly with regard to the importance of surgery?

Rumi told me transwomen had played an important role in identifying transmen, particularly in the years before the transmasculine networks had become such organized forums.

'When we go district by district, doing training and workshops, often hijras will immediately spot these people who are the exact opposite of them,' R said. 'And many transmen don't even know that this concept of transition exists. They don't know about the surgery. And if they know, they usually can't afford it. There is no real community or network, as there is with hijras. We're really not able to come together as a community across states or whatever. So we have to work very differently with this community. We can't use the same strategy which the HIV prevention process uses, in terms of peer educators and so on and so forth. That won't work for us.'

There were various combinations of information and intent: those who did not know they had options to medically transition and didn't want to, those who did not know but desperately wanted to, those who knew but did not want to, those who knew but could not afford to, those who knew and did want to and did save for it and did it.

When I asked Rumi about the conflicts between pre-operative and post-operative transmen, R was not forthcoming. R believed that just as they had been able to deal with gender chauvinism in terms of transmen displaying toxic machismo, they would be able to deal with such intra-community prejudices.

'It's something we want to handle ourselves,' R said. 'I don't see why the world should know about it. See, you can't expose everything about a person just because it's a question of something new.'

There were so many pressures involved in transitioning that someone who had been through all that was perhaps bound to feel a certain triumph. And since it was so new, with hospitals and doctors often experimenting on transpeople in order to hone their craft, there were huge risks involved; the triumph of having crossed all the hurdles sought expression, and the means of channelling that expression were yet to be found.

I asked Bittu about the hierarchy that others had spoken of, where those who had had surgery or at least desired surgery were considered more authentically transmale than those who did not. 'I haven't faced that personally, as someone who hasn't wanted that,' Bittu said. 'I think more than any other place, people have been really accepting of variation in the trans community in India.'

But they could face discrimination in other ways. Doctors, for instance, were looking for a particular narrative in order to certify someone as trans. Desiring surgery was part of it; so was interest in women. To desire men while being a transman could be seen as less masculine, both within the community and by doctors. Doctors play a particularly important role in the lives of transmen, not just to give them certificates, but also to counsel them. As an identity without a lineage or role models, it could be confusing for a lot of those who experience it. And most psychiatrists are not equipped to handle gender dysphoria, which Bittu described as 'in the context of being trans, it's not a general unhappiness, but it's an unhappiness with parts of the body that are not just gendered, but are sexually dimorphic'.

Even in the case of discrimination within the community, I wondered whether class played a role. Rumi, Sunil and Bittu are English-speaking, high-profile activists. Charupriyan's experience with discrimination had been rather different.

Caste, too, appears to play a role in one's acceptance within the transmasculine community, in terms of how one lives, and even job opportunities.

'With my trans brother who was in the Telangana Hijra Transgender Samiti, we would find that even in the course of trans organizing, the way in which activists whom we both knew reacted to the two of us was very different,' Bittu said. 'And he always felt that it was my caste and class privilege which played a role in this. Like I would sometimes say, "Oh, this person is quite trans-friendly," and he would say, "Maybe he's trans-friendly to you. But he's not to me." And I realized that the differences in our privilege were affecting how people reacted even to the work we did *around* transition.'

Bittu acknowledged that very few transmen identified on the spectrum and that they did try their best to keep the conversation going on what it means to be trans, through their social networks as well as face-to-face interactions, where transmen of various orientations and opinions on the binary met each other in person. But it *is* a contested space, and people do have trouble seeing gender as a spectrum rather than a collection of discrete identities.

'The conversation hasn't really happened in terms of in-depth understanding of what it means to be trans- and intergender, non-trans and intergender,' Bittu said. 'I think there's a misconception that people who are on the spectrum are somehow more radical in their gender identity than people who are more binary identified. And I think that that's wrong, and that sort of thing is just dysphoria. And the reason that I have been able to survive in this field is just because of the privilege that comes from having weaker dysphoria than many other transpeople.'

There was no real label for people identifying somewhere in the middle of the spectrum, who did not desire surgery, either. Revathi had coined the term 'kotha' to describe Bittu and Sunil, as a parallel to 'kothi'.

While speaking to Bittu, I had referred to the kothi identity as a 'bridge identity', and Bittu asked, 'But a bridge between what and what?'

It was moments like these, years into my research on trans issues and months into the book, that I would realize how much I subscribed to, perhaps not heteronormative notions, but certainly rigid notions of gender identity. For all our discussions on gender as spectrum, I could not entirely remove the boxes from my mind.

Perhaps that was why it was so difficult for us to simply do away with boards in bathrooms. Why could we not have single stall bathrooms, which were unisex? Had we come to see bathrooms not just as functional spaces, but community spaces, where we in some sense needed to feel a 'sisterhood', in re-applying makeup and combing our hair before the mirrors, or the fraternization of hearing each other pee, which appears to be the main socializing activity in men's restrooms?

~

'Ma'am,' the cab driver said, after we had dropped off an interviewee at a cafe en route to my friend's home, 'Was that a boy or a girl?'

I hesitated. 'Oh . . . a very young boy,' I said, with a laugh. I hadn't been thinking. But I felt protective of the person in a shirt and dhoti, with the androgynous manner and no biological identifiers of transition.

The cab driver nodded. And I felt ashamed. I had had an opportunity to educate someone, and I had blown it. Why did I expect so little understanding from the world?

Glass Ceiling

The NALSA judgment could be interpreted to entirely do away with gender as a criterion for consideration; if a person who has the anatomy of a woman can identify as a man and vice versa, gender as a category makes no sense and becomes irrelevant. What application does this have in professions that are gendered, such as sports and the armed forces?

As early as February 2017, trans rights activists whom I interviewed were in touch with Sabi Giri, a transwoman who was in the Indian Navy and had been locked up in an institutional psychiatric facility in Visakhapatnam, in the male ward, and was not allowed to interact with anyone. She had managed to reach out through a social network.

She was released in April, underwent surgery, and was discharged from the navy in October 2017. When she appealed against her dismissal, Sabi Giri became something of a household name. The case went to the Delhi High Court, but the navy offered her a job in a private company before it was heard.

How many others were trying to break barriers that the judgment had rendered pointless, and how successful were they?

∼

New Delhi

9 July 2017

Sometime in May, I heard of the transmale bodybuilder who was trying to get special permission to participate in male bodybuilding competitions. His name was Aryan Pasha, and he was said to have quite the following on Instagram. I wasn't entirely convinced I had found the right Aryan Pasha until I came across a before–after picture he had put up of his transition. It was rare to find transmen proudly displaying pictures of their transformation—most of my interviewees did not like looking at old pictures, let alone put them up for public consumption.

Our first interaction was over the phone. His voice was not the adolescent one of early transition, and that surprised me because, at twenty-five, he was one of the younger transmen I was interviewing. He laughed and told me he had started his transition when he was eighteen, had finished surgery at nineteen, and joined college under his male name, complete with a new set of identification documents.

He was keen on participating in the Musclemania bodybuilding competition, a series that would start in mid-September 2017. If he did not feel he was ready on time, he would give it a shot next year, he said. He nursed no hope of winning. All he wanted was to prove that transmen were no different from cismen. His cismale brother, at seventeen, had biceps the same size as his, and hardly had to work for it, he said. 'His body is producing what I have to take externally.'

Aryan's biggest worry was the regulation about testosterone intake. It has taken him more than three years to build his muscles, with testosterone. His dosage is currently Sustanon 250 mg every twenty-one days.

Bodybuilding competitions are mandatorily steroid-free. But testosterone does qualify as a steroid. His eligibility would depend on whether they measured the steroid level against the natural testosterone level of the male body or imposed a blanket ban on steroid intake.

Toning his body was particularly hard because his mastectomy had left him with scars on his chest where the muscle could not develop. After his hysterectomy, he had some pain while doing abdominal exercises.

'Surgery leaves some cuts on your body, and even when they've healed, it's not the same as never having had that. It's depressing because I don't produce my own testosterone. And any sort of building requires extra steroids anyway. Even cismale and female bodybuilders take additional testosterone to build muscle.'

The organizers had told him they did not mind what his gender was. It was open to all athletes. The NALSA judgment had paved the way for transpeople to switch to the gender category they deemed correct. 'But people are not trying as yet. That's why I want to prove it's possible.'

Schuyler Bailar, appearing on *Ellen* shortly after his switch from the women's to the men's varsity swim team, said the change of category meant he had gone from being an Olympic hopeful in the women's team to an also-swam in the men's team, getting the sixteenth place in his most recent swimming competition—a rank that he had never encountered as a female swimmer.

To switch gender in sports could be daunting. But it felt right to Aryan.

'I've explained my situation to the organizers,' Aryan said. 'I know I won't get a (podium) position. But I just want to try it out. Maybe next year, I will be at a certain level and can perform well. This time, I just want to participate, to show the world that a transperson is not less than you.'

He was working with an NGO, Multiple Action Research Group, which works for the legal empowerment of vulnerable and marginalized communities. He had quit the organization a couple of days before we spoke, so that he could focus on bodybuilding. He had never wanted to be a lawyer, he said, but he had had no choice. When he had transitioned and insisted on going to college with his new identity, Rizvi Law College in Bombay was the only one at which he'd felt he was treated with dignity during the admission procedure. His first choice of subject was sociology at Delhi University, but he would be eligible for admission only as a girl. This was, of course, before the NALSA judgment.

Through most of his life, he had passed himself off as a boy. When he was six years old, he told his parents he would only wear male clothes to school.

'My father knew I'm a stupid ass, and I won't go to school if he doesn't take me seriously,' Aryan told me, laughing. 'So it's better to change my school and everything and let the (school authorities) think I'm a boy.'

His father thought it was a phase he would outgrow. His parents divorced when he was a child, and he was raised by an aunt and uncle until he was in his teens. There was no pressure at home to dress in a particular way, and no restrictions on his playing sports with the boys. Even his teachers did not realize he wasn't male, he said. In school, he played basketball in the boys' team. They called him by his surname 'Pasha', and his given, female name was mispronounced over time so that it sounded male. He even represented his school in zonal competitions, without revealing his gender identity.

'My teachers in Class 10 and Class 12 got to know, because the board exam form needs you to specify gender, and mine was listed as female in my birth certificate,' he told me. 'But they were very understanding. They would call me to another room to sign, so that my classmates would not get to know.'

The only activity that triggered his dysphoria was skating. He was a national-level skater, and he had to participate in the girls' category. He did not represent his school, but was being coached privately.

The first time he had participated in a zonal competition, it was in the under-10 age group. His coach had registered him in the girls' competition. He initially refused to participate, but his coach and aunt persuaded him to let it go this once. From the next time on, he would be allowed to participate in the boys' category.

'I was mad at the time for skating. It was my passion. And as a kid, I just wanted to participate, so I said okay,' Aryan said. 'In that race, I was selected for (the) nationals. The national competition would be in Chandigarh, and when I found out I had to participate as a girl, I started crying. I told them they had promised me I would participate in the boys' category.'

They had assured him that this was the last time. It was a continuation of the competition, and so he didn't have a choice this one time, they said. He won a medal, and his coach told him it would be impossible to change his gender now. He had a national rank.

'So then I decided I'm not going to participate in anything. I started missing my races. If the competition was for five days, I would only attend on two days. Because it was very difficult for me to stand in the girls' race. Whenever I used to participate, I couldn't concentrate on my race, because people—other parents and coaches—would start shouting that a boy is participating in girls' category and protest against it. At one point, I just could not go any further. I was selected for an international competition, but I dropped it. I couldn't be in the girls' category. I think I was sixteen–seventeen when I finally quit.'

Puberty didn't affect his appearance much. His involvement in basketball and skating had made him lanky, and his chest was so flat he did not need a binder even in his late teens. But puberty did take its toll on him. Menstruation upset him so much that he was nearly suicidal, and it coincided with an otherwise turbulent time. He had moved back into his father's house, and had a new family to which he had to get accustomed—a stepmother and half-siblings.

'But my stepmother is a psychologist,' he said. 'And she knew what I was going through. In fact, she is the one who told me about gender dysphoria, and found out that I could take hormones and do surgery. At that time, the internet was not like it is now, and I didn't know what I was feeling and why I was feeling like this. Like I would get very angry, furious, if someone referred to me as a girl. I would fall into depression often. She's the one who guided me.'

When he was in Class 12, some of his classmates found out that he was biologically female. For the first time in his life, he was being bullied.

'They would comment on me, and tease me, and once some of them even threatened rape,' he said. 'I decided I could not study with them. So I dropped one year. Because even if I wrote the exam and passed, I could run into them in college, in the same year. I didn't want them in my life at all. But I didn't want my parents to know about the bullying. So I just told them I wasn't selected for the nationals this year in skating. I made sure I got the third position because the first and second would be in the nationals, and I had to show my father I had a valid reason for dropping one year. My father knew it was the kind of thing I would do, drop a year just so that I could have a second chance at nationals. He never thought I could be going through something else.' He laughed.

Around this time, his parents began to make enquiries to find doctors who could aid his medical transition. He did not know any other transmen back in 2010. His parents met an endocrinologist, who explained the procedure.

'It was really difficult to get a psychiatrist who handled gender issues. I wasted some two–three months just trying to find someone who could give me my GID (Gender Identity Disorder) certificate. One doctor thought I was a guy who wanted to become a girl. And when I told him it was the opposite, I think he was just in such total shock, he just gave me the letter. I got it in forty-five minutes. Most people take six months to a year. This psychiatrist hadn't seen anything like this before, he did not know transmen existed. But I got the certificate I needed and started hormone replacement therapy.'

In 2011, once he had written his Class 12 board exams, he had his mastectomy and hysterectomy, both in the three-month gap between school and college.

'The problem with college admissions was that back then, pre-NALSA, they were not aware of sex change,' Aryan said. 'They wanted me to write a letter to Delhi University, and that meant I would have to waste another year. We considered fighting a case in court, but then there were two things: everyone knew me as a guy, so it would be like coming out as trans and (my parents) didn't want that; also, a court case would also drag on for some time, and I would have to wait until the verdict to apply.'

He came out to some of his classmates in college, and they accepted him without reservations, he said. Someone even put him in touch with another transman. He was introduced to activism in Bombay, too, through trans rights activists Laxmi Narayan Tripathi, Atharv Nair and Abhina Aher. Finally, he had a community of people who could understand what he was going through, and he grew increasingly confident. He even stayed in the boys' hostel during his exams, he said.

He would have a chance to start skating in the male category as an adult, but his coach discouraged him. 'He said it might become complicated because people had seen me participating in the female category. And now, if I switched suddenly, it would again become a big deal. I think I was also not ready for any of these things at that time.'

Being a skater had also placed restrictions on the kind of exercises he could do at the gym. He had always wanted to be broad and muscular, but a skater had to focus on his core—abs, thighs, and lower back—and cardio; he was not allowed to work on his shoulders, chest, or arms. He bowed out of competitive skating.

'Now I can't play basketball also, because you need flexibility for it, and my muscles are too stiff now,' he said. 'So my entire focus is on bodybuilding. And I'm very particular that I want to participate in the male category. There are lots of bodybuilding competitions for transmen, but I'm not interested in those now. I want to make history. I want to show the world something.'

9 August 2017

I was all set to meet Aryan when he sent me a text.

He was leaving for his grandparents' home town. Things did not look good. He needed to invest money in the training, and being financially dependent on his father made him feel guilty, particularly when he wasn't sure he would be allowed to participate in the bodybuilding competition.

He wanted to go away for a few days to clear his head.

3 September 2017

'All good now,' said a text from Aryan.

He had started his training. His father and he had spoken, and his father was happy to support him.

15 October 2017

WhatsApp text

Hi Nandini. Competing this year is not in my luck. I was hospitalized for dengue and missed my selection trials and I have lost so much muscle that I won't be able to recover soon :(

~

Madras, Tamil Nadu

He had been in the police force for nearly ten years, after being recruited through the state examinations in 2008. Sub Inspector D.M. Sairam[1] had joined the Tamil Nadu police eight years before Prithika Yashini, who became the first transwoman in the police force in 2016. Prithika is best known for a case she filed in the Madras High Court, *K. Prithika Yashini vs the Chairman, Tamil Nadu Uniformed Services Recruitment Board*, asking to be recruited in the women's cadre. On 3 November 2015, the verdict was that she should be allowed to write the police recruitment examination as a woman.

Sairam is officially in the women's cadre, but he had the advantage of a unisex name, and his transition began quietly. He had been taking testosterone for six months when I met him. He was initially worried about how his colleagues would take it, whether they would notice the change in his voice, the appearance of a moustache. But he felt he had waited too long already, and he decided to go ahead with the change, and 'wait for the law to switch to our side'.

---

[1] This person's name has been changed on request.

'I changed my name last month,' he said in September 2017. The suffix to his given name had indicated he was female, and he changed it with a gazette notification.

'I'm waiting until January to change my gender,' he told me, 'because the next promotion in our batch, to Inspector, is due to come to me. I'm the topper in the exam, and in second place overall. So even if five people are promoted, I will be among them. The lawyer has asked me to hold on till the outcome is known. On 18 January 2018, I will complete ten years in the force, and I don't want to take risks now. But there are lots of organizations trying to fight a case in our favour, so that gender becomes irrelevant in service. If that works out, I can disclose everything. I've always wanted to tell people the truth about myself. I've never cared what they say. But I do want to help younger community members, to know that they can follow any profession they want and be out, irrespective of gender.'

'Being a policeman has advantages,' he said, with a laugh. No one would dare pass a snide remark in the presence of an officer in uniform. His juniors in the force wouldn't dare mess with him, and his seniors needed his help, he said grinning. 'I went to a convent school, so I speak and write English well, and I'm the only one they can depend on to write reports. Everyone else writes reports that no one can understand.'

Living Smile Vidya mentions him in her memoir. They had both worked in the same bank in Madurai. Strangely, she did not seem to sense he was a transman, though she describes her colleague as a woman who would 'only wear pant-shirt' and had 'a boy cut'. In the book, she says Sairam planned to write the Indian Civil Services recruitment examination, and join the police. Sairam had ambitions of becoming a Kiran Bedi, she writes, and is, in all ways, the *'pudumai penn'*—modern, empowered woman—whom Bharathiyaar had envisioned in his poetry.

Sairam had not always wanted to join the police, though.

His uncle is a retired inspector general of police, and his father is an engineer in the railways. He was determined to become an officer of the Indian Administrative Services.

'But my struggles took me about fifteen years,' he said. 'So many setbacks. So much to overcome. And I've lost all this time, too much time to figure out what I could do with my life.'

He had been accepted in his family early on. He was born in 1984, and had a brother three years younger. The brother passed away suddenly, and then his parents began to find some solace in Sairam wearing boys' clothes. He was their only son now. But that didn't make school or college easier.

'I have been through the same struggles any other thirunambi has,' he said. 'I knew education was my only way out, my only way to achieve my goals, and so I endured everything. I studied in a convent because that was the best school in my district. I was the school topper and state second rank holder in Class 12. I adhered to the dress code for women in college because I needed my degree. But it was hard. I tried to wear jeans and T-shirt, but they would not allow me to. Ragging was an issue in college. I retreated into a shell, though that's absolutely not my personality, you know?'

He threw himself into his studies, earning degree after degree, by correspondence once he was done with college.

'I have an MA, an M.Phil. through correspondence, an Executive MBA, a "proper" MBA, a diploma course in foreign trade, and now I've joined a three-year law course by correspondence,' he said. 'Basically, I want to guide our people on legal issues. I've always believed: *Money does many things. Without money, we cannot do anything.*' He recited it like a slogan, with accompanying gestures. 'And this is for my people. Back in the village, our family has lots of land. Eventually, I'm going to establish a business there, employing only transpeople.'

'What kind of business?'

'I haven't decided yet. I get new ideas all the time. Sometimes, I think I'll start a restaurant. At other times, a magazine. And then I think the best thing would be to train transpeople in various skills, so that they can get jobs in the field they want. So I want to start a training centre.'

It was only in the last couple of years that he had met other transmen, he said. He had known several transwomen in his line of work.

'The strange thing is, usually, the police are against them. I've come across cases where (transwomen) have been arrested and beaten up. I do my bit when I can. I've given my personal number to many of them, asked them to call me if they have trouble with the police. I have called up constables and told them not to create problems for thirunangais. The problem is, no one has any awareness. I've been telling people in the department about myself. I have nothing to hide. The mistake is not mine. God's design is wrong, I tell them. If you have a problem with me, it's your perspective that needs fixing, not me. Even before my transition, I would ask my juniors to call me "sir", not "madam". Being called "madam" irritates me like nothing else. I've asked my friends to say "ji" instead of "di" or "pa". These things are important. Everyone cooperates if you explain and ask politely.'

He had always wanted to be a teacher, and he was now an instructor in the department's training programme.

'I do basic training as well as weapons training. When I have the students with me, I use the opportunity to throw in my "bit".' He grinned. 'I tell the trainees it is important to be a straightforward officer. You will have various opportunities to go the wrong way, to accept bribes and so on. Don't take them. Each batch of trainees has some boys who come up to me and say, "Sir, we want to be like you." And to whatever extent I can, I speak about trans rights—subtly, of course.'

Once, when I phoned Sairam to fix our next meeting, a subordinate answered.

'Sir is speaking to the DSP (deputy superintendent of police), madam,' he said. 'I'll ask him to call you back once he's done.'

When Sairam called back, I told him the constable had referred to him as 'sir'. I had also sensed in the constable's tone a certain deference typically reserved for male superiors. What if it had been a senior police officer who'd phoned, I asked, wouldn't he be outed?

'If I am, I don't care,' he said. 'I think life is more interesting when you have problems. That's why I'm speaking to you for the book. I don't know whether my senior officers will read your book. But if they do, it will make them think about their rules, it may sensitize them to the needs of people like me. I don't hide my identity. I go to LGBTQ rallies and participate. I've given speeches in some. I've told my juniors to treat me like a normal SI. A normal, male SI.'

When I finished my final interview with him, Sairam held out his hand. 'Pray to god. Pray that no one should be born like us, should suffer like us. You speak of our achievements, but think: people with so much spirit, so much determination—if we had not had to waste so many years fighting society and nature, how much more we could have achieved.'

~

Bombay, Maharashtra

2018 was the year Rachel Morrison made history by becoming the first woman to be nominated for the Academy Award for Best Cinematography in its ninety-year history. If it was this hard for a woman to break the glass ceiling in Hollywood, how much harder was it for a transman in India, I wondered.

Satya Rai Nagpaul is one of the most respected cinematographers in the country, having been director of photography on several award-winning and acclaimed films. He has a Filmfare Award and a National Award to his credit. He started working as a researcher on wildlife-environmental films in a small company in Delhi in 1995, where he would eventually handle film production. This was before he had begun his transition. He has written several articles about the prejudice he faced, over his gender as well as over his transition. A producer once wanted to compare 'dick sizes' after learning of his transition.

Sustaining him through all this was his love of cinematography, a passion he has pursued for twenty-three years.

'The journey has been a very, very long one and I owe it totally to some key people who came along at different points in time,' he told me. 'The love for cinematography is really a love for light. Light holds everything within it: time, space, movement and the liminal. At best, this love is inexplicable. It's an instinct that one knows of, even at a moment when one's craft skills are absolutely absent. The long gestation years are an exercise in actualizing the instincts. Of giving the instincts a material direction. It's an intensely interdisciplinary position. One is encompassed by the script, which at the very beginning, has to be imagined; by the vision of the director, who is the film's first and final author; and the hard substantive boundaries that the production puts on you and those you cannot cross.'

It was the love of light that sent him from Delhi to Pune. After working as an assistant director with political documentary film-makers in the capital, he wrote the entrance test for the Film and Television Institute of India (FTII). He graduated in 2004, and spent the next six years 'assisting some of the best Indian and international cinematographers'.

I asked him about his time in FTII. The early years of the millennium were a period when the institute groomed several sharp, talented minds who have gone on to become legends in cinema. I had gathered, from alumni I knew, that the culture at FTII had always been about opening oneself to cinema of various kinds. With exposure to so many different perspectives on life, it must surely have had an effect on acceptance of the non-normative?

'The answer is yes. And no,' Satya said. 'Yes, for the reasons you just stated. And also because, if you have gone to FTII, it "constitutes you forever". Its histories inhabit you, irrespective of which genre(s) of cinema you spend the rest of your life in. Like they say, "It's a country by itself." The answer is also "no", for the reason that it doesn't challenge patriarchy enough. The "entitlement of maleness" is preserved and celebrated, especially in specializations like cinematography. And it continues to be in utter denial about sexual harassment on campus.'

In 2010, he was director of photography on his first feature film, *Anhey Ghode Da Daan*, and won the National Award for Best Cinematography. Seven years later, he won the Filmfare Award for *Chauthi Koot*.

'I can't complain any more!' he said, with a laugh.

Imphal, Manipur

He was a national-level athlete who had been recruited into the CRPF through the sports quota. He had played hockey for the state, and had got through most of his school and college on sports scholarships. When he told me his name was Jibolata, the femininity of it sat oddly on the tall, broad, strong-jawed person who responded to it.

Jibolata was forty, and hadn't been living at home since he passed out of school. A scholarship had got him admission to the Sports Academy of India complex hostel in Imphal, and he spent ten years representing the state.

He told me he loved being in athletics, but the hockey team occasionally made him feel awkward, because the ciswomen in the team outnumbered the transmen.

'So there were other transmen in the team?'

'Many,' he said. 'We like sports. And the coaches like us too. We do better than the girls, because we want to prove we're men, right? So we keep pushing ourselves to better our timings, our performances. In fact, in athletics, only two or three of those in the team were not transmen. The girls in the hockey team were friendly too. It's just that . . . sharing a dressing room is a bit odd.'

Once he was recruited to the CRPF, he was stationed in Delhi. The security lines in malls were a pain, he said, and there was some racism against people from the northeast in Delhi, but being a member of the armed forces had its privileges. People didn't bother frisking CRPF personnel.

He had never worn a *mekhla*. 'For as long back as my memory goes, I've been a man,' he said. And because he spent more time on the sports field than in the classroom, his school was happy to exempt him from the uniform.

He retired voluntarily from the CRPF after a decade of service. He missed home. He had been away too long. He wasn't eligible for a pension, but he liked working in the fields. He showed me a picture of his wife, taken on holiday in Kanyakumari.

'I met her four years ago, through friends, when I moved here,' he said. 'We got married. And she's treated as the oldest daughter-in-law of the family.'

Nanao gasped. 'They accept you both?'

Jibolata nodded. They had the master bedroom. His family had always accepted his identity, and never treated him as female.

'You must be the only one with such a supportive family,' Nanao said.

'I think it's because I always did well in sports,' Jibolata said, with the analytical air of speaking about someone else. 'If I hadn't represented the state, or stayed in hostel, or been recruited by the CRPF, and made my own money throughout, I may have had problems. They know I've always chosen the right path.'

Manipur was largely accepting of transpeople, he said. The only problem he had faced was in the sports academy hostel, where the warden was strict. With a grin, he added, 'She didn't like the way I looked at the girls. I like girls with long hair, and she noticed that I would keep flirting with them.'

In Delhi, he met far fewer transmen. The ciswomen found his behaviour odd.

'I think it would have been very difficult to live in Delhi if I were not in the CRPF,' he said, again. 'There's so much difference, so much prejudice, there. I met some other transmen in the CRPF, and we all would hang out together.'

He was rather disapproving of the younger transmen he had met, both in the CRPF and through athletics. They seemed only interested in checking women out, he said. Either they claimed to be in love and spent all their time and money on girlfriends, neglecting work, or they chased women to the point of harassment.

'How can an officer behave like that?' he said, shaking his head. 'I used to tell them to focus on their careers, to treat women with respect, and not to use intoxicants. But they don't listen. The younger ones simply don't listen.'

'You'll meet some in my house tomorrow,' Hemabati told me. 'You'll see what he means.'

'You're lucky that you don't have any problems,' Nanao said again.

'So far,' he said. 'But I'm the oldest of my siblings. Once my brothers get married, I may have problems. I also worry because I don't have a pension, and the tradition is that the land goes to the boys. I think the higher authorities should make some provision for us, you know. We can't have children, so we don't know who will look after us in old age. My brothers are loving, they're respectful, for now. But what if their wives have a problem with me?'

'We're speaking to the government about this,' Hemabati said. 'We want facilities for surgery and hormone treatment here in Imphal. And we want them to issue directions about inheritance. There is a long way to go.'

Jibolata nodded. His wife was working in the fields, he said, and couldn't join us. She liked to sew. He showed us some curtains she had made.

'Sister,' BD nudged me, 'since he doesn't have many problems, shall we leave now? We have to show you our sacred place.'

∽

Imphal, Manipur

We were passing a busy market on our way to the fort, when Hemabati suddenly asked the driver to stop.

'Here, here, let me see if they're home.' He jumped off the car, and then ran into a food shack. He gestured for us to join him.

Joymati was wiping his hands on a towel. A woman was cooking something on a stove behind him.

'He has a very interesting story,' Hemabati said.

Joymati had never had problems at home. He had flatly refused to wear the mekhla. His sisters and mother had given up on turning him into a woman, and he was rather proud of it.

'I fell in love with a woman,' he said. 'And she loved me too. But then her family forced her to marry someone else.'

She had had an unhappy marriage, which produced a child. But ten years ago, her husband had passed away. She was no longer bound to anything. She had come away with her six-year-old child, to live with Joymati.

'She's the one you saw at the shop,' Joymati said. 'And now we have a son. He's in Class 11. We've worked very hard to raise him. I am not entitled to any property, and every paisa we have, we have earned. It's hard for us to make money. We can't do physical labour easily. I don't have the energy of a man, though I feel like a man. We had to borrow money, and we're slowly building a life for ourselves. But at least we have a son, who will look after us when we're old. And now we have an organization to ask for rights, maybe for some pension, from the government. If nothing else, we have a community, where everyone has the same problems. After my partner got married to that other man, I felt so alone, so alone. No one needs to feel that way now.'

As he was speaking, a friend of his, with short hair and a masculine face, but wearing a mekhla, had come to sit by us, nodding quietly every now and again.

'He is also like us,' Joymati said. 'He's Nebe. Nebenita, we call him Nebe.'

'I've always felt like a man,' Nebe said, softly. 'But I have many brothers and sisters. They forced me to wear the mekhla instead of long pants.'

He was forty-eight years old. I asked him why he still wore the mekhla. Surely his siblings couldn't force him to do anything now?

'I've given up.' He smiled sadly. 'I fell in love with a girl. But her parents persuaded her to leave me. They said she cannot have children with me, so what was the point of a relationship? She married a man, and I decided I would not have girlfriends again. I can't take the heartbreak. Now I don't care what happens to me, I don't care what I wear.'

It was the saddest sentence I had heard, I thought. *I don't care what I wear.* There were so many kinds of glass ceilings, at work, in life. So much depended on the most private parts of us, parts we hid behind clothing. And yet, those organs, whose shape and size we concealed from the world, determined what careers we chose, whom we could love, how we lived.

Joymati packed us some food. He waved me away when I reached for my purse. 'I won't take money from a guest,' he said, and then pointed to the plate. 'This is our life. Taste it. You will be tasting our life. This is how we live. I don't want anything from you. All that I want, I want from the government.'

Tell her to taste this. To taste our life. This is how we live. This is the food that gives us our livelihood. No! No! I will not accept money to feed a guest. Whatever I want, I want from the government, not from her.

~

It was their first trip to the fort. By the time it had sunk in that it was no longer an army camp and was truly open to the public, by the time its name had shed the dread for so long associated with it, Kangla Fort had become a tourist attraction, which locals didn't visit.

As we sat on the benches, I couldn't help but notice how the transmen among us splayed their legs, almost as a conscious departure from the behaviour into which they were conditioned in childhood.

'Sister, do you want Manipuri pizza?' BD grinned.

When I squinted, he ran to a cart and brought back a packet. 'Pakoras, peas cake, and homemade wild apple *aachaar* (pickle),' he said. 'This is our fast food.'

We finished the fast food, went to the temple inside the fort, and crowded together for photographs.

'You should go to Moirang, Sister,' BD told me the next day. 'The first Indian flag was unfurled there by Netaji Subhas Chandra Bose. But India doesn't recognize us. Also, near that place, you can see the memorial of Khamba and Thoibi—the Manipuri Romeo and Juliet.'

'Who's the girl, Khamba or Thoibi?' I asked.

Everyone began to laugh.

'Thoibi is the girl,' BD finally said.

'I was confused because we met Thoibi yesterday and . . .'

'Yeah, yeah, it's so difficult to get any documents, we don't even bother with the (formalities of) name change.'

'I don't like my name,' Hemabati said, smiling at me. 'Everyone calls me "Yambung". Uff, yesterday night, I didn't sleep at all. So many calls from midnight. Yambung, happy birthday, Yambung, happy birthday . . .'

It was the thirteenth of August—Martyrs' Day in Manipur, and Hemabati's birthday.

Safety

6 September 2017

Rommel had been hoping to visit home for Eid. It was a sad day for his family—his father had passed away on the eve of Eid, 2013. But he was worried about clearing immigration checks at the airport. He could not afford any red flags. Besides, his brother would insist he wear female clothes, complete with a hijab, to enter the house and meet his mother. He did not want to be a stranger in his own home. He did not want to be the girl who cried before the mirror every night.

27 October 2017

Rommel had been looking forward to a camp for transmen arranged by APTN in Thailand. But there was no Bangladeshi consulate in the country where he was posted, and he could not apply for a visa. He would have to travel to a nearby country to apply, a process which usually took six days. But this time, he was told the visa would take three weeks to be processed. He had not taken leave since the previous December, when he started work, waiting for the camp. He was gutted. Ten months was a long time to go without leave—he had been on call and had outpatient duty even on his days off. He had been waiting for the two-week holiday.

29 November 2017

'Just one more month,' he texted.

He also sent me a selfie.

His face had begun to look different. The angles were accentuated, and shaving had made his cheeks rugged. When I told him, he sent me a series of smileys.

'Nowadays the workload is less,' he added. 'On this chance I m watching walking dead. My fav serial :-) :-) B-).'

3 December 2017

WhatsApp message at 10.20 a.m.
Didi , i am worried about
transgender bill of india. I m already
in suffering.
Do u think i can go any other
country where its already accepted..
?
I m quite tensd.. :-(:-(

He asked if I could visit him. I was keen to. He would be in the country till the middle of January, when one of his friends would be back in Bangladesh. She had been doing her post-graduation abroad. He would not be allowed into his house, and needed a place to stay, and he was banking on staying with her.

20 December 2017

WhatsApp message at 3.34 p.m.
Didi, i m leaving _____ on 26th. There
r some urgency to go. Later, i will tell
u Details.
I m okey. Dont worry.

The next time I checked, he had deactivated his Facebook account.

Young and Bound

31 October 2016

'Aren't you both ashamed of yourselves?'

'How do you people plan to have sex?'

'I will tear off my slipper and hit you with it!'

'I will break your legs to show what happens to people who are a blot on the great Indian culture.'

'You call yourselves parents? You allow her to talk like this? First up, get her married off! And lock this creature up, this creature who claims to be a boy and is ruining your girl!'

'Homosexuals and transgender people are disgusting. A woman cannot feel like a man. A woman cannot love a woman. God has made us what we are for a reason.'

Geetha was fuming. She had been a relatively successful actress in the '80s and '90s in all four south Indian cinema industries. She now hosted a show on Zee TV Telugu, *Bathuku Jataka Bandhi*, a sort of Oprah-meets-Judge-Judy.

The couple were harangued and harassed for weeks after the show. Various LGBTQI organizations filed complaints against the episode and issued notices against the channel for airing it. There were calls to cancel the show. Eventually, the episode was removed from digital media websites, but Geetha continued to play host, and the show was not cancelled.

September 2017

The couple now work in a different state, one at a petrol station and the other at a hotel.

I met them late at night, when they had finished their shifts and returned to the home of an activist who was helping them out.

'It was a frightening experience,' he said, 'to be under the arc lights, and to have this actress saying we should be beaten up, we should be married off, we should be locked up. The day that happened, I thought I would kill myself.'

'I just wanted to run away,' she said. 'Not go home, not speak to anyone. Just run away with him. And the moment we saw another soul, we would kill ourselves. That was our plan.'

~

It is the curse of the young, to have all the passion and none of the power. Young people typically rebel against the world, and are met with indulgence at best. There is no 'at worst'. One only has to look to regions of conflict, Kashmir and Syria and several countries of Africa, to know just how dire the world can be for the young with conviction.

For young transmen, across socio-economic groups, there is little to no parental or familial support. In the rare case that a family does accept a transman's gender identity, the affirmation can be 'life-saving', Satya told me. In the absence of such support from natal families, transmen often run away from home. In many of these cases, this entails abandoning school or college, and without an education, they are forced to turn to the unorganized employment sector, exposed to exploitation for the rest of their lives.

~

The lottery was popular in Manipur. It was not the regular lottery, but a game of chance that anyone could start. Each person would contribute a certain amount, perhaps Rs 500. They would pick out a name, as in tombola. The winner would get the money. But it was a loan, not a gift. Over time, they would put in the money with interest, until everyone had got something out of it.

He was twenty-seven. He and his twenty-one-year-old partner had taken a loan of Rs 10,000 from a bank, opened a small shop selling cigarettes, magazines, snacks and betel leaves. They had joined the lottery several times, and expanded into a hundred-square-foot shop which did brisk business.

Even in the first few minutes of our interview, he was interrupted thrice by customers. A friend tried to help him out, but he decided to close the shop for a while. Watching him leap up a pole to bring down the shutters and tie the awnings, I saw nothing of the woman in him. There was something beautiful and capable about his litheness, the athleticism of the teenage boy who was all arms and legs. His voice was husky. Had he started medical transition, I asked, and he grinned and shook his head.

'We started the shop last April,' he said. 'And this April, they took her away.'

They had been dating for a couple of years, and had lived with each other for a year. His parents did not mind, he said. He was one of seven siblings, and had two brothers and four sisters. His parents hadn't had the time to harass him.

'Up to Class 4, I wore trousers to school. Then my father scolded me and said I should behave like a girl. But then I refused, even when he beat me, and he gave up.'

It was compulsory for girls to wear mekhla in Class 9 and 10. He didn't like it. Wearing a skirt upset him so much he didn't pursue his studies after Class 10, he said. It made more sense to start a proprietory business. He had worked in several shops, to learn the trade secrets, and finally found the confidence to invest in one himself.

His partner and he had wanted to get married, but her parents refused and took her back home. Both their Facebook profile pictures were couple photos, and they had written that they were engaged to each other, he said, and showed me on his phone.

'If I were a "born man", I would have gone to her house with my parents and asked for her hand in marriage,' he said. 'She loves me, and she has promised to wait for me. We have such a lovely story—we fell in love, we took a loan, and built a small shop. We used to live in that little space, sleeping among the packets of chips and biscuits and cigarettes. And we made a life for ourselves. But now, they won't let us get married.'

He was luckier than some transmen, he said. His parents had not disowned him. But when his partner's parents asked him how he would protect her, how a woman could roam freely at night, he could offer no reply.

'What can I say? My own parents ask me those questions: you look like a man, but you can't go out at night and be sure you'll be safe. Unless I change my organs, I can't live as a man. And there are no facilities to do the operation here. We don't have a free surgery scheme. I want to save money for our life together. But I also want to be a man. Once I have the surgery, society can't say anything about me. I won't lack anything.'

A dog wandered in and settled down on his lap. He stroked her fur. 'This is the woman of the house now,' he smiled. 'Bala.'

Everyone else laughed in delight. 'Bala is a famous Manipuri actress,' BD explained. 'Very beautiful.'

'My partner is more beautiful.'

~

'I think people who have partners, their lives are very hard,' BD said, as we left. 'I have a girlfriend, so my life is happy. But to live alone, it's a big, big, decision. So much responsibility, and so little money. That's why the young transmen and lesbians, they're coming to Yambung's house to meet you. Their houses will be very, very small, I think.'

BD began to tell me about his girlfriend, interrupting himself often to make a comment on politics or prejudice, whenever we passed hoardings or places that triggered such reflection.

'I met her at a wedding during my Class 12 board exams,' he said. 'They give you lots of holidays, na, to study? So instead of studying, we started texting. That girl waited for me all the time I was in college. I'm her first boyfriend, and she's my first girlfriend. We love each other a lot. She gets very angry, though. Sister, don't you think that guy we just met had a really nice voice? Mine is *poora* (entirely) female. Once, in school, I had a fight with a guy because both of us liked the same girl. I wanted to call him up and tell him to back off, but then because my voice is so high, he will only laugh at me. So I made Aily call him, because Aily's voice is deeper. So Aily said, "Keep away from my girl."'

'And then you asked her out?'

'Oh, no, not that girl. Some other guy became her boyfriend. Not the one I called, not me. So, I told you my girlfriend gets very angry? Once, because I didn't message or call her for a day, she started a fight with me. I told her I was busy, and we started quarrelling by the roadside. She threw my scooter key into the river by the bridge. Thank god it wasn't monsoon. I asked for a polythene bag, and got it back.'

'Ah, young love,' I said, and Hemabati laughed.

'What do you mean, sister?'

'When you're older, you just want peace from a relationship. No quarrels.'

'That is correct,' Hemabati said. Aily laughed and shook his head. BD grinned. 'But fighting is also fun.' He paused. 'Sister, you know Irom Sharmila also fell in love and she wanted to marry that NRI *ladka* (boy) and called off her fast? I think instead of standing for elections to the state assembly, she could at least have tried to become an MP. Then everyone would have supported her.'

'Why do you have a problem with her falling in love?'

'No problem. But she fought so hard for fifteen years. Why waste it? Manipur became famous because of her. She should have represented us as an MP. No one knows about Manipur. You know, this Manipuri woman who played hockey for India is now a ticket collector in the railways.'

〜

There is a song I dedicate to all the partners of transmen. Shall I play it for you?

Hemabati's house was beautiful, BD had said. Even the annexe was lovely. If he had been a son, what a nice room he and his wife would have had, BD rued.

'The young couples we are going to meet now, they said their homes are not big enough for more than two people to sit inside. Because we are transmen, see how difficult our lives are. Their parents are not so poor. But they are.'

I could hear the voices even as we crossed the courtyard—a tricky business. It had rained the previous night, and we had to jump from stone to stone. I saw everything Nanao had spoken of the previous day—the shrine she had made for her home, the 'Welcome' mat, the patio they had improvised, and a separate electricity connection.

Inside, three couples were chatting with Nanao. The boys wore sports jackets and running shoes. They were all sportsmen, BD told me. One was a boxer and volleyball player; another was into taekwondo; another was into football.

The girls wore frayed but pretty clothes, and had make-up on. All the girls, I noticed, had very long hair.

'Sonia and Rishi.' BD pointed them out. 'Rishi is a football player; he played in our exhibition match. Tony and Tilottama. Malem and Prabha.' He told them something, and Prabha remarked excitedly. 'It seems they ran away to your city,' BD said.

Malem was twenty-five, and Prabha nineteen. Their parents had been against the match from the start.

They couldn't remember how long they had been dating, but it was several years, Prabha said. There was a time when their relationship had been accepted by family. Her father had met with an accident and could not work. Malem had helped the family out financially. He had even moved into the house, and for a time, her parents seemed to approve.

'But once my father got better, he used to ask me, "How long will your friend stay? When will she leave?" He said "she",' Prabha said.

They had decided to run away from home in September 2016. Malem's parents figured out they had eloped, and didn't worry too much. Prabha's father insisted on putting a missing persons advertisement in the newspaper.

'My father didn't want to publicize it,' Malem said. 'He thought we are young, it could affect our futures if our photos came in the paper. So he thought he would ask friends and find us. But her father wanted a report, and so my family agreed. My father told the newspaper to put it in two different columns, not both of our pictures together. It might cause trouble. But then, her father went and gave the ad again, this time saying our pictures should come together and it should say both of us were missing, and to please inform them if anyone saw us.'

Prabha and Malem had come across both advertisements. Panicking, they had left the state.

'We went from Imphal to Madras,' Malem said with a laugh. 'I have a friend there. He got me a job. I said please don't let anyone see me, I want to do some work inside, in a hotel kitchen or something like that.'

They were in hiding for a couple of months. Eventually, their parents agreed to let them stay together, in Prabha's home, they said.

'It was too difficult, to make money for food, rent, clothes, everything,' Prabha said. 'He had to work very hard. So we decided to come home. Now, my father makes comments, he says it's not okay for a transman and lesbian to live together and all that, but they let us live at home.'

'Even though I work in a shop and I earn my own money,' Malem added.

Tony, twenty-two, and Tilottama, nineteen, had not yet moved in together. Her parents did not know about them, but his parents did, and they didn't mind. They were waiting for Tony to get his new identity documents, so that they could have a court marriage, they said.

'There will be problems from my side,' Tilottama said, shyly. 'My parents will not support us. So once we get married, we will leave Manipur. It's better to work outside. No one will know about us. They will think we're a "normal" couple.'

Tony was still in college. They would get married as soon as he was finished and had found a job, he said.

Rishi, nineteen, and Sonia, twenty-one, had been trying to elope for three years, BD told me, and everyone laughed. 'They're so young, and they didn't plan properly. Her entire family is in the police—father, brother, uncle. So they found them, and beat them up, and said they would put them in jail, even.'

'They put us inside a cell,' Sonia added. 'That was the second time. The first time, they just scolded us. Then we ran away a third time, and then they gave up.' She laughed. 'We have been running away since August 2015. Exactly two years.'

After the beating at the police station, Sonia's phone had been confiscated.

'But she called Rishi from a friend's phone and they made a plan to run away,' BD said.

'The movies teach us everything,' Nanao said, laughing.

'Only my mother supports us,' Rishi said. 'My aunty went and told Sonia's parents to separate us. It is not good for these two girls, they're spoiling each other, things like that. My mother even told her to stop. I don't know why they have a problem. I am working and earning for both of us. We are living off that money.'

They had considered living elsewhere, but both of them liked home. They didn't want to leave Manipur.

'But they don't know whether they are safe, because of the police connections,' BD said.

Prabha touched my arm. 'You know something? The transmen can say "We are like this", and finally the parents will accept them. But for us lesbians, it is not like that. Their families also scold us for spoiling them. And our families also scold us and say, "You don't want a future or what? Why do you want to be with a transman, you should be with a real man." Things like this happen.'

'Uff,' Nanao said. 'Yesterday, I was telling her about the *jatra* tradition. The first person to do important rituals has to have a first-born son. Our entire lives, we can't do those rituals. We are making all these sacrifices for our love. And how many problems we have!' Suddenly, almost eerily, we heard a baby squealing.

'My brother's baby,' Hemabati explained.

Nanao spoke rapidly in Meitei, through a mouthful of paan, and BD began to laugh. 'Bhabhi is saying in a very funny way, she feels like she gave up *everything* in her life, she is sacrificing *all* for the transmen's love. She is going to play a song. She says she dedicates it to all the lesbian partners.'

She was scrolling on YouTube, and began to sing the lines. Apparently, the song was quite popular. I had never heard it.

The song started off rather sentimentally, and we were laughing at the first stanza. 'How much I love you,' the woman sang to her lover. 'A hundred times in a moment.' If he were to go, she said, leaving her behind, she would desire nothing but death.

The chorus rang out, and the girls began to sing along. It was standard Bollywood fare, maudlin and hyperbolic. The woman wailed that she loved him so much she had given up the world for him; her breath began and ended with him, and he could never fathom how much she wanted him.

None of us could imagine any circumstances under which a sane cisgender couple would sing such things to each other. But, in the case of such unconventional couplings as those I had encountered that day, and in the preceding months, every stanza seemed to ring truer, without exaggeration. As the song played on, we stopped laughing, even singing, and sat in silence.

The world was nothing, the heroine swore, the hero was the only thing which was alive to her. Where could she possibly want to go, she asked, when he was her final journey. I found it strange that she referred to him as 'journey' and not 'destination'—the latter would have been more in keeping with logic and lyrical sentimentality. Relationships were a journey, fair enough. But were partners a 'journey'? Perhaps they were, particularly when a relationship had to be recalibrated with physical changes in one partner.

'We want children,' Prabha said, suddenly. 'Not adoption. We want to do IVF (in vitro fertilization). One child from each of our eggs. Because if we adopt a child, people could change the baby's mind about us. The child may think it's wrong for a transman and a lesbian to marry. But a "bloodchild" will always love us.'

Rishi and Sonia wanted the same thing. They would save up money to have a baby, first, they said, and then think about everything else.

'My first priority is to buy a house,' Tony said. 'Before surgery, even. What is the use of having male organs if I cannot provide for her? If we have a house, even if I die, she will have a place to live.'

'Too many expenses,' Malem said. 'We all need land. We all need houses. We all need children. We all need surgery.'

'We had group discussions about this, sister,' BD said. 'For as long as we live with family, we have to worry that there will suddenly be a big quarrel and they will ask us to get out, or separate us. Mostly, the male child gets the property here, even if it's a very large property. So transmen are saying we should have the same rights as a male child. It's okay if the wives don't get it from their families, but we transmen at least should get the land. And we should be able to put our names down as head of the family on BPL cards, ration cards, and food security cards.

'Surgery is another thing. We all want hormone therapy and surgery. A few months back, we took it up with the government and they promised financial aid for medical transition. But we don't even have the facilities for transition here. Even if we go to RIMS (Regional Institute of Medical Sciences), they just refer us to bigger hospitals in other states.'

It was time to cook, Nanao announced. Hemabati switched on the TV, and left the boys and me to watch it. Nanao, he, and the three girls went into the kitchen. I wandered in after a few minutes and offered to help. They refused to allow me to.

It would take them hours to prepare and cook the meal.

I struck up a conversation with the boys in Hemabati's room. Did they think cooking and cleaning were women's jobs?

'I don't think much about it,' Rishi said. 'We're husband and wife. So if she's not well or something, I will do it. Even when my mother is not well, my father helps. It's not wrong.'

But none of them liked the idea of their wives working.

'I will make her live happily. I won't feel good if she works,' Rishi said, and Tony nodded.

'I'm okay with my wife working,' Malem said. 'We have to save a lot of money, so it's better for both of us to work. But not too much. She should not tire herself out. I want to look after her. Prabha likes to work. She says, "One hand cannot clap."'

The girls laughed when I asked them for their opinions. Sonia wanted to work, she said, but Rishi had refused to allow her to. She liked the idea of a double income; they could save faster, and move closer to the life they dreamt of having. Did she also like the idea of being independent? She blushed and giggled.

'I can't allow Tony to earn money for both of us, and sit doing nothing,' Tilottama declared.

'Are you okay with that?' I asked Tony.

He thought for some time and then said, 'Not in front of the eyes of others. She can work, but no one should see her.'

'You should all be living with your parents,' Nanao said. 'It's a hard life, living alone. Why waste money on rent?'

'Bhabhi gives good advice,' BD said. 'She even tells these lesbians, only date transmen if you're serious about them. Don't do it for fun. They're more sensitive than other boys, don't play with their feelings. If you're going to leave them, leave them now.'

Nanao was about to say something, when Hemabati suddenly swooped down and kissed her cheek. She swatted him away, smiling.

~

On my last day in Imphal, I dropped into the SAATHII office to see Randhoni and Santa.

Randhoni smiled when I told her how keen the younger transmen and their partners were on hormone therapy, surgery, and eventually children.

'Adoption?' she asked.

'They want to have biological children,' I said. 'The older ones would like to adopt, these kids want their own DNA.'

For many years, people had simply been worried about being accepted by their families, Randhoni told me, just acceptance and perhaps a little room to stay. The activists had not really thought about fighting for adoption rights.

'The frisking has come down now, but earlier, there was a *lot* of it, which would have been very painful for them. Even the women's cell in the police station has come up very recently, maybe a year old. Earlier, there would only be men in the police holding cell, and even if there is no physical harassment, there would be a lot of name-calling and ridiculing, which takes an emotional toll.'

Because so much of Manipur was remote, almost inaccessible for months at a time, she couldn't be sure how many transmen were in the hillier regions, not connected to ETA, perhaps lonely and confused. But there had always been a tendency for them to get into sports and into the military, paramilitary, or police forces, where their masculinity could find expression.

Recently, ETA had organized a football match between women and transmen—an exhibition match as part of a larger football tournament. The youth sports clubs in Manipur were very active, and they had no problem finding volunteers to participate in the match. It was held in a village on the outskirts of Imphal.

'It's a good opportunity to speak about transgender issues, when the entire village has come to see the match,' Randhoni said. 'To tell them it is not something new, that it is common, there is such a thing as transmen in our society, in our families. So it becomes a kind of sensitization programme for the whole village. It also encourages other people who are trans to come out.'

~

A transboy who (has) come (to) the exhibition on the economic inclusion of Gender and Sexual Minorities along with his mother to observe the event.. _____, 13 years old studying (in) 7th std, was bullied in school bcos of wearing boy's clothing, which has made him reluctant to go to school. Both ETA and AMANA members (are) helping him (by) encouraging (him) to continue education.

—Facebook post by Santa Khurai

To Love and to Cherish

1 December 2017

'Hi, Akka. I have very good news to share with you. I'll tell you in person ☺'

Keerth had taken to calling me 'akka'. We had met often in the last months, and I'd begun thinking of him as a little brother.

'Don't do this, man!' I replied to his text. 'Shall I call?'

'Oh no. I should see the expression. If you're coming tomorrow afternoon, it's not even twenty-four hours.'

2 December 2017

'So what do you want to eat?' Keerth grinned. We were sitting in the IIT canteen, as usual.

'What is the good news?'

'Ah. The *news*.' Keerth gave me a feline smile, and then took a deep breath. 'My mom and dad have agreed for surgery.'

My response—'*What are you saying?*'—was loud enough for several people to turn their heads.

He laughed. 'But then my dad said he can't call me by whatever name I choose for myself. So he went and sat with some astrologer, and spent some half a day working out the numerology, and finally I'm calling myself Kirithick Rajkumar. I'm going to sign all my poems like that now.'

'How did it happen?'

'I think . . . in some ways, my dad had always wanted a son,' he said, contemplatively. 'They've agreed to the hormone therapy and everything. I think if I had been a boy and then wanted to change into a girl, it would have been a very different story. I could not have convinced them. But with this . . . sometimes I even felt my dad was elated to have a son, you know?'

The issue of relative privilege for trans children of the two inclinations—male-to-female and female-to-male—had come up often during discussions of this sort. Bittu had once spoken to me about the effect of patriarchy playing out as both disadvantages and advantages to the two. While transmen's families could accept expressions of masculinity in people they saw as daughters, transwomen's families were deeply unhappy with expressions of femininity in people they saw as their sons. The difference was that transwomen, for as long as they were seen as boys, had the freedom and even encouragement to go out into society on their own, to take risks, to move away from their families to study; transmen, for as long as they were seen as girls, were often 'raised in environments where there isn't a sense of how to function in the outside world', to the extent they didn't even know where or to whom they should turn when they wanted to transition.

A factor that had worked in Keerth's favour was that he had recently been diagnosed with Poly-Cystic Ovarian Syndrome, and the doctor had explained to his parents that his body naturally produced more androgen and testosterone than the average woman's. The doctor had also suggested retinitis pigmentosa often presented with 'gender disorders'. He told Keerth's parents that he knew an intersex person with RB.

'People somehow find it easier to accept if it is biological,' Keerth said. 'And they can also tell my relatives that I have changed naturally. Most people aren't aware that hormones are taken externally. They think you're intersex, or you change organically. They don't know you choose to transition. It was quite good, this visit to my mom's and dad's. By far the best, I'd say. Because my dad took me to the men's section and got me clothes. See, this T-shirt I'm wearing now, it's what he got me.'

During his last visit home, for Deepavali, in October 2017, the
salespeople at the store had assumed he was a boy and said they would
have to go to the seventh floor. 'They were all staring at me. And my
father was picking out salwar-kameez and skirts and showing me and
I said, "Choose whatever you want." But this time, he actually finally
took me to the seventh floor.'

For the first time, his mother had not asked him to wear earrings.
And they would get his name changed on all his certificates and
identity cards.

'I even spoke to the dean of students yesterday,' he said. 'The
institute is very supportive. He said, "We as an institute want you to
graduate, and we want you to get a job." I will be the first transman, I
think first transperson, to graduate from IIT.'

~

28 December 2017

> Hello.
> Didi
> I have come to the country I told you I might go.
> To one of my very best friend's home.
> Tomorrow we r going to his village home.
> My return is January 20.
> I will be active again in Messenger.
> How r u??
> Don't worry about me
> I m safe here
> Your brother Rommel

~

*It was the big, fat wedding his family had always loved. He stood by her
side, and their parents beamed as they spoke to the more recognizable of the
hundreds of people who had gathered there. She wore the bridal veil that*

had been handed down generations of his family, daughter to daughter to daughter. But Aashish was not a daughter, and so his bride wore the veil. Perhaps they would have a daughter who would inherit it some day. They planned on having two children through a surrogate, one for each. Once she had a child who looked like her husband, no one could suspect that he had been assigned female at birth.

A section read 'Name and Parentage of Parties'. Under 'Husband', he wrote 'Aashish Arora, S/O Sushil Arora'. Under 'Wife', she wrote 'Aanchal Arora, D/O Manish Gupta'.[1]

'Congratulations,' the registrar said.

⁓

15 January 2018

Didi

i have something to share with u

1 week after i came here, (something happened to) one of transman in bangladesh who is very close to me. whatever activity we r doing . I was behind d screen as i was in _____ . He used to go front. That night when he was going back home was attacked by 5/6 people. They threat him and said they r looking for others specially main one. So its not at all safe for me to go back. Here my friends they r very scared about my return. So, they r searching for immigration option in _____ regarding me. What do u say?

Your brother Rommel

---

[1] All names have been changed to protect privacy.

Citations

- 1969 official 'certified copy' of Dr Karl M. Baer's corrected entry in the German Births Register Arolsen (Hesse), obtained from Wikimedia Commons
- Chimamanda Ngozi Adichie's Facebook post: https://www.facebook.com/chimamandaadichie/photos/a.469824145943.278768.40389960943/10154893542340944/?type=3&theater
- Facebook page for the Stop the Transgender Bill 2016 campaign: https://www.facebook.com/stopTGBill/
- Full text of the Transgender Persons (Protection of Rights) Bill 2016: http://orinam.net/content/wp-content/uploads/2016/08/TGBill_LS_Eng-1.pdf
- Gee Semmalar's article on the Transgender Persons (Protection of Rights) Bill 2016: http://orinam.net/apathy-farce-trans-rights-bill-standing-committee-report/
- Jamal Siddiqui's blog: https://jamalsiddiquiblog.wordpress.com
- Jamal Siddiqui's article for Gaylaxy Mag: http://www.gaylaxymag.com/blogs/queer-spaces-can-transphobic-open-letter-transman-felt-violated-idahobit-event/
- 'Rajveer And Shivangi's Unique Love Story Will Make You Tear Up', published in *The Quint* website on June 6, 2017.
- Raquel Willis' tweets can be found on this thread: https://twitter.com/RaquelWillis_/status/840369626487783425

Bibliography

- Bentz, E.; Hefler, L.; Kaufmann, U.; Huber, J.; Kolbus, A.; Tempfer, C. (2008). 'A Polymorphism of the CYP17 Gene Related to Sex Steroid Metabolism Is Associated with Female-to-male but not Male-to-female Transsexualism'. *Fertility and Sterility.* 90 (1): 56–9. doi:10.1016/j.fertnstert.2007.05.056. PMID 17765230.
- Hare, Lauren; Bernard, Pascal; Sánchez, Francisco J.; Baird, Paul N.; Vilain, Eric; Kennedy, Trudy; Harley, Vincent R. (2009). 'Androgen Receptor Repeat Length Polymorphism Associated with Male-to-Female Transsexualism'. *Biological Psychiatry.* 65 (1): 93–6. doi:10.1016/j.biopsych.2008.08.033. PMC 3402034. PMID 18962445.
- Mohan, Sunil with Murthy, Sumathi (Harish, Rumi) (2013). *Towards Gender Inclusivity: A Study on Contemporary Concerns around Gender.* Published by Alternative Law Forum and LesBiT, Bangalore, India.
- Penrose, W. (2001). 'Hidden in History: Female Homoeroticism and Women of a "Third Nature" in the South Asian Past', *Journal of the History of Sexuality,* 10:1, 3–39.
- Phillimore, Peter. (1991). 'Unmarried Women of the Dhaula Dhar: Celibacy and Social Control in Northwest India'. *Journal of Anthropological Research* 47 (3): 331–50.
- Revathi, A. (2016). *A Life in Trans Activism.* Zubaan Books.
- Sharma, Maya (2006). *Loving Women: Being Lesbian in Unprivileged India.* Yoda Press.
- Vidya, Living Smile, *Naan ~~Saravanan~~ Vidya: Oru Thirunangaiyin Ulukkiyedukkum Vaazhkkai Anubhavangal* (2008). Kizhakku

Pathippagam. *(Available in English as* I am ~~Saravanan~~ Vidya: A Transgender's Journey (2013). *Rupa Publications).*

- Zhou, Jiang-Ning; Hofman, Michel A.; Gooren, Louis J.G.; Swaab, Dick F. (1995). 'A Sex Difference in the Human Brain and its Relation to Transsexuality'. *Nature.* 378 (6552): 68–70. doi:10.1038/378068a0. PMID 7477289.

Videos:

- All about our Famila: Documentary by Chalam Bennurkar: https://www.youtube.com/watch?v=PmXsYt6drTk
- Bathuku Jataka Bandhi, episode aired on 31 October 2016, no longer available on Zee TV's official site or YouTube.
- Interview with Chimamanda Ngozi Adichie: https://www.youtube.com/watch?v=KP1C7VXUfZQ
- Dr Sanjay Pandey's YouTube channel: https://www.youtube.com/channel/UCWt7JGMIy17fbMzCSXxKbnw
- En Aasai, En Kanavu: Short film by Charupriyan: https://www.youtube.com/watch?v=LpoSxmUBkjo
- Gee Imaan Semmalar's talk at the TransForm National Conference: https://www.youtube.com/watch?v=jc2p2ySX0gA&t=0s&list=PLqox2uc-20JKpO4oPdGxqQoU0GTxKhtEK&index=9
- Jamal Siddiqui's YouTube channel: https://www.youtube.com/channel/UC9CWN9zI_hzbeI51E7aM_5w
- M/F/?: Documentary by Nandini Krishnan

All illustrations and translations in the book are by the author, unless otherwise specified.

Acknowledgements

My first thanks are due to my 'gurus', Amit Chaudhuri and Patrick French, for counsel, encouragement, laughs, and more. Shreekumar Varma, Shree Uncle to me, and Geeta Aunty believed I was a writer a decade and a half before it was true, and their love and support means the world to me. I'm grateful to Dr Kavery Nambisan, for constantly encouraging me to push my boundaries; to Manu Joseph for various conversations over the years, for his invaluable feedback on my writing, for being the editor who assigned me my first long-form stories, and for so kindly consenting to write the foreword to this book.

This work would have been impossible without the initial enthusiasm from Meru Gokhale, and immense thoughtfulness from Manasi Subramaniam. I owe Dr Javeeda Habeeb, my Urdu teacher, for her friendship and guidance, for helping me with translations from the Q'uran and interpretations of Islam. I made more friends through this book than I have in years, and I thank all my interviewees for letting me into their lives; I reserve a special hug for Satya Rai Nagpaul, my little Keerth (officially Kirithik Shiva), and 'Rommel', whose name I cannot reveal for reasons of his personal safety. Dr L. Ramakrishnan and Selvam facilitated many of my interviews, and I am grateful to them.

My primary research entailed weeks of travel, and I thank my parents for looking after my various species of fur babies in my absence. I owe a debt I can never repay to Shakthi Girish, Dinesh Baba, Gopalakrishnan, Sujatha, Mani and Sai Prem for giving me those babies, who have shown me the purest love I know.

Much of the planning for the book and mulling over its form happened at the Amakshi Residency, and the friendship of Amandeep Sandhu, Lakshmi Karunakaran and Jaspreet 'Minni' Kaur has been invaluable.

The book started with a long-form story I wrote for *Fountain Ink* magazine, and its editors Saurav Kumar and Gopal Rao, also dear friends of mine, have been kind enough to allow me to cite from the piece.

I've been lucky to have friends who've opened their hearts and homes to me. I'm beholden to Swathi and Arjun, Nidhi and Dev, Iswar and Anushka for love, laughs and conversations; to Aniruddhan Vasudevan for always being there; to Vandana Krishnan, who put a roof over my head when I first began to research transgender issues, and has given ear to me before and since; to Ranjitha Gunasekaran, who is never more than a text away; to Lakshmy Venkiteswaran, for the world's warmest hugs; to Akhil Katyal, whose poetry has got me through many a dark day; to Moushumi Ghosh and Anupama Chandrasekhar, for all that has been spoken over long lunches, through long years; to Karthika Naïr and D.P. Prashant, for so much more than can be put into words; to Gauri Burde, who knows exactly what I mean when I trail off, "You know . . ."; to Nishant for all that he is, not least of which being my favourite travel companion, fellow insomniac and provider of 4 a.m. laughs, and for promising to read my first draft (he didn't); to Raghu, who spins everything I need to hear into sentences I want to hear, for all that he has done for this book, which includes spending a brave evening photographing me and my Chaitanya to our satisfaction, reassuring me every time it seemed I would never finish it, and promising to read my first draft (he claims he 'read parts'); to Poornima Muralidhar, Khaled Ezzelarab, Manuela Gsponer, Miho Abe, Richard Webster, Ikramuddin Sarwary, Archana Ram, Ratna Rathore Tanwar, Idrees Lone and Sabahat Zakariya, my oldest and dearest friends, whom no oceans and calamities and time zones and work schedules can ever separate from me.